Things Boundaries are Allowed to Do for Kids

(An Incomplete List)

Ben Kucenski

Things Boundaries are Allowed to Do for Kids

(An Incomplete List)

Paperback Edition: 979-8-9939525-2-9

Copyright © 2025 Ben Kucenski

All rights reserved.

No part of this publication may be reproduced, stored, or transmitted in any form or by any means without the prior written permission of the author, except in the case of brief quotations used in reviews or scholarly work.

A boundary is something that helps people take care of themselves and each other.

Pages are deliberately left with plenty of space to draw and color whatever the child wants while the content of this book is being presented by a safe adult.

Kids are allowed to decide who touches their body.

Kids are allowed to say no to hugs.

Kids are allowed to change their mind.

Kids are allowed to step back.

Kids are allowed to say "stop."

Kids are allowed to not explain their no.

Kids are allowed to move away from someone.

Kids are allowed to keep their body to themselves.

Kids are allowed to notice when something feels weird.

Kids are allowed to trust that feeling.

Kids are allowed to feel uncomfortable.

Kids are allowed to leave when they feel unsure.

Kids are allowed to say something feels wrong.

Kids are allowed to ask for help.

Kids are allowed to expect adults to keep them safe.

Kids are allowed to say no to adults.

Kids are allowed to talk to more than one adult.

Kids are allowed to ask another adult for help.

Kids are allowed to tell a trusted adult when something happens.

Kids are allowed to be believed.

Kids are allowed to be protected.

Kids are allowed to have adults listen to them.

Kids are allowed to tell about secrets that make them uncomfortable.

Kids are allowed to talk about anything that worries them.

Kids are allowed to tell even if someone said not to.

Kids are allowed to talk about mistakes.

Kids are allowed to talk about confusing things.

Kids are allowed to leave a room.

Kids are allowed to go find another adult.

Kids are allowed to change activities.

Kids are allowed to stop playing.

Kids are allowed to go home.

Kids are allowed to say "I want my parent."

Kids are allowed to take up space.

Kids are allowed to be serious.

Kids are allowed to be quiet.

Kids are allowed to be themselves.

Kids are allowed to ask questions.

Kids are allowed to matter.

Kids are allowed to be safe.

www.ingramcontent.com/pod-product-compliance
Lightning Source LLC
Chambersburg PA
CBHW080946050426

42337CB00056B/4858

من ذره بدم ز کوه بیشم کردی

پس مانده بدم از همه پیشم کردی

درمان دل خراب و ریشم کردی

سرمست و دستک زن خویشم کردی

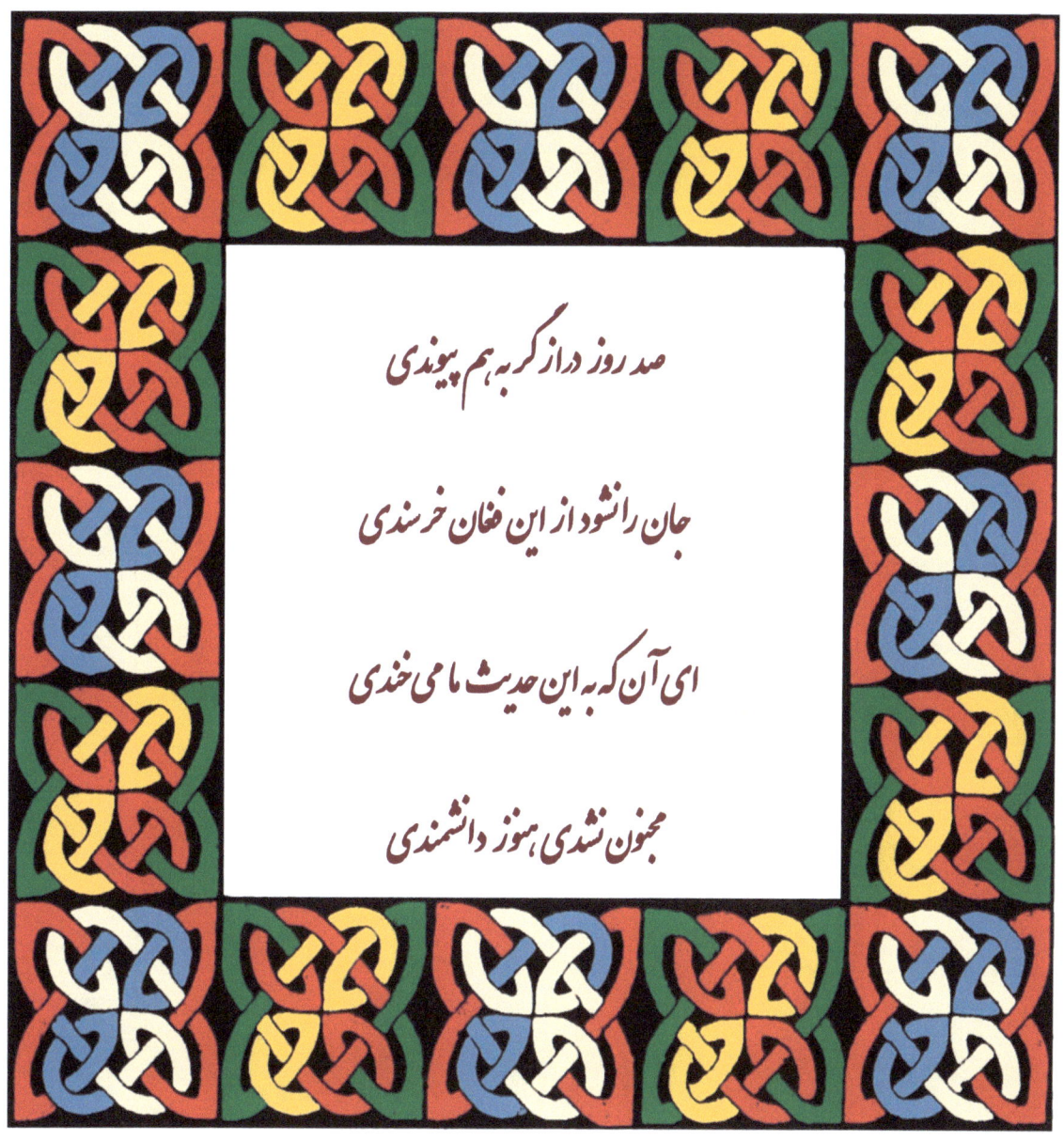

صد روز دراز گر به هم پیوندی

جان را نشود از این فغان خرسندی

ای آن که به این حدیث ما می خندی

مجنون نشدی، هنوز دانشمندی

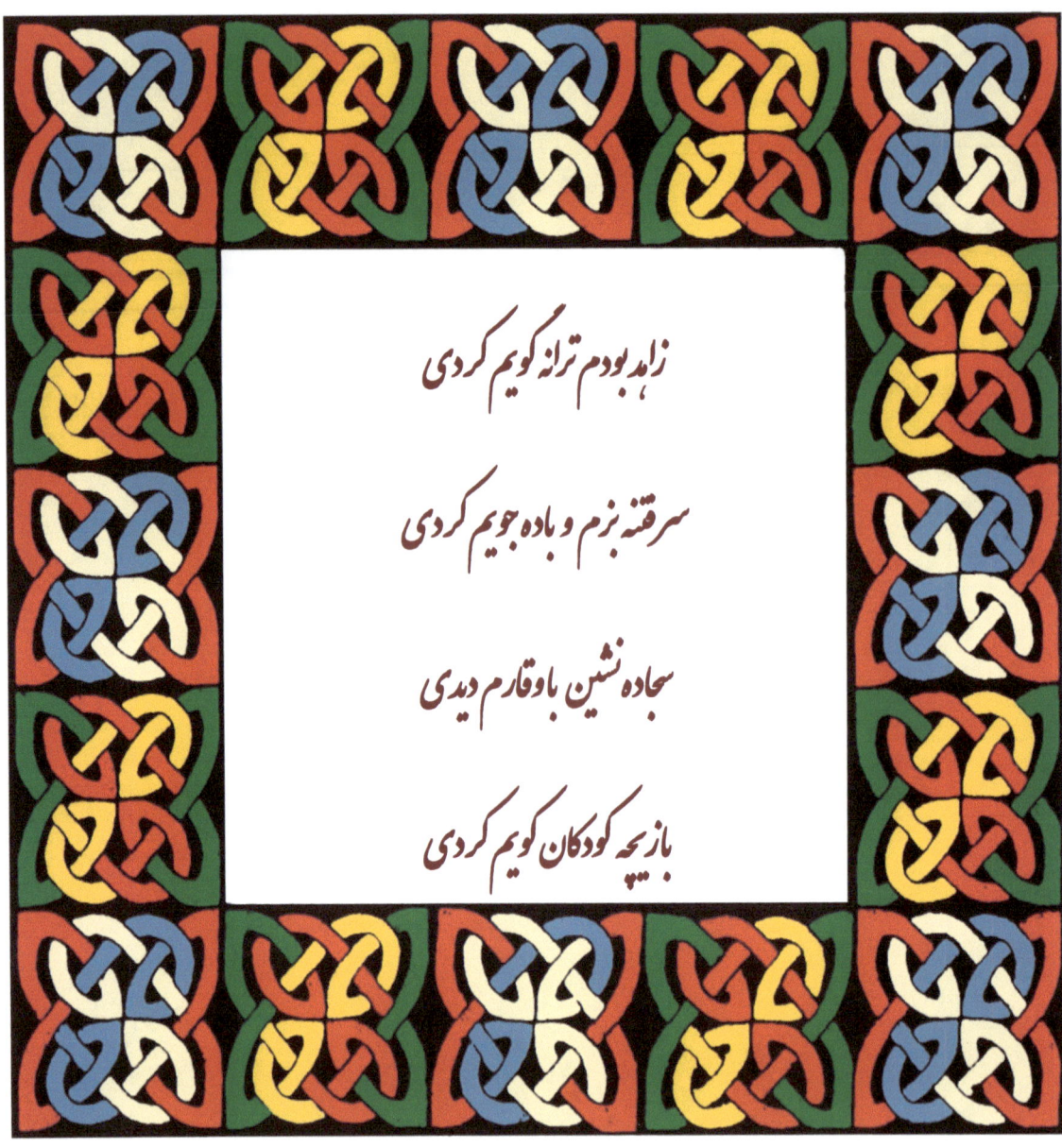

زاهد بودم ترانه گویم کردی

سرقبهٔ بزم و باده جویم کردی

سجاده نشین با وقارم دیدی

بازیچهٔ کودکان کویم کردی

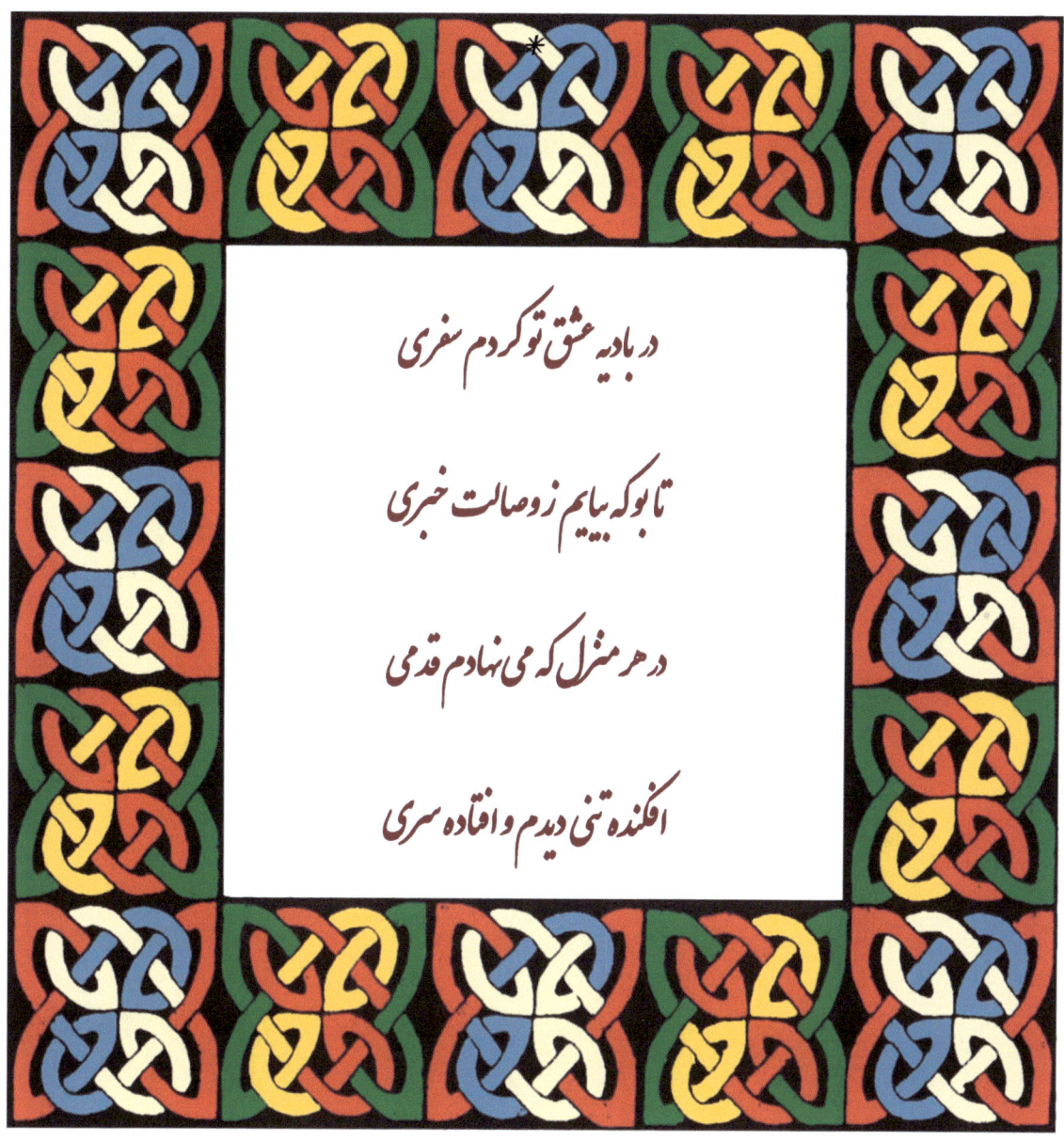

در بادیهٔ عشق تو کردم سفری

تا بو که بیایم ز وصالت خبری

در هر منزل که می‌نهادم قدمی

افکنده تنی دیدم و افتاده سری

تا هشیاری به طعم مستی نرسی

تا تن ندهی به جان‌پرستی نرسی

تا در غم عشق دوست چون آتش و آب

از خود نشوی نیست به هستی نرسی

با یار به گلزار شدم رهگذری

بر گل نظری فکندم از بی خبری

دلدار به من گفت که شرمت بادا

رخسار من اینجا و تو بر گل نگری

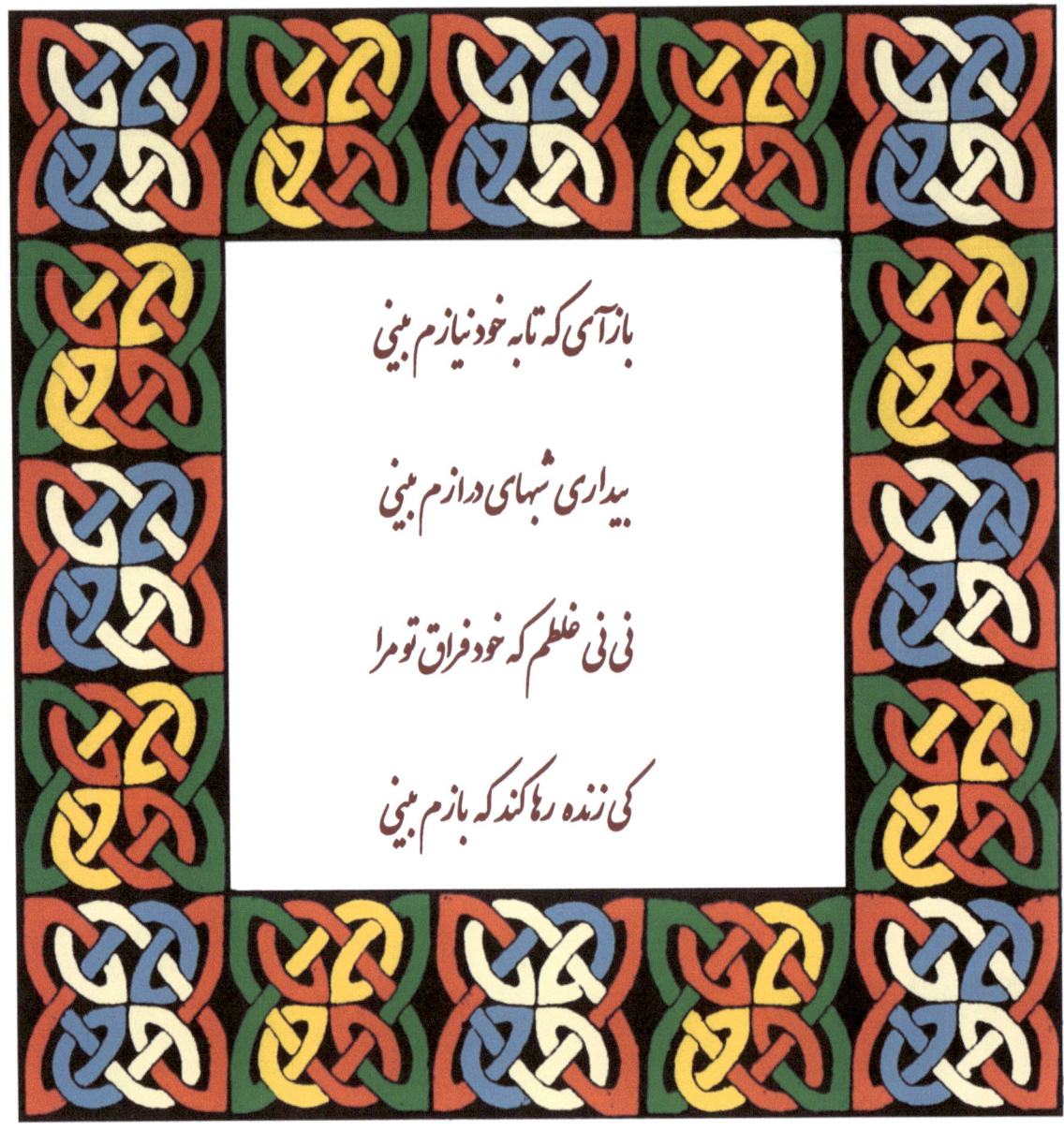

بازآئی که تا به خود نیازم بینی

بیداری شبهای درازم بینی

نی نی غلطم که خود فراق تو مرا

کی زنده رها کند که بازم بینی

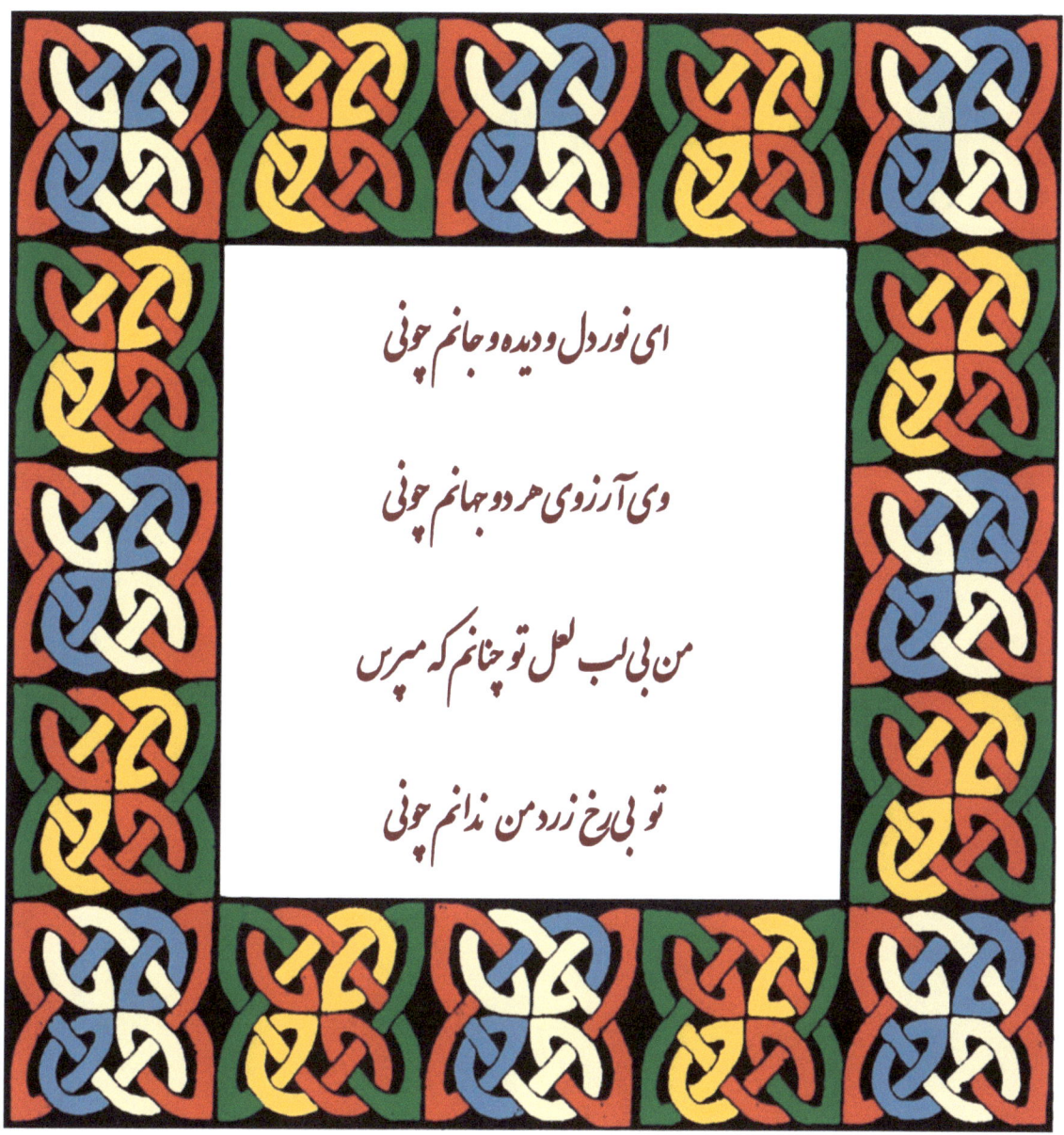

ای نور دل و دیده و جانم چونی

وی آرزوی هر دو جهانم چونی

من بی لب لعل تو چنانم که مپرس

تو بی رخ زرد من ندانم چونی

ای زندگی تن و توانم همه تو

جانی و دلی ای دل و جانم همه تو

تو هستی من شدی از آنی همه من

من نیست شدم در تو از آنم همه تو

ای جان جهان جان و جهان بندهٔ تو

شیرین شدهٔ عالم ز شکر خندهٔ تو

صد قرن گذشت و آسمان نیز ندید

در گردش روزگار مانندهٔ تو

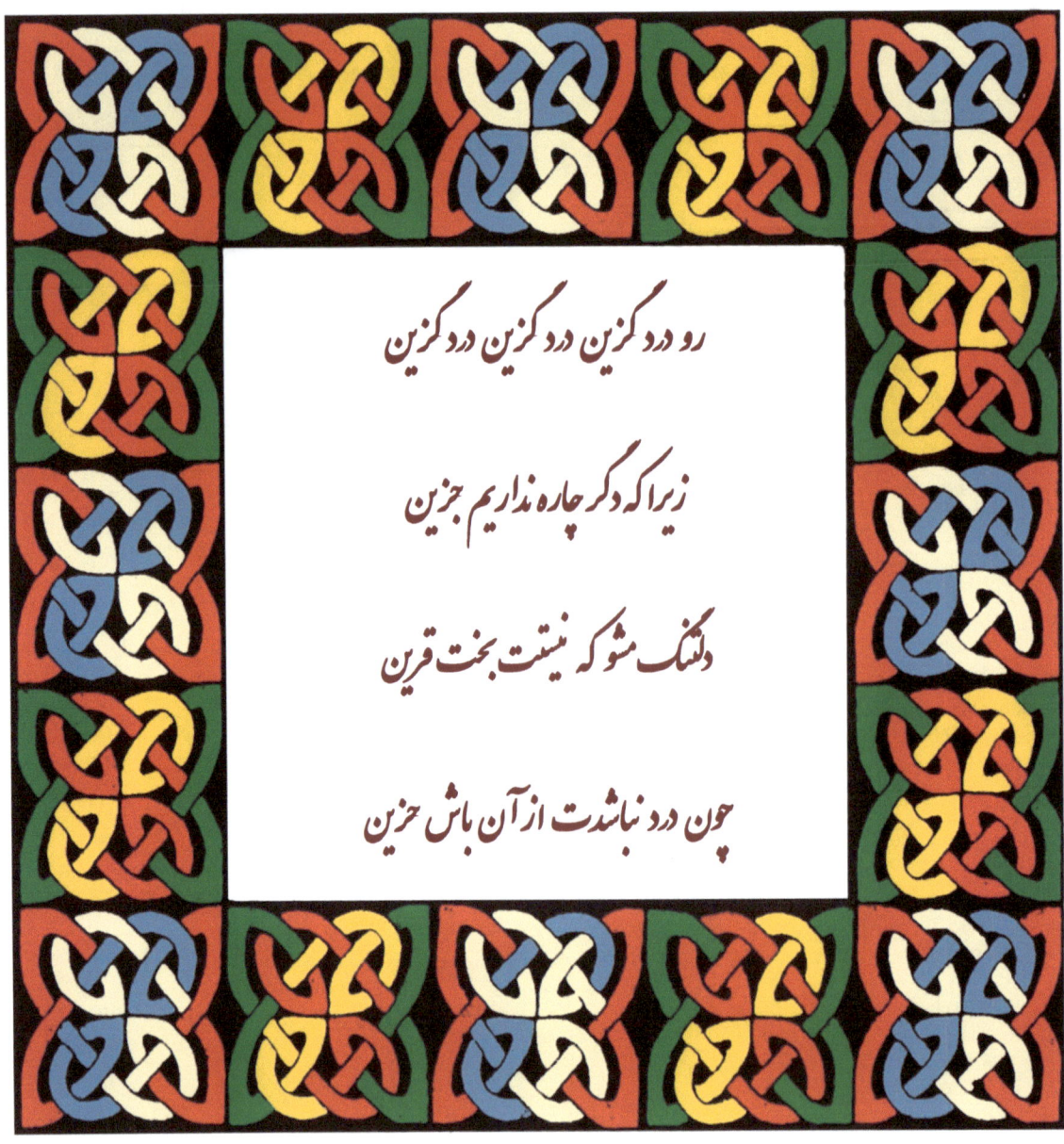

رو درد گزین درد گزین درد گزین

زیرا که دگر چاره نداریم جزین

دلتنگ مشو که نیستت بخت قرین

چون درد نباشدت از آن باش حزین

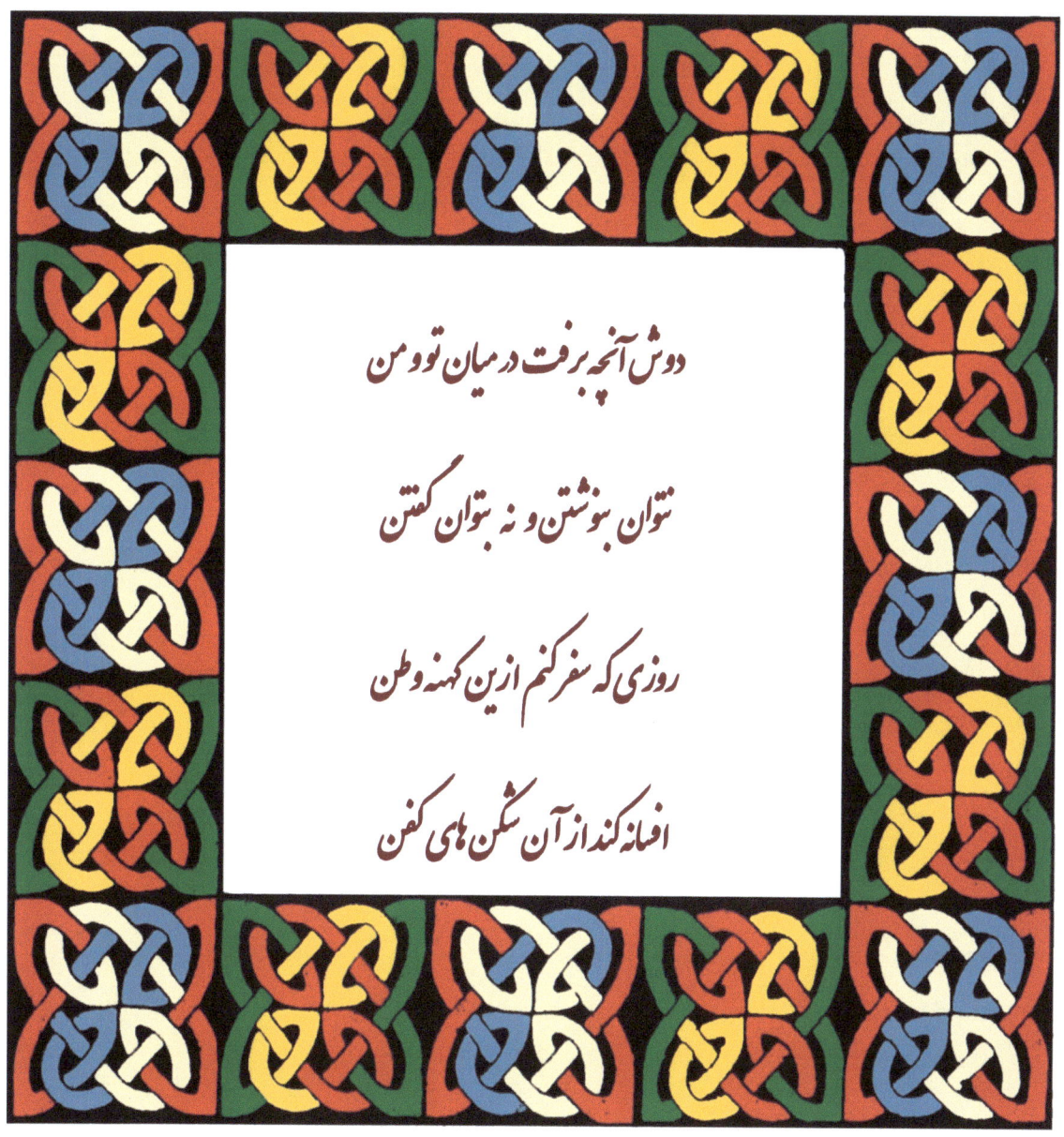

دوش آنچه برفت در میان تو و من

بتوان بنوشتن و نه بتوان گفتن

روزی که سفر کنم ازین کهنه وطن

افسانه کند از آن شکن های کفن

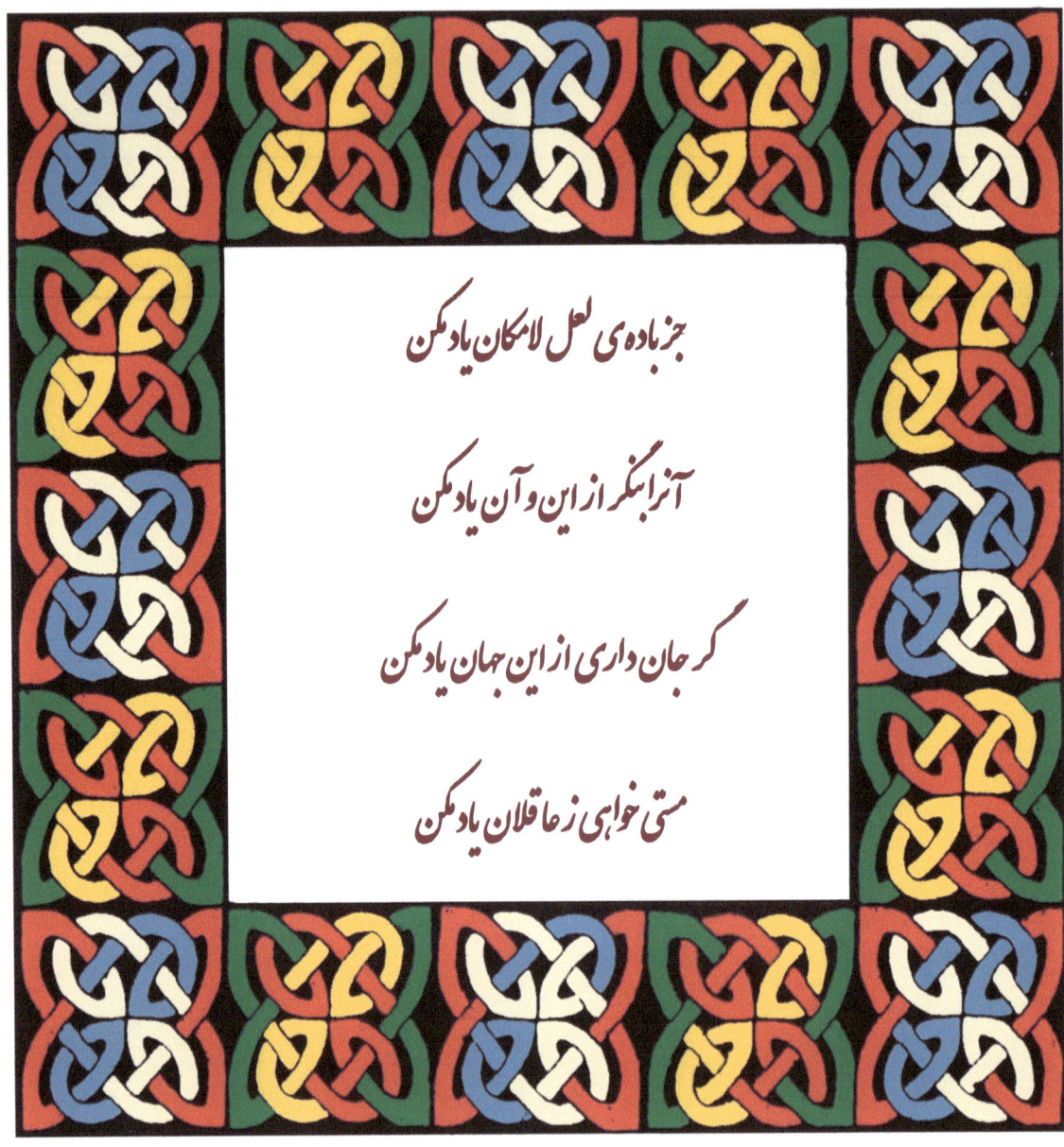

جز باده‌ی لعل لامکان یاد مکن

آنرا بنگر از این و آن یاد مکن

گر جان داری از این جهان یاد مکن

مستی خواهی ز عاقلان یاد مکن

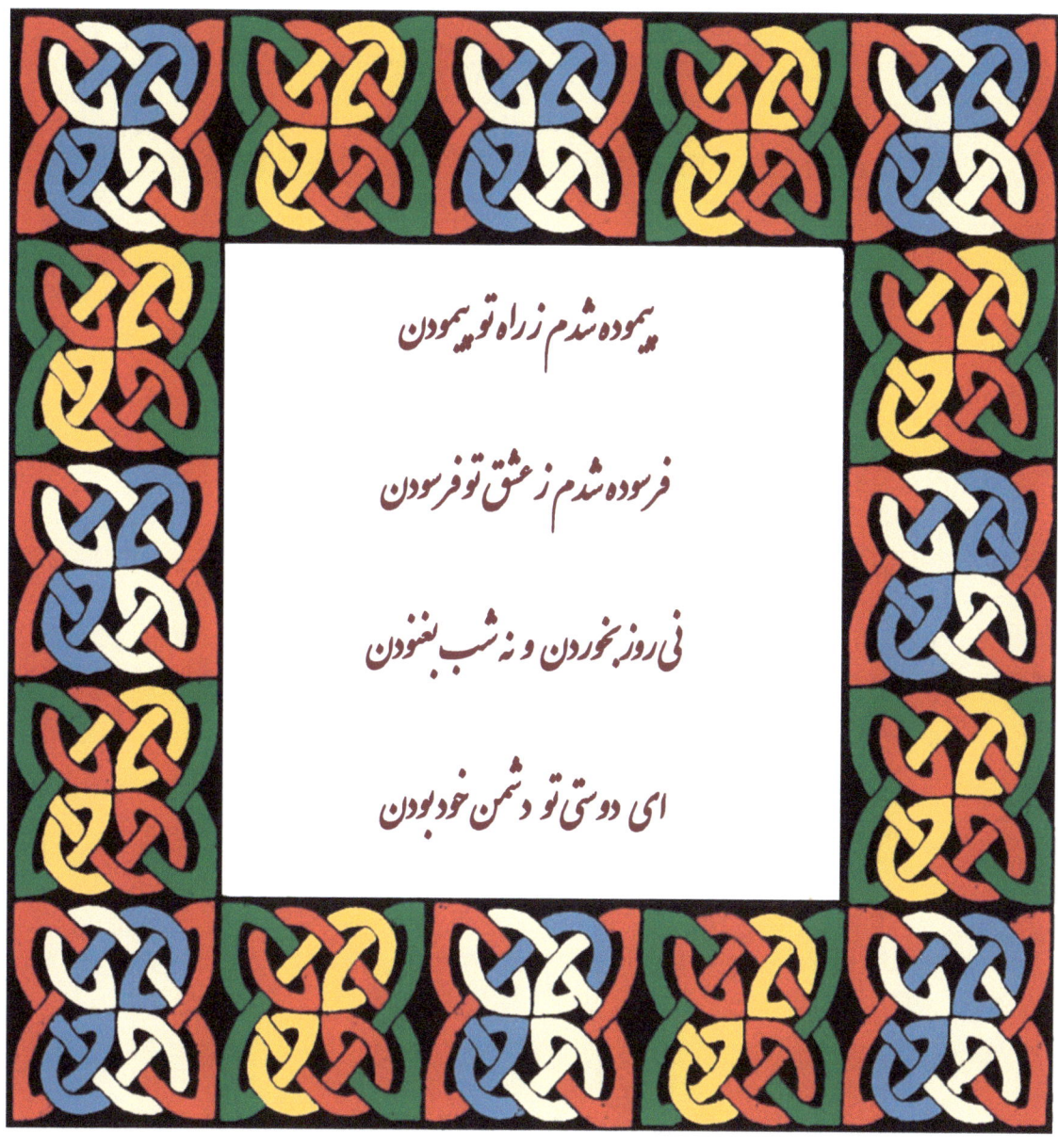

پیموده شدم ز راه تو پیمودن

فرسوده شدم ز عشق تو فرسودن

نی روز بخوردن و نه شب بغنودن

ای دوستی تو دشمن خود بودن

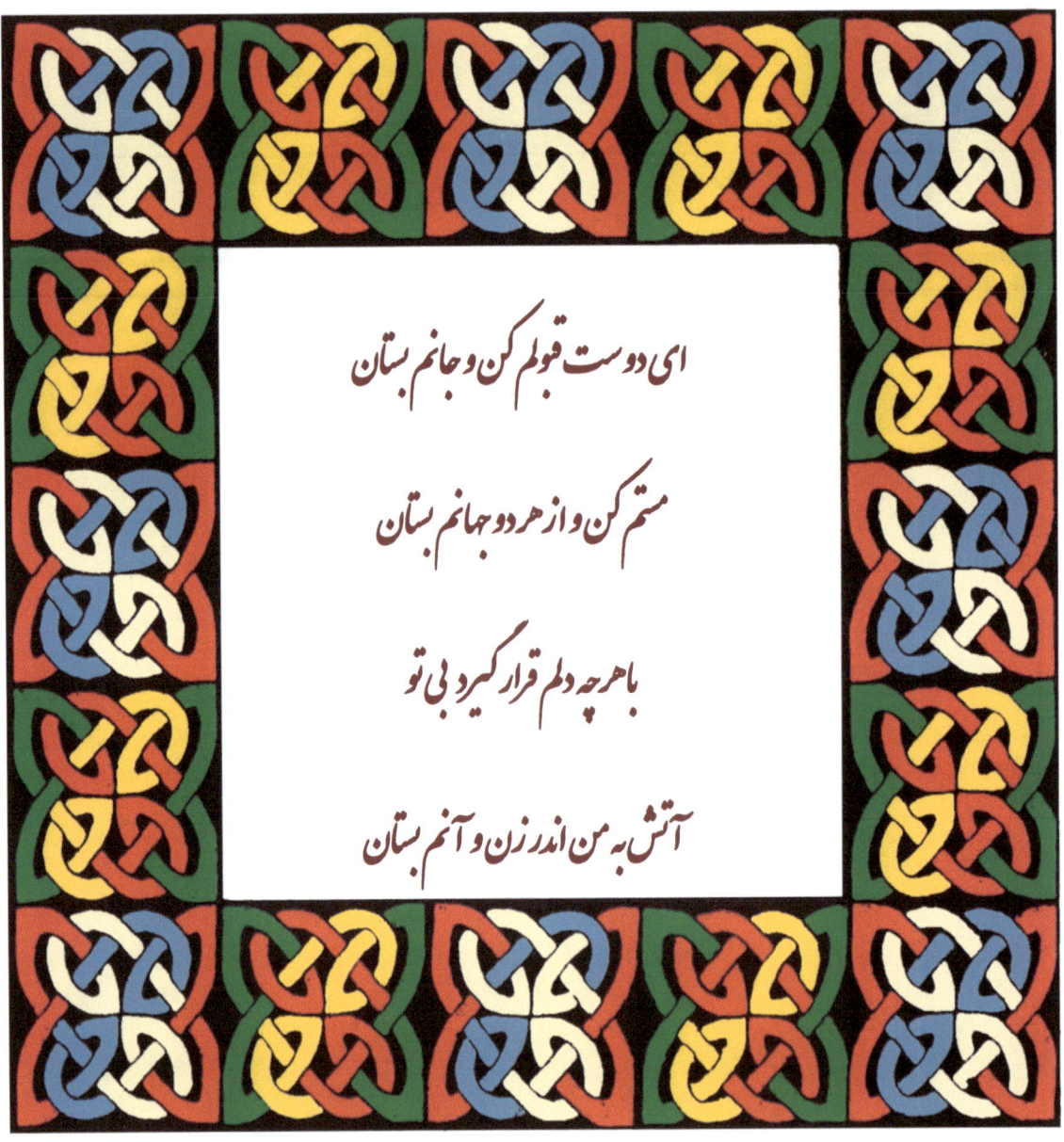

ای دوست قبولم کن و جانم بستان

مستم کن و از هر دو جهانم بستان

با هر چه دلم قرار گیرد بی تو

آتش به من اندر زن و آنم بستان

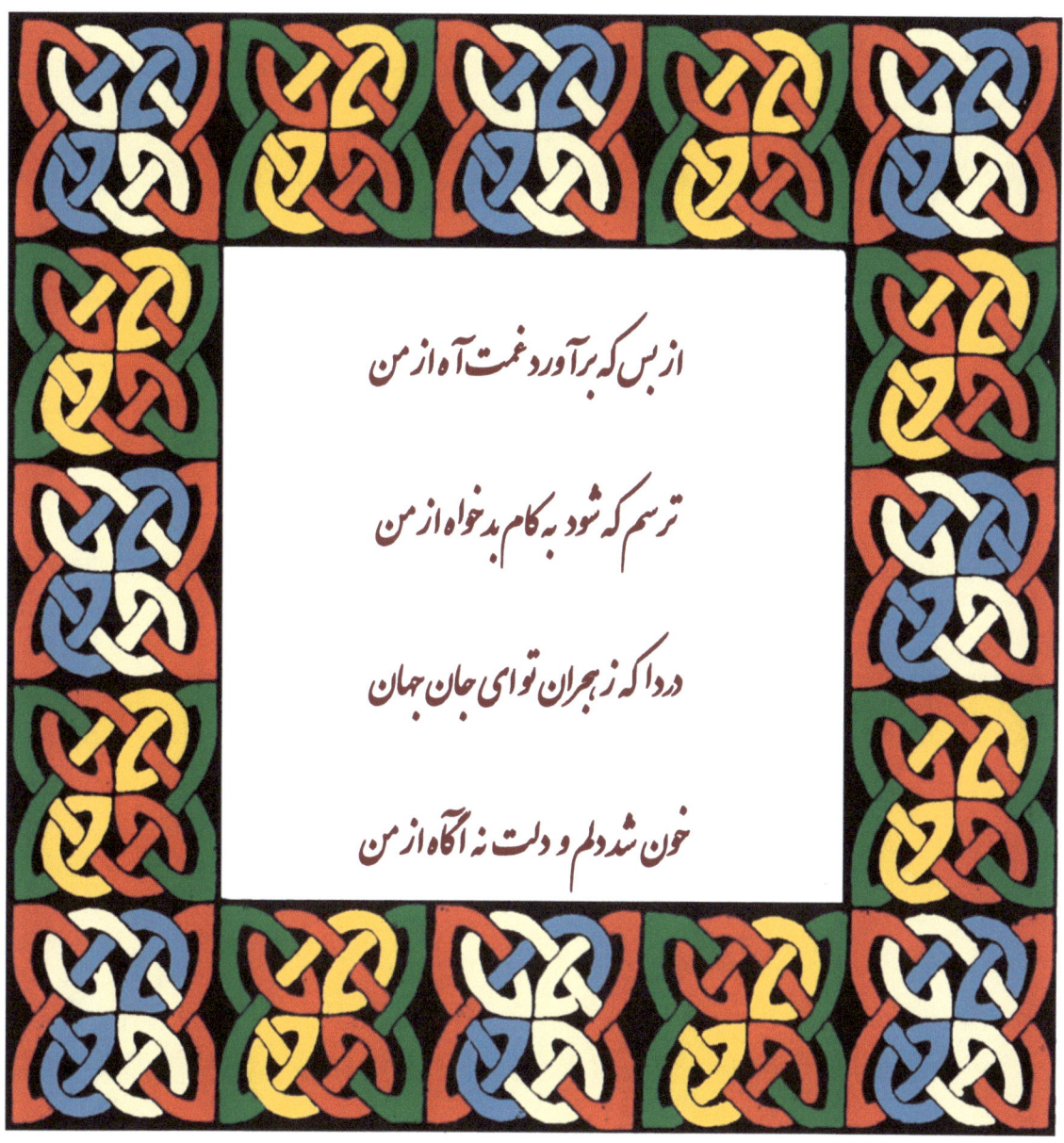

از بس که برآورد غمت آه از من

ترسم که شود به کام بدخواه از من

دردا که ز هجران تو ای جان جهان

خون شد دلم و دلت نه آگاه از من

می‌پنداری که از غمانت رستم

یا بی تو صبور گشتم و بنشستم

یا رب مرسان به هیچ شادی دستم

کز یک نفس از غم تو خالی هستم

من درد ترا ز دست آسان ندهم

دل بر نکنم ز دوست تا جان ندهم

از دوست به یادگار دردی دارم

کان درد به صد هزار درمان ندهم

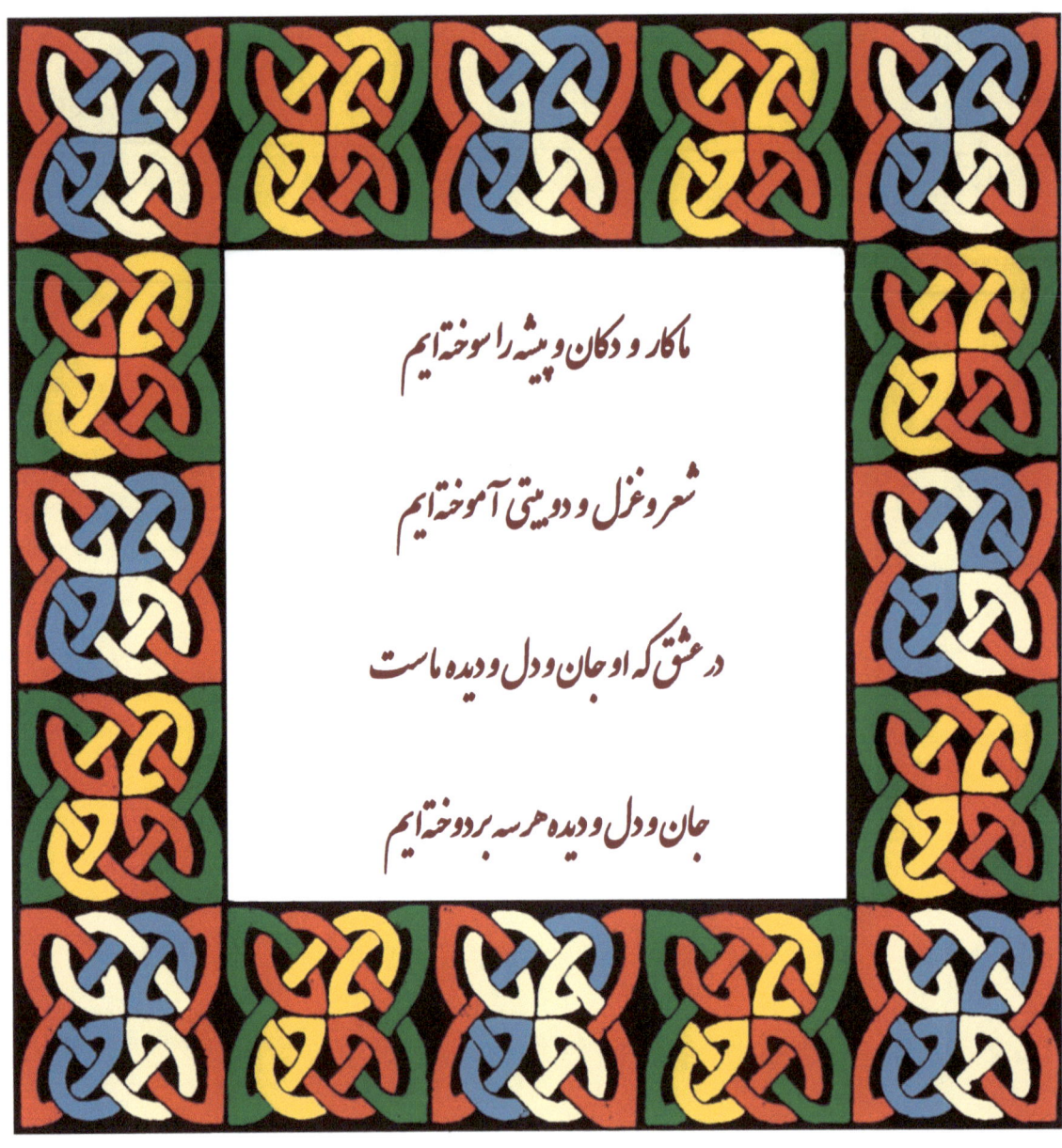

ما کار و دکان و پیشه را سوخته‌ایم

شعر و غزل و دوبیتی آموخته‌ایم

در عشق که او جان و دل و دیده ماست

جان و دل و دیده هر سه بردوخته‌ایم

تا چند چو دف دست ستمهات خورم

یا همچو رباب زخم غمهات خورم

گفتی که چو چنگ در برت بنوازم

من نای تو نیستم که دمهات خورم

بخروشیدم گفت خموشت خواهم

خاموش شدم گفت خروشت خواهم

برجوشیدم گفت که نی ساکن باش

ساکن گشتم گفت بجوشت خواهم

با درد بساز چون دوای تو منم

در کس منگر که آشنای تو منم

گر کشته شوی مگو که من کشته شدم

شکرانه بده که خونبهای تو منم

گفتم چشمم گفت که جیحون کنمش

گفتم که دلم گفت که پرخون کنمش

گفتم که تنم گفت در این روزی چند

رسوا کنم و ز شهر بیرون کنمش

هستم ز غمش چنان پریشان که مپرس

زانسان شده‌ام بی سر و سامان که مپرس

ای مرغ خیال سوی او کن گذری

وانکه ز منش بپرس چندان که مپرس

من بودم و دوش آن بت بنده نواز

از من همه لابه بود و از وی همه ناز

شب رفت و حدیث ما به پایان نرسید

شب را چه گنه حدیث ما بود دراز

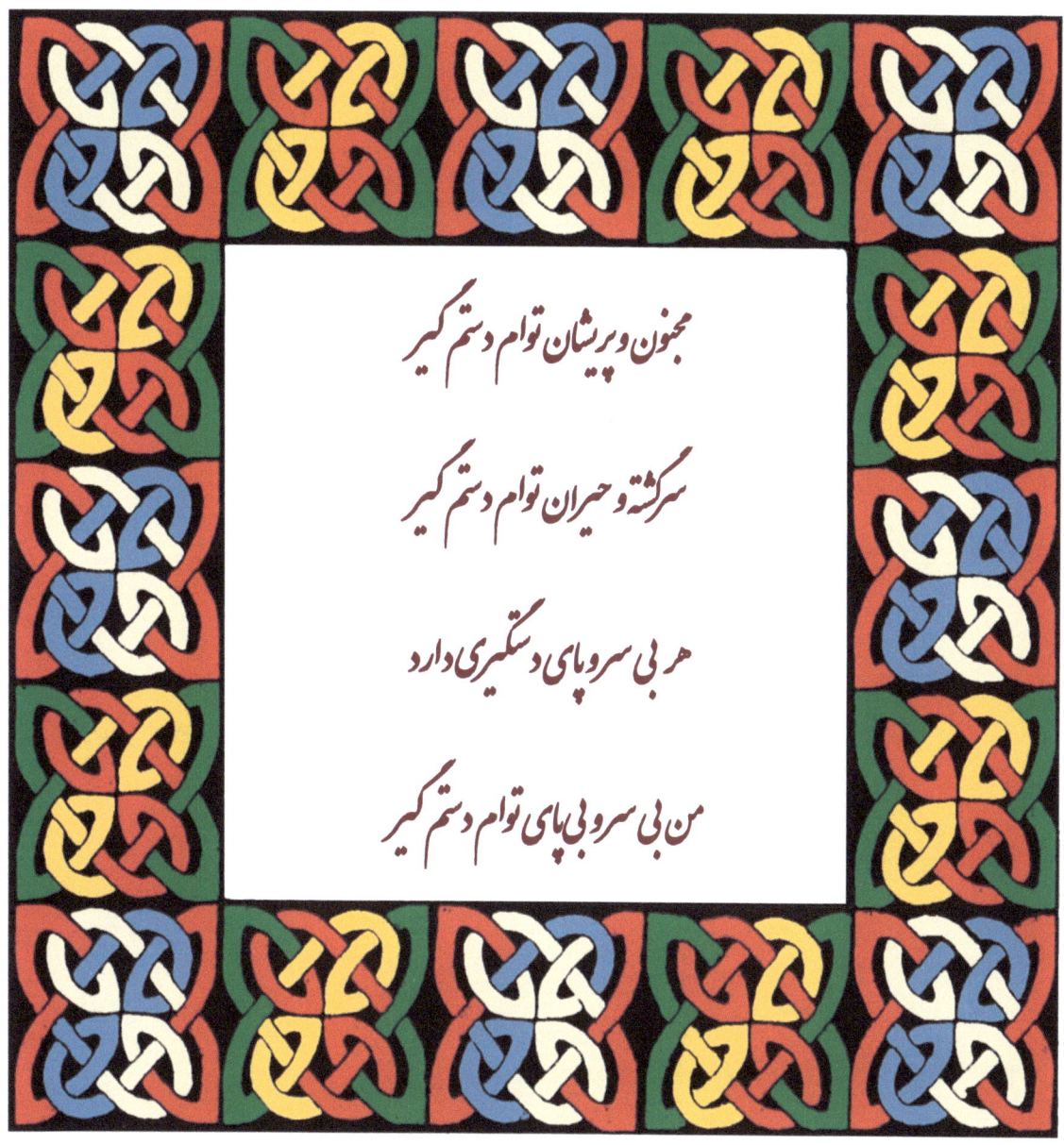

مجنون و پریشان توأم دستم گیر

سرگشته و حیران توأم دستم گیر

هر بی سر و پای دستگیری دارد

من بی سر و بی پای توأم دستم گیر

دست و دل ما هر چه تهی تر خوشتر

و آزادی دل ز هر چه خوشتر خوشتر

عیش خوش مفلسانه یک چشم زدن

از حشمت صد هزار قیصر خوشتر

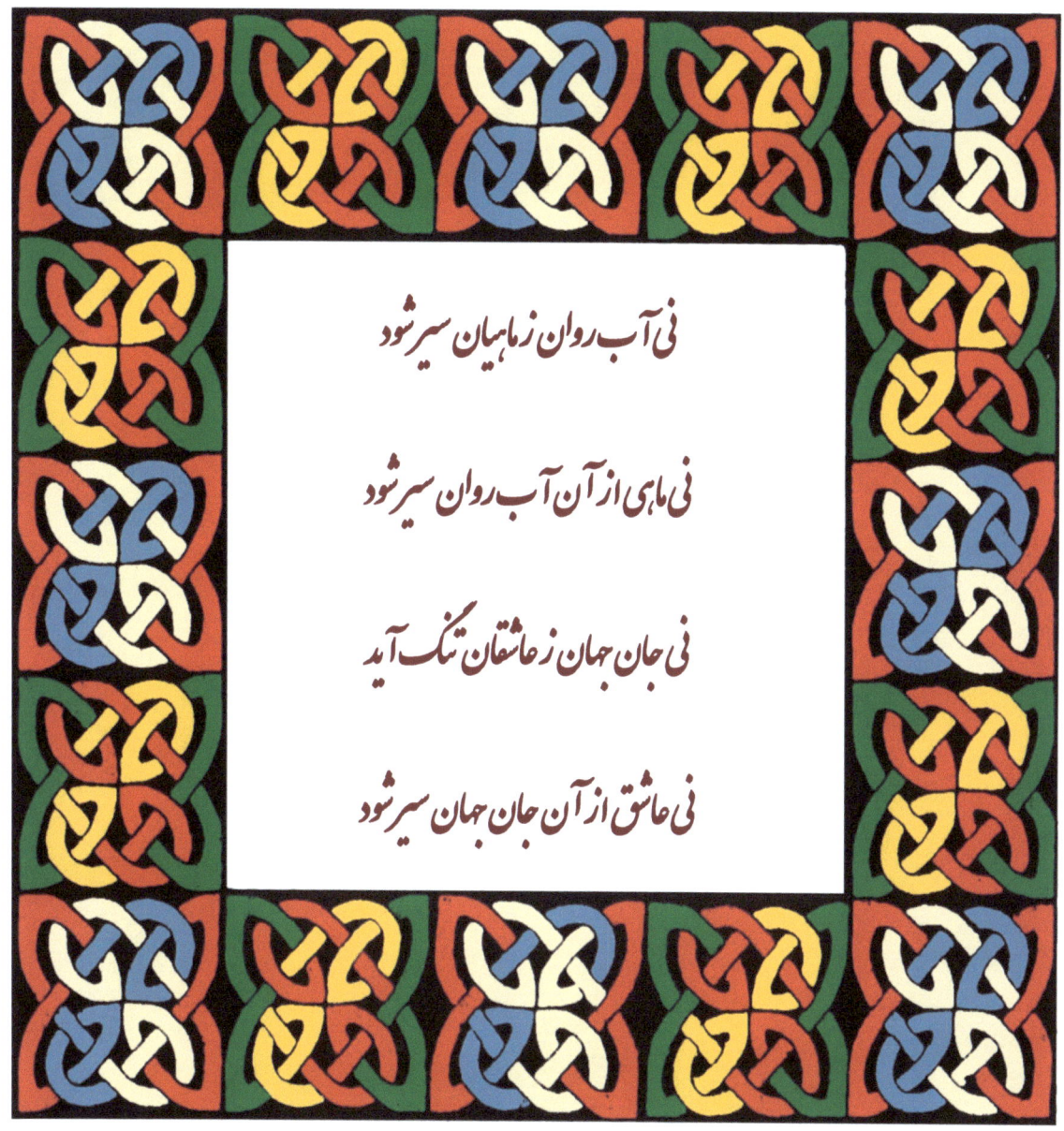

کشتی چو به دریای روان می‌گذرد

می‌پندارد که نیستان می‌گذرد

ما می‌گذریم زاین جهان در همه حال

می‌پنداریم کاین جهان می‌گذرد

سودای تو را بهانه‌ای بس باشد

مستان تو را ترانه‌ای بس باشد

در کشتن ما چه می‌زنی تیغ جفا

ما را سر تازیانه‌ای بس باشد

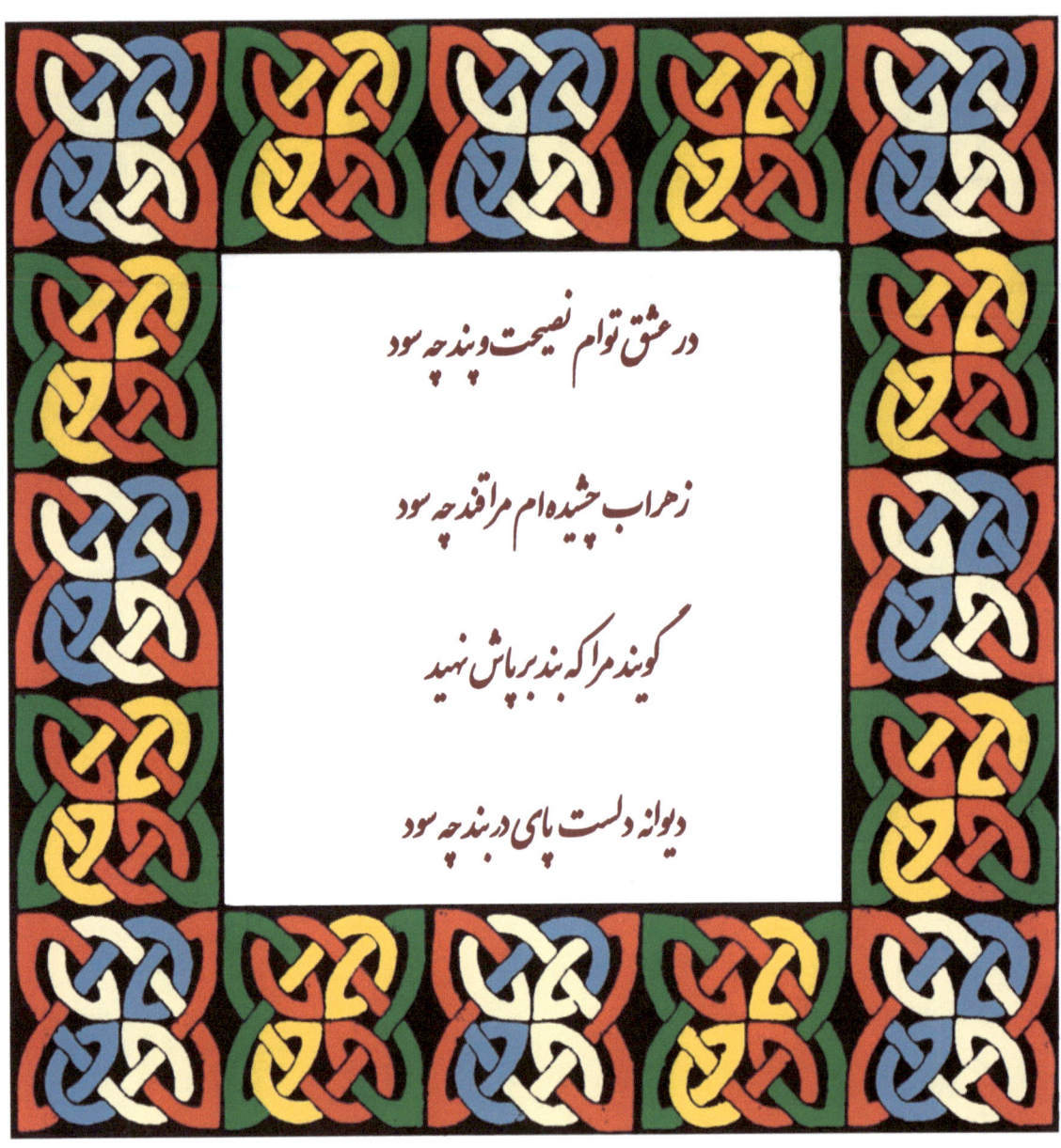

در عشق توام نصیحت و پند چه سود

زهراب چشیده‌ام مرا قند چه سود

گویند مرا که بند بر پاش نهید

دیوانه دلست پای در بند چه سود

چون خمر تو در ساغر ما در ریزند

پنهان شدگان این جهان بر خیزند

هم امت پرهیز ز ما پرهیزند

هم اهل خرابات ز ما بگریزند

تا با غم عشق تو مرا کار افتاد

بیچاره دلم در غم بسیار افتاد

بسیار فتاده بود اندر غم عشق

اما نه چنین زار که این بار افتاد

اندر دل بی‌وفا غم و ماتم باد

آن را که وفا نیست ز عالم کم باد

دیدی که مرا هیچ کسی یاد نکرد

جز غم که هزار آفرین بر غم باد

از شبنم عشق خاک آدم گل شد

صد فتنه و شور در جهان حاصل شد

صد نشتر عشق بر رگ روح زدند

یک قطره از آن چکید و نامش دل شد

آن کس که تراشناخت جان را چه کند

فرزند و عیال و خانمان را چه کند

دیوانه کنی هر دو جهانش بخشی

دیوانه تو هر دو جهان را چه کند

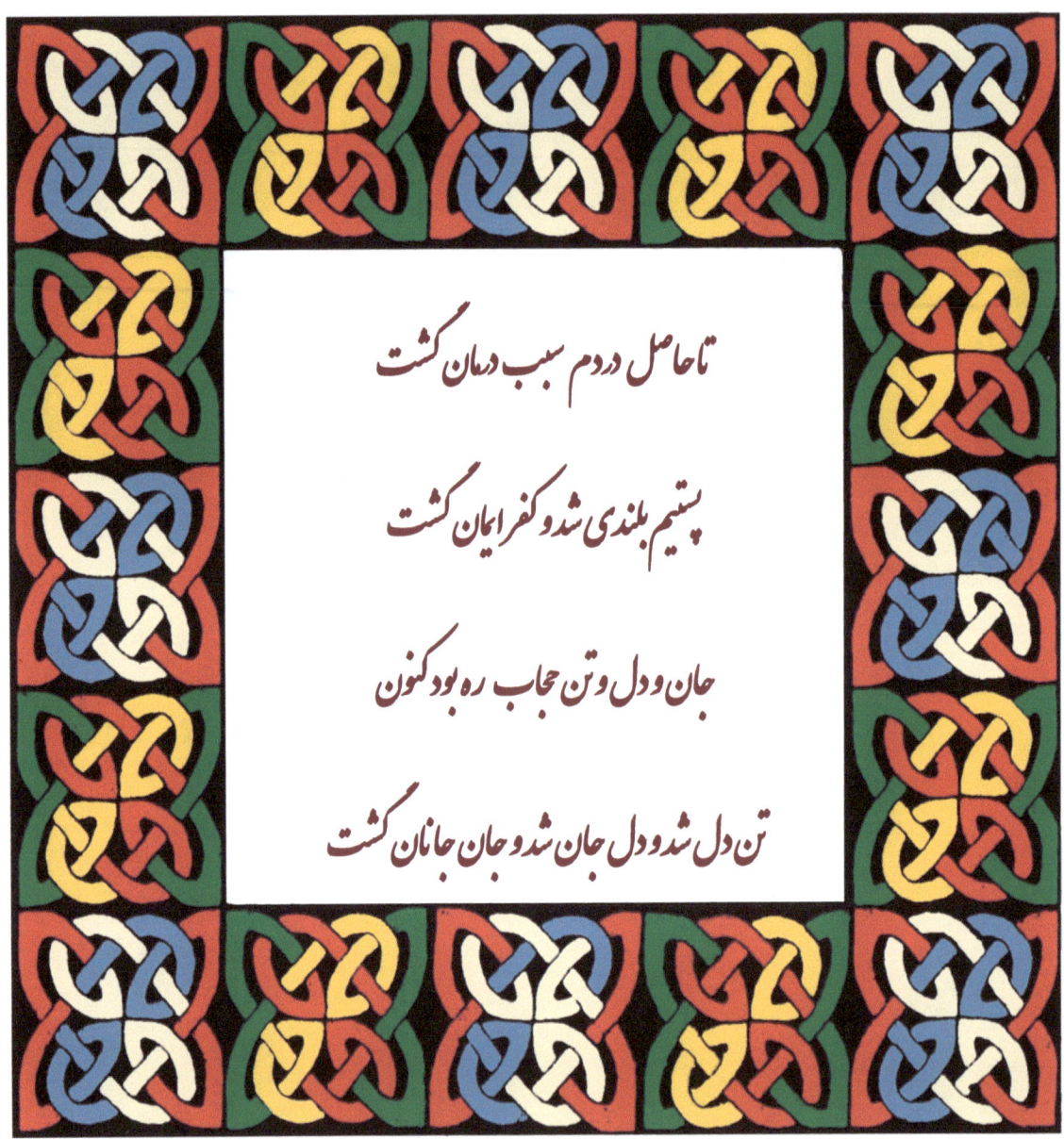

تا حاصل دردم سبب درمان گشت

پستیم بلندی شد و کفر ایمان گشت

جان و دل و تن حجاب ره بود کنون

تن دل شد و دل جان شد و جان جانان گشت

هر روز دلم در غم تو زار تر است

وز من دل بی رحم تو بی زار تر است

بگذاشتیم غم تو نگذاشت مرا

حقا که غمت از تو وفادار تر است

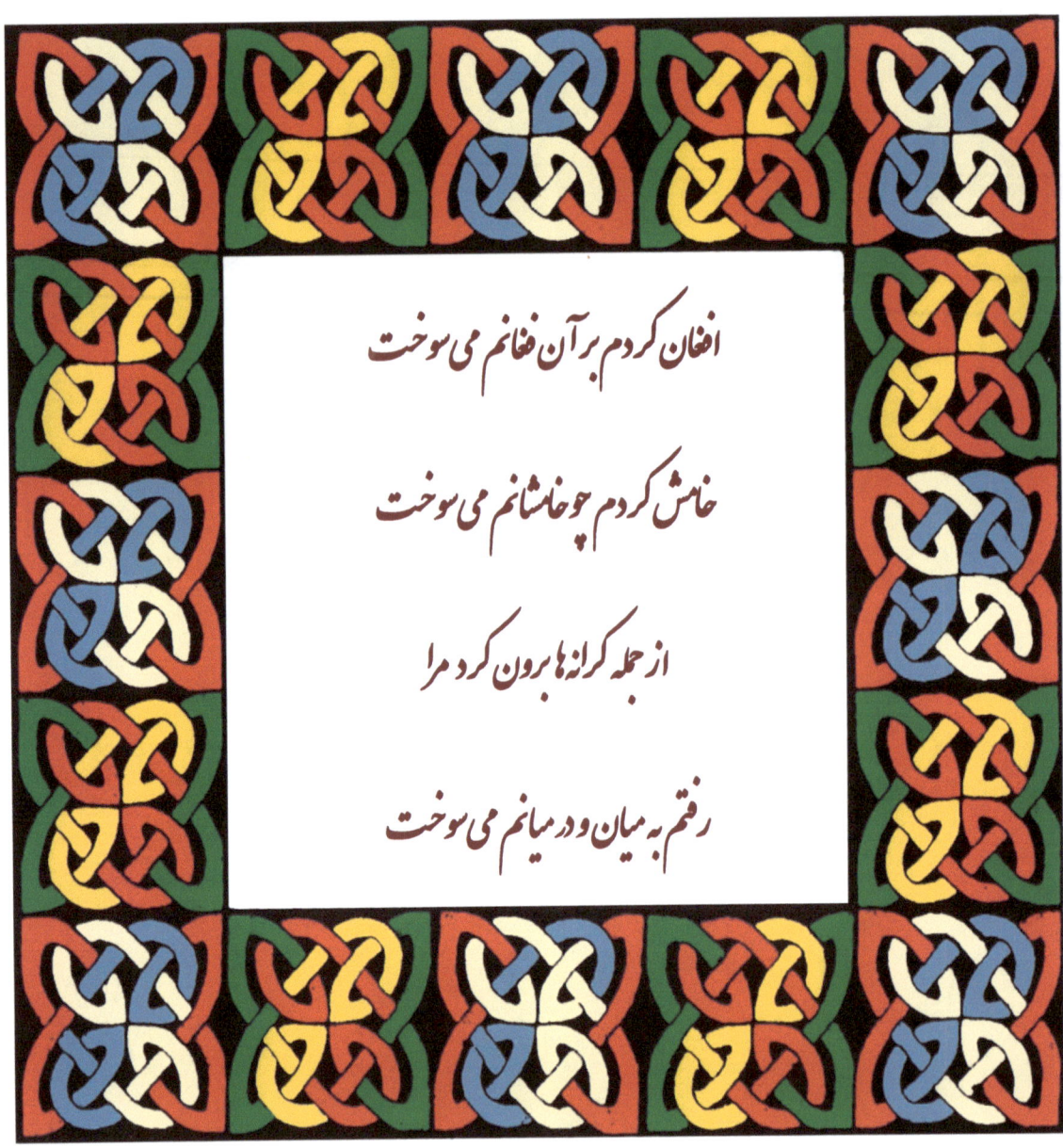

افغان کردم بر آن فغانم می‌سوخت

خامش کردم چو خامشانم می‌سوخت

از جمله کرانه‌ها برون کرد مرا

رفتم به میان و در میانم می‌سوخت

حاجت نبود مستی ما را به شراب

یا مجلس ما را طرب از چنگ و رباب

بی ساقی و بی شاهد و بی مطرب و نی

شوریده و مستیم چو مستان خراب

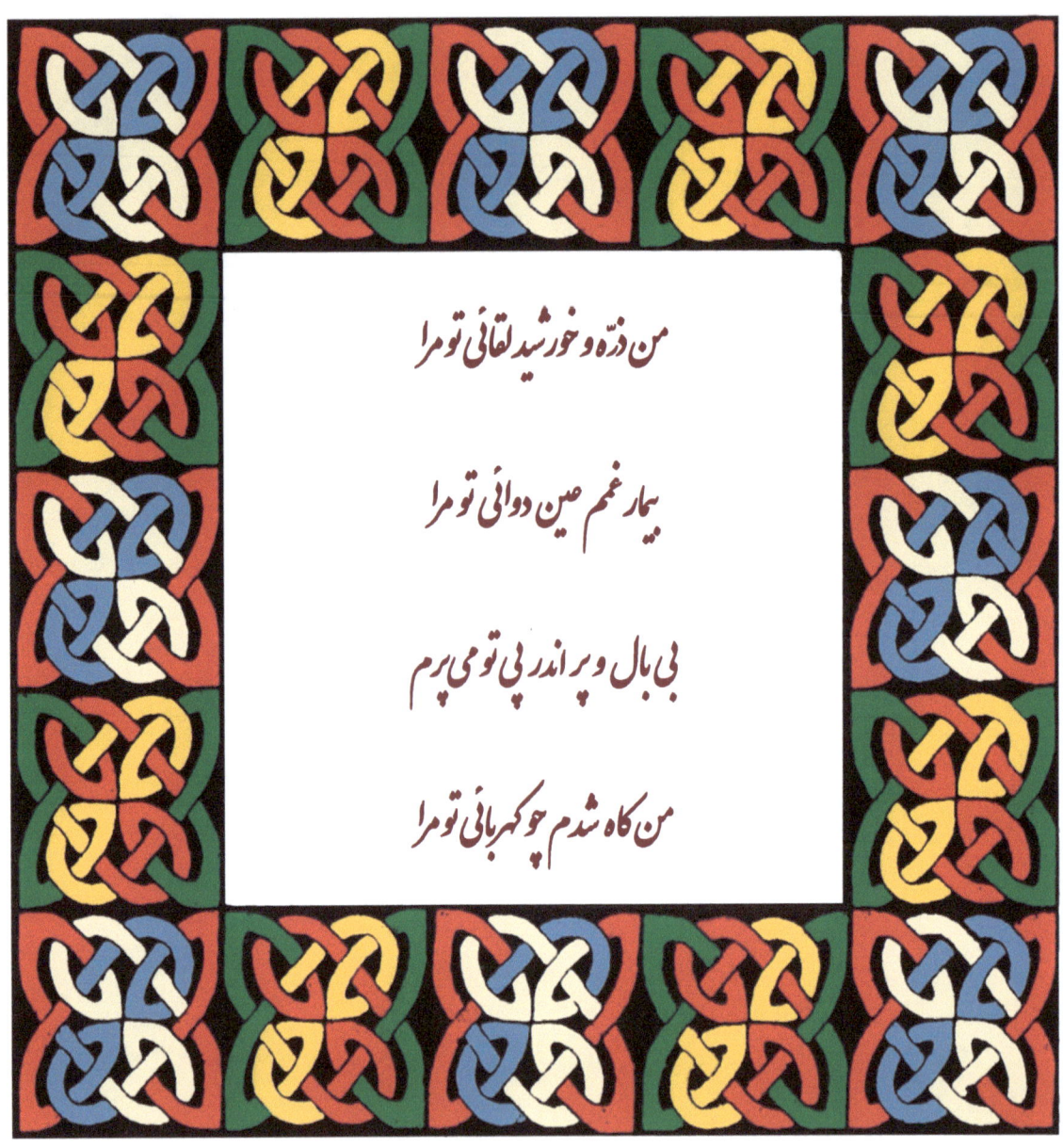

من ذرّه و خورشید لقائی تو مرا

بیمار غمم عین دوائی تو مرا

بی بال و پر اندر پی تو می پرم

من کاه شدم چو کهربائی تو مرا

عاشق همه سال مست و رسوا بادا

دیوانه و شوریده و شیدا بادا

با هشیاری غصه هر چیز خوریم

چون مست شویم هر چه بادا بادا

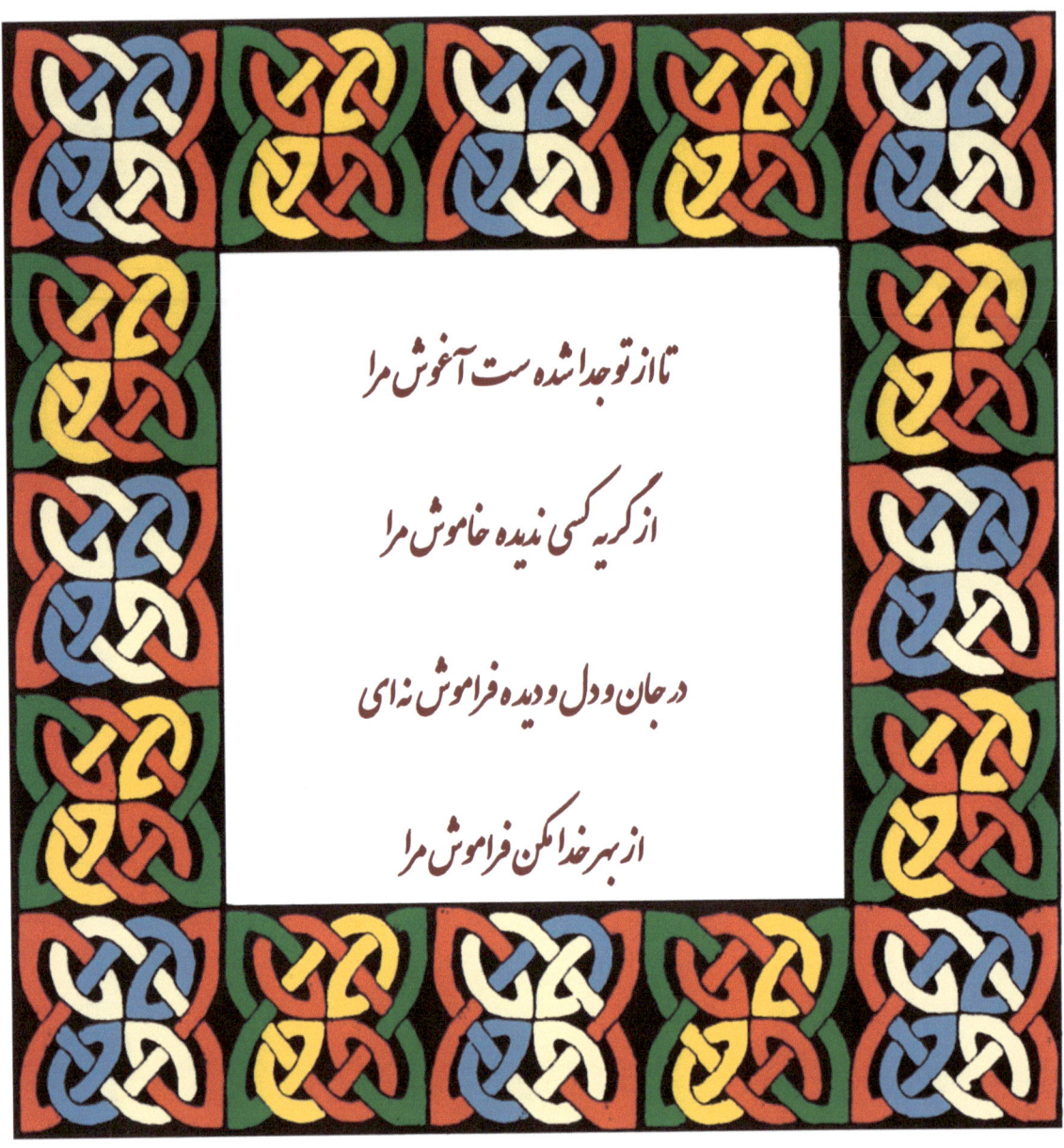

تا از تو جدا شده‌ست آغوش مرا

از گریه کسی ندیده خاموش مرا

در جان و دل و دیده فراموش نه‌ای

از بهر خدا مکن فراموش مرا

ای سبزی هر درخت و هر باغ و گیا

ای دولت و اقبال من و کار و کیا

ای خلوت و ای سماع و اخلاص و ریا

بی حضرت تو این همه سوداست بیا

ای آنکه چو آفتاب فردست بیا

بیرون تو برگ و باغ زردست بیا

عالم بی تو غبار و گردست بیا

این مجلس عیش بی تو سردست بیا

منتخب رباعیات

مولانا جلال‌الدین محمد بلخی رومی

This book remains the property of the publisher and copyright holder, Bahar Books, LLC.
All rights reserved under International Copyright Conventions.
No part of this book may be used, distributed or reproduced in any forms or by any means without the prior written permission of the publisher.

ISBN-10: 1939099110

ISBN-13: 978-1-939099-11-2

Copyright © 2012 by Bahar Books, LLC.

Published by Bahar Books, White Plains, New York

منتخب رباعیات

مولانا جلال‌الدّین محمّد بلخی رومی

Bahar Books

www.baharbooks.com

www.ingramcontent.com/pod-product-compliance
Lightning Source LLC
Chambersburg PA
CBHW040026050426
42453CB00002B/20

other animals. Like radiation, which is invisible, vast quantities of microscopic plastic have entered the food chain, affecting marine life, water quality, and ultimately human and animal circulatory systems. One source of microplastics is the "Great Pacific Garbage Patch," a continent-sized patch of plastic waste in the Pacific Ocean that serves as a stark symbol of humanity's collective failure to manage our waste.[7]

As we republish *Island of Dreams* in this Fiftieth Anniversary Edition, we invite readers to remember Japan's environmental crises of the past and reflect on the global implications of these stories. We hope that making *Island of Dreams* available again will offer readers valuable insights to help us come together and protect our global environment into the future.

Norie Huddle
Michael Reich
2025

FOREWORD BY PAUL R. EHRLICH

Since the end of World War II, man has gained increasingly vast powers over nature. But power is not control, and man's fate remains inextricably tied to nature and the ecological systems that are necessary for human survival on earth. These systems cannot be assaulted with impunity. When quantities grow—and shrink—exponentially (as, for instance, do human population size and petroleum resources in today's world), limits tend to be reached suddenly, and these limits are converging in the form of the ever-deepening population-resources-environment crisis that now confronts us.

Japan is in many respects the front-runner in this crisis. First of all, she is vastly overpopulated. The degree of overpopulation of a country is frequently judged by its population density—and by that standard Japan certainly qualifies. A century ago, Japan had a population density four times the present density of the United States; today, at nearly 290 people per square kilometer (750/sq. mile), her population density is 13 times that of the United States. The grossly overpopulated Netherlands has well over 300 persons per square kilometer, but since only 16 percent of Japan's land is arable and suitable for habitation, Japan is, in terms of habitable land, by far the most densely populated of the earth's major nations.

A much more meaningful measure of overpopulation than density is the relationship between numbers of people and the availability of resources to sustain them. While all industrial nations are to some degree dependent on imports, those that are unable even to come close to supporting their populations on internal resources are in the most precarious position if the world trade system breaks down or ocean fisheries collapse. It is in this context that the true degree of Japanese overpopulation becomes clear. Although Japan is self-sufficient in rice, she imports massive amounts of other grains and legumes, and with only 5 percent of the total Asian population she absorbs well over half of all food and feed flowing into the area. To keep the all-important flow of fishes moving toward her overpopulated islands, Japan has spread her fishing operations around the world—to the Mediterranean, the South Atlantic, the Caribbean, and the waters off Baja California.

The Japanese situation with regard to other resources is similar. In 1970, Japan produced less than 17 percent of the energy she consumed. She must import all of her bauxite and most of her copper. Japan imports about ten times the value of forest products that she exports, which has helped to drive the price of lumber in the United States to record highs.

There is a third standard by which Japan is vastly overpopulated—and that is the way that the Japanese overstress the natural ecological systems of their islands. That they have an enormously deleterious impact on their environment is hardly surprising, considering the amount of industrial activity that is compressed into a small space. Energy consumption per unit of land area is eight times higher than that of the United States, 2.5 times that of the United Kingdom, and 1.8 times that of West Germany. Even within Japan's limited land area, the activities are concentrated, with about 60 million people living and working in the Tokyo-Osaka megalopolis alone. Tokyo-Osaka produces roughly the same amount of steel as all of England. The miracle is that the famous Tokyo smog is not even worse!

If, however, Japan has been a forerunner in overpopulation, she has also shown the way in population control. Awareness of population problems among the Japanese people played a major role in the passage of the 1948 "Eugenic Protection Law," which legalized abortion and sterilization. This law also set up an office under the Ministry of Health and Welfare that established a network of some 850 centers distributing family planning information throughout the nation. As a result of these measures, the birthrate dropped precipitously from over 34 per thousand in 1947 to less than 18 in 1960, and the net reproductive rate (NRR) has fluctuated around 1.0 since about 1955. If the NRR remains around 1, Japan may reach ZPG (a stationary or non-growing population) before 2025.

The other overdeveloped nations of the world can thus look to Japan for portents of their own future. The public health problems associated with environmental deterioration in Japan have received worldwide attention: extreme air pollution, mercury poisoning, and cadmium poisoning are outstanding examples. The Japanese are also serving as guinea pigs for experiments on the long-term effects of chlorinated hydrocarbon poisoning.

It seems likely that the more subtle and perhaps more dangerous ecosystematic effects of human abuse of the environment will appear in Japan and in the adjacent oceans before they appear in many other areas of the world. It would behoove Japan and perhaps the United Nations to carry out intensive monitoring programs in the hope of providing other nations with some warning of expected patterns of breakdown.

Japan also provides an excellent microcosm in which to study the behavior of a highly literate, technologically sophisticated people facing problems that will soon be ubiquitous in the overdeveloped world. For

Foreword *xiii*

instance, the government in Japan is controlled by industry to an even greater degree than that of the United States. Therefore the patterns of government-industry interaction in Japan as she comes to grips with pollution and the demographic changes associated with an approach to ZPG will be of great interest to Americans and Europeans. Will American politicians, for instance, prove to be as naive in population matters as former Prime Minister Eisaku Sato, who, in 1969, at the behest of business interests, called for an increase in the Japanese birthrate because of an impending "labor shortage"? Needless to say, the most elementary ecological analysis indicates that any attempt to increase the Japanese population is utter insanity.

Japan in many ways is making the same mistakes the United States has made. There is, for instance, the interest among Japanese politicians in "solving" population problems by population redistribution. Such a "solution" is popular in American government circles also. Unfortunately, many of the most serious problems associated with overpopulation (such as the environmental deterioration associated with the use of pesticides in agriculture) are little affected by population distribution, and others (such as the loss of agricultural land due to construction) would be exacerbated by population redistribution. Redistribution may be beneficial in certain special circumstances (such as relieving congestion and concentration of air pollution around Tokyo), but by no stretch of the imagination can it "solve" the problems of overpopulation in either Japan or the United States.

A pronounced drop of the birth rate in 1966, the year of Fire and Horse (thought to be unfavorable for having female children), indicates that the Japanese people have considerable control over their fertility. It seems unlikely, for instance, that exhortations from business or government are likely to produce a significant upturn in fertility unless the population as a whole sees benefit in it. It remains to be seen whether they can attain similar control over their environment, especially when changes to deal with ecological imperatives often will be opposed by industry and an extraordinarily economocentric government. But ecological and consumer activism is on the upswing, and the courts have begun to compensate the most severely affected victims of environmental abuse.

The most important question about Japan, however, may be that of her future international behavior. Japan is the ultimate example of a highly industrialized, resource-poor nation playing the role of an economic "middleman." From the parochial viewpoint of the classical economist, Japan may appear to be in a strong position. From the broad viewpoint of the ecologist, she teeters on the brink of disaster. The soybean "shokku" of 1973, followed a few months later by the Arab oil embargo, was an early warning of what is coming. Japan's response in both cases was disheartingly slow and inadequate. It was as if the Japanese could not believe what was happening. Now that they have been somewhat alerted, will their responses fit the situation?

What, for instance, will the Japanese do as the world fisheries move inexorably toward collapse from overfishing and destruction of oceanic productivity by pollution? Where will Japan turn for food if exporting nations such as the United States find they require more of their own supplies domestically? Or if they must make such difficult decisions as whether to limit supplies sold to Japan or the Soviet Union? How long can Japan maintain the resource flows of all kinds upon which she is utterly dependent in a world of increasing scarcity and competition?

It will be most interesting to see whether Japan plunges on in search of an ever greater Gross National Product, constantly increasing her dependence on imports. Will her already legendary economic aggressiveness continue to increase? Will the Japanese turn to military aggressiveness as suppliers become unwilling or unable to maintain flows? Will they move toward an equilibrium, low-throughput economy? Will they do everything possible to lessen their dependence on imports? Will they become leaders in establishing international controls over the exploitation of fisheries and the pollution of atmosphere and oceans? Will they fall back on their enormous cultural resources and return to valuing beauty and tranquillity more than an expanding GNP? Knowledgeable people in other industrial countries will be watching Japan closely, much as old-time coal miners once watched the canary in the cage.

Paul R. Ehrlich
1974

PREFACE, 1975

Although the Japanese comprise little more than three percent of the world's population and inhabit a narrow chain of islands remarkably unendowed with natural resources, their impact upon modern history has been imposing. The boldness, energy, and speed with which they have absorbed and adapted the precepts and practices of modernity have amazed both scholars and laymen alike. Indeed, their economic recovery since the end of World War II has been called "miraculous," and their economic performance has inspired futurologist Herman Kahn to envisage the dawning of a "Japanese century."

There are, to be sure, many aspects of contemporary Japanese culture that deserve appreciation, many unique cultural institutions, the products of a merging of East and West, that are worthy not only of probing analysis, but, perhaps, even of emulation. Why, then, the reader may ask, have we chosen to air so unpleasant a subject as environmental deterioration in Japan, an issue the Japanese themselves are understandably reluctant to publicize? First, it is because we think that environmental problems comprise a focal point for understanding contemporary Japan. But more important, it is because we are convinced that many of the problems faced by "spaceship Japan" today will be faced by all of us on "spaceship Earth" tomorrow. In telescoping economic and industrial development, the Japanese have brought ecological catastrophe—the other side of the balance sheet—into clear view; we like to believe that perhaps by studying history we will not be condemned to repeat it.

In the past century, the Japanese have embraced Western capitalism's economic values, they have adopted its productive technology, and they have pursued its goals in the marketplace—all with resounding success. But while their cultural underpinnings have given impetus to this process, the disadvantages of limited space and resources, coupled with the Japanese enthusiasm for the game, have resulted in environmental deterioration unparalleled elsewhere. This is the tragedy lurking behind Japan's GNP statistics. And if present global trends continue, if we are to allow unlimited growth in population, resource exploitation, and industrial production in a world that is finite and limited, it is inevitable that, at some point in time, we will all meet with the same or a similar set of difficulties.

To analyze the development and present status of Japan's environmental disruptions holistically, we have tried to cope with the cultural and linguistic barriers often standing between the Japanese and the rest of the world. Throughout, we have attempted to convey the universality of the Japanese predicament. For in living and working in Japan, we know that beneath the cultural overlay throbs the heart of humanity: men and women pursuing health and happiness, security and peace, and a sense of dignity and real worth. When it is suggested that not all their activities as a modern, industrial people are conducive to the realization of these ends, many are set to thinking about what true welfare, both for themselves and for future generations, really means. Is this unique to Japan? We think not.

In sum, we hope that the story which unfolds in the following pages will broaden our perspectives regarding the choices that will have to be made in the future and will, while we still have the chance to choose, help tilt those choices in favor of survival.

Norie Huddle
Michael Reich
1974

INTRODUCTION, 1975

Adept at working together to realize their communal aspirations, the Japanese are a goal-oriented people. During the first half of this century, they pursued a dream of imperial status and military conquest, a dream that ended in nightmare. In the postwar period, under the tutelage of the United States, they have sought national economic power and material well-being, and this dream has ostensibly been realized. But Japan's much-admired economic success has brought with it a wide array of severe environmental disruptions. And having come to know as realities many of the environmental hazards only forecast elsewhere, the Japanese are racing ahead of the world into a potentially calamitous future.

A survey of Japan's experiences with environmental disruption, population growth, and diminishing resources casts into sharp relief the problems common to all industrialized and industrializing nations. Moreover, the negative consequences of Japan's rapid growth policies may well foreshadow an advanced stage of our planetary predicament. If so, they offer a glimpse into a future for which few of us may be adequately prepared.

The Japanese environment is so riddled with industrial effluent and agricultural chemicals that in 1973 the entire populace panicked before the threat of a nationwide epidemic of "pollution diseases," incurable human disorders resulting from exposure to intense environmental pollution. "Yokkaichi asthma," one such disease, demonstrates the effects on man of extreme overexposure to industrial air pollutants. The notorious "Minamata disease," whose destructive potential is suggested by cases of occupational mercury intoxication such as America's "Danbury shakes," reveals the dangers inherent in mercury contamination of the food supply. And Japan's "oil disease," the result of an industrial accident that could occur anywhere, and that in fact closely resembles the contamination of two million West Virginia broilers with PCBs in 1971 and of 20 million Mississippi broilers with the pesticide Dieldrin in 1974, demonstrates how social attitudes, governmental bias, and industrial irresponsibility can combine to transform an accident into a lethal epidemic.

The physical suffering—the painful strangulation by sulfur oxides, the crippling effects of organic mercury poisoning, the permanent disfiguration caused by ingestion of PCBs—is only the surface of the tragedy. In proportion to their severity, pollution diseases are inevitably accompanied by loss of economic livelihood, social ostracism, psychological desperation, and, in the early stages, self-defeating efforts at concealment. The full tragedy of pollution diseases is magnified when they strike the young or the unborn, depriving them of their incentive for life and divesting them of their humanity. Environmental consequences of this magnitude have yet to be experienced in the West. Forewarned by their example, the public's vigilance should be reinforced.

But is it fair to extrapolate from Japan's experiences to throw light on future conditions in other parts of the world? Unfortunately, the answer is yes. For Japan's environmental problems reflect the assumptions underlying modern industrial society everywhere. They have simply been allowed to work themselves out rapidly, unrestrained by "external" considerations. It is true that geographic circumstances, economic opportunity, and the demands of cost efficiency dictated a strategy of industrial concentration along Japan's seacoasts, and that it is this design that hastened and exaggerated environmental decline. But the economies aimed at by this arrangement were achieved; in economic terms, the strategy was a winning one. Now that the competitive forces, and energy and resource limitations that recommended this strategy to Japan twenty-five years ago bear on all industrialized nations, similar designs are being adopted wherever possible. Consider, for example, the sixty-odd 150,000 barrel-a-day refineries called for by 1985 by the American National Petroleum Council, installations potentially disruptive to the environment and earmarked for American coastal locations.[1]

Indeed, the economic effectiveness of Japanese patterns of industrial organization has gained increasing recognition. Many developing nations openly aspire to fashion their own futures after the Japanese blueprint, choosing to cope with pollution control only after a high economic growth rate is achieved. Nor are Japan's admirers restricted to the leaders of the world's developing nations. In 1971, James M. Roche, on his retirement from the presidency of General Motors, expressed his concern about America's diminishing competitive structure in world markets and urged "closer cooperation between government, business and labor to weld a Japanese-style corporate America."[2]

But the value of Japan's economic gains cannot be measured if they are viewed in isolation from the total Japanese experience. More and more Japanese are questioning the assumptions of "Japan, Inc.," and are concluding that government must regulate rather than facilitate industrial activities that threaten the health and welfare of present and future generations. Pollution problems have thus begun to generate unprecedented changes in Japanese social values. As nation after nation plunges after the goal of ever-increasing material affluence, local and global ecological systems come under ever greater assault. The Japanese experience should alert us to some of the dangers inherent in a continuation of our present style of economic life, and should serve as an incentive to us all to reassess our economic, social, and political objectives. Such a reassessment should be carried out with dispatch—before we reach the unknown limits of nature's tolerance.

Norie Huddle
Michael Reich
1974

CHAPTER ONE

THE INDUSTRIAL BARONAGE

Not a few workers are still lying in their beds, completely deprived of their normal human functions and unable to see the last days of the mine for themselves. Downstream on the Watarase River, local residents continue to suffer from copper poisoning brought to them by the continuous flow of the river. The mine shaft has been sealed up, but the mine's history and its identity as the birthplace of pollution in Japan can never be buried in the darkness of the shaft.

—MAINICHI SHIMBUM
February 25, 1973

In Japan, as in other nations, the development of pollution prevention technology was simply not a major concern in the early stages of modernization. Growing volumes of factory effluents were handled according to the principles of convenience and minimal cost: treatment facilities were usually nonexistent and areas bordering industrial sites invariably bore the burden. To a large extent, the entrepreneurs of the Meiji era (1868–1912) were unaware of the hazards caused by discharging untreated wastes into the environment. Production during the earlier feudal period had remained on a relatively small scale so that pollutants were often purified by natural systems. Environmental damage, when it had occurred, was generally limited in scope and severity and was often curbed by the protests of the victims, mostly farmers and fishermen. This situation changed dramatically after the Meiji Restoration in 1868. Mining and manufacturing replaced agriculture as the nation's top priority industries and farmers lost a great deal of their political power and social prestige. A powerful partnership of central government and private industry now concentrated its full efforts on rapid industrial growth, and the number of pollution victims grew apace. Victims who attempted to halt environmental abuses and gain compensation for their sufferings found themselves socially isolated and politically overpowered.

More often than not, the environmental consequences of rapid industrialization during the Meiji era were considered unavoidable and were endured as necessary for the sake of the state. The deeply ingrained Japanese sense of obedience to a strong central authority, compounded by a cultural heritage of fatalistic resignation, deterred those harmfully affected by the new enterprises from protesting. Nor did the managerial level of society look at the matter much differently, as revealed in the following story told about Eiichi Shibusawa, one of the most important industrialists of the period. Sometimes called "the father of Japanese capitalism," Shibusawa was instrumental in establishing many of the new Meiji enterprises and eventually rose to control the Oji Paper Company. In 1891, he decided to build a home near the factory. His biographer describes the scene:

> The smoke from its chimneys was such a nuisance that it sometimes brought complaints from his family. His son recalls that his father would reply, "Why do you complain? The smoke comes from the chimneys of the factory which I built with the greatest of efforts. Therefore, no matter how it may smoke, *bear with it patiently*."[1] (emphasis added)

This spartan attitude, penetrating all levels of society, contributed to Japan's industrialization efforts. And to the extent that "the virtues of endurance and perseverance, the capacity to put off pleasure and to endure suffering, characterize Japanese culture to a degree not paralleled elsewhere,"[2] so they were to prove conducive to ecological catastrophe.

But one area of economic development during the Meiji period provoked significant social protest against environmental pollution. Expansion of the mining industry during the decade of the 1880s brought with it severe environmental damage, including air pollution, water contamination, and continuous ground sinkage. The Ashio Copper Mine incident, while not the only example, is one of the best documented cases of early industrial pollution. It glaringly represents the mood of the time, the overriding goals of the nation, and the difficulties encountered by early pollution victims in their struggle for recognition and an equitable solution to their plight. It set a pattern that would be followed for almost a century.

In 1610, the farmers of Ashio, a village located some 100 miles north of Tokyo, discovered a rich vein of copper ore on the border between Tochigi and Gumma Prefectures. A mine was soon built near the headwaters of the Watarase River, and for nearly two centuries was managed by the Tokugawa central government. Even during these early days, the Ashio Copper Mine caused serious damage to the surrounding area, and in 1790, protests by local farmers forced the facility to stop operations.

With the Meiji Restoration in 1868, the copper mine was reopened, and, along with other mines and early industries, was turned over to the new government in Tokyo. Nine years later, it changed hands again when the government sold its rights to Ichibei Furukawa, a forward-looking silk merchant on intimate terms with several influential Meiji oligarchs. Although the copper mine was little more than a dead pit when he purchased it in 1877, Furukawa foresaw that growing demand for copper in electric machinery and wiring would provide rich possibilities for future growth. Investing huge sums of money in enlarging the mine and importing new equipment from overseas, Furukawa steadily increased production. Within 20 years, Ashio's yield was 44 percent of Japan's total copper production, and the mine soon became famous for being one of the largest enterprises of its kind in the Far East.

Increased production naturally meant an increase in the volume of wastes from the mining and refining processes. These were unceremoniously dumped into the nearby Watarase River, the major source of freshwater fish and irrigation water for the farmers and fishermen living downstream. In the past, the river had frequently overflowed its banks, depositing rich soil on the fields, which, in turn, gave hardworking peasants the rice crops needed to support their families. To expand its facilities, however, the mining company stripped surrounding mountains of their timber, and once the new refinery began its operations, sulfur oxides in the exhaust gases destroyed the remaining vegetation. With no more natural ground cover to help absorb periodic downpours, the moderate overflows of the past gave way to disastrous floods after every heavy rainfall. Severe erosion of the barren mountains soon became widespread.

As early as 1878, one year after Furukawa took over management of the mine, signs of copper pollution were already appearing. That year's flood waters subsided slowly, leaving many copper-poisoned fish in their wake. The men and women who bathed in the river developed painful, festering body sores. By 1880, the Tochigi prefectural governor, appointed by the central government, became sufficiently concerned about the pollution of the Watarase to issue a decree forbidding all fishing in the river. He also announced his intention to investigate the causes of the river's sudden degradation, but was mysteriously transferred to another prefecture before the investigation could begin.

The problem worsened with each passing year, and the symptoms of copper poisoning were seen in plants, animals, and humans alike. Kanson Arahata, a contemporary socialist and author who investigated the Ashio problem firsthand, describes the aftermath of the floods of 1888, 1890, and 1891:

> Farm land was made desolate and unproductive. Epidemics killed many domestic animals, and human beings, too, sickened and died. Other victims of the manmade disaster were left in the depths of misery, without clothes to wear or food to eat.[3]

In 1890, residents of the village of Agatsuma located downstream, believing that the Ashio mine was the source of their misery, filed a petition with the prefectural governor calling for an end to the mine's operations. Their request was summarily refused. Other farmers asked the Ministry of Agriculture and Commerce to analyze samples of river water and soil to demonstrate scientifically that crop and health damages were a direct result of the mine's activities. In 1891, the ministry replied that it was unable to undertake the analysis, and requested the farmers' "understanding." Two professors at Tokyo's Imperial University School of Agriculture, however, conducted an independent investigation of the samples, and their published results unequivocally traced the origin of the poisonings, which had by then spread to 28 villages, to the mine. The Ashio case became a national issue.

In December 1891, Shozo Tanaka, representative from Tochigi Prefecture to the newly formed Japanese parliament, known as the Diet, publicly interrogated the Minister or Agriculture and Commerce about the Ashio incident.* Proclaiming his conviction that the role of the Ministry and the new Diet was to protect the people's livelihood and well-being, Tanaka condemned the government's failure to enforce the Mining Ordinance. For did it not stipulate, he demanded, that "if a business of... mining is hazardous to the public benefit... the Agriculture and Commerce Minister may revoke its authorization to operate"? But before the minister could formally respond to Tanaka's pointed appeal, an interparty clash over budgetary issues brought on the Diet's dissolution. The minister's official response, published after the Diet recessed, conceded that there had been damage to the farmlands along

---

* Shozo Tanaka, it should be noted, was no ordinary politician. He was elected to the Diet in Japan's first parliamentary elections in 1890 by a large majority after serving as the Chairman of the Tochigi Prefectural Assembly. A popular leader and advocate of citizen's rights, he dedicated his life to fighting the Ashio Copper Mine pollution.

the Watarase, but maintained that the cause of the damage was "not yet certain." Experts were still examining the situation, and the mining industry, the minister said, had "taken every possible preventive measure." No further action would be taken by the government at that time, and further debate was deferred until the next session of the Diet.*

Tanaka was reelected and again attacked the government's passivity. The new Minister of Agriculture and Commerce refused to respond to his interrogations in person, but stated in writing that even if the copper poisoning were caused by a single source, the issue of compensation for damages would have to be settled privately. Furthermore, he proclaimed, the government would not order the suspension of industrial operations. As a result, Tochigi's governor and prefectural representatives formed an arbitration committee to settle the dispute between Furukawa and the afflicted farmers. When agreement was finally reached, the farmers were granted a bulk indemnity of approximately 7,000 yen ($4,900), and the company promised to install equipment to collect the poisonous mineral residues and prevent further contamination of the river. The amount of compensation was minuscule when compared to the damages, estimated at a total of 11 million yen ($7.7 million). The company's new equipment, moreover, proved abysmally ineffective. Between 1891 and 1897, the area of contaminated agricultural lands grew from 2,000 to 40,000 hectares, affecting five prefectures and reaching all the way to Tokyo.[5]

Japan in those days, however, was hardly concerned with the farmers' misfortune. In 1894, the nation plunged into war with China. Copper, a strategic metal, came into increasing demand. It was accepted that no single region's suffering—no matter how great—should stand in the way of Japan's ultimate victory. Money diverted from production into pollution control equipment meant diminished productivity, and therefore less copper for the war effort. The farmers, too, accepted the necessity of the war and believed it was their duty to "make no waves." After all, Ashio's copper production, they knew, was nearly one-half that of the nation as a whole. Silently enduring the spreading contamination of their fields, the farmers nevertheless hoped that when the war was over they might receive just compensation for their patriotic sacrifices.

In the fall of 1896, two devastating floods deposited heavily contaminated silt over wide areas of farmland near the river. The following February, nearly two years after the China adventure had been brought to a successful close, Representative Tanaka once again demanded that the govern-

---

* It so happened that the minister in question was the father of the adopted heir of the Furukawa family.[4]

ment put an end to the the mine's operations because they were "damaging to the public interest." The government responded firmly that the matter was closed, for the private parties involved had already concluded a settlement to the dispute!

Enraged at the government's continued inaction, some 800 farmers undertook a three-day pilgrimage to Tokyo, where their representatives appealed directly to the Minister of Agriculture. The minister promised to visit Ashio and examine the problem personally, while the government established the Ashio Mine Poisoning Investigation Council.

Even with Tanaka leading the debate in the Diet, however, no headway could be made, and in March 1897, one month after the first mass protest, over 3,000 farmers set out for a second demonstration in Tokyo. The government responded with an order to prevent further flooding by contaminated waters and with a tax exemption for damaged lands. A protective flood embankment was built along the river and seemed to be effective, but a disastrous flood in 1899 inundated vast areas of previously unscathed farmland.

In February 1900, some 3,000 victims gathered for another march to Tokyo. This time, however, even before they left the prefectural boundaries, they were confronted by a cordon of armed military police dispatched by the central authorities. A one-sided struggle ensued: "One old man was picked up by five policemen and thrown into the river. Others had their faces pasted with mud, their mouths filled with sand and dirt. The wounded lay in their wretchedness on both sides of the road, while the road itself was stained with blood for more than ten kilometers."[6] Sixty of the protest leaders were arrested, and during the next two and a half years a series of trials and appeals were held. The case was finally dismissed, but never in the process were the mine's activities challenged by the courts.

Widely publicized by contemporary journalists, the Ashio case developed into one of Japan's most urgently felt social problems. Sympathizers organized a pollution investigation committee and the Women's Christian Temperance Union formed a relief group. Speeches and meetings were held by Christian social activists, and hundreds of students from the Imperial University and other schools, defying a Ministry of Education decree to the contrary, swarmed to the area to provide moral support. Tanaka, who converted to Christianity during the protest, remained at the head of the Ashio movement until October 1901, when, disillusioned with the Diet and the government's evasiveness, he resigned his public office at the age of sixty-one. Two months later, still committed to continuing the struggle as a private citizen, Tanaka tried to bypass the parliament and appeal directly to the Emperor. Although the imperial guard prevented him from accomplishing his goal, the daring attempt climaxed a decade of struggle on behalf of Ashio's victims.

In March 1902, while the government was finally moving to establish a mine pollution committee in the cabinet, nature intervened. A major flood of the Watarase brought soil from lands above the mine and left deposits of fresh silt over the contaminated earth. Farmers could once again plant their crops. The government and Furukawa were quick to proclaim that the copper poisoning had been "corrected." To their mutual relief, public criticism over the issue soon subsided. And, as if taking no chances on a recurrence of the problem, the government announced plans to transform Yanaka village, which had been at the center of the protest movement, into a reservoir to absorb future flood waters. But this only triggered a new dispute. Tanaka moved into the village and joined those who were to be dispossessed. Despite a desperate struggle, however, some 450 households were forced to sell their lands to the government and were relocated in 1907 to the northernmost island of Hokkaido—Japan's Siberia.

For many years, the displaced villagers continued to write to the families and friends from whom they had been torn, promising that they would someday return to the land their ancestors had tilled for centuries. But with the passage of time, even these ties—the strongest and most vital for rural Japanese—gradually weakened. The relentless power of central government and industry had decisively won out.

To this day, the hills around Ashio bear the scars of centuries of heedless exploitation. The region is disfigured by huge grey mounds of slag, and its mountains are still barren from years of exposure to sulfur oxides emitted by the refinery's stacks. Rice plants grown in nearby paddies are still stunted by use of the river for irrigation. The mine continued in operation until February 24, 1973.

2.

The ecological crisis in which Japan finds itself today is not simply a product of rapid postwar economic growth. It is the culmination of a century of modernization molded by historical circumstances of much longer duration. A brief foray into those circumstances is indispensable for an understanding of the directions Japan has taken in modern times and of the forces still moving her decision-makers. For although industrial in its capital infrastructure, modern in its use of technological amenities, and Western in many aspects of external appearance, contemporary Japan continues to be strongly influenced by patterns of social organization that are firmly rooted in premodern times. Japan's industrial society rests on a solidly feudal framework. And while enabling Japan to achieve a high pitch of industrialization, these durable aspects of Japanese psychology and social behavior have been nearly insurmountable barriers for those who have been the victims of that rapid development.

Perhaps the main characteristic that has influenced Japan's cultural development has been its geographic setting. With a total area about the size of California, Japan's main islands are separated from Korea, the nearest continental neighbor, by straits some 150 kilometers wide. In ancient times these straits and the surrounding seas imposed formidable barriers to international travel, contributing to a culturally self-centered orientation toward the rest of the world, something the Japanese themselves refer to as an "island mentality."

Japan's insularity, however, was by no means an absolute barrier. On five occasions in historical times the nation experienced what British historian Richard Storry has aptly termed "cultural invasions." During these periods foreign concepts and modes of life penetrated the country and were accepted to varying degrees. The first such invasion occurred during the sixth century A.D. when the Chinese system of writing and many of the doctrines of Buddhism entered Japan through Korea. By the mid-ninth century, a period of relative isolation set in, during which the cultural borrowings were absorbed and modified to fit Japan's peculiar requirements. In the twelfth century, Japan revitalized its contacts with the continent, and during the next two centuries underwent a second "invasion." Trade with Asia continued, expanded now to the Indochinese peninsula and the Philippines. By the time European adventurers entered Far Eastern waters in search of the fabled treasures of the Orient, the area was already widely traveled by seafaring merchants from Japan.

In 1453, a small Portuguese boat heading for Macao was blown off course by a gale and, quite by accident, "discovered" the southern tip of Japan. Portugal soon established profitable commercial ties and the British and Dutch quickly followed suit. For several decades, Japan's feudal leaders continued to permit and even welcome trade with the West. Then, after Ieyasu Tokugawa unified the nation at the turn of the seventeenth century, Japan's rulers became increasingly fearful that the European predilection for colonialization might extend to Japan. The Tokugawa government therefore expelled all "barbarians" from the islands and prohibited all but a select handful of Japanese from going overseas. Thus, the Tokugawa overlordship plunged Japan into the security of more than two centuries of isolation. The third cultural invasion had been cut short well before it could exert its maximum impact.

A small number of Chinese and Dutch traders were allowed to stay, however, confined to special compounds facing Nagasaki harbor, Japan's "window to the West," on the southern island of Kyushu. The limited contact with Holland during this period of renewed isolation was not insignificant, for some Japanese came to exhibit a keen interest in what was called "Dutch learning." The latter was to be the principal means by which the more open-minded among Tokugawa intellectuals came to learn of Western scientific and technological developments. Despite formidable opposition from the central government, a number of progressive fiefs sent students to Nagasaki to absorb Western knowledge, especially of medicine and armaments. Among those fiefs whose leaders were the first to grasp the importance of the "Dutch learning," several were situated in Kyushu. There and elsewhere a few modest strategic industries (iron smelting, casting, and manufacture of armaments) based on the imported technology were set up before the end of official isolation in 1853–54. These industries, though for the most part militarily oriented, helped lay the foundation for subsequent industrialization.

Although the developments in Kyushu were to be important in the later Meiji era, the mainstream of Tokugawa Japan was hundreds of miles away, in central Honshu. The Tokugawa administration (1600–1867) centralized governmental power in Edo (later renamed Tokyo) through an efficient bureaucracy, and then sustained a long period of political and cultural stability primarily by means of a rigidly hierarchical social structure. This structure, based on a revival of Chinese Confucian doctrine, divided the population into four classes. Highest in status were the samurai soldier-administrators. They were followed by the peasant farmers (the primary producers). Next came the artisans (the secondary producers), and finally the merchants—whose benefit to society was considered dubious. Strict observance of elaborately detailed social mores emphasizing duty, loyalty, and obedience to superiors was required of each class. Those in superior positions were expected to bestow paternalistic benevolence upon their inferiors, while the latter were charged with the duty of repaying that benevolence with unquestioning service. Obedience to authority and the fulfillment of social obligations were strictly enforced; personal feelings which might interfere with the execution of one's duty were to be suppressed.

The land was apportioned as fiefs among some 260 *daimyo*, or feudal barons. Each daimyo, appointed by the Tokugawa bureaucracy in Edo, was imbued with autocratic albeit local power. The daimyo, in turn, numbered in his personal entourage lesser hereditary vassals of the samurai class. The highest ranking of these served as his councilors and executives in carrying out local and centrally decreed policies. With severe limitations placed upon foreign trade, and domestic commerce benignly neglected, the Tokugawa government was for the most part financially dependent on the nation's agricultural base. Peasants were often ruthlessly exploited by exorbitant taxes which aimed, according to a popular saying of the times, to "keep the farmers neither dead nor alive." Each daimyo was ranked according to the productive capacity of his fief, measured in terms of the taxable rice yield. Until the end of the Tokugawa period in 1867, the samurai class, amounting to only some five or six percent of the total population, exerted predominant political and social control.

The basic component of Tokugawa society was the family, infused with the Confucian concepts of paternal authority and filial piety. Families in turn were linked externally into hierarchical clans. Family-to-family relationships within the clan repeated the paternalism of parent-child and master-servant relationships. This rigid vertical organization of society, while drawing impetus from similar arrangements in earlier periods of Japanese cultural history, crystallized under the Tokugawa regime. The value system it spawned, *bushido*, or the "way of the samurai," was accepted not only by the samurai class, but by the lower social classes as well. With its enthronement of the virtues of self-sacrifice in the service of one's patron and the fulfillment of duty to lord, family and society, bushido was to become a touchstone of Japanese psychology that persists even today.

In tandem with the spread to the lower classes of the samurai values of obligation and self-discipline, village life came to be organized in a system of group harmony achieved through collective mediation. A five-man unit system of collective responsibility sprang up in rural villages. Typically, this system designated five men, each the head of a clan, collectively responsible for the actions of all members of their community. The "five-man unit" discouraged socially deviant behavior so effectively that the central authorities rarely, if ever, had to intervene in village life. Indeed, harmonious participation in the group was considered so important that exclusion was generally felt to be one of the most extreme forms of punishment. Internal group harmony came to be of paramount importance; disruptive personal ambition was suppressed by mutual agreement, while social confrontation was viewed with abhorrence. The individual was valuable insofar as he served the group: social ostracism meant psychological death.

Thus, the Tokugawa feudal system gave every man his place within a group, and every group its place within the entire social hierarchy. Behavior was dictated in detail by social regulations calculated to keep society running in line with the policies of the ruling authorities. As a result, the Japanese developed a pattern of situational ethics—unlike the Western-style system of universal principles—that defined "right" and "wrong" in terms of social position and class prerogative. Behavioral guidelines and restraints issued from a group's need to maintain its security and position within the overall framework. Untrammeled by the sense of "sin" embodied in the Judeo-Christian tradition, the individual was impelled by his desire to avoid the shame of failing in his social obligations. Positively expressed, he sought to win the honor to be had by accomplishing as much as, if not more than, expected of him. While endowing individuals with a sense of duty and honor, the rigidity and formalism of Tokugawa ethics was also to implant in them a tendency "to sacrifice moral principles and true courtesy to a punctilious observance of form and etiquette."[7]

Despite its isolation from the rest of the world, the domestic economy of Tokugawa Japan continued to grow, particularly during the seventeenth century. Agricultural productivity increased due to improved methods of farming, and village industries specializing in silk production, cotton spinning and weaving, and *sake* brewing arose under the direction of wealthy landowners. While many fiefs jealously maintained strict trade barriers, a national market nevertheless grew in size and importance. Money and banking, the institutions of a nascent capitalism, likewise flourished. Japanese society became increasingly urbanized, and population increased disproportionately in the cities. From the mid-eighteenth century, however, disasters, crop failures, and widely practiced infanticide and abortion held Japan's population relatively steady at an estimated 25 to 30 million, while the ossification of the Tokugawa system slowed the momentum of economic growth.

Tokugawa society, dependent upon rigid social control and an orchestrated power balance among regional lords, survived as long as it did by grace of its freedom from external influences. Its isolation was made possible, in part, by Europe's preoccupation with colonizing more accessible parts of Asia. By the mid-nineteenth century, Japanese isolation became more difficult to sustain. The Americans, after settling the entire breadth of their own continent, were now eyeing the Far East as they increased their involvement in the Pacific whaling and fur trades. The American government was eager to secure the use of Japanese ports as supply bases for American vessels operating in northern Pacific waters, while businessmen were eager to engage in what promised to be a lucrative trade. The earliest American diplomatic attempts to persuade the Tokugawa government to loosen its regulations against foreign contacts met with rebuff. Further unsuccessful overtures by the British and the Russians convinced the American government that only a dramatic display of force could change the Tokugawa policy.

Thus, in 1853, Commodore Matthew Calbraith Perry, under orders from his government, steamed into Tokyo Bay with a squadron of four black warships and pried Japan open by means of an overt gunboat diplomacy.

Once the barrier of isolation was penetrated by the Americans, other Western powers—England, Russia, France, Prussia, and Holland—successfully pressed their own demands for similar diplomatic recognition and trade. This intrusion of foreigners into Japan upset a regime that by the mid nineteenth century had already weakened considerably. In the decade and a half following Perry's arrival, discontented members of the samurai class proclaimed it necessary to return the Emperor to genuine rather than merely symbolic authority. In collaboration with powerful regional lords, they succeeded in engineering the downfall of the Tokugawa government and in "restoring" the Emperor to sovereign rule. With the wolves howling at the door, these revolutionary samurai believed that decisive reform was imperative to avoid foreign domination.

In the spring of 1868, the young Meiji Emperor announced the Charter Oath, a statement of the new government's general intent. The oath appealed to the nation to unite, promising that the new government would dedicate itself to abolishing "base customs of former times." By declaring the nation's resolve to "seek knowledge throughout the world," the oath officially consummated the reopening of Japan and set the tone for a strong centralized government that was to undertake and guide the process of modernization. In the following year, imperial edict removed the feudal daimyo from their positions of hereditary authority (although some were reappointed as "governors" of their former fiefs), and the populace was instructed to redirect its allegiance from the defunct feudal baronies to the Meiji nation-state and the Emperor. In effect, the entire nation was to become one integrated clan, with the Emperor at its head.

3.

This shift in power, known as the Meiji Restoration, marked the beginning of Japan's fourth cultural invasion and signaled the rearrangement of certain fundamental social institutions. The primary objective of the new government was clear: to maintain Japan's cultural integrity and national security in the face of the West's superior military strength. Japan's new leaders, with a high degree of flexible pragmatism and foresight, replaced the feudal policy of isolationism with a vigorous program of domestic reform calculated to "modernize" the nation. As one means of doing so, they dispatched hand-picked teams of investigators to cull from the Western world those social and technological advances best suited to Japan's needs. Not long thereafter, Bismarck's Prussia, its strong central government linked to a well developed industrial base, was selected as the most appropriate political system upon which Japan might model herself. As in Prussia, universal primary education and compulsory military service were established.

From the outset of the Meiji period (1867–1912), Japan's natural and human resources were mobilized by her national leaders to achieve "a wealthy nation and strong army," a posture of defensive militarism. The purpose of modern industrialization was not to achieve the well-being of the populace per se, but rather to provide a basis for military strength and earn Japan equal status in the community of modern nations. Every member of Japanese society was expected to contribute his utmost toward achieving this national goal. Hard work and self-sacrifice, values ingrained during the earlier feudal period, remained the people's social obligation, only now it was a duty to the nation and the Meiji Emperor. Labor was sanctified; complaint was sacrilegious. The nation was primed and unified behind a national policy of security in tune with the requirements of a modern age.

When Japan entered the Meiji period, it already possessed several iron foundries, iron-ore smelters, mechanized spinning mills, iron, coal and copper mines, and some shipbuilding facilities, legacies from the later feudal age. In line with the feudal pattern of government management of mining and heavy industry, the Meiji government at first assumed ownership of most major industrial enterprises. It also occupied itself with the rapid development of what were viewed as urgently needed elements of a modern industrial infrastructure—railroads and other facilities for internal communication, mining, shipbuilding, and the manufacture of armaments. In addition, to stimulate economic activity and provide models for private enterprises, it invested directly in light industries specializing in textiles and other manufactured goods initially imported from abroad.

Toward the end of the 1880s, the government discovered that most of its enterprises were operating at a loss, and decided to sell all but a few strategic industries to private individuals. Most of these relatively large-scale enterprises were "entrusted" (sold at extremely low prices) to friends and relatives of the men in power. This created at a very early stage in the development of Japanese modernization close ties of obligation between government and industrial officialdom. The arrangement ensured that economic leaders would continue to support government policies, effectively laying the foundation for the extremely close relationship—some have called it "incestuously intimate"—between government and big business that has persisted to the present day. Thus, unlike early Western capitalists, Japan's early entrepreneurs could begin operations without the socially disruptive necessity of struggle against feudal powers. On the contrary, they were aided by a government established by men some of whom themselves had been relatively high in the feudal hierarchy, and who, because of their impassioned desire for modernization, passed laws and provided contracts, loans, and subsidies to stimulate industrial growth.

The nation's new leaders in government and commerce had come to a consensus regarding the direction Japan was now to take, a direction motivated both by the dread of foreign domination and the goal of maximizing industrial productivity and profits. Many former samurai, stripped of their feudal status, fell naturally into the role of the "new samurai" of the Meiji era: the entrepreneurs. However, many of the new samurai also came from the merchant class which, by the end of the feudal period, was economically experienced and financially well off, and from the ranks of wealthy landowners. And it was the values of the former merchant class—nominally the lowest caste during the Tokugawa period—that now became supreme. Heavily influenced over the years by the bushido ethos of the samurai elite, these values differed primarily in their emphasis on profit maximization. The Meiji political leaders, men who were deeply inculcated with the values of bushido and the attitudes of an earlier age, thus contributed to investing the Japanese businessman-industrialist with the authority and prestige that were formerly the exclusive prerogatives of the samurai-warrior. The businessman's responsibility to administer the nation's well-being enabled him to rise to the top of the social totem pole. The totem pole, however, was to remain firmly in place.

As long as the Meiji government owned and managed the nascent industries, the pattern of employer-employee relations was similar to that of the late feudal period. Its roots deeply embedded in the hierarchical clan system, the manager-worker relationship closely resembled the feudal ties between master and servant or between craftsman and apprentice, which were based primarily on a highly developed sense of reciprocal obligation. After the Meiji government sold its industrial installations to private interests, manager-worker relationships underwent a change. The immediate increase in the scale of production required large numbers of new workers who were drawn primarily from the agricultural sector or hired indirectly from special labor contractors. Ties of empathy and mutuality between management and labor grew tenuous. Since labor was viewed as little more than a tool for maximizing productivity and profits, private management felt little direct commitment to its welfare. Workers, on the other hand, continued to be generally respectful of managerial authority, a tradition they and their ancestors had been born and reared in.

Work conditions reached their nadir in the years between 1890 and 1910. At times, workers rose in violent protest, but such uprisings were sporadic, disorganized, and usually ineffective. Around 1900, journalists began to rally public sentiment against poor working conditions, and the government slowly began to show some concern, primarily for pragmatic motives:

> The government's concern was largely prompted by fear that the maltreatment of workers would have serious effects on the achievement of the national goal of "building a wealthy nation and a strong army." The continued harsh exploitation of labor, it feared, might too seriously deplete human resources and thus slow down Japan's industrial progress. Also, the government became aware of the need to protect the health of young female factory workers—the future mothers of the country's soldiers—from industrial abuses and maltreatment.[8]

Subject to popular criticism and impelled by the need for skilled long-term employees to operate increasingly sophisticated machinery, business leaders sought ways to ensure their workers' loyalty and obedience. They soon found the answer in the traditional structure of the family, the core of Japanese social values. Management undertook a deliberate campaign of praising the feudal family structure and the virtues of using it as a model for employer-employee relations. The company came to be regarded as one vast family with management playing the benevolent father role and the workers accepting the submissive role of children.[9] The new system appealed to employees, too, because it guaranteed them life-long employment and regular wage increases based on length of service. Migrants from rural areas found security in the familiar family ideology, which helped them adjust to an impersonal and alienating urban setting. The "new" philosophy gained ground quickly after World War I. The individual was expected to identify completely with the corporate collectivity and strive for harmony and cooperation. Individual freedom and independent action were to be willingly surrendered for the common good.

Thus, the corporate "family" that continues to dominate Japanese economic organization to the present day took form relatively early. Its structure paralleled that of the feudal fief: the samurai-executive exercised benevolence, and the peasant-laborer, tied emotionally as well as economically to the corporate house-clan, returned loyal service. Professor Tadao Umesao of Kyoto University has pointed out that even today the words used for corporate executive (*juyaku*) and director (*torishimariyaku*) are "the exact words used in the fief government for its key administrators."[10] Even the ranking of these new corporate domains was to reflect the earlier pattern, with each firm and its executives graded in accordance with productivity (later, market share) measured, of course, in taxable yield.

Among the notable changes in the wake of the Meiji Restoration, mention must be made of the resurgence of population growth. An important factor impelling the renewed growth in human numbers was the prohibition by imperial edict of abortion and infanticide, deemed "offensive" to non-Japanese sensitivities. Other factors were improved hygiene and medical practices, and increased agricultural productivity. Japan's population swelled from 34 million in 1890 to 44 million in 1900 and 64 million in 1930, nearly doubling in forty years.

This population growth was skillfully manipulated by Meiji leaders to serve the nation's program of modernization. After the turn of the century, heavy taxes, poor harvests, unstable crop prices, and rising rents forced tenant farmers to migrate to the cities in droves. While in 1873 only 16 percent of the population had lived in cities and towns of 10,000 or more, by 1913 this proportion rose to 28 percent. During the years 1900 to 1910, the number of factory workers doubled, and more than doubled again in the next decade.

The bulk of the rural population inflow was absorbed by the larger urban areas of the main central island of Honshu, especially the Tokyo and Osaka regions. These areas, formerly under the direct rule of the Tokugawa bureaucracy, were already important manufacturing centers at the outset of the Meiji era. By 1920, the cities of Tokyo and Osaka had a combined population of 6.8 million, or 12 percent of the nation's total. The region's pre-existing financial and manufacturing infrastructure, central location, and proximity to good ports soon led the government to adopt a deliberate policy of developing the Pacific coastal belt into Japan's industrial heartland. This policy was to have an important bearing on the development of the severe environmental problems that have plagued Japan during the latter half of the twentieth century.

4.

The outbreak in 1894 of the Sino-Japanese War marked the beginning of a transition from the early policy of defensive militarism to a posture of military expansionism. As Japan grew stronger, her perception of the West gradually changed. The goal of defense against Western colonialism shifted to one of imitating those very expansionist policies. Victory in 1895 over a decadent China and Korea was followed in 1905 by the defeat of Russia, the first Asian triumph over a major Western state. These military successes, coupled with the annexation of Taiwan in 1895 and of Korea in 1910, nourished the nation's self-confidence and made credible the shining vision of a Japanese destiny to be made manifest in Asia, a destiny that seemed a necessary requirement of the burgeoning industrial state.

Although a small domestic market materialized in the period before the Second World War, Japan's industries were almost wholly dependent on exports. Economic growth and the accumulation of capital did not imply an equitable distribution of the nation's wealth. Low wages and meager domestic purchasing power thus forced Japan to seek markets overseas.

Dependence on foreign markets was paralleled by a reliance on foreign sources for raw materials. Yet, after the end of the First World War and under the influence of a rapid influx of Western democratic ideas, Japanese businessmen tended to reject colonialism and military conquest as a way to expand markets and stabilize the flow of resources. Instead, they decided to develop a massive export trade through peaceful diplomacy. During this period, referred to as Taisho Democracy, militarism entered a latent stage as a wide array of social and cultural changes transformed the surface of Japan, particularly in the cities. But a reaction to the period's heady political and intellectual liberalism soon set in. Hostility to "foreign" values grew among army and navy officers, low-ranking government officials, rural landowners, and small-town, lower middle class citizens. Educated during the earlier Meiji period and imbued with its strong nationalistic values and militaristic inclinations, these groups viewed liberalism as "weak" and "cowardly," and looked back with nostalgia to the strong authoritarian rule and expansionist ideals of the Meiji oligarchs. An ominous current of ultranationalist and militarist sentiment slowly undermined the tenuous mood of liberal democracy.

In the midst of this rising domestic reaction came the Great Depression of 1929; foreign demand for Japanese goods fell off sharply, a serious setback for a nation striving for wealth and prestige through commercialism. In their attempts to recover from the international crisis, many nations felt a need to protect their domestic industries by raising import barriers. Since Japan depended so heavily on foreign markets, these restrictive tariffs had a devastating impact on her domestic economy. It became painfully clear to many that the program of economic expansion through peaceful export trade was dependent on too many factors beyond the control of Japan's policymakers.

Adding to the pressure on her internal resources was Japan's burgeoning population. Both Australia (1908) and the United States (1924) had enacted legislation restricting immigration and barring Asians. This not only made reduction of Japan's population pressures more difficult but also struck a serious blow to Japanese pride. By the early 1930s, a growing number of Japanese had concluded that the only answer to rising tariffs and exclusionist immigration policies was for Japan to resume its former program of colonial expansion and to win for itself the land, resources, and markets needed for self-sufficiency and invulnerability as a world power. Extremists argued that unless Japan extended its empire, it was only a matter of time before the nation would be reduced to a perennially poor standard of living and a subjugated international status. The converging crises of population, resources, and markets demanded immediate action, and in September 1931, Japanese army units stationed in Manchuria took the first steps in initiating a period historian Shuichi Kato has designated one of "hysterical militarism."[11] The way leading to the invasion of Manchuria and China was opened. Development priorities shifted to meet its demands.

The outbreak of war in Europe and the fall of France in 1940 signaled the start of a gradual Japanese military and economic invasion of Indochina. The risk of a major war in the Pacific grew, as America decided in 1940 not to renew its commercial treaty with Japan. Realizing that Japan was stockpiling oil and strategic war materials imported from the United States, the American government began slowly to exert economic pressures in an attempt to halt further aggression. Licenses were required for the purchase of oil and scrap iron; scrap iron, iron and steel were then embargoed; by December 1940, steel articles and tools were cut off. In a few months, the list had grown to include almost all the materials vital to Japanese production. The most serious blow was dealt in June 1941, when shipments of the most essential item—oil—were stopped; soon thereafter, Japanese financial assets were frozen. The oil embargo and freezing order were decisive. Six months later came the surprise attack on Pearl Harbor, destroying or immobilizing 90 percent of America's air and surface strength in the Pacific.

The Japanese moved quickly. By the end of April 1942, Hong Kong, the Philippines, Malaya, Singapore, the Dutch East Indies, and Burma were under their control. Japan's military policymakers envisioned that the entire area would eventually comprise a Greater East Asia Co-prosperity Sphere, with Japan, Northern China, and Manchuria forming its industrial center. Other nations in the sphere would serve as sources of raw materials and as huge consumer markets for the goods manufactured in the heartland. But the ideal of "East Asia for the Asians" proclaimed by intensive Japanese propaganda never materialized, as the brutality and arrogance of Japanese troops disillusioned the populations that fell under their control.

Japan's leaders seriously miscalculated America's psychological reaction to the Pearl Harbor attack. The United States navy and air force in the Pacific were rebuilt faster than anticipated, and by the summer of 1942, American troops had stopped the Japanese advance and taken the offensive.

By 1944, American warplanes were conducting frequent bombing raids over Japanese cities, slowly destroying the nation's industrial base. In the next year it became clear to many that Japan, with most of its industrial and urban centers heavily damaged from incendiary bombing raids, had lost the war. Nevertheless, the general public was constantly assured by government propaganda that "they could win the war, if only they would make a supreme effort—sometimes it was called a supreme sacrifice—in their own defense." Intensive propaganda backed by centuries of tradition convinced the bulk of the populace that the individual existed for the sole purpose of service to the state and glory to the Emperor.

On August 6, 1945, the United States exploded the first atomic bomb over Hiroshima; the gruesome sequel at Nagasaki took place three days later. On August 15, despite diehard opposition by military extremists, Emperor Hirohito took an unprecedented action: in a radio broadcast he personally announced Japan's unconditional surrender. Stunned by the sudden and unexpected announcement and prepared for the worst, the Japanese public fearfully awaited the arrival of the occupation forces, their first conquerors in centuries of history. Still, they were buttressed by the Emperor's call to "endure the unendurable and suffer what is unsufferable"; they would continue to serve.

And the future would indeed bring great suffering, but of a grotesque and unexpected variety.

CHAPTER TWO

A MILLION DOLLAR NIGHT VIEW

> ... the city authorities saw the possibility of transforming Yokkaichi into a great industrial center. A group of "regional development" experts was commissioned to draft a "Yokkaichi Master Plan," and a gigantic piece of reclamation was begun along the scenic seashore. The "plan" spoke of "a birth of a new industrial city with abundant sunlight and green spaces," but foresight was lacking.
>
> —SHIGETO TSURU
> "Kogai," UNESCO Courier
> July 1971

In many ways, the history of Yokkaichi encapsulates the story of Japan's rapid development into an industrial state. Located at a central crossroads on Japan's main island, the Yokkaichi region was noted for many of its natural features. Sparkling beaches studded with pine trees twisted from years of exposure to strong sea winds stretched for miles along the coast of Ise Bay. The bay's clear waters teemed with life and the lands bordering it were rich and fertile. Spreading between the Pacific coast and the Suzuka mountains to the north lay a thriving patchwork of tiny rice paddies, bordered here and there by broad expanses of yellow rapeblossoms.

Life was never easy for Yokkaichi's inhabitants. Since long before feudal times, the local villagers, like most other Japanese, eked out a meager existence by cultivating the earth or engaging in simple fishing. Browned from the hot sun, farmers worked long hours planting, thinning, weeding, and harvesting their precious grain. In the early morning, fishermen cast off from the shore in small boats to throw out their nets, hauling in mackerel, flatfish, sea bream, and octopus from the coastal waters. Life was lived close to nature; the residents of Yokkaichi enjoyed its beneficence and endured the occasional havoc of floods, earthquakes, and typhoons.

Because of its key location for both land and sea transport, Yokkaichi early developed into a commercial center. The local market opened the fourth, fourteenth, and twenty-fourth of every month, giving Yokkaichi its name, "market of the fourth day." The cottage silk industry provided the peasantry with an additional source of income. Fed mulberry leaves, the silkworm was carefully tended until it spun a cocoon of silk which in turn could be spun into thread and sold to local weavers. Gradually, as Yokkaichi's trade grew, its merchants accumulated enough wealth to virtually control the town.

In the early seventeenth century, Yokkaichi was designated one of the 53 stops on the famous *Tokaido*, the eastern coast road that stretched from the city of Edo, center of Japan's feudal administration, to the ancient capital of Kyoto, residence of the Emperor. Along this route passed dignitaries on political, military, or commercial missions, and the handiwork of a burgeoning commerce. In towns and villages located at convenient intervals along this route there sprang up numerous inns, restaurants, and entertainment houses designed to meet travelers' needs. Because of its proximity to the Grand Shrines of Ise, a sacred place for Japan's native Shinto religion, the village of Yokkaichi had by the mid-seventeenth century grown into a town, an important stopover for feudal lords and their samurai retainers on visits to the shrines.

The Meiji era brought the first trappings of modernity. Large cotton mills were set up by local community leaders with the encouragement of the nation's oligarchs. Newly imposed land taxes forced many rural women and children into the mills to work long hours of grueling routine for pitifully small reward. The dedicated industriousness of the peasant workers yielded good returns, and Yokkaichi's trade expanded rapidly. Cotton and woolen cloth quickly became important items of domestic and international commerce, and ships from other parts of Japan as well as many foreign countries were soon dropping anchor in Ise Bay. Tiny sampans loaded with rolls of cloth, rapeseed oil, and *bankoyaki*, red earthenware for which the region was famous, scurried out to service and trade with them. In exchange, they returned to the tiny wharf heavily laden with sugar and rice from Taiwan and Thailand, raw cotton from India, and wood and wool from Hokkaido.

It was during these early years of the Meiji reign that a wealthy Yokkaichi landowner, Emon Inaba, hit on the idea of constructing a harbor deep enough to accommodate even the biggest trading vessels. Inaba reasoned that modern facilities would make Yokkaichi more attractive to foreign shipping, while transforming it into a haven for marine traffic during the frequent summer and early autumn typhoons that swept Japan's Pacific coast. The town's leaders realized that since the completion of the Tokaido railway, which bypassed Yokkaichi, the region's commercial center had shifted to the neighboring port and rail city of Nagoya. Improving Yokkaichi's harbor had become a matter of economic survival. Inaba supplemented large sums of city tax money with personal contributions and called in the most sophisticated experts available to design the new port. When finally completed, it was boasted to be one of the best in Japan, second only to those of the major commercial areas of Tokyo and Osaka.

As Inaba had foreseen, profitable trade and commerce increased. The city's population grew as better sanitation and improved medical care lowered the death rate, and as newcomers from all over Japan migrated to the bustling new metropolis to set up shops, work in the mills, or join in the thriving trade. Schools were built to provide compulsory primary education. By the turn of the century, the electric light bulb had replaced the old-fashioned rapeseed and whale oil lamp by which the children had formerly studied. The modernized educational system taught the values of deference, obedience, and dedication to hard work as the means by which to build Japan into a great nation. Above all, the children of the era were imbued with an unbounded reverence for the Emperor, whose inspired leadership had started Japan on the road to becoming a member of the community of modern nation-states.

The decade of the 1920s brought further changes to Yokkaichi in the wake of growing economic power and heightened international status. As in other urban centers, Occidental manners of behavior and dress were unabashedly affected by the urban classes. The rural peasantry, however, still committed to the orthodoxy of hard work, austerity, and conservative values, looked on disapprovingly, and with the onset of worldwide economic depression in 1929, contributed to the process of social and political reaction that resulted in the new order of the 1930s.

In 1937, Ishihara Industries, one of Japan's "new" zaibatsu conglomerates which arose in the period of military expansion, built an oil refinery in Yokkaichi on reclaimed land off Shiohama. The following year, the Imperial Navy selected the city as the site for a large petroleum refinery and oil storage depot. Local farmers and fishermen were ordered to sell their land to the government and were relocated to other areas nearby. Although in the privacy of their homes many complained about having to forfeit property that had been in their families' possession for generations, in public the necessity of selling was accepted as a gesture of patriotic support. Indeed, for only too many reasons, refusal was unthinkable. The new depot was built, and the rumor spread that when the Navy had filled the huge oil tanks, the war would begin.

With the attack on Pearl Harbor in December 1941, Yokkaichi's eligible men were called to the front, the women, children, and elderly remaining behind to begin their long vigil. By 1944, American bombers were flying nightly overhead, bound for Nagoya and points east. Because of the oil refinery's obvious strategic importance, many of Yokkaichi's residents feared that their turn would come. And on a hot June night in 1945, American B-29s leveled the city. "Always before," a witness recalls, "the planes were just dots in the sky, but that night they swooped down like terrible, monstrous birds. The noise was deafening. All around, houses burst into flames."

2.

Almost the entire city was destroyed in the firestorm. Where the oil depot once stood, only the blackened metal framework of the refinery remained, a desolate skeleton near the mouth of the Suzuka River. Katsuro Yoshida, Yokkaichi's mayor (1934–46, 1955–58), felt that his city had been destroyed and many of its residents innocently killed because he had personally allowed the oil depot to be built. He apologized to his constituents for the devastation that had befallen them. For a number of years after the war, the broad expanse of charred land where the depot had stood lay idle as rice paddies were reclaimed, houses rebuilt, boats repaired, and a modest trade was slowly revived.

The Korean War and the intense economic activity it stimulated in Japan revived Yokkaichi's appeal among industrial policymakers. The petrochemical industry had been selected as the focal point for reorganizing and strengthening Japan's zaibatsu after the Occupation period, and large expanses of flat land were needed to construct the new factories. In 1955, government and industrial planners selected Yokkaichi and the site of the former Imperial Navy oil depot to be the home of the largest of Japan's first petrochemical complexes. The people of Yokkaichi, their energy and efforts now to be used for purposes of peaceful reconstruction, felt deeply honored that their region had been chosen to serve in the forefront of the struggle to create a "New Japan."

Mayor Yoshida had long urged that the petrochemical complex be built and was gratified that his negotiations with the nation's new political and industrial leaders had ended in success. For finally, he reasoned, he could make amends for the great wartime suffering of the people under his protective charge. Indeed, official promotional campaigns promised that the project would bring great material wealth to Yokkaichi and place it on the map of a reviving Japan. The city's residents were pleased that a large new railroad station and wide modern highway would accompany the complex. Government-issued brochures announced that Yokkaichi would be a "city of sunlight and greenery," an urban model for the New Japan. The site of the oil depot in Yokkaichi's Shiohama District was soon cleared of rubble, and in May 1956, construction of the new oil refinery was begun.

Across the river from the bustling construction site lay the small fishing village of Isozu. When inclement weather prevented them from going out to sea, Isozu's fishermen signed on as day laborers at the Shiohama complex to earn some extra money. During a lunch break one such day, a British engineer directing them on the Showa Oil Refinery project, a joint venture with British Shell, gestured in the direction of Isozu and announced, "Someday that little village might become unlivable." When the remark was translated, Isozu's fishermen laughed in disbelief. "*Masaka!* You must be kidding!" After all, their forebears had lived for generations in Isozu, earning a livelihood from the sea and cultivating small patches of sandy earth behind their homes. The fishermen were confident that their centuries-old pattern of living would go on as before: change of such vast proportions was unthinkable. Construction, and their participation in it, continued, and in April 1958, the refinery was ready for operation. As other industries grew up around it, the area developed into a full-fledged petrochemical complex. Hereafter it would be referred to as a *kombinato*, in conscious imitation of the Russian *kombinat* used to describe such sprawling industrial centers.

The concept of the integrated industrial kombinat was embraced by Japan's postwar leaders as the most efficient means to recover a powerful economic base rapidly. Believed to be a triumph of "rational technology," the kombinat combined the best elements of the decade's engineering know-how. Yokkaichi's kombinat, like others being set up at strategic locations along Japan's Pacific coast, clustered petrochemical-related industries in a design that vastly enhanced productive efficiency (Fig. 1). Huge port facilities were constructed at each site to accommodate greatly increased imports of precious raw materials (primarily petroleum) and facilitate the export of finished products. Coastal locations also offered the advantage of readily available water resources for use in cooling machinery. Similarly, participating factories could conveniently dump liquid and solid wastes into nearby "common" waters.

By 1958, huge tankers were calling regularly at Yokkaichi, piping their liquid cargo to the newly constructed Showa Oil refinery. Showa Oil distilled the crude into heavy oil, gasoline, and kerosene. A fourth product, naptha, key to the petrochemical industry, was transferred to the Mitsubishi Petrochemical plant where it was processed into ethylene and other intermediate materials used in the production of synthetics. Some of the heavy oil was piped to a neighboring thermal electric power plant to produce electricity for the city's homes and offices and for the operations of some 200 kombinat-related factories. The products of these kombinat industries were then shipped by sea and land to nearby industrial areas. In Nagoya, for example, small factories used Yokkaichi's products to churn out millions of plastic buckets, table mats, utensils, and other household items for domestic consumption and export.

Fig 1. The Yokkaichi Kombinat

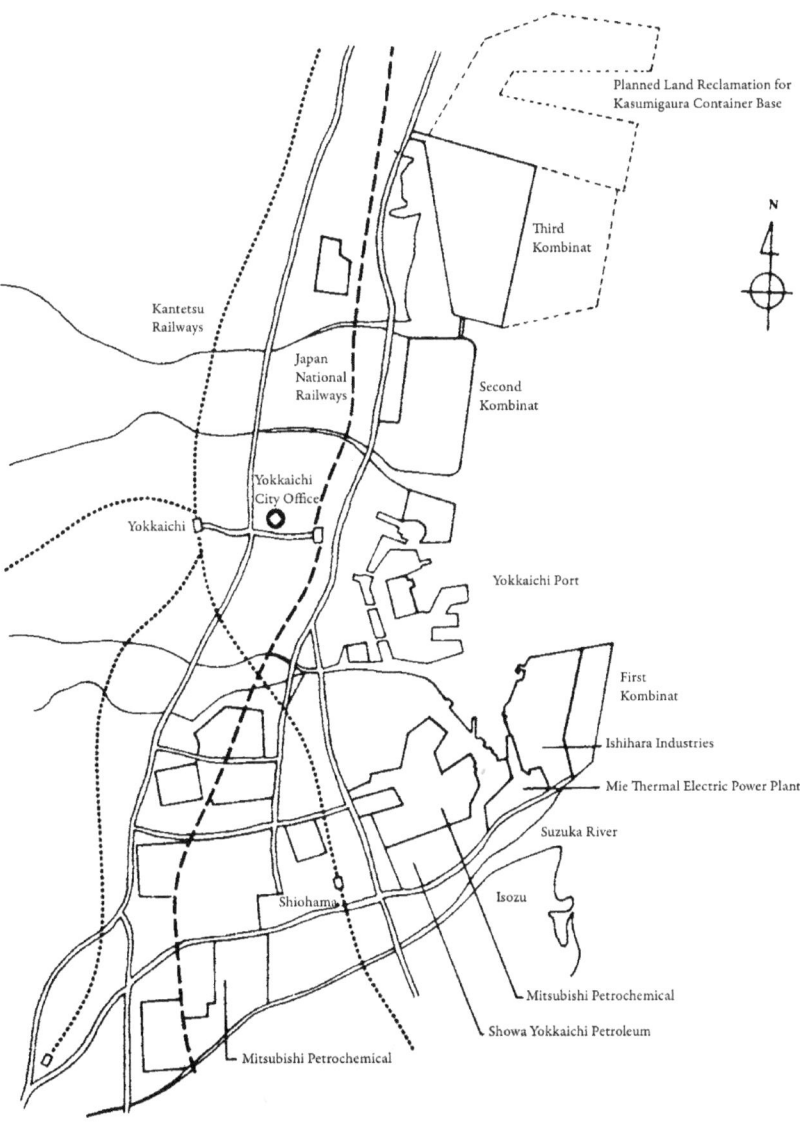

In 1959, Yokkaichi's kombinat went into twenty-four hour operation, and its night lights were turned on for the first time. Nearby residents marveled at how beautiful the factories were, their lights sparkling like jewels against the backdrop of the night sky. Isozu's 3,000 inhabitants were considered the luckiest because, being close to the complex, they could enjoy the nightly vista with the least inconvenience. The "million dollar night view" soon became a source of pride for Yokkaichi's citizenry, even attracting sightseers from other parts of Japan.

But the kombinat brought more than twinkling lights and envious sightseers; nor was Isozu's enjoyment of the "night view" to remain painless. As kombinat operations expanded and intensified, Isozu's residents found it difficult to sleep because of harsh odors and window-rattling noises emanating from the site across the river. Women working in their vegetable gardens noticed that when the wind blew from the direction of the complex, it bore with it an unpleasant chemical smell. By April 1960, Isozu's residents felt impelled to make what they felt was a reasonable appeal to Yokkaichi's municipal office requesting that something be done about the disagreeable odors and noises produced by the kombinat.

Although city officials were sympathetic and vaguely reassuring, no concrete countermeasures were forthcoming. Aware that the power to solve their problems really lay at the prefectural capital, Isozu's leaders lodged an appeal with higher officials. Their request evoked surprise and noncommittal allegations of ignorance. Isozu's spokesmen judged the prefectural officials' assurance that they would investigate the situation to be little more than a polite dodge. They knew that the prefectural budget, authorized several months earlier, was committed to "first priorities"—roads, port facilities, and more land reclamation—and left no funds for dealing with Isozu's unprecedented complaints. They were also aware that the prefectural and municipal governments received large tax revenues from companies in the petrochemical complex and that, on a personal level, close contacts and a spirit of intimate cooperation existed between government officials and industry executives. In Japan, they knew, these relations traditionally had far more influence on the policies of government than did the plight of ordinary citizens. Although government officials might sympathize with them, on an official level the ties of social and professional obligation were too strong to allow them to restrict kombinat activities. Discouraged, Isozu's delegates returned home.

After much debate, it was decided to appeal directly to the factories and the good will of the officials in charge. But time after time Isozu's representatives were met with the same reply: "We're not causing the problem; perhaps it's the factory next door." Months of fruitless effort persuaded the frustrated fishermen that apparently nothing could be done. It soon became clear, however, that the problem was not only Isozu's, for one day in July the entire area west of the Shiohama kombinat was blanketed by heavy fumes. The Mihama primary school was compelled to suspend classes, its frightened children directed by their teachers to keep very still and "breathe as little as possible."

As more and more Shiohama residents appealed to the city office for relief from the noise and increasingly frequent attacks by fumes from the kombinat's factories, Yokkaichi's new mayor reluctantly concluded that something had to be done. In August 1960, the Yokkaichi City Pollution Countermeasures Council was established to investigate the situation. Composed of four city councilmen, four factory representatives, and three professors from Mie Prefectural and Nagoya Universities, the council held its first meeting in October and began exploratory studies the following month. Because the professors were in the employ of the municipal government, however, their sole responsibility was to report to the city office. In March 1961, they submitted a brief interim report of their findings, confiding to city officials that the level of sulfur dioxide in Isozu's air was six times greater than that found elsewhere in Yokkaichi. Unseen by the general populace, the study's conclusions underscored the undeniable seriousness of the problem and a more detailed survey was immediately commissioned. In the meantime, the people of Isozu, waiting patiently for the results of the report, were told nothing; the contamination of their living environment simply grew worse.

3.

By early 1961, mothers in Isozu were beginning to notice that their children caught colds more easily and that the colds seemed to last longer than ever before. Swollen tonsils were common. In the past, the victim of a cold would simply rest, allowing the body's natural defenses to achieve a cure. But this new type of cold refused to respond to traditional treatment. People started coughing, and some found it more and more difficult to breathe. Rumors spread that this mysterious lung disorder was a "new"—and severe—form of asthma.

In Isozu, as elsewhere throughout Japan, it was known that hereditary asthma struck less than 1 percent of the general population, with children tending to be the most affected. Indeed, residents could identify certain families as traditional "asthma sufferers." But in 1961, it seemed that an epidemic had broken out, and the traditional classifications became meaningless.

Coughing and gasping for breath, a victim seeking treatment from Isozu's only doctor would be shocked to see others—people like himself who were not from an "asthma house"—suffering from the same disorder. Something was definitely wrong, they agreed. This was no ordinary asthma.

When modern medicines failed to bring relief, people turned in desperation to folk cures, drinking the water of a shrine famous for its healing powers or eating the ashes of the cremated. Nothing seemed to work, and the number of victims rose dramatically during the spring and summer of 1961. There seemed to be no way to prevent the coughing and no way to cure it once it started—at least not as long as the patient remained in Yokkaichi.

Slowly, however, the bewildered fishermen of Isozu, among whom the incidence of the new disease was highest, began to piece together the telltale evidence. One victim went to Hokkaido to visit relatives and reported that within a month his coughing stopped. A week after returning to Yokkaichi, however, it recommenced with renewed intensity. The mother of a stricken infant was advised by her physician to take the child to the mountains for a rest. As she relates it, "I had no relatives there and very little money, so I could only go for a couple of days. Still by the second day, my child was coughing only half as much. I hated to bring him back to Yokkaichi, but I had no choice."

As the situation worsened, Isozu residents began to point accusing fingers at the factories, and the Shiohama Federation of Village Councils decided to conduct its own investigation of the health problem. Developing a questionnaire based on the probe used by the doctors representing the city council, they began interviewing from door to door throughout Shiohama. The results of their survey were shocking. Respiratory abnormalities were reported in 48 percent of children under ten, 30 percent of those over sixty, and 19 percent of those in their twenties. Furthermore, residents' opinions regarding the factories had changed. People no longer believed that attracting more industries would necessarily contribute to the development of the city, and what they wanted most urgently were administrative measures to control pollution. Armed with their survey, representatives of the federation once again confronted the city office, this time, with an even stronger appeal. The city, they said, should pay for necessary medical care of asthma victims. City officials, however, responded as they had before, apologizing for whatever discomfort was being undergone and asking for patience. Experts, it was explained, were investigating the health problem, but had yet to complete their probe. There was still, they insisted, "no scientific evidence proving that the disease was actually caused by the activities of the factories." Until such conclusive scientific evidence was available, they were powerless to act.

Five months after the presentation of the citizens' data, the interim report of the council's year-long study was submitted to the municipal government. Its findings were portentous: the amount of sulfur dioxide in Yokkaichi's air was greater than that at Kawasaki, Japan's largest industrial center; Yokkaichi's death rate from respiratory diseases, which in 1955 had been significantly lower than the national average, was now up to the national level; and while the death rate from respiratory diseases was falling in suburban areas, in contaminated regions, particularly in Isozu, it was on the increase. The Yokkaichi Medical Society analyzed the data and recommended that people living in Isozu, Shiohama, and other highly polluted areas nearest the factories be moved en masse to healthier grounds. The Englishman's prophecy was coming true.

Neither the report nor its recommendations were made public. When Isozu's residents requested to see the results, the city government refused. Angered, a member of the opposition Socialist party confronted the ruling Liberal Democratic party members in the city assembly and challenged their justification for keeping the results secret. The ruling party replied that the report was commissioned for government use only and that, if the findings were published, the "people might worry unnecessarily." But the citizens of Isozu and Shiohama persisted, forcing the city government to issue a short statement saying that the present stage of the investigation indicated that the prevalence of asthma in Isozu was somewhat higher than the national average. This brief, statement, issued under duress, was the extent of official compromise; nothing further was divulged.

The Shiohama Federation responded to the official statement by making another appeal to municipal authorities. This time they requested that a public hospital provide free examinations for pollution victims, that a city ordinance to control pollution be enacted, and that the mayor submit a statement to the central authorities and request their official opinion on the pollution problem. In August, when still no relief for the air pollution victims had been found, the federation decided to submit a similar petition to the Mie prefectural governor. Confronted once again with evasive responses, the citizens' patience finally snapped. For the first time, angry voices demanded an end to polite appeals that got them nowhere. The federation's representatives threatened that if the government would not listen and respond reasonably, they would have to resort to direct action "forcing it to do something." In an attempt to mollify them, the prefectural governor agreed to free medical examinations for all victims of the new disease. The representatives returned home with what many considered "a mere bone the government had thrown them."

By the end of 1962, the fundamental environmental problems besetting the region had not improved at all.

Although medical checkups were now free, residents of Yokkaichi were still falling ill, and new victim; were forced, as before, to bear the full costs of medicine and hospitalization. Indeed, Yokkaichi's air pollution was getting progressively more serious. The Shiohama kombinat, using Middle East crude oil with a high sulfur content, was spewing pollutants from short smokestacks only 30 to 50 meters high. Winter winds blowing out to sea blanketed Isozu with contaminated air, and summer winds carried the poisonous gases into homes in Shiohama. The concentration of invisible sulfur dioxide in the air over Isozu and Shiohama frequently exceeded the tolerance level of 0.1 parts per million (ppm) and reached the extremely dangerous levels of 0.5 to 1.0 ppm for hours on end. Totally engulfed by hazardous industrial pollution, the once quiet fishing village had become part of a human experiment.

Nevertheless, the Yokkaichi city government continued to expand industrial production. In 1963, the *second* petrochemical complex began operations in the Umaokoshi area just to the north of Shiohama, and the region's respiratory disease, previously known as "Shiohama asthma," now became "Yokkaichi asthma." The painful coughing would not yield to treatment, and the number of victims rose relentlessly.

4.

Nor were polluted air and the disease it gave rise to the only problems confronting Isozu. Already in late 1959, fish caught at the mouth of the Suzuka River, Isozu's traditional fishing grounds, came up bearing a disagreeable odor and taste. In March 1960, Isozu's catch was refused at Tsukiji, Tokyo's central fish market, and the fishermen suddenly found their economic livelihood gravely threatened.

Called in to investigate the situation, the Mie Prefectural Fisheries Bureau reported that 100 percent of the fish within four kilometers of Yokkaichi's coast smelled foul, while 70 percent of the fish as far as eight kilometers from shore were inedible. Markets around the country began refusing Isozu's produce, and in order to reach marketable supplies, the men were compelled to rise earlier—at two or three in the morning—to motor out to the cleaner waters of Ise Bay. By April, it had become almost impossible for Isozu's fishermen to market their fish, even when uncontaminated, because of the reputation now associated with the area. To publicize the need for corrective measures, the Federation of Ise Bay Fishermen's Unions held a fish-tasting party in June, to which they invited some fifty members of the Prefectural Sanitation Department. Two or three hours after eating the fish, several of the government officials came down with painful stomach cramps and diarrhea. Clearly, something was wrong.

In December 1960, the prefecture formed the Council to Promote Countermeasures Against the Contamination of Ise Bay, with the prefectural vice-governor at its head. The problem of analyzing the cause of the offensive fish odors was assigned to Mie University Professor Katsumi Yoshida, who was also supervising studies on Yokkaichi's air pollution. In April 1961, Yoshida presented his report on the connection between factory effluents and the oily fish. The results squarely indicted the kombinat, particularly the Shiohama petrochemical factories. With this report in hand, 15 fishermen's unions formed their own solidarity league and demanded that the responsible kombinat industries pay them a total of three billion yen ($8.3 million) in compensation. In addition, they insisted upon direct negotiations regarding compensation, an end to all pollution, and purification of their fishing grounds. Not surprisingly, their demands fell on deaf ears.

In January 1962, a mediating committee formed by the prefectural government proposed a settlement of 100 million yen ($275 thousand)—one-thirtieth of what the fishermen originally demanded. This sum, it said, would be distributed evenly among the 15 unions whose members fished the seas along the northern coast of Ise Bay. Reflecting close government-industry ties, the committee stipulated that payment would be shared equally by the prefecture, the municipality, and the participating industries, and would be made over a four-year period. The proposed settlement, however, included no provisions for antipollution or clean-up measures, nor did it provide funds for retraining those fishermen who wanted to change their occupation. Isozu's fishermen, the most adversely affected by the pollution (their losses in 1960 alone totaled some 100 million yen [$275 thousand]), staunchly opposed the mediation agreement. But their outcry was muffled by the other unions, whose members far outnumbered them and whose losses were much smaller. In the end, the plan was adopted, although as one Isozu participant put it, the settlement "solved nothing and was just another payoff from government and industry." Because no efforts were being made to control the discharge of pollutants into the Suzuka River or to detoxify the fishing grounds, Isozu's future remained dismal.

Thus, when the final agreement was signed on March 21, 1962, two years after the contaminated fish catches had become a major problem, Isozu's ancient fishing grounds were polluted, its economic losses were rising, and its fishermen had to go farther and farther from shore to cast their nets. Even here, however, they found they could not escape the ever-widening circle of pollutants.

The final straw came in June 1963, when the local Yokkaichi fish market refused to buy fresh muck, a small white fish, from Isozu, but bought the same fish from a neighboring village. Isozu's fishermen exploded in rage. Packing their polluted fish back into their boats, they made a beeline for the house of Yokkaichi's mayor, situated near a fishing port to the north of the kombinat. Arriving early in the morning, they pounded on the mayor's door. Still half asleep, the mayor appeared in his nightclothes to inquire what the fuss was all about. A fishermen thrust a particularly evil-smelling fish into the mayor's face and said angrily, "*This* is the matter. And we have thousands more that no one will buy from us. It's *you* who brought those factories here. It's *your* responsibility." Still in his nightclothes, the mayor was led to the boats moored nearby, where he counted pile after pile of foul, unsalable fish. Now wide awake, he could measure the fishermen's fury, and in an effort to calm them, he offered to buy the morning's catch himself. Temporarily mollified by the mayor's paternalistic response, the fishermen accepted his offer and, following his instructions, dumped their catch back into the sea. But still equivocating, the mayor insisted that conclusive evidence linking the factories to the problem had yet to be supplied.

The fishermen were convinced that the Mie electric power plant, supplier of energy to the Shiohama kombinat, was the principal source of contaminants. With their own eyes they could see the yellowish effluent gushing day and night from its drainpipe into the Suzuka River directly above their fishing grounds. In reality they were mistaken. The power plant was only an intermediary, pumping water from Yokkaichi harbor to cool its generators, and then discharging the hot water into the river. The problem was that the harbor's shallow waters were already highly polluted from four years' accumulation of effluents from the various kombinat factories.

Yet Isozu's fishermen's union was unable to make a formal appeal to the power company because of an agreement between the two made several years earlier. In exchange for 2.6 million yen ($ 7,200), the union had promised not to make demands for compensation due to power plant effluents. This pact strait-jacketed the union's leaders: they could neither initiate nor participate in negotiations. Consequently, the rank and file members were forced to act. On June 3, 1963, some 400 fishermen went to the power plant for a meeting with its officials; the following day, 150 union members visited the city office. Later, 24 representatives met with the prefectural governor. On each occasion, the fishermen demanded that the waste outlet be moved. But the company refused, claiming that such a procedure was technically difficult and far too expensive. The government kept asking the fishermen for more time.

Exasperated, the fishermen decided to take the matter into their own hands. They had tried their best to be patient and to negotiate rationally with industry representatives. For over three years they had paid repeated visits to the factories and city and prefectural offices. Time after time they had been met with the same runaround and plied with vague promises. They now set June 21 as the last day they would try negotiation as a means of solving their problems. If a concrete decision were not reached that day, the long-suffering fishermen agreed, they had no recourse but to take direct action.

> ... Beginning early that morning, the loudspeakers atop Isozu's fishermen's union building were calling the people together. The village bristled with electric energy, the fishermen determined to do what had to be done... Finally, the announcement came. The final round of talks between the company and the union ended in deadlock. Shortly after three o'clock the long-suppressed anger of the fishermen at last exploded.[1]

Twenty young representatives of the union marched to the plant's gate and announced they were going to take direct action, while a group waiting on a nearby embankment signaled to others manning boats on the Suzuka River. In response, some 300 young fishermen in a fleet of vessels bore down on the offending drainpipe. As their onlooking women cheered, men armed with hoes and shovels marched across the bridge toward the electric plant.

The power company was not caught off guard. Inside its gates stood 80 riot policemen and 30 plainclothesmen who had been called in earlier by worried officials. A messenger was quickly dispatched to the home of Yoshi-ichiro Imamura, president of the Shiohama Federation of Village Councils, and representative of the fishermen in negotiations with industrial and governmental officials. A local political figure, Imamura was known to command the fishermen's respect and, perhaps more importantly from the factory officials' point of view, their obedience, both because of his political prestige and because of his steadfast efforts to negotiate on their behalf. After three years of dealing with Imamura, company officials felt they had come to know him well and considered him a reasonable man. Although they knew he represented the interests of the people in his district, they were convinced that he could also understand their own position.

While the officials waited anxiously for his arrival, the fishermen continued to move. An old boat filled with 2,000 sandbags was pushed steadily toward the drainpipe. The union's young spokesmen announced that the company had ten minutes to respond to their demands or they would plug up the pipe. Confident of victory, the fishermen counted the time. The ultimatum was met with silence; the electric company's only response was to turn up the plant to full power, causing the polluted discharge to pour even more forcefully from the huge pipe.

As the boat approached its target, Imamura suddenly appeared standing near the drainpipe. In a gesture of supreme humility, he bowed deeply before the startled fishermen, kneeling and touching his forehead to the ground in the manner traditionally reserved only for one's superiors. Pleading on the basis of their shared humanity, Imamura gave the fishermen his word that they could meet with the prefectural governor and have an opportunity to voice their complaints. Were they to insist on "committing this act of violence," however, he implored that they kill him first.

Had the young men been confronted by force, there is little doubt that the day would have ended in violence. But Imamura's humble plea came as a complete shock, putting them at a loss for what to do. The power of tradition, which called for obedience to superiors, and the ties of duty and obligation to their leader proved decisive. The fishermen swallowed their pride and retreated. Four and a half hours later, reduced to angry impotence, they were back in their village across the river, while the harbor's pollutants continued to foul their fishing grounds. One chronicler of the incident concludes:

> Thus, after suppressing their anger for so long, the fishermen had finally been forced to take direct action. Face to face with the police, they had reached a peak of tension unequaled in ten years of Yokkaichi history. But, alas, it ended in nothing.[2]

Two days later, as Imamura had promised, the governor of Mie Prefecture and two officials from the power plant met with the frustrated men at another fish-tasting party. The governor took one bite of the freshly caught fish, then quickly removed it from his mouth, gasping, "It's terrible!" Factory officials, however, downed their portions expressionlessly, praising the fish for its delicious taste. The fishermen were at first incredulous, then overcome with a feeling of great pity. They suddenly realized that the company officials believed that a public admission of how bad the fish tasted was tantamount to betraying the company and felt obliged to eat it even at the risk of their health. Ironically, the fishermen found themselves sympathizing with the company's loyal employees, who they realized for the first time, were also victims of industrial irresponsibility. The meeting ended with the governor's promise of compensation, and a prefectural committee was established to mediate the dispute.

A year and a half after the first fateful meeting with Mie's governor, the compensation issue was finally settled, at least as far as the prefectural administration was concerned. In January 1965, the mediation committee awarded the fishermen a total of 36 million yen ($100 thousand), a sum that put a mere 40 to 50 thousand yen ($100–150) into the hands of each of the young fishermen who had fired the abortive effort at direct action. Many were dissatisfied with the decision: "Just like all the other damned agreements and settlements, this one completely missed the point. There were still no attempts to stop the pollution or to pipe the polluted water somewhere else. Nothing changed. Our fish still smelled and tasted bad, and no one wanted to buy them from us. We didn't want their money, but we had to take it because our losses continued to rise and we had so many medical bills and debts to pay. What we really wanted was for the company to stop polluting and give us back our clean sea."

5.

During 1963, the prevalence and severity of Yokkaichi asthma worsened considerably. In August, the Shiohama Federation agreed to contribute 200 thousand yen ($550) from its treasury to help poorer victims cover the costs of medical care. It was hoped that this voluntary contribution might shame both government and industry into accepting some responsibility for the increased incidence of the disease, or at least into helping defray the continuously mounting treatment costs. Unfortunately, the federation's attempt lasted only three months, due to its feeble financial base. But about the same time, members of the Yokkaichi Medical Association, who had their hands full treating the victims, began entering the phrase "industrially caused asthma" onto medical history forms, also in an effort to exert pressure on the factories. For by then, despite numerous government and industry denials, it was taken for granted by Yokkaichi residents and medical practitioners that the disease's origin lay in the chemical pollutants discharged in the kombinat's operations.

In January 1964, epidemiologist Katsumi Yoshida examined thirty-one Isozu residents. According to his findings, the condition of eight patients was so serious that if they did not receive proper medical attention, they would probably die from the pollution-induced respiratory disease. Yoshida subsequently met three times with the prefectural vice-governor demanding better care for the victims and more research funds. Finally, the prefecture agreed, providing him with money to expand his investigations and set up a special "pollution-free" room in the Shiohama Hospital. When the air was especially bad, those plagued by disease in Isozu and Shiohama could escape to this asthma ward, where purifying machines turned Yokkaichi's poisonous air clean again. For many, the hospital became a necessary part of daily life. Isozu fishermen began to spend their nights in the ward, leaving early in the morning to fish far out in Ise Bay where the air was still fresh and returning to the hospital in the evening. Some returned to their families only once a week; some never returned. On April 2, after a particularly heavy smog had blanketed Yokkaichi for three consecutive days, sixty-two-year-old Yoshiro Furukawa died in the Shiohama ward. The autopsy, performed at Furukawa's deathbed request, identified the cause of death as emphysema and chronic bronchial inflammation of the lungs. He was Yokkaichi's first known pollution disease fatality.

Furukawa's death incited new protests from local residents, medical practitioners, and outside scholars. A visit in June of progressive intellectuals of the Statistics Research Council focused national attention on Yokkaichi's pollution and the totally inadequate countermeasures. Under increasing public protests coupled with greater news media coverage, Yokkaichi's city government at the end of 1964 established Japan's and the world's first pollution disease system. Recognizing publicly the link between kombinat industries, air pollution, and respiratory disease, the city agreed to take responsibility for the health impairment. Those who met medical criteria were now officially designated "pollution disease victims" and were authorized to have their medical expenses paid by the city government. Japan's first petrochemical kombinat had given rise to Japan's first pollution disease.

Although this shift of policy seemed like a breach in the formerly impenetrable alliance between local government and industry, in reality it was not. The new system was not accompanied by forceful attempts to control pollution. The city bore all the medical costs, while industry spokesmen continued to deny that their factories were at fault. Moreover, although by 1965 the city had finally agreed to pay the medical expenses of official victims, at the same time it was recruiting more industries for a *third* petrochemical kombinat to be constructed just north of Umaokoshi.

On April 2, 1965, the anniversary of Furukawa's death, Yokkaichi's asthma victims formed the Society to Protect Yokkaichi Pollution Patients. Its members realized that things could not continue as they were: receipt of free medicine and the official recognition that it implied were not in any way improving the quality of Yokkaichi's air. Factory officials, despite the fact that they had begun to raise the height of the exhaust stacks—an indirect acknowledgment of culpability—persistently denied any and all responsibility for the disease. While the stacks' new height reduced the concentration of sulfur dioxides in the most polluted areas, the total volume of pollutants continued to climb as the kombinats expanded production. The taller stacks only dispersed the poisonous gases over a wider area, and the new disease they engendered spread in proportion to the kombinats' commercial success.

Michitaka Akin, a noted legal scholar and member of the Statistics Research Council, suggested during his visit to Yokkaichi in June 1964 that the Society to Protect Yokkaichi Pollution Patients take the case to court. The society's reaction to this piece of advice was shock. Not only was a trial inordinately long and expensive, but Japan lacked a strong legal tradition in civil cases and mere presence in court involved a serious loss of face for both the plaintiff and defendant. How could its members, average citizens at best, initiate legal proceedings against top-level industrial officials? Yokkaichi's citizens stood in awe of the formidable body of civil law and the complicated court procedures. Dreading a decisive confrontation with the industrial and governmental establishment, a confrontation that would of necessity lead to public embarrassment and possibly total defeat for one of the parties involved, they preferred to continue their efforts to reach an acceptable solution in the more traditional manner. Hence their reliance on public and private forms of discreet "mediation" in search of a compromise solution. Grateful for the suggestion, however, the society decided to reserve it as an alternative of last—desperate—resort.

Sufficient desperation was not long in coming. On July 10, 1966, two years after Kaino had advised recourse to the courts, Usaburo Kihira, an elderly and impoverished asthma victim, committed suicide quite literally in the shadow cast across his home by the Daikyo Petroleum refinery. Kihira hanged himself, leaving a note explaining that in the next world things would be easier because medicine and money would no longer be necessary. Four days later, one Kazuhiko Otani bore a black-framed ceremonial death picture of Kihira at the head of a procession that wound its way silently through the city. Its representatives confronted city hall with four urgent demands: a guarantee of pollution victims' welfare, the establishment of an emergency refuge near the mountains, a change in the type of fuel being burned by the factories, and a halt to further industrial expansion. But the mayor failed to appear that day, claiming to be too busy to give a definite answer to the victims' demands. During 1966, the city government continued to push for approval of plans for the third kombinat and in February 1967, despite strong opposition from local residents, achieved its goal through a forced vote in the city council.

Kihira's suicide once again raised the idea of taking the pollution issue to court, but no one was yet willing to step forward and serve as plaintiff.

Otani, who carried Kihira's picture in the death march, was the wealthy owner of a confectionery business and one of the society's most energetic leaders. Like many others, his breathing grew increasingly painful as the air around Yokkaichi became laden with sulfur dioxide gases. Indeed, he was known on occasion to be seized with a paroxysm of coughing that would last for hours. But Otani was fortunate. He had more money than most, and when the discomfort grew unbearable, he would escape to the nearby mountains. It was just like the war, he reflected, when people ran for their lives to escape America's B-29s. From his refuge, Otani would call home to inquire whether it was "safe to return."

On June 3, 1966, Otani entered the following in his diary: "After five in the afternoon the smog became terrible. Because of the sulfur dioxide, I couldn't stop coughing. Packed lunch and left my home as fast as I could. It's a shame. Even though I want to be at home, I have to come to this lonely place. Damn! Why doesn't Mayor Kuki try asthma and see what it's like? Then would he understand? . . . Ah, but I don't want to die from the pollution. . . ."

Late May and early June 1967 brought a long stretch of smog-filled days. Otani's lungs knew little rest as a thick gray mist shrouded the city. On the morning of June 13, he awoke and peered despondently at the polluted sky, mumbling, "The air is bad again today." As he bathed, then ate his morning meal, persistent coughing racked his body. He left home silently and walked to his place of work, there to become Yokkaichi's second suicide, another death by hanging.

Otani's death finally shocked the asthma sufferers of Yokkaichi into action. When Kihira died, there was, it is true, brief but indecisive talk of taking the problem to the courts, but with the loss of Otani, an active, highly respected man still in the prime of his life, a new resolve was born. The society decided that there was indeed no other alternative. It would be the first time in Japanese history that a pollution suit would be brought collectively against several corporations at once, and the asthma sufferers were not optimistic about its outcome. But in Otani's suicide, and in Kihira's, they saw reflected the utter desperation of their situation. Their recourse to the courts could be justified by the seriousness of their plight. It had, after all, become a matter of life and death.

In August 1967, an association to support the pollution litigation was organized with progressive public employees' labor unions—particularly the teachers and city government workers—at the core. Fifty-six lawyers formed the legal team, based on the Takai Labor Litigation Group, which agreed to handle the case, although they were dubious about the chances of success. The victims were even less hopeful, as they had known only failure in a decade of efforts to stop the pollution of their environment.

But the impoverished residents of Isozu had tried everything else, to no avail. On September 1, 1967, despite their many misgivings, a group of nine Yokkaichi asthma victims filed a civil damage suit against the six companies of the Shiohama kombinat. A new social consciousness born of rapid industrialization was slowly taking shape to challenge the established power structure through what were, for Japan, revolutionary new forms of communal action and protest.

CHAPTER THREE

THE MASTER PLAN

"Japan is not really a developed country; industry has developed but the country as a whole has not. Our economic growth rate and GNP may well make the government proud, but the living conditions of the people should cause it shame."

—A HIGH-RANKING MEMBER OF JAPAN'S
NATIONAL INSTITUTE OF PUBLIC HEALTH

Ever since the United Nations Stockholm conference on the Human Environment in 1972, Japan's postwar economic experience has often been cited in the debate over the issues of economic growth and environmental disruption. It has been pointed to both as an envied example of the positive gains to be reaped from accelerated development and as an archetypical case of the negative consequences of excessively rapid growth. Of course, Japan has been by no means unique in its industrial expansion or in its relative disregard of environmental problems. But it has been unique in the amazing speed at which both have advanced and in the critical point the interrelated process has reached. Fundamentally, both Japan's rapid industrialization and its ecological decay have come about as a result of the peculiar characteristics of Japanese society and its response to the fifth "cultural invasion."

During the early Occupation years Japan knew extreme poverty, psychological depression, and an overwhelming sense of defeatism. Indeed, the end of the war meant more than losing to a stronger military power. It signified the defeat of an entire consciousness. The Japanese had blindly trusted their wartime leaders and the act of surrender, which violated every principle, set off a potent psychological reaction against the political and cultural doctrines that had led Japan into war. Masao Kunihiro, a well-known educator and cultural anthropologist, describes the Japanese defeat in the Pacific as a "baptism into the age of materialism, for Japan's surrender was perceived as a total spiritual surrender to the United States, viewed as the 'citadel of materialism.'"[1] It marked the start of a series of surface transformations of social, cultural, and political institutions and the adoption of a new national goal, initiated once again from above but this time by foreign forces.

In the first three years of the Occupation, General Douglas MacArthur, the Supreme Commander of the Allied Powers (SCAP), instituted programs aimed at democratizing and decentralizing Japan. His efforts have more than once been described as "one of man's most ambitious attempts at social engineering."[2] In the attempts to wipe out all traces of feudal authoritarianism, SCAP left few aspects of Japanese culture untouched. Political scientist R. E. Ward describes the extent of the Occupation reforms as follows:

> ... the purge of upwards of 200,000 individuals from public office or the possibility of acceding thereto; the writing of a completely new constitution; the drastic decentralization of what had been a highly centralized system of government; a complete reform of the entire national and local civil service; an attempt to establish a new democratic system of political parties and to regulate abuses associated therewith; *the introduction of a completely new concept of civil rights, human rights, the rights of women, and the rights of labor*; a complete overhaul of the judicial and legal system; a deliberate inversion of the theoretical position and powers of the Emperor; the dissolution of the system of giant cartels, known as the *zaibatsu*; the drastic reform of the land tenure system; the promotion of labor union organizations and collective bargaining; stringent control of credit and inflation; a total reform of the education system from kindergarten through graduate school; an attempt to substitute the Latin alphabet for the traditional writing system; campaigns to eliminate tuberculosis and other epidemic diseases; and even an attempt to persuade the Japanese to give names to at least the main thoroughfares in their major cities. This is a highly selective list that could be multiplied many-fold.[3] (emphasis added)

In short, SCAP attempted to transform Japan's semi feudal society into a "little America." Although many of SCAP's efforts may be characterized in retrospect as an attempt to force Japan's right foot into America's left shoe, they nonetheless succeeded in abruptly providing a new structure for Japanese society. This structure permitted the release of liberal tendencies and personal desires suppressed by years of militarism and centuries of cultural indoctrination.

Ironically, losing the war provided Japan with several long-term economic advantages. One such benefit was an enforced ceiling on military expenditures. Even in the relatively peaceful years of 1934–36, Japan had allotted approximately 7 percent of her GNP for military purposes; by 1944, the military budget claimed 68 percent. The postwar cut in military expenditures to less than 1 percent of the GNP (now for "self-defense") freed available funds for investment in modern industrial equipment and contributed to increasing the annual economic growth rate by an estimated 2 percent. The end of hostilities also freed Japan's top scientists and engineers from the requirements of designing military hardware; they could now engage in the production of consumer and industrial goods. The application of wartime technological experience to peacetime production provided a powerful stimulus to the electronics, camera, automobile, and shipbuilding industries.

Another factor contributing to recovery was the attitude of the Japanese people. The return of disciplined troops from the battlefield and experienced administrators from foreign colonies expanded the labor pool with dedicated and capable men willing to work hard for low wages. For the second time in a hundred years, the Japanese sense of loyalty, devotion, and self-sacrifice, rather than dissolving into a moral vacuum, found a new form of expression. Loyalty previously exercised for the sake of the Emperor would now be offered to the goal of economic recovery. In a review of postwar economic policies, Saburo Okita, one of the prime architects of Japan's remarkable growth, stated that because of defeat, the Japanese "were more easily convinced [of] ... the necessity of harder work, austere life and larger savings."[4]

The first steps toward economic recovery were taken in 1946 when SCAP directed the newly formed Japanese government to establish an Economic Stabilization Board to prepare a program for economic rehabilitation. In 1948, during the brief tenure of Japan's only nonconservative government in the postwar period, the board presented its draft Economic Rehabilitation Plan: 1949–53. The conservative government that came to power in November 1948 retained the basic concepts of the Socialists' plan and upheld its main objective, a recuperation of the prewar living standard of 1934–36. Both socialists and conservatives agreed on the basic approach to be taken in rebuilding Japan's economic power: rapid expansion of the heavy and chemical industries.

During the first stage of postwar recovery (from the beginning of the Occupation in September 1945 until the outbreak of the Korean War in June 1950), Japan's policy leaders drew up an industrial blueprint for the future. American advisors contributed to the plan by instituting firm controls on inflation and by arbitrarily establishing the exchange rate at 360 yen to the dollar. The only formidable barrier remaining was Japan's desperate shortage of foreign capital, forcing the nation to rely heavily on American aid. From 1945 to 1951, the United States loaned Japan some two billion dollars and purchased supplies for the Occupation Forces worth an additional three billion dollars. Japan's former enemy had become a crucial partner.

By 1949, Japan was already uneasy with her reliance on American aid and eager for greater economic independence. The outbreak of the Korean War in June 1950 provided an opportunity to initiate a second stage of economic recovery, the "self-supporting" period. The new Asian war transformed Japan into a supply, service, and operations depot for United Nations forces. "Special procurements" contracted for in Japan supplied the necessary foreign currency to pay for nearly half Japan's total imports during 1952–53, stimulating an economic boom with an average growth rate during those two years of some 10 percent.

Moreover, with the advent of the Korean conflict, America's attitude toward Japan's rehabilitation underwent an important change. In late 1949, following the military success of Mao Tse-tung's Red Army in mainland China, the United States drastically revised its foreign policy in the Far East to meet what it termed the "threat of an advancing red peril." Intensification of the cold war abroad and the McCarthy hearings at home created a new American world view in which Japan was cast into the role of a "bastion against communism in Asia." This sudden change of heart meant a revision of SCAP efforts at democratization, which reversed the trend toward liberalization of controls over the Japan Communist Party and labor unions.*

---

* Another manifestation of the new policy was the establishment in August 1950, at the urging of American military officials, of a paramilitary national "police force" of 75,000 men. Because one Occupation reform was a new Constitution that specifically renounced war and the nation's right to maintain military forces (Article 9), the formation of this force marked the beginning of a constitutional controversy that has yet to be resolved. The government argued that Article 9 did not prohibit "self defense" and therefore permitted the establishment of a National Police Force (1950). This gradually developed into the National Security Force (1952) and then into the present-day Self Defense Forces (1954). Japanese leaders in the postwar period, realizing that domestic and international reactions to a rearming Japan might well interfere with the reestablishment of trade relations and obstruct economic recovery, played down the role of this

On September 8, 1951, representatives of 48 nations meeting in San Francisco signed a treaty of peace with Japan. At the same time, the United States and Japan concluded the US-Japan Security Pact, which promised American military protection in exchange for the right to maintain American military bases in Japan. This security pact set in motion two important long-term trends. First, it allowed Japan to minimize defense expenditures and devote its full labor force, capital supply, and psychic energy to economic growth and development. Second, the military agreement became the basis for a unique relationship between Japan and the United States, supplemented by economic aid and, for the most part, mutually beneficial ties. The wartime "enemies-to-death" relationship was replaced by a teacher-pupil relationship in which Japan remained economically, militarily, and diplomatically dependent on American leadership.

During the second stage of the postwar period, the Japanese economy, in spite of high growth rates recorded in 1952–53, was not yet self-supporting. The country remained heavily dependent on UN procurements for its foreign exchange, and the Korean armistice in 1953 precipitated a serious depression. But the government's determined efforts to attain a positive balance of payments without reliance on foreign aid were beginning to take effect. By 1952, when the Occupation had ended, many economic indicators had come to equal the prewar levels of 1934–36, and Japanese industry was regaining a degree of its former self-confidence. This second stage reached a peak in 1955, with the announcement of a Five Year Plan for Economic Self-support, the first postwar economic blueprint designed solely by Japanese planners. The realization of its goals a mere two years later signaled the end of the postwar recovery period.

2.

A powerful mechanism for implementing postwar economic growth was the restoration of a three-way partnership among business leaders, bureaucrats, and politicians. Although the Occupation forces had initially attempted to dissolve the prewar financial cliques, even American military leaders grew to realize their advantages in terms of "organizational efficiency." By 1952, antimonopoly restrictions were being relaxed and the combines were beginning to reappear. Although the reorganized corporate groups differed

---

paramilitary force and conscientiously avoided involvement in world politics. They chose, instead, to remain in the protective shadow of the United States, while advocating policies of "non-aggressive" military strength and "economic diplomacy."

from their predecessors, they eventually grew to control Japan's world trade. At home, too, they entered into nearly every field of production from noodles to missiles. By 1972, Japan's six major trading firms virtually monopolized the country's economy, controlling more than half of the companies listed on the stock exchange, and handling about half of Japan's imports and exports.[5]

The merger of Japan's two conservative parties in 1955 to form the Liberal Democratic party—said by its critics to be neither liberal nor democratic—facilitated single-party rule and contributed to an atmosphere of security in the business world and the bureaucracy. The Conference for Economic Reconstruction was established the same year by businessmen to serve as a financial channel between the business community and conservative politicians. In 1973, this fund-raising body, renamed the People's Association (Kokumin Kyokai), reportedly collected nearly 20 billion yen ($56 million) from Japan's big businesses and was seeking to raise its monthly "dues" fourfold in 1974.*[6] With this immense financial backing, and with decisive electoral support in rural communities, the LDP has been able to dominate national and local politics in Japan for nearly two decades. Noting that Japan has "one party that only knows how to govern and others that only know how to oppose," political scientists Robert Scalapino and Junnosuke Masumi have labeled the Japanese political setup a "one-and-a-half party system."†[7]

One of the first redevelopment policies agreed upon by the triumvirate was to increase the nation's energy supplies. During the early 1950s, an ambitious program was adopted to construct more than 50 multipurpose dams throughout the country. This project, modeled after America's Tennes-

---

* Heavy criticism leveled by the general public against corporate donations, combined with LDP election losses in 1974, has resulted in the dissolution of the Kokumin Kyokai and the formation in January 1975 of a new organization which announced it will channel funds to all political parties that support parliamentary democracy.

† A further mechanism for strengthening the bonds between the ruling elites has been the practice known colloquially as the "descent from heaven," i.e., the flow of personnel from the bureaucracy to private and public corporations. The early retirement age (55) for government employees, coupled with inadequate pension plans, encourages them to seek post-retirement employment—which industry is only too willing to provide. Public enterprises, such as the Japan Housing Corporation and other corporations charged with specific development projects, commonly serve as resting spots for "retired" bureaucrats. Not surprisingly, this tradition is often criticized by opposition parties as a breeding ground for business-bureaucracy-LDP collusion. The ex-bureaucrat can influence his former colleagues remaining in the government, while bureaucrats defer to business interests to lay the foundations for a comfortable post-retirement life. Similarly, business promotes its interests in the Diet through financial contributions to LDP factions, while politicians court the favor of bureaucrats who make the day-to-day decisions of government. Thus, throughout the postwar period, important policy decisions have typically been arrived at by compromise and consensus among LDP politicians, government bureaucrats, and financial and business leaders.

see Valley Authority, was purportedly aimed at increasing agricultural production and improving rural living standards through electrification and improved irrigation, while laying the foundations for industrial growth. The fact is, however, that these dams were often designed and located without regard to agriculturally beneficial objectives such as flood control, water use, and water conservation, in favor of the development of a cheap supply of industrial electricity. During the early 1950s, dams in western Japan caused, rather than prevented, widespread water and flood damage, and similar incidents continue even today.[8]

The hydroelectric power development program has been cited as typical of the central government's one-sided emphasis on the growth of secondary industries at the expense of farming and fishing. In the 15 years between 1955 and 1970, the percentage of national income earned by primary industries (agriculture, fishing, and forestry) decreased from 22.0 to 7.5 percent, while that of secondary industries increased from 30.1 to 38.0 percent. Over the same period, the proportion of the population occupied in primary industries decreased from 42.0 to 19.3 percent, while the proportion occupied in secondary industries increased from 22.7 to 33.9 percent. Thus, while production in the primary industries almost trebled during these 15 years, that of secondary industries increased more than tenfold.

Taking hydroelectric power development as a case in point, it is significant that 70 percent of the necessary capital came from the central government, with private power companies supplying the rest. Centralizing bureaucratic control over the projects served to lighten the financial burden on the electric power industry and accelerated its rehabilitation. At the same time, it provided cheap electricity to those industries regarded as "basic" for economic recovery: coal, ferrous metals, fertilizer, electric power, and shipbuilding. During the economic boom of the 1950s, the central government controlled an estimated one-third or more of the nation's investment spending.[9]

The government, in turn, obtained its funds from private savings deposited in postal savings accounts, life insurance programs, and the like. For given per capita income levels, the frugal Japanese have consistently put relatively high proportions of their income into savings which have indirectly provided the foundation for industrial investment. This high savings rate (rising over the past two decades to 20 percent of disposable income) is attributed to various organizational characteristics of modern Japanese society: the payment of large semiannual bonuses to most company and governmental employees, anxiety due to an inadequate social security system, a low level of consumer or mortgage credit, the high cost of land, and outright governmental inducements favoring long-term deposits. This steady flow of funds into public and private financial institutions has been redirected by government ministries into chosen industries.

Stimulated by relatively low interest rates and high credit availability, industries came to rely heavily on these external sources of capital. This resulted in a situation of "over-loaning" by banks and "over-borrowing" by enterprises.* This phenomenon has made it necessary for Japanese firms to grow at extraordinarily high annual rates simply to service the interest on their huge loans: The result is a vicious circle, referred to as "bicycle operations," in which companies initially borrow money to expand their facilities, and then must continue to expand to pay back their growing debts. The company that stops growing, like the bicycle rider who stops pedaling, wobbles and eventually falls unless there is some outside prop to lean on. Thus, large-scale annual growth is essential to the very survival of Japanese firms in a way not paralleled elsewhere.

Another factor promoting postwar economic growth has been the persistence of the traditional "double-decker" structure of the Japanese economy. This structure is characterized by very large gaps in political power, wages, and working conditions between big business on the one hand and small- and medium-sized enterprises on the other. Small and middle-sized manufacturing enterprises, dependent on their "big brothers" in getting subcontracts and the like, have served as shock absorbers for the economy. Their expendability allows larger firms to react to changes in domestic and international market conditions with greater flexibility. While many small firms operating on a low capital basis file for bankruptcy every year, big businesses are usually protected from insolvency by their sway in political circles. The smaller firms, typically family-based contractors operating with minimal safety and health measures, produced the cheap "made in Japan" sundry goods that flooded world markets during the postwar period.

Manipulation of the economy's double structure served not only to perpetuate the social and health-care inequities but also contributed to the general disregard of environmental pollution. In many instances, the big firm could claim that it was cleanly operated only because the dirty work was subcontracted to smaller factories.† These smaller industries typically lack

---

* Even today in Japanese banks the ratio of loans to deposits exceeds 100 percent, while private enterprises commonly function at a debt-equity ratio of 70:30, the opposite of what is considered in the West to be a "stable" financial basis.

† Electrolytic plating work for the automobile industry, for example, which uses highly toxic metals such as chrome and zinc, has been largely handled by small and middle-sized factories.

both the financial resources and the expertise to provide pollution abatement equipment. Consequently, they end up not only polluting the surrounding environment but their own internal environment as well, affecting the health of their workers. The fact that larger concerns refuse to hire those not in excellent physical condition further reinforces the problem, because the already weak and rejected can only find work with the dirtier small firms.

Expansion of Japan's domestic consumer market also contributed to postwar economic growth. Before the war, Japan had conceived of itself as a middleman in international trade, importing raw materials, manufacturing finished goods, and then exporting them to foreign markets. While this pattern continued into the postwar period, the Japanese consumer began to experience the rising personal expectations associated with economic growth. When Japanese big business discovered this "new" market, it lost no time in flooding it with wristwatches, radios, televisions, cameras, stereos, washing machines, refrigerators, and all manners of other goods. With the growth of the plastics industry, inexpensive substitutes for goods once made exclusively of wood, clay, leather, and bamboo gradually found their way into every home.

After 1955, when the government first announced its plans to expand the petrochemical industry, there was an accelerated shift away from coal and hydroelectric power in favor of petroleum as the major source of the nation's energy requirements. Having no significant petroleum resources of its own, Japan successfully negotiated with the seven major international oil cartels for its supplies. In the buyer's market of the 1950s and 1960s, Japan took full advantage of the large volume of oil available at relatively low prices.* The switch to petroleum steadily increased Japan's dependence on foreign supplies of raw materials, but postwar Japanese leaders, now under the protective wing of the United States, took the same approach that had led to the prewar vulnerability of its industrial base to the Allied oil embargo. Business leaders, in cooperation with the Ministry of International Trade and Industry (MITI), increased petroleum imports almost fiftyfold in twenty years.†

---

* This policy, however, was not without its domestic as well as international costs. The most immediate dislocations occurred in Japan's domestic coal industry. Hundreds of mines shut down and the cities and towns they supported in the two major coal-producing areas of Kyushu and Hokkaido were thrown into depression. The economic boom of the early 1950s, however, provided many displaced miners with ready employment opportunities in the construction industry.

† Only when Japan was struck by the short-lived oil embargo of late 1973 did she begin to seriously reexamine the implications of her total dependence on foreign oil and the possibilities of returning to coal or moving more rapidly to adopt nuclear or other forms of power (see pp. 305–308).

While the switch to petroleum was an economically expedient strategy, it totally ignored environmental considerations. The result was economic success coupled with vast environmental deterioration. Oil spills and the discharge of untreated bilge waters devastated coastal inlets, bays, and beaches. Sulfur and nitrogen oxides and organic chemical wastes discharged during refining and processing operations contaminated both water and air; the widespread use of petroleum products as fuel for production and transportation fouled urban and rural air; and solid waste problems grew to enormous proportions from the widespread use of non-biodegradable plastics in the mass production of consumer goods. Until the late 1960s, voices calling for greater attention to human health and the quality of the environment were lost in the roar of machinery. Indeed, nowhere in this complex program for national recovery were environmental considerations given any attention.

Japan's official plans for the petrochemical industry designated three former Imperial Navy fuel depots (in Yokkaichi, Tokuyama, and Iwakuni) for reconstruction as petrochemical kombinats. These industrial complexes were designed to compensate for Japan's paucity of resources and distance from foreign markets. Its format based on the latest principles of economic rationality, the kombinat was devised by government and industry planners to incorporate the most advanced manufacturing technology. The latter was largely imported at relatively little cost from the West, particularly from the United States, which was eager to see its non-Communist ally prosper. Planners restricted imported equipment to that directly related to production, and while they frequently provided ingenious efficiency-heightening modifications, they tended to consider any cost-incurring accommodations to safety and environmental protection as "self-defeating." In many cases, they actually removed such accommodations from imported blueprints.[10]

The government provided participating companies with high depreciation allowances and long-term, low-interest loans, while protecting their domestic markets by imposing high tariffs on imported goods and restricting foreign investment. Local governments contributed to the communal effort by assuming many of the costs of providing industrial infrastructure. The kombinats specialized in the production of new synthetic materials considered to have the highest future growth potential.

In deciding on appropriate sites, industrial planners chose areas with abundant and inexpensive water supplies, low land prices, and a relatively well-developed infrastructure of roads, railways, and harbors. To further minimize overhead investment, the kombinats were located near existing urban centers to provide a ready source of labor. The kombinat was to be

Japan's economic salvation, a strong pillar upholding the nation's postwar policies of growthmanship and the "production first" economy.

3.

In May and June 1960, Japan was rocked by violent antigovernment riots occasioned by the renewal of the US-Japan Mutual Security Pact and the planned visit of President Dwight D. Eisenhower. The government ratified the treaty on June 23, but subsequent violence forced the cancellation of Eisenhower's visit and was a major factor in compelling Prime Minister Nobusuke Kishi to resign. Nevertheless, in general elections held the following November, Hayato Ikeda, recently elected president of the LDP, received overwhelming popular support, and his party's landslide victory was a glaring contradiction to the anti-LDP riots that had exploded only six months earlier. By campaigning on the promise to double incomes in ten years, Ikeda united the populace with the goal of meeting consumer expectations and returned the country to the business of economic growth.

Under Ikeda's leadership, the indices of growth reached new heights, as the government encouraged the trend of concentrating industrial production near urban centers. The Income Doubling Plan, moreover, proposed to link the four existing industrial areas along the Pacific coast—Tokyo, Nagoya, Osaka and Kitakyushu—into one massive Pacific Belt industrial area. This would be done by constructing, in addition to the Yokkaichi, Iwakuni, and Tokuyama kombinats, several new industrial complexes in relatively underdeveloped urban areas between the four cities. The industrial build-up of the Pacific Belt was aimed at realizing a sustained annual growth rate of 7 to 8 percent, ensuring full employment, reducing regional disparities, and improving the nation's living standard.

Announcement of the Income Doubling Plan stimulated a burst of new capital outlays and overall productive capacity; the major goal of doubling per capita income was achieved by 1968, two years ahead of schedule. By 1970, per capita income had reached $1,658, almost quadruple the 1960 figure! The doubling plan was less than successful, however, in spreading the qualitative benefits of development. The location of kombinats near large population centers caused severe pollution problems and aggravated urban-rural disparities.

By 1962, pressures exerted by rural governments on the nation's bureaucracy and political leaders to remedy this inequitable distribution of the benefits of modernity led the government to announce the National Comprehensive Development Plan. This regional plan proposed a nationwide network of new urban centers to be established near preexisting regional cities. These new centers would host heavy industrial and petrochemical complexes which, government planners reasoned, would attract other industries to the area. They would thereby increase local living standards through "multiplier effects" in which the original funds invested in new industries would set off chain reactions throughout the local economies. The plan also aimed to prevent further expansion of the metropolitan areas around Tokyo, Nagoya, and Osaka, already beset with serious environmental disruption.

The final plan designated fifteen "new industrial cities" and six "special industrial areas," and its passage into law sparked fierce competition among prefectural governments to attract industries and persuade the central government to designate a portion of their prefectures for development. Local governments spent some 600 million yen ($1.5 million) in lobbying efforts alone, a sum that rivaled the total funds granted by government for new industrial infrastructure during the first year of the program. Thus local governments in areas not chosen lost huge sums of money, but the winners suffered even more serious financial difficulties. For one, individual prefectures were expected to provide the bulk of the necessary infrastructure through local funding. In addition, as part of the effort to entice enterprises to the new industrial areas, the prefectures reduced their taxes (particularly fixed asset taxes) by large margins for participating companies. Finally, Japan's centralized taxation system, which earmarks 70 percent of local taxes for redistribution through the central government, exacerbated the problem, by increasing the burden on local governments and making them extremely vulnerable to central government control. As a result, regions favored with development projects often found themselves unable to afford adequate investments in housing and health-care facilities, or in improvements in the living environment and educational facilities.

Yet, in overall economic terms, the National Development Plan was highly successful. During the 1960s, Japan coped with heightened international competition by constructing some of the world's largest steel factories, petroleum refineries, and petrochemical plants, all elements of huge kombinats. She increased her share of world trade from 3.6 to 6.9 percent, her GNP rose nearly four times, unemployment dropped from 2.1 to 1.1 percent, and a positive balance of payments was reached in 1965 for the first time in the postwar period.

But the grand kombinats also brought with them health and environmental hazards, and by the mid-1960s, their popular image as the symbol of Japan's return to industrial power was being tarnished by widespread press coverage of Yokkaichi. The kombinat now brought to mind images of asthma victims, nets full of oily, inedible fish, and small enclaves of houses huddled miserably in the shadows of huge factories. Although the prefectures were supposed to design and control their own regional development plans, most lacked the necessary expertise and experience to coordinate the complicated kombinat planning. They were therefore obliged to depend upon central government and industry planners for guidance. In practice, plans for construction and design were decided upon by the respective industries involved, financial circles, and the central government (particularly the Ministry of International Trade and Industry [MITI] and the Economic Planning Agency), and then were "reviewed" and approved by local officials.

Even with consensus among these groups, however, planning tended to be piecemeal, resulting in the not-uncommon pattern of building an industrial plant and not providing it with waste treatment facilities until several years later. One commentator writes with regard to the Japan Housing Corporation (a public enterprise) that,

> In many cases the JHC constructs houses according to its own housing plans without any consideration to city planning at the prefectural level... Still worse, prefectural authorities have to expend large sums of money for constructing public facilities such as schools, highways, water and sewage lines, etc., after construction of housing by the JHC—the JHC considers its job is only to build houses and not to provide public related facilities.[11]

Pollution control measures also lagged. The major air-pollution prevention device eventually adopted in kombinats constructed during the 1960s—taller smokestacks—was justified by considerations of concentration rather than of the total volume of pollutants released and the capacity of a given area to absorb them. The tall stacks, unable to change the quantity of pollutants but capable of dispersing pollutants over a wider area, improved conditions in some areas while worsening them in others.* This pattern was clear in Yokkaichi, where the increase in the height of stacks between 1966 and 1970 was accompanied by an expansion of the area burdened with high concentrations of sulfur dioxide from 26 to 67 percent of the city. More than one health expert has pointed out, however, that while the tall stacks are

---

* When environmental standards are based on the concentration of air pollutants in exhaust fumes from a given smokestack, it is possible to increase the total volume of discharged contaminants by dilution or by adding another smokestack. This is also true in the case of liquid effluents; the concentration of pollutants is often reduced by pumping up clean groundwater to dilute effluents.

limited in effectiveness, they are very visible in environmental reports and in the annual budget report, where they serve as good public relations gimmicks. Their construction also contributes to the nation's GNP.

Another widely used antipollution measure in the late 1960s consisted of green belts, or strips of land planted with trees and intended to separate industrial from residential areas. These, too, were found to be of limited effectiveness. The limitations were especially evident in the older industrial areas, such as Yokkaichi, where there is not even space enough to construct such a belt. In 1970, the population density in Yokkaichi had risen to 1,192 persons per square kilometer (3,099 per square mile), and the number of officially recognized pollution victims was increasing at the rate of twenty per month. Although planting trees may help to curtain some noise or particulate matter from nearby residences, green belts used in highly congested areas are of questionable effectiveness in significantly reducing damage from toxic exhaust gases; a number of green belts, in fact, themselves have succumbed to the poisonous fumes.*

In less congested industrial complexes constructed in the middle and late 1960s, however, green belts could theoretically serve to exchange oxygen for discharged carbon monoxide, provide some protection against accidental fires and industrial explosions, reduce noise somewhat, and give a natural warning system for sudden changes in the kind or amount of air or water pollution released by neighboring factories. Nonetheless, it requires ten years before a green belt can offer minimal protective results, and thirty years before it is optimally effective. The scrawny saplings now visible in many kombinats can do little to reduce contemporary pollution problems but, like tall smokestacks, they make for good public relations.

4.

The kombinat has been characterized by its critics as a form of colonial exploitation of "underdeveloped" regions. It is pointed out, for example, that company employees and their families generally live apart from the "native

---

* The response of industry to this contingency has at times been rather ingenuous. A pollution control official of one of Japan's major steel producers with a factory in Kawasaki suggested in an interview that his firm was considering planting trees that are "resistant to pollution." Ecologist Akira Miyawaki, the main proponent of the green belt idea in Japan, commented in an unrelated newspaper interview that the result of such thinking may be that "even if the trees survive, the people may die."[12]

residents" of a given area.* Participating firms import skilled labor to fill high-level managerial positions and operate sophisticated industrial equipment, while employing only a relatively small proportion of the local labor force. The latter are usually restricted from rising very high in the company hierarchy, and those who have not graduated from a "good" university rarely, if ever, become part of the Tokyo office managerial staff. Instead, a kombinat corporation utilizes local residents indirectly as subcontractors or in service industries; many are employed simply as menials.

Local governments tend to adopt a subservient attitude toward the incoming industries. Kombinat installations often belong to such powerful combines as Mitsubishi, Sumitomo, and Mitsui. The latter wield enormous political power through their ties to the central Tokyo bureaucracy and the LDP, a combination for which local politicians are no match. Few city and prefectural government officials, therefore, are willing to express overt resistance to the demands made by the emissaries of big business. On the contrary, they tend to treat their "invited guests" with deference and respect. In short, most do (or at least try to do) as they are told.

Resident industries exercise an even more direct influence over local politics through their employees and subcontractors. In Oita, located on the southern island of Kyushu, the city council in 1972 was composed of 21 conservative and 21 progressive members. Nevertheless, the council passed phase two of its controversial kombinat expansion program because its Socialist progressives represented kombinat labor unions and, following company directives, voted in favor of the measure. Housing all company employees in a single complex also benefits the company, as it is thus assured elected representation in city, and often prefectural, assemblies. Big business has also exploited the double structure of the economy to enhance its influence. In many older industrial areas, subcontractors commonly stop work at election time to campaign full time for company-sponsored candidates. In sum, big business profits from the traditional Japanese attitude which views the electoral process not as an individual decision based on the policies of candidates, but as an "impersonal action connected with group behavior and the ratification of authority."[13]

The hierarchical organization of Japanese companies further discourages the feeling of "belonging" to local communities. Company employees, particularly upper executives who are typically rotated through various corporate installations in different parts of the country, tend to identify more

---

* In Yokkaichi, for example, the employees of kombinat industries live in company housing separated from the factories by a safe distance of five to ten kilometers!

with the company than with the city in which they happen to be living at a particular point in their careers.

Local governments are caught in a double bind by the taxation system, which further exploits native residents. In order to invest in social overhead, local governments must increase their tax revenues, which means either increasing population and/or individual taxes or raising income from fixed asset taxes by recruiting more industries to settle in the area. This continual drain on local finances led Yokkaichi's municipal government, despite the city's severe pollution problems, to construct its third petrochemical kombinat in the mid-1960s.

In short, most areas that recruited kombinats during the 1950s and 1960s have relinquished their local autonomy to corporate, bureaucratic, and political decision-makers in Tokyo. The kombinat has thus tended to perpetuate Japan's traditional double structure of government, in which local authorities are obedient "subcontractors" for the ruling Tokyo triumvirate.

Although some Japanese were beginning to question the kombinat formula by the mid-1960s, the first legal challenge did not come until July 24, 1972, when a decision was handed down in the Yokkaichi litigation. After nearly five years of legal debate, Judge Kiyoshi Tonemoto awarded the 12 plaintiffs in the case a total of 88 million yen ($286,000) in damages to be paid jointly by the six major firms of the petrochemical complex. This epoch-making ruling in Japan's first multiple-source air pollution suit held the industries "collectively responsible." Furthermore, it recognized epidemiological data showing a relationship between sulfur oxides discharged by the industries and the incidence of respiratory disease as legal proof of causation. The court concluded that the participating factories were collectively responsible for damages because they located in Yokkaichi without first conducting joint studies of the effects of their operations on the local environment and because they failed to use the most advanced pollution control equipment available. The decision was a major triumph for victims of Yokkaichi asthma, supporting all the plaintiffs' allegations except that of "*intentional* negligence."

The implications of this victory extended far beyond Yokkaichi. Once their legal responsibility was publicly confirmed, government and industry officials throughout the nation were forced to consider effective countermeasures for similar pollution problems. The Environment Agency (established in July 1971) reviewed, then strengthened national air pollution regulations; reevaluated sulfur dioxide standards; drafted legislation to regulate contaminants by total volume rather than by concentration; and declared the necessity for more extensive use of low sulfur oil. In addition to increased attention to pollution control on the part of industry, the Yokkaichi decision raised the possibility that industrial complexes might be restricted in size to meet regional environmental limitations—a development that could negate the kombinat's basic rationale. Furthermore, the Yokkaichi precedent left industries in other kombinats vulnerable to similar damage suits brought by air pollution victims. Even those factories complying with exhaust regulations could now be sued if the combined effect of all installations at a given kombinat could be shown to be detrimental to the health of local residents.

The kombinat formula was further challenged by a highly abnormal succession of 26 industrial accidents in chemical and petrochemical factories from July to October 1973. Explosions and fires claimed a total of eight lives, caused injuries to many workers, and on two occasions forced the evacuation of nearby residents. The Japanese weekly magazine *Ekonomisuto* (Economist) cited a number of factors responsible for the accidents.[14] In designing factory layout, it pointed out, Japanese industrial planners had crowded Western production facilities, including highly flammable and explosive equipment, into one-quarter of the space commonly allotted similar installations abroad; moreover, little or no consideration was given to the distance separating residential from industrial areas. While computers automated and further "rationalized" industrial operations, it claimed, the quality of workers was allowed to decline. Furthermore, enterprises had obstructed government safety inspections because of a fear, fed by excessive competition, of exposing their technological secrets to "industrial spies." Excessive competition was also said to have driven industries to operate old equipment at rates exceeding safety levels in their passion to meet strong market demand. Finally, the *Ekonomisuto* criticized the perennial laxity of MITI inspections and controls, the ministry's close relationship with kombinat industries, and the tendency for industry to report accidents as "handling mistakes," shifting responsibility onto lower managerial employees. But the fundamental cause of the accidents, concluded the *Ekonomisuto*, was the same as that underlying the problems of air pollution, defective merchandise, contaminated foods, and traffic accidents: a single-minded emphasis on economic growth that ignored all its negative effects.

The Yokkaichi decision and this string of accidents exposed fundamental problems inherent in the kombinat formula of industrialization and regional development. In response, the press conducted campaigns for stricter control of pollution in industrial areas and for greater concern for the health and safety of the public. But government reaction was cursory and conservative at best. Indeed, industry and government commitment to the kombinat-style industrial complexes has remained unshaken, and, as we shall see in Chapter 7, new economic policies call for the construction of even larger "industrial parks."

CHAPTER FOUR

TRAGEDY AT MINAMATA

... I had never been sick before. Before this started, my hands, my legs—every part of me was good and strong. Now I feel as if my body is gradually drifting away from this world. I have no grip. I can hold nothing in my hands or arms, not even my husband's hand, not even my own dear son. I might be able to endure that, but I can't even hold a bowl of rice—the chief food in my life-or my chopsticks. When I walk, I don't feel as if I'm walking with both feet on the ground. I feel as if I'm on my own, a long way from the earth. I feel so alone...

—MICHIKO ISHIMURE
Kukai Jodo Waga Minamata Byo
(Suffering Sea, Pure Land: Our Minamata Disease)

The high toxicity and wide industrial applicability of mercury have for centuries given rise to occupational diseases. One early case report comes from the Italian physician Ramazzini who, in the eighteenth century, described the agony and death of young miners and gilders who had absorbed the heavy metal in the course of their work. In the nineteenth century, a mercuric nitrate solution was widely used in the felt hat industry, and workers in these factories, too, were commonly stricken. Excruciating complaints were so common in the American hat-making city of Danbury, Connecticut, that the symptoms became known as the "Danbury shakes." In 1940, the English researchers Hunter, Bomford, and Russell reported four clinical cases of mercury poisoning in workers at an agrochemical plant, thereby establishing the symptomatic criteria for identifying organic mercury intoxication.

Minamata disease, however, was the first recorded incident of mass mercury poisoning due to *indirect* transmission of the heavy metal from industrial wastes through the environment. The Minamata tragedy alerted the world to the dangers of environmental mercury pollution. But Japan had to experience two deadly outbreaks of the disease, one in Minamata and the other in Niigata, before its government gave serious consideration to the need for effective measures to bring industrial contamination of the environment by heavy metals under control.

The production facilities of the Chisso Corporation—gray blocks wrapped in a massive collage of intertwining pipes and stacks—dominate Minamata, a small city on the western coast of Kyushu. The Minamata installation was established in 1908 by the Japan Fertilizer Company (renamed Chisso in 1965) at the request of the town's leaders. The plant specialized in the production of nitrogen-lime fertilizers and industrial chemicals including explosives, and as both domestic and international demand for its products increased, the company's Minamata facilities expanded. Supporting the rising tide of colonial expansionism of the late 1930s, Japan Fertilizer followed the nation's victorious armies to the Asian mainland and built production facilities overseas, particularly in Korea. During the Second World War, all chemical imports to Japan were halted and the domestic industry boomed. Nearly half of Minamata's chemical yield went to fill military orders until, in 1945, American bombs put a temporary end to the factory's operations.

The nation's defeat threatened Chisso's existence, for it lost foreign holdings amounting to some 80 percent of total assets. Postwar rehabilitation efforts, however, soon created a new prosperity for the company. Government economic policies, giving special emphasis to the expansion of the chemical industry to meet the brisk demand for nitrogen fertilizers and organic chemicals, fueled a sharp production rise at the rebuilt Minamata plant. By the early 1950s, the factory was manufacturing ten major synthetic chemicals, and by 1960 production figures for many of them had increased from five- to tenfold. Two "big growth" chemicals at the core of Chisso's operations were polyvinyl chloride and acetaldehyde, used in the production of plastics. Chisso's rapid growth gained it an envied reputation as one of Japan's top electrochemical manufacturers, and it was soon attracting the most promising graduates in chemical engineering from Japan's best universities.

But accompanying Minamata's industrial growth is a history of pollution problems. As early as 1926, and again in 1943, local fishermen demanded and received monetary compensation from Chisso for losses attributed to factory-induced deterioration of coastal waters. Chisso's rapid expansion after the Second World War naturally led to an increase in the volume of effluents it poured into the sea, until in 1949 and 1950, damage to the local fishing industry was once again conspicuous. Sea bream, shrimp, sardines, and octopus disappeared completely from Minamata Bay, fishing nets rotted in the sea, and dead fish floated near the factory's drainpipe. The evidence convinced Minamata's fishermen that Chisso's wastes were responsible for the damage, particularly since no other major industrial installation was operating in the area. In 1949, the local fishermen's union appealed to the company for compensation and an end to the pollution. But factory management, claiming that the allegations lacked a scientific basis, denied responsibility for the bay's deterioration.

Dr. Masazumi Harada, assistant professor at the Kumamoto University Medical School and a researcher in clinical electroencephalography and neuropsychiatric defects associated with the intake of toxic materials, later criticized the company's response. In his book on Minamata disease, Harada stressed that "the facts as perceived by the fishermen, based as they were on their direct experiences, were indeed very scientific."[1] Harada points out that in fact the company had admitted to polluting coastal waters in 1943 when it settled with the Minamata union by purchasing the union's fishing "rights" to one portion of local waters. This transaction did not carry with it an overt admission of responsibility for environmental problems per se, but the company did concede through its payment that its factory wastes were causing damage to the fishing industry. One clause of the agreement stipulated, however, that in exchange for the compensation, the union and its members would promise to make no more reparation demands.

The reorganization of Minamata's fishermen's union in 1949 under a new "democratized" Fisheries Law raised the question of whether the union was bound to adhere to the 1943 agreement and occasioned renewed demands for compensation.* The compensation negotiations begun in 1949 ended in deadlock, Chisso apparently believing that the earlier agreement was still in force. When the union encountered financial difficulties in 1951, however, the company provided it with an interest-free loan of 500,000 yen ($1,400). This loan was made on the condition that the union make "absolutely no objections" to factory activities, even if they eventually produced "toxicity

---

* According to the American-inspired revisions of the Fisheries Law, union members for the first time elected their leaders and gained control over the rights to commonly held fishing grounds. These rights, which had existed before the war, resembled a license and were granted by prefectural authorities to prevent other fishermen and industries from encroaching on a union's particular fishing grounds. If an industry desired to occupy a given coastal area, for example, it was first required to purchase the fishing rights from the appropriate union. The decision of whether to sell or not, previously made by the union's leaders, now required approval of two-thirds of the full membership.

damages" within the union's fishing grounds, and that the union "positively acquiesce" to company plans for land reclamation in the future.

In 1954, in order to reclaim land for expansion, Chisso applied to the union to purchase fishing rights it held in the Hachiman Sea area. Seeing in this application an opportunity to pressure the company to meet its former demands, the union refused to relinquish the area unless, it bargained, Chisso agreed to pay the yearly sum of 500,000 yen ($1,400) to compensate its members for past and future damages. The company proposed a sum of 400,000 yen ($1,100) on the condition that "even if further damages were to occur in the future, no new demands would be made." The financially desperate fishermen accepted the offer.

Thus, Chisso and the fishermen's union engaged in compensation negotiations on four occasions, in 1926, 1943, 1951, and 1954. During each session the company reportedly promised to survey its effluents, install appropriate treatment equipment, and carry out pollution countermeasures to prevent damages. In fact, no such investigations were made, and although countermeasures were discussed, the company deemed certain damages to the local fishing industry as simply unavoidable.[2] According to a study carried out by Minamata's municipal government, the total number of fish caught in Minamata Bay decreased some 40 percent between 1953 and 1954, and by 1956 was less than one-quarter the haul of 1952. Fishermen's annual incomes declined accordingly and, by 1956, had fallen by one-half or more from their former levels. But even these shocking statistics failed to elicit the immediate and thorough analysis of factory wastes that was obviously required. The deterioration of Minamata Bay continued.

2.

By 1953, ominous evidence appeared in Minamata. Birds seemed to be losing their sense of coordination, often falling from their perches or flying into buildings and trees. Cats, too, were acting oddly. They walked with a strange rolling gait, frequently stumbling over their own legs. Many suddenly went mad, running in circles and foaming at the mouth until they fell—or were thrown—into the sea and drowned. Local fishermen called the derangement "the disease of the dancing cats," and watched nervously as the animals' madness progressed.

Inexorably, the dancing cats disease spread to humans. By the early 1950s, a number of Minamata fishermen and their families were experiencing the disquieting symptoms of a previously unknown physical disorder. Robust men and women who had formerly enjoyed good health suddenly found their hands trembling so violently they could no longer strike a match. They soon had difficulty thinking clearly, and it became increasingly difficult for them to operate their boats. Numbness that began in the lips and limbs was followed by disturbances in vision, movement, and speech. As the disease progressed, control over all bodily functions diminished. The victims became bedridden, then fell into unconsciousness. Wild fits of thrashing and senseless shouting comprised a later stage, during which many victims' families, to keep the afflicted from injuring themselves or others, resorted to securing them with heavy rope. Around 40 percent of those stricken died.

Because the horrifying ailment was confined to a group of families in the fishing villages on the outskirts of Minamata City, the city's urban residents and those unaffected attributed its cause to hygienic deficiencies within the stricken households. Believing the disease to be contagious, they cautiously avoided and eventually ostracized the afflicted. Shopkeepers refused to serve them or their families, and when the victims passed along the street, their awkward gaits and physical deformities brought stares, smirks, and harsh ridicule from onlookers. Because the cause of the disease was obscure and it had no name, it was simply referred to by the press, medical authorities, and victims as the "strange disease."

In the conservative society of Minamata, not only the victims of the disease but also other family members became social outcasts. For, as in most parts of the world, in rural Japan the reputation of the family as a whole determines the social fortunes of its individual members. In arranging a marriage, for example, it was traditionally more important to select a good family than a good mate, marriage being not simply the union of two individuals but the joining of two families. Good physical health has always been an especially vital requirement in matchmaking among the Japanese, who place great importance on maintaining the genetic integrity and strength of their progeny. In this context, families with a disease victim in their midst lost all prospects for a "good" marriage or for general social acceptance; they were eventually ostracized outright. Victims were guilt-ridden because of the stigma they had unwittingly brought upon their families, and were mortified before outsiders when unable to control their movements or physical functions. Under the intense pressures of Japan's group-centered social order, the victims' families took every measure open to them to try to avoid social ostracism, including hiding the sick from public view, often even refusing doctors the permission to examine them.

Discrimination against disease victims and their families was compounded by the alienation of city dwellers from the villagers of outlying fishing districts. Although neighboring villages were merged into the administrative borders of Minamata City in 1949, they remained physically separate from the central area of the city. Their inhabitants were socially segregated from urbanites in general and from Chisso's employees in particular. Indeed, it can be said that while Minamata City prospered because of Chisso's presence as the major source of financial support for the local government and of employment for the city's residents, the fishermen were barely managing to survive because of it. The long controversy over damages caused by untreated factory wastes had already fostered deep animosities between the two groups and brought into clear relief their conflicting interests and allegiances. But while suspecting the cause of their problem lay in the factory, the fishermen nonetheless at that time shrank from openly accusing the factory of causing the disease. In part this reluctance reflected their desire to avoid the glare of national attention. They feared such exposure might tarnish the name of Minamata and thereby threaten the survival of the tourist trade and possibly even that of their own already handicapped industry.

The late Dr. Hajime Hosokawa, former director of Minamata's Chisso Hospital, is credited with the official "discovery" of the "strange disease." In May 1956, a delirious six-year-old girl came under Hosokawa's care. Finding a degree of brain damage more extensive than that associated with encephalitis and aware of recent reports of similar cases, Hosokawa formally notified the Minamata Health Center of the outbreak of a disease characterized by severe damage to the central nervous system. Within a month, the Health Center organized a Council on Strange Disease Countermeasures, enlisting the cooperation of the Chisso and municipal hospitals, the local Medical Associations, and the municipal government. The council initiated an intensive epidemiological survey of the nearby fishing villages and, to its surprise, identified 52 victims of the disease by the end of the year. Despite the council's progress in describing the course of the disease, however, its precise cause remained unknown.

Suspecting the disorder to be contagious, the council initially quarantined the affected areas. When test results were negative, however, the quarantine was lifted. The researchers took another tack, heeding rumors then current among the fishermen that the cause might lie in contaminated fish. In the fall of 1956, the council reported its conclusions to the Minamata Disease Medical Research Society, which was composed of Kumamoto University Medical School scientists requested by the prefectural government to research the disease's cause. The report stated that the original hypothesis of a contagious disease due to bacterial or viral infection was highly unlikely, and suggested the cause might be heavy metal intoxication from eating contaminated fish. After the local council presented its report, the university researchers, representing every major department—internal medicine, pediatrics, neuropsychiatry, hygiene, public health, pathology, microbiology—assumed the central role in investigating the disease.

Although the university research group received research and financial support from the Ministry of Health and Welfare (MHW) and the National Institute of Public Health, the scientists encountered great difficulties in isolating a specific metal as the cause. But they did succeed in reproducing the symptoms in cats fed fish caught in Minamata Bay. In February 1957, the group strongly recommended that fishing in the bay be suspended. Although such a prohibition would seem to have been reasonable, the recommendation led to no decisive action.

The proposed fishing ban was complicated by two problems. First, Japan's Foodstuffs Hygiene Law stipulated that conclusive identification of a specific causative agent of illness was required before the government could take any administrative action, such as prohibiting fishing. Second, the Fisheries Law provided that compensation be paid to any union restricted from operating in its legal territory. But who would provide this compensation? In August 1957, the Kumamoto prefectural government banned fishing in Minamata Bay, but subsequent Diet debate forced the prohibition to be rescinded. Instead, the prefecture adopted a policy that forbade only the sale of fish. The local fishermen's union was therefore forced to "voluntarily restrict" its activities within the bay—with no compensation for resulting losses.[3]

Since decisive countermeasures awaited the scientific identification of the disease's cause, all subsequent investigatory work focused on this objective. Various theories pinpointing heavy metal consumption were proposed as university researchers performed toxicology tests on compound after compound. In 1956, manganese was the first metal to become suspect, followed in 1957 by two others: selenium and thallium; in 1958, thallium alone took prominence. Finally, in 1959, organic mercury came under suspicion.

The sudden and intense interest in organic mercury was occasioned by the visit to Minamata of a British neurologist. In March 1958, Douglas McAlpine spent two days in Minamata investigating the mysterious nervous disorder. In his report published in the September 20, 1958, edition of *The Lancet*, a British medical journal, McAlpine suggested for the first time that Minamata disease might be caused by the excessive concentration of organic mercury in nerve tissue. He pointed to similarities between Minamata disease and the well-documented cases of organic mercury poisoning known as the Hunter-Russell syndrome. In particular, Minamata disease's characteristic concentric constriction of vision was symptomatic, he believed, of mercury-related neural damage. Although cautiously worded, McAlpine's report had great impact on the history of Minamata disease research.

The period dating from the official recognition of the disease in 1956 to the first proposal in 1958 that organic mercury might be its cause was marked by intensive but inconclusive laboratory research. The scientists at Kumamoto University had been basing their studies on an analysis of factory effluents conducted by the Chisso Corporation and made public in October 1956. In the list of heavy metals the company identified in its waste waters mercury was conspicuously absent. Furthermore, according to Harada, most of the medical scientists investigating the new disease knew almost nothing about Chisso's equipment and manufacturing processes. They naively assumed that mercury was too valuable a substance to be discarded in the industrial process. After publishing its own analysis, Chisso prevented independent researchers from sampling wastes within the factory to determine if and how organic mercury was being produced.[4] Chisso's uncooperative attitude, the researchers' imperfect knowledge of the factory's operations, and the concentration on laboratory research (while failing to perform epidemiological field surveys) delayed serious consideration of organic mercury until McAlpine's visit.

Once McAlpine published his report, however, Kumamoto University researchers moved quickly. Within a week they declared it necessary to investigate the possible role of organic mercury compounds. At a meeting of the research group in late 1958, Professor Tadao Takeuchi, head of Kumamoto's Department of Pathology, asserted authoritatively that the symptoms of Minamata disease and those of the Hunter-Russell syndrome were indeed identical, and in early 1959, published the first Japanese report implicating organic mercury as the likely causative agent.

Official research on the "mercury theory" began in January 1959, with the formation of the Minamata Disease Food Poisoning Subcommittee. This research team, made up of both medical and physical scientists from Kumamoto University, served under the Health and Welfare Ministry's Foodstuffs Hygiene Investigation Council. Its findings were finally divulged in an interim report issued on November 12, 1959, after several bureaucratic delays imposed by government officials and an attempt by Kumamoto's prefectural governor to postpone the announcement even further. On the basis of pathological, clinical, and experimental data, the subcommittee concluded that the causative agent involved in Minamata disease was indeed organic mercury. Although the report failed to mention Chisso's possible role in releasing this substance into the environment—indeed it took pains not even to mention the company's name—the Ministry of Health and Welfare disbanded the subcommittee the day after the report was published. The question of the disease's cause was removed from the jurisdiction of the Ministry of Health and Welfare and was referred for "reexamination" to the Ministry of International Trade and Industry, the Economic Planning Agency, and the Ministry of Agriculture and Forestry.

Five months before the Food Poisoning Subcommittee submitted its official report to the Ministry of Health and Welfare, the Minamata Disease Research Group from Kumamoto University issued a similar document indicting organic mercury compounds. This earlier report had furthermore cited Chisso's effluents as the "likely source" of such compounds found in the environment. Although the researchers were admittedly unable to explain how the inorganic mercury used by Chisso had been transformed into the organic mercury found in the environment, their report and its implied indictment of Chisso had caused an uproar. Using the findings of the report as justification, fishermen and disease victims intensified attempts to gain compensation from the company. The Chisso Corporation, meanwhile, stepped up its defensive counterattacks, issuing denials of responsibility for the occurrence of the disease and rejecting outright the entire "mercury theory."

3.

In August 1958, Minamata disease victims and their families had formed the Mutual Assistance Society to negotiate with Chisso for compensation, but their initial approaches were rebuffed. In early August 1959, shortly after publication of the independent university report, Minamata's fishermen's and fish dealers' unions demonstrated at the factory's gates, demanding 100 million yen ($277,000) in compensation for economic losses, the purification of Minamata's fishing grounds, and the installation of improved pollution abatement equipment within Chisso's facilities. The company's reply stressed that the cause of contamination was still scientifically ambiguous. Chisso therefore offered a solatium of 500,000 yen ($1,400), later raising it to 3 million yen ($8,300). It doggedly maintained that it could not independently undertake to purify the bay, however, because, after all, it was public domain. The fishermen reacted by storming the factory. When, at a third meeting, the company did no better than to increase its offer to 13 million yen ($36,000), the fishermen stormed the factory again, holding its executive director hostage overnight and demanding that all three of their conditions be met. Finally, representatives of the two sides agreed to settle the controversy through a mediation committee consisting of Minamata's mayor and local delegates to the prefectural assembly.

Chisso's insistence on making payment in the form of a "solatium" (*mimaikin*) rather than a "compensation" (*hoshokin*) was rooted in a critical cultural distinction between the two. The need to pay compensation is recognized only when responsibility for causation has been legally established or admitted to in writing. A solatium, on the other hand, is perceived as a humanitarian expression of sympathy for another's misfortune. A popular element in traditional gift-giving patterns, it implies no legal responsibility. Thus, for Chisso, payment of a solatium propagated a corporate image of social concern, while at the same time subtly denying responsibility. Playing on the Japanese sense of *giri* (unspoken ties of social indebtedness for favors received), the company assumed that payment would inhibit subsequent complaints, while freeing the company from formal responsibility and the humiliating ritual that would accompany it: a ceremonious act of apology to common fishermen.

"Entrusting" the resolution of the conflict to an ostensibly neutral mediating committee was expected to be another corporate plus. Jun Ui, an instructor at Tokyo University's Department of Urban Engineering and one of Japan's foremost antipollution activists, stresses that "neutrality" in such cases could only be an illusion. According to Ui, Japan's pollution problems tend to polarize government, industry, and citizenry into two antagonistic groups: polluters or "assailants," made up predominantly of the industry-government complex, and the polluted "victims," comprised of a hapless citizenry. Minamata, he explains, is a good example of this polarization, for the city is characterized by a de facto company control of local government. The city's mayor from 1950 to 1957, and again in 1963, for example, was Hikoshichi Hashimoto, a former director of the Chisso factory. The company was well represented on the city council by Socialist party members, who came directly from the company-controlled union. Because Chisso employed, either directly or indirectly, seven or eight of every ten Minamata residents, other "independent" councilmen representing the city's urban wards invariably supported company policies. Opposing the "progressive" company representatives were "conservative" city councilmen elected primarily from outlying farming and fishing districts.

The "third party" mediation committee convened and after only ten days of negotiations proposed an economic settlement specifically disregarding the victims of Minamata disease. Chisso agreed to pay the 270 members of the Minamata City Fishermen's Union an initial compensation of 35 million yen ($98,000) followed by annual payments of 2 million yen ($5,600). But other fishermen's unions in districts around Minamata Bay were left out in the cold and protested the settlement, demanding compensation for their own pollution-attributed losses. When, in October 1959, the company dismissed these demands, 2,000 of these neighboring fishermen rioted, forcing their way into the factory compound. In November, union members again demonstrated, and when the company announced its refusal to negotiate, the fishermen climbed over barricades blocking the factory's gate and stormed into the buildings, causing extensive damage.

The riots focused national attention on the sharpening conflicts in Minamata. The eruption of violent confrontation and intensive press coverage embarrassed Minamata's local government into action. By the end of November 1959, the Kumamoto prefectural governor had appointed a second mediation council. The mediators' initial purpose was to settle only the fishermen's dispute, but disease victims, through a widely publicized sit-in at the Chisso factory gate, pressured the local government into agreeing to mediate the issue of medical compensation as well. The victims' demands totaled 230 million yen ($650,000) or some 3 million yen ($8,300) per person.

On December 16, the mediation council announced its decision. It recommended a payment of 74 million yen ($206,000) to the disease victims, and 35 million yen ($98,000) to the fishermen. The unions, lacking the means for a continuous lobbying effort, signed the agreement. But the victims' Mutual Assistance Society, judging the sum offered to be ridiculously small, refused it and resolved to block the government's efforts to settle the problem by the New Year.

On December 27, Minamata's mayor and city councilmen, stressing the Japanese tradition of clearing the slate at the end of every year, prevailed upon the victims' organization to accept the mediation pact and settle their dispute with the company before the year ran out. Threatened with the possible dissolution of the committee, the victims relented. Many, unable to work and shouldering rising debts, concluded that to receive a little money, especially during the New Year season, was better than to receive none at all. On December 30, representatives of Chisso and the victims' organization signed the agreement and a truce was declared.

The agreement, couched by the mediation committee in terms of a "solatium," fueled a heated controversy and became a nagging source of discontent. It provided for payments of 300,000 yen ($800) for deaths, and annual award of 100,000 yen ($280) for adult victims, 30,000 yen ($83) for children, and 20,000 yen ($56) for funeral expenses. Since these solatium payments were never intended as formal compensation, questions related to

Chisso's responsibility were left ambiguous. Two clauses appended to the agreement in fact tilted it blatantly in favor of industry:

> CLAUSE 4: In the future, if Chisso's factory effluents are decided not to be the cause of Minamata disease, the solatium agreement will be dissolved immediately.
>
> CLAUSE 5: In the future, if factory effluents are shown to be the cause of the disease, no further demands for compensation will be made.

Thus, the truce was in reality an enforced peace, and the signing of the solatium agreement marked the beginning of a dormant period in the social history of Minamata disease. Receipt of the small annuity from Chisso successfully quelled overt protest; frustrations and grievances were suppressed on behalf of social harmony. Minamata Bay, however, remained contaminated, its fish unmarketable. In attempts to market their catch, some local fishermen sailed to distant ports, concealing the origin of their fish. Others, who could no longer earn enough money to feed their families, sold their boats and went to work for Chisso's subcontractors. The lives of recognized victims were eased somewhat by the annuities, but many unrecognized victims remained. The solatium agreement had solved nothing.

4.

Not until 1968 did the central government officially recognize the disease's causative agent to be organic mercury or its source in the Minamata environment to be the Chisso plant. Awaiting a scientific consensus on these two points, the government insisted upon categorizing Minamata disease as an isolated phenomenon that had been "settled" privately by the 1959 solatium agreement. Nonetheless, it would seem only reasonable that local or national authorities should have undertaken at least the following measures during the period 1959–68:

1. A comprehensive epidemiological survey of all potentially susceptible residents in the Minamata area, followed by clinical examinations of all suspected poisoning cases;
2. A detailed examination of Chisso's production history and machinery to determine the content and amount of industrial wastes discharged;
3. A complete examination of local food and water supplies to

determine sources and total intake of mercury and other possible contaminants;
4. An investigation of methods to remove contaminants from seawater and seabed sludge;
5. A program of compensation and assurance of fishermen's welfare;
6. A nationwide survey of industrial installations and production processes similar to Chisso's that used mercury.

While the scholars debated, however, not one of these measures was enacted.

After McAlpine's initial suggestion of methyl mercury as the cause of Minamata disease, both Japanese and foreign researchers began to produce important scientific data indicting organic mercury compounds. In particular, timely support for the mercury theory came from the work of Leonard Kurland, director of the Epidemiology Branch of the United States National Institute of Neurological Diseases and Blindness. After conducting a study in Minamata in September 1959, Kurland published articles in the *Mainichi* and *Asahi* newspapers tracing the cause of Minamata disease to organic mercury compounds in Chisso's effluents. Six months later, he published a full report in *World Neurology*, lending additional weight to the theory.

Kurland's reports were influential because they were the opinions of a foreigner, an unbiased third party to the Minamata dispute, and because they appeared at a time when the volatile debate over the causative substance had become acutely politicized. Industry-supported scientists had proposed the theory that the mercury found in fish and disease victims originated from the decomposition of explosive materials dumped by the government into Minamata Bay at the end of the war. Another popular theory had it that the poisonous agent was not mercury at all, but toxic amines from putrified fish. Most of these hypotheses, according to Ui, had little scientific basis and were merely attempts to discredit the mercury theory and attack Kumamoto University researchers while protecting Chisso. Charges against the Kumamoto research team culminated in 1960 in the cancellation of research grants given it by the Ministry of Health and Welfare. During the next three years, Kumamoto University investigators, generally looked down upon by central authorities and the Tokyo academic elite for belonging to a "hick college," were forced to rely upon financial support from the United States National Institutes of Health. This American grant money was instrumental in helping the research team produce conclusive results.

The major problem facing Minamata disease researchers was to explain how the inorganic mercury used by Chisso in its industrial processes was transformed into the organic mercury found in local fish, shellfish, and disease victims. The presence of methyl mercury in disease victims had been traced to fish and shellfish, the plankton on which the latter fed, and then to the water and sludge in Minamata Bay. But there was still a missing link that obscured the direct cause-effect relationship between the manufacturing process and the disease.

Three discoveries were to fill the gap. The first important breakthrough occurred in 1958, after Chisso stopped dumping wastes from the acetaldehyde process in Minamata Bay via the Hyakken harbor. Instead, the company began to divert them to a settling tank, eventually releasing them into the Minamata River. The company's action, referred to by Harada as a "human experiment," resulted in the outbreak of Minamata disease in new areas along the Minamata River, demonstrating only too clearly the existence of a cause-effect relationship.

The second important discovery occurred in 1959 and disclosed that mercury was greatly concentrated as it passed up through the food chain. Thus, although water in Minamata Bay contained about 0.1 microgram of mercury per liter (0.0001 ppm), the amount of heavy metal in local fish rose to 50 ppm in wet weight—a concentration some 500,000 times greater. Mercury discharged by the factory was selectively filtered out of the water by plankton and gradually concentrated at higher levels of the food chain. Eventually, this mercury reached its highest concentrations in animals that consumed large quantities of seafood—cats, birds, and humans.* Ironically, when the first symptoms of the "strange disease" appeared, some afflicted families increased their consumption of fish in the hope that the trusted staple would cure them. In fact, however, it only hastened the malady's course.

The third and clinching discovery was the detection in 1962 and 1963 by Katsuro Irukayama, a member of the Kumamoto University research team, of organic mercury compounds in the factory's effluents and in reaction tubes used in Chisso's equipment for acetaldehyde synthesis. Since the factory refused to allow outside investigators to enter its production facilities, it was pure chance that Irukayama discovered a sample of sludge from the acetaldehyde reaction tubes, a sample which had been obtained from the factory several years earlier and was gathering dust on a university laboratory shelf. Further investigation of the acetaldehyde process revealed a previously unknown side reaction in which the inorganic mercury catalyst was indeed

---

* This rapid absorption of mercury and other contaminants into the food chain would tend to discredit the reliability of measuring water samples to determine the ppm of various contaminants and of using this as a pollution-level indicator.

converted into organic methyl mercury. Ui has estimated that about 5 percent of the inorganic mercury catalyst was converted into its organic counterpart, so that 15 to 50 grams of organic mercury were discarded for every ton of acetaldehyde produced. Production of acetaldehyde using a mercury sulfate catalyst began in 1932.* In 1973, the Ministry of International Trade and Industry announced that during 33 years of operation before Chisso ceased acetaldehyde production at its Minamata facilities in 1965, the factory had used a total of 1,180 tons of inorganic mercury catalyst and discharged an estimated 80 tons of organic mercury into the shallow waters of Minamata Bay!

These pieces of the Minamata puzzle were not to be fitted together until several years after their discovery. After the publicity given the 1959 fishermen's riots and the victims' sit-in, the Minamata problem seldom appeared in the news media and the Japanese public largely forgot about it. The specialized reports issued by Irukayama elicited little public reaction and the economic plight of the victims was generally ignored. The victims, subdued by the solatium pact and their annuities (which were periodically readjusted for inflation), had been neutralized. It seemed that only another powerful shock could awaken the press, the public, and the government to the real dangers of mercury contamination.

The shock came in late 1964, when another "strange disease of unknown cause" was discovered in Niigata Prefecture along the Agano River near Niigata City. Preliminary examinations of the new victims, poor farmers and fishermen who lived near the river and depended on fish as a staple in their diet, revealed symptoms similar to those of Minamata disease. Soon thereafter, the Niigata University Medical School began investigating the possibility of mercury poisoning. In June 1965, Hosokawa, who had retired from his post as director of Chisso's Minamata Hospital, confirmed that the victims were indeed suffering from Minamata disease. Independent investigator Ui then initiated research to determine local sources of environmental mercury contamination and soon found an acetaldehyde factory, using an industrial process identical to that employed by Chisso's Minamata facilities, located upstream and owned by the Showa Denko Corporation.

The Ministry of Health and Welfare responded to the new outbreak by officially commissioning the Niigata University Medical School to research the disease and determine its cause. The course of events that followed, however, repeated the pattern set in Minamata. The medical school's interim report, which cited Showa Denko's acetaldehyde process and its mercury

---

* It is more than ironic that the inventor of this production process for converting acetylene to acetaldehyde was Hikoshichi Hashimoto, Minamata's mayor when the disease first appeared.

wastes as the most likely cause of the disease, was opposed by the powerful Ministry of International Trade and Industry, and was consequently suppressed. In mid-1966, the Ministry of Health and Welfare discontinued its funding of the Niigata Medical School research team, and the scientists were forced to proceed at their own expense. For three years, Niigata victims, like those in Minamata, encountered corporate denials, obstructive cooperation between government ministries and industry, and interventions of "objective" scientists who supported the company's claims.

Finally, in April 1967, despite strong resistance from upper-level bureaucrats in the Ministry of Health and Welfare, the final report of the Niigata University researchers was made public through the efforts of a progressive Diet member. Nevertheless, Showa Denko announced that even if the Ministry of Health and Welfare should accept the scientists' report as the official government opinion, the company did not intend to recognize its conclusions.

After the Niigata University report was made public, the victims' attitude quickly radicalized. Relying upon a fairly strong local support group,* they initiated legal proceedings against the company in June 1967. It was the first large-scale civil suit brought against a polluter in postwar Japan, predating by some three months the suit declared in Yokkaichi. The legal initiative taken by Niigata victims was a major turning point in the social history of pollution in Japan. Their suit was to become a first step, quickly followed by that of the asthma sufferers of Yokkaichi, toward "modernizing" the image of the courts as vehicles for the resolution of pollution problems.

In late 1967, victims in Niigata and Minamata began to correspond by mail; several months later, Niigata victims traveled to southern Japan to join hands with their fellow sufferers. This historic meeting, which reminded Minamata's victims that Chisso still refused to accept responsibility, rekindled a spirit of protest. In January 1968, the two groups vowed to persevere in their fight against pollution and corporate irresponsibility.

Eight months later, on September 26, 1968, the Japanese government officially recognized organic mercury compounds as the cause of Minamata disease. Twelve years after the discovery of the "strange disease," eight years after Kurland attributed the cause of the disease to organic mercury, six years after the detection of organic mercury compounds in Chisso's effluents and the reaction tubes of the acetaldehyde process, four years after the second outbreak of Minamata disease, and one year and three months after the Niigata victims filed suit against Showa Denko, the government finally

---

* The Niigata Prefecture Democratic Congress for Minamata Disease Countermeasures.

announced that, in its official judgment, the Chisso and Showa Denko acetaldehyde factories caused the disease by discharging organic mercury compounds into the environment. Minamata disease was designated the world's first official mercury-pollution disease.

5.

The central government was not alone in its protracted refusal to recognize the causal relationship between Chisso's effluents and the debilitating disease. Minamata citizens also waited 15 years after the outbreak of the disease before organizing a group to assist the victims. Even after 1968, most of the city's inhabitants and local political parties remained aloof. In addition, Chisso's labor union followed the company line until 1968, and at times was overtly antagonistic toward the fishermen. Throughout the debate over the disease's cause, Chisso's workers faithfully guarded corporate secrets. Only after a bitter wage struggle in 1962–63, during which management formed a new "number two" union to quell the protests, did alienated workers remaining in the original organization begin to assist the victims.*

Coming in the wake of these local developments, the government's long-delayed announcement in September 1968 had important consequences. It generated a much sought-after sense of justification among disease victims. They could now face the world with greater self-confidence; the government had officially declared that the disease was not due to any "fault" of their own. Moreover, government recognition of organic mercury as the cause of the Niigata outbreak served to support the legal claims that were still under litigation. Finally, the government's decision renewed the issue of compensation for victims in Minamata.

After the government's announcement, Chisso and the Minamata victims entered into renewed negotiations, but were unable to reach agreement. In late 1968, the Ministry of Health and Welfare intervened, proposing that the Minamata compensation dispute be settled by a new mediation committee. The ministry stipulated, however, that the patients entrust the selection of the committee's members solely to the ministry's discretion and agree beforehand to abide by the mediators' conclusions. One group of victims agreed to these conditions, but 28 families, harboring bitter memories of the 1959 solatium agreement, refused to relinquish their rights to the government. On June 14,

---

* This group, as a result of its own struggle with corporate irresponsibility, came to identify with the plight of the disease victims and in August 1968, proclaimed its full support of the Mutual Assistance Society's efforts to gain fair compensation.

1969, this group, following the lead of the Niigata victims, filed a legal suit against Chisso.

This disagreement among the victims marked the beginning of an intense factionalism that has endured to the present day and is likely to persist well into the future. By March 1973 the 397 officially designated victims of the new pollution disease in Minamata were split into six distinct factions, while support groups were bitterly divided along political lines.* When in November 1971 Chisso failed to meet the demands of the "direct negotiation" faction, its members, with student and other antipollution group support, initiated much-publicized sit-in demonstrations in front of both Chisso's Minamata factory and the company's main office in Tokyo. These lasted nineteen months, until July 1973.

A major focus of dissatisfaction reflected in the victims' factionalism has been the procedures employed in designating "official victims." Minamata's original Countermeasures Council successfully identified victims of the disease, and the council's original criteria remain the basis for identifying Minamata disease. By December 1956, the council had recognized 53 victims. When the problem was transferred in 1957 to Kumamoto University researchers, however, Minamata disease entered its two-year "scientific research" phase, during which only 26 more victims were officially recognized. From the end of 1959 until the central government's announcement in 1968, the local administrators, fearful of placing too heavy a burden on Chisso, recognized only 32 new victims. Sixteen of them, designated in 1962, were children born with severe physical and mental deformities due to congenital mercury poisoning. The heavy metal, passing through the mother's placental barrier during pregnancy, had concentrated in the unborn baby causing irreparable damage. By 1968, 22 children born as Minamata disease victims had been officially recognized.

---

* Factionalism among the victims was exacerbated by support groups active in Minamata. The Association to Indict Minamata Disease, formed in April 1969 after the victims had decided to start legal proceedings, initiated a variety of research, publication and protest activities to assist in the struggle against Chisso's irresponsibility. Soon after its inception, prefectural political groups—labor union federations, the Socialist party, and the Japan Communist Party—organized still another council to support the litigation which was being undertaken largely by lawyers associated with the JCP. The relationship between these two organizations was strained from the outset. The former is dominated by "non-sect radicals" who tend to be highly critical of what they consider to be the political parties' manipulation of the victims to enhance their own popularity, while the latter denounce the Association's use of "extreme tactics." The Citizens' Council for Minamata Disease Countermeasures, a local support organization formed in January 1968, tries to maintain a neutral stance between the two groups. On several occasions antagonisms between these two camps have degenerated into outright violence, and disease victims associated with one group or the other have inevitably been drawn into these conflicts between outsiders.

With the passage of the Pollution Victims Relief Law in December 1968, the central government became responsible for designating official victims. But central government participation in the identification process by no means ended the burden of unrecognized sufferers; bureaucratic difficulties in gaining recognition remained:

> ... when Kawamoto (one of the victims) went to the City Office to pick up an application form for another victim, the officials in charge told him that unless the applicant appeared in person, they could not hand over the form. The applicant, however, was confined to bed and was totally unable to get to the City Office.[5]

Finally, in late 1971, designation criteria were liberalized, and the number of recognized victims more than tripled from 121 in July 1970 to 397 in March 1973.

This change in the government's attitude was not unrelated to the decision handed down in the Niigata trial on September 19, 1971. A legal victory for the plaintiffs, it upheld the three contested points of causation, corporate negligence, and corporate legal responsibility. In addition, the decision aroused popular support throughout the country for the protest movement against mercury pollution. The Niigata victims, however, were dissatisfied with the ruling because it ordered payments far below their original demands. When their lawyers were unwilling to appeal their case, the victims decided to protest the decision directly at Showa Denko's main offices in Tokyo. After Haruo Suzuki, the company president, refused to meet with them, the protesters declared their intention to wait for him and began a sit-in demonstration in the firm's offices. Late that night, Suzuki finally relented and in the course of an emotional meeting kneeled in apology. His traditional act of contrition was splashed across the following day's front pages.

The Niigata results set the stage for the decision that was to come a year and a half later in Minamata. On March 20, 1973, after more than 17 years of debate over the cause of Minamata disease, Judge Jiro Saito of the Kumamoto District Court settled the question once and for all. He found Chisso guilty of "gross negligence" for discharging mercury wastes into the environment and upheld the plaintiffs on all points. The decision ordered Chisso to pay more than 937 million yen ($3.6 million) in compensation to the 30 families represented in the trial. Saito ruled that studies prior to discharging the wastes could have predicted the effects of mercury on the human body and that the company had operated in total disregard of the health of local residents and the welfare of the environment. During the course of the proceedings, Chisso formally admitted its responsibility, for the first time acknowledging the cause-effect relationship between factory effluents and Minamata disease.

Saito's decision nullified the solatium agreement of 1959 and declared that Chisso had taken advantage of the victims' ignorance and poverty. The judge based his opinion on a chilling disclosure that surfaced during the trial: as far back as 1959, while in both its public statements and its negotiations Chisso was adamantly denying responsibility for causing the disease, company officials *knew* that their factory's effluents were indeed responsible. For in testimony given from his hospital deathbed in 1970, Dr. Hajime Hosokawa revealed that after establishing the Strange Disease Research Room in Chisso's company hospital in July 1959, he conducted experiments in which he fed cats waste water from different production processes in the factory. Experimental records indicated that on October 7, 1959, cat number 400, after being fed each day for 78 days 20 grams of waste water collected from the acetaldehyde process, developed the symptoms of Minamata disease. Ironically, on the same day Chisso, in presenting its case to the prefectural government, sought to pin the cause of the mercury poisoning on explosive materials dumped into the bay at the close of the war. Hosokawa testified that when he informed management of his results, he was ordered to keep them secret and halt his experiments. Hosokawa complied. Although the doctor discreetly released the experimental findings following his retirement and they were published by Ui in 1968, it was not until his testimony that Japanese society was shocked into awareness of the full implications of the loyal adherence of Chisso's employees to the inhuman demands of corporate secrecy.

When the decision was announced at Kumamoto District Courthouse, the victims recognized that it was a limited success at best because it applied to only one faction and ignored ecological considerations. Nor, they knew, did it solve Minamata's problems. Many victims were reportedly still being hidden by their families, and existing medical and rehabilitation facilities were grossly inadequate. The issue of compensation was not resolved, and Minamata's fishing grounds remained contaminated by about 80 tons of mercury mixed into an estimated 600,000 tons of sludge at the bottom of Minamata Bay.

On the day of the court announcement, members of the "first trial" and "direct negotiation" factions traveled to Tokyo, and two days later their representatives met with leading Chisso executives. With their legal victory behind them, the victims now had the upper hand, and 20 years of tension and frustration came to a climax. After five hours of negotiations, Chisso President Kenichi Shimada signed a statement promising that "compensation for all damages related to Minamata disease will be carried out in good faith."

But it was only after Shimada kneeled before the victims and apologized that they accepted the promise.

The pressure of the negotiations, which sometimes lasted all night, was apparently too great for Chisso's executives to handle alone. When Shimada asked for a recess in mid-April, the Director-General of the Environment Agency, Takeo Miki, offered to mediate a final agreement. Signed on July 9, 1973, it marked final and unambiguous victory for the victims of Minamata disease. In its preamble, Chisso admitted that it had failed to treat harmful industrial wastes properly and that its effluents had contained organic mercury compounds which were the cause of Minamata disease:

> CLAUSE 2: Because Chisso did not take sufficient measures to prevent the spread of Minamata disease after its official discovery in 1956, did not undertake to investigate the cause of the disease and did not provide patients with sufficient relief aid, the extent of the damages increased even further. Moreover, even when the causative substance had been confirmed and the disease became a social problem, Chisso continued to maintain a regrettable attitude toward its solution. Chisso will reflect upon these actions, with heart-felt sincerity.
>
> CLAUSE 3: Chisso deeply apologizes to those patients and their families, already in great poverty, who experienced further suffering from contracting Minamata disease, who suffered as a result of Chisso's attitudes, who were subjected to various types of humiliation and, as a result, suffered from discrimination by local society.
>
> Furthermore, *Chisso deeply apologizes to all of society... for its regrettable attitude of evading its responsibility and for delaying a solution*, as this caused much inconvenience to society. (emphasis added)

Chisso agreed to pay high compensation to all persons recognized at present and in the future as victims of Minamata disease (16-18 million yen [$51-59 thousand], according to the severity of the victim's condition). The pact also included lifetime pensions to be adjusted biannually to match rises in the cost of living; a 300 million yen (about one million dollars) fund to provide victims with medical and economic aid; and a promise by Chisso to search for and extend relief to unidentified victims. The company pledged to enter into antipollution agreements with local governmental bodies, and to undertake the clean-up of Minamata Bay in cooperation with central and local governmental authorities.

The signing of the indemnity pact ended an era in Minamata. A health survey of people living near the bay was finally taken, and there were industrial and governmental efforts to alleviate environmental contamination of the area. Moreover, Chisso began paying financial compensation to an ever-increasing number of official victims. By January 1975, there were 793 certified and about 2,700 uncertified Minamata victims, and Chisso had paid out over 20 billion yen ($66 million) in compensation.* Still, medical authorities estimated that an additional 10,000 residents of the area were latent victims and could well develop full-fledged symptoms of mercury poisoning in the future.

Nevertheless, the personal and social conflicts of Minamata remain: factionalism among the victims, antagonisms dividing support groups, and deep-felt enmity between Chisso and the stricken fishermen of Minamata. It will be a long time before the areas' residents forget who took which side in the bitter dispute that stretched through two decades. Most tragic is the plight of those who have had the crippling debilities of mercury poisoning since birth or the plight of those lingering in the last stages of unconscious writhing. For them, Chisso's monetary compensation is meaningless and its proffered consolation inaudible. They remain a testament to man's refusal to recognize the dangers to human health implicit in environmental pollution.

---

* The large indemnities have significantly destabilized Chisso's financial position, even raising the possibility of bankruptcy, which would foreclose further compensation to victims of Minamata disease. A January 1975 request by Chisso for a government loan of 3.9 billion yen ($33.3 million), ostensibly for the reconstruction of one of its plants, was seen by many as an attempt to enlist government aid in meeting its responsibilities in the face of mounting deficits. Also, in an attempt to escape the burdens of liability, Chisso has been spinning off its more profitable subsidiaries into new companies. This may set a pattern for other corporations confronted with large pollution indemnities. Finally, it is worth noting that protesters have also directed demonstrations against Chisso's major financial backers, such as the Industrial Bank of Japan, in an attempt to force them to accept some of the responsibilities for their client's activities.

CHAPTER FIVE

A QUESTION OF AUTHORITY

> "This disease is not merely a case of food poisoning, as the government claims. It is another kogai byo—a pollution disease—just like Minamata disease and Yokkaichi asthma. As in Minamata, the victims unknowingly ate contaminated food, and once they became sick, no one would accept responsibility for causing or treating the disease. It is this social abandonment of the victims and the refusal by industry, government and society at large to accept responsibility for the disease that have turned an 'accidental food poisoning' into a full-fledged case of kogai byo."
>
> —NAOHIDE ISONO
> *Biologist, Tokyo Metropolitan University*

When first synthesized in Germany in 1881, the chemical substances known as polychlorinated biphenyls (PCBs) were a scientific novelty, and their uses were limited mainly to the electrical industry. After the Second World War, however, technological advances provided PCBs with more varied applications, and by 1970, production had reached a peak of 38,000 tons in the United States and 11,000 tons in Japan.

PCBs are closely related compounds belonging to the chlorinated hydrocarbon family. Other chlorinated hydrocarbons in common use include insecticides such as DDT and BHC (benzene hexachloride), herbicides 2,4-D and 2,4,5-T used as defoliants in Vietnam, mustard gases employed during World War I, and polyvinyl chloride used in the manufacture of plastics.*

The chemical and physical properties of PCBs make them very adaptable. At room temperature, they form a colorless fluid (increasing in viscosity with the number of chlorine atoms) that does not conduct electricity or undergo chemical decomposition even at very high or low temperatures. PCBs are nonflammable and can theoretically be recycled. They have been used industrially as a heat-transfer medium, an insulator in condensers, transformers, and other electrical appliances, and as an additive in paints, insecticides, lubricating oils, plastics, and inks used in the manufacture of "carbonless" copy paper. Thus, during the last 25 years, PCBs have on all counts become a technological success.

It is just these technologically advantageous qualities, particularly their virtual indestructibility, that make PCBs a dangerous environmental contaminant. Once discharged into the environment, they are extremely difficult to destroy, retrieve, or render harmless. Furthermore, they concentrate as they move up food chains and are even harder than DDT for living systems to metabolize. High-chlorine PCBs accumulate in fatty tissues and are not readily excreted through urine or perspiration. The effects of PCBs on biological systems are thought to be similar to those of DDT: they interfere with sex hormone activities, exert a deleterious effect on liver enzymes, and are potentially carcinogenic.

The first warnings of PCBs' highly toxic effects came in 1936, when industrial health hazards, particularly a severe skin disease known as chloracne associated with the production and handling of the compounds, were reported in the United States. "By the end of the war," writes ecologist Barry Commoner, "it was well established from the workers' experience that PCBs were so toxic that industrial techniques ought to be controlled to avoid exposure."[1] For twenty years or more, however, these early warnings were ignored. In 1953, Japanese workers in an Osaka-based factory producing PCB-containing electrical condensers fell victim to a skin disorder identical to that suffered earlier by American workers, but reports of this incident were suppressed until 1969, when a far more widespread disturbance, the subject of this chapter, had already become a major social problem.

---

* Theoretically, some 240 different structures and isomers of the PCB molecule exist, varying according to the number and arrangement of chlorine atoms around two benzene rings. The PCBs sold on the market are a mixture of a number of these different forms. A detailed analysis of Arachlor 1254, a PCB preparation commonly marketed in the United States, for example, showed over 69 different chemical structures.

In the United States in the last few years, excessive PCB levels have been found in milk, broilers, turkeys, and eggs in various parts of the country. In early 1971, 140,000 contaminated New York State chickens were slaughtered and buried. Later in the year, a heating system in a Wilmington, North Carolina, fish meal pasteurization plant leaked PCBs into chicken feed. Twelve thousand tons of feed were contaminated, nearly 124,000 pounds of eggs were removed from the market, and one producer was forced to destroy 88,000 broilers.[2] Chance discoveries followed by quick government and industrial intervention prevented these contaminated foods from reaching consumers and causing a massive outbreak of human PCB poisoning. Until recently, however, the potential hazards of PCBs were not commonly recognized in the United States or elsewhere. It was Japan's tragic experience in 1968 that alerted the world to the acute danger posed by this technological wonder.

One area affected by Japan's PCB catastrophe was the isolated fishing village of Tama no Ura, set on a far corner of Fukue Island in the Goto Archipelago some 120 kilometers west of Kyushu. The village is a good six hours' journey by ferry, bus, and small fishing trawler from Nagasaki and, since the end of the Second World War, only a few of the local inhabitants' relatives, some tourists, and a handful of hardy salesmen have bothered to make the trip. At first glance, Tama no Ura's seclusion might be expected to have protected its 4,000-odd residents from the harsher realities of modern life. The village's air is clear and pure, and the fish caught off its shores are relatively free from contaminants.

Early in 1968, however, some of Tama no Ura's residents were struck with a strange ailment. They lost their appetites; then their bodies broke into a drenching sweat. Extreme fatigue set in, and they could no longer work. Fishing trawlers and gardens were left untended as entire families were reduced to helplessness. It seemed as if a curse had suddenly descended upon the village.

The victims resorted to every imaginable cure—Chinese herbalism, Western medicine, prayer—but nothing seemed to work. Ugly boils exuding a strong-smelling pus appeared over every part of the body. Vision deteriorated, and from the eyes streamed a viscous discharge that quickly hardened into a paste. As incomes plummeted, it became increasingly difficult to support the children away at school or even to secure food. And with increasing pain came desperation.

One victim described the onset of the disease as follows: "Around March 1968 the members of my family began to feel unusually fatigued. Eventually, we could hardly work at all, for every movement required a very great effort. We lost all desire to eat and couldn't even force food down: my oldest daughter lost thirty-five pounds, my wife lost twenty-eight, and I lost twenty-two. We'd wake up in the morning but it would take hours before we could open our eyes, since our eyelids had been sealed by glue-like secretions during the night. And even when we opened them we couldn't see more than four or five yards ahead of us."

But the biggest problem was the boils that covered our bodies from head to foot. After June, squeezing them became the biggest task of the day, and it was always put off until evening. The work and pain were unbearable. One of us would always start to cry, and by the end of the evening we were all in tears. We did this for two or three hours every night before going to bed; any part of our body that came into contact with a hard surface stung with pain."

Western medicine was unable to identify or treat this strange disease, and baffled doctors debated its cause. Some labeled it a skin disease; others felt it was a liver or kidney disorder. Rumors spread that it was syphilis or leprosy. Medicines provided only temporary and partial relief, if any at all. "We had peace only when we slept. But we always awoke to more pain and more agony. It was hell."

For seven months, suffering ravaged the village. Since few of its residents regularly read newspapers and relatively little information entered or left the village, they endured alone, gradually losing all hope. Then, on the evening of October 10, 1968, a televised news report reached them of a strange disease, reportedly caused by contaminated cooking oil, that had struck communities in northern Kyushu. To their amazement, the symptoms described were identical to their own. Two days later, an instructor at the island's high school brought twelve of his students to the Fukue Health Center, where he declared them to be victims of the newly identified Kanemi cooking oil disease, named for the company that produced the contaminated oil. Although the specific substance causing the disease was still unknown, its victims were given hope that their illness could be treated and cured.

Only after the October 10 news announcement did the scale of the disease begin to become clear. The Ministry of Health and Welfare initiated an intensive survey of potential victims: within two weeks, over 12,000 people throughout southwestern Japan—in Shikoku, western Honshu and Kyushu—appeared at local health centers. By 1973, over 1,000 had been designated as "official victims," although from 3,000 to 5,000 more are believed by medical authorities to exist. Why, one must ask, did it take so long to uncover the victims of an "accidental case of food poisoning," when the number of afflicted was of near-epidemic proportions? How could it be that even in modern, developed areas like northern Kyushu, the disease had not been identified or reported to the public until October—over seven months after its initial outbreak?

Part of the answer lies in the attitudes and behavior of the victims themselves. The following account was repeated with only slight variation by almost all those interviewed: "Before the October announcement, I made every effort to conceal my unsightly face and body from society. After the boils appeared on my daughter, she could no longer bear the sight of her own face and feared to look into the mirror. It reached the point where she forgot what her own face looked like. On the train to the hospital, she hid behind a newspaper or a handkerchief, and my wife served as a screen. When she had to go out shopping, she always came back home in tears. What could we say when she cried, 'Strangers stare at me, and I can't stand the way their stares cling to my body.'" Children, too, were subjected to social pressure. A young boy told of the special routes he took to and from school to avoid meeting people along the way, and of how, during classroom recess, he would wait until his healthy classmates had left the lavatory before entering—in order to be by himself.

Such attempts by the victims to escape the "coldhearted eyes of others" contributed to delaying recognition of the disease and clarification of its origin. Indeed, victims were so successful in isolating themselves from both society and each other that, until October, many families believed that they alone were stricken! Gradually, however, sufferers who chanced to meet at hospitals recognized their common plight. It was these rare contacts that eventually led to the discovery of the disease's origin—a discovery made not by medical or scientific authorities, food industry representatives, or government agencies, but rather by one of the victims.

Tadashi Kunitake, a low-ranking employee of the Kyushu Electric Power Company, pieced the mystery together. When, in early 1968, Kunitake and his entire family fell victim to the disease, he began a search for an explanation. As the symptoms worsened, Kunitake suspected leprosy or syphilis, but by August, finding no corroborating evidence for this theory in his family's medical history, he decided to submit to an examination at the outpatient dermatological clinic of the Kyushu University hospital in Fukuoka. Here, to his surprise, he met others with symptoms identical to his own. His talks with them revealed a common characteristic shared by all their households: the daily consumption of a high proportion of deep-fried foods. This led him to the conjecture that contaminated cooking oil might lie at the root of their common ailment.

Kunitake remembered that six months previously, when he had been living in company housing in Fukuoka (before being transferred to nearby

Omuta), he and his fellow employees had divided up a large drum of Kanemi rice oil. He knew that since that time his own family had used this oil continuously in the preparation of tempura and fried vegetables. To corroborate his suspicions, Kunitake returned to his former compound to visit the families still living there, and found that every household that had used the oil was stricken with the disease. Thoroughly convinced by the end of August that his theory was correct, Kunitake brought a sample to doctors at Kyushu University who were treating victims of the disease and asked for an analysis. Days went by without a response. Kunitake then delivered a second sample to the Omuta Health Center, where he was reportedly told to come back after the summer vacation.

Kunitake's mother, an instructor in the traditional tea ceremony and art of flower arrangement, was naturally distressed by the plight of her son's family. Convinced that his association of the disease with the cooking oil was correct, she tearfully pleaded with her students to discard any Kanemi brand oil they might be using. On October 8, one of these students, a housewife, telephoned an old friend to inquire after her family's health and, in the process, spread the warning regarding Kanemi oil. The friend's husband happened to be a reporter for the prestigious *Asahi* newspaper. And it was this reporter, Masaki Abe, who followed up the lead, resulting in the revelation of October 10.

The victims avidly welcomed the Asahi report. "The fear of a contagious disease was gone. We no longer had to put up with the cold stares of society. We knew that others like us existed, that we were not alone. But most important, we felt that it was just a matter of time before the authorities identified the poison and we would be cured. It was a great relief."

The doctors at Kyushu University, however, did not welcome the report so warmly. According to Ryuzo Kamino, former head of the National Federation of Kanemi Rice Oil Victims Associations, the scientific authorities were distressed because the announcement was not "medically oriented" and because they had lost face in not being the first to publicly identify the disease and its cause. Mikio Nishimura, an *Asahi* correspondent, reported that although some doctors had by mid-summer known of the disease and had apparently suspected its connection with Kanemi oil—in fact, had advised victims to discontinue using the oil—they had failed at the time to publicize the matter. They were waiting to announce their findings at the annual meeting of their academic society (to be held several months later)—a forum considered more appropriate.

Eight days after the *Asahi* scoop, the national media carried a report that revealed the role of government agencies in the tragic history of "oil disease," as it came to be called. It was a report that suggested governmental ineptitude, if not malfeasance, in the handling of early warning signs. For in February 1968, over 400,000 chickens had died throughout western Japan, and more than 2 million had fallen sick with something similar to chick edema disease. The Ministry of Agriculture and Forestry responded to the crisis by immediately initiating an intensive investigation. By mid-March, the study was almost complete, and on the basis of experimental data, an ingredient of the birds' feed was isolated and suspected of containing the causative agent. By the end of April, all feed products that included this substance, called "dark oil," were recalled, and damage to chickens ceased. In May it was officially confirmed within the Ministry of Forestry and Agriculture that "dark oil" was indeed responsible, and it was postulated that the causative agent contained in it was a chlorinated hydrocarbon. "Dark oil," a product of the Kanemi Corporation, was a byproduct of the process that transformed rice bran into cooking oil intended for human consumption!

Despite this early discovery of the cause of the chicken epidemic, Kanemi's main product apparently went unsuspected of contamination. It was not recalled from the market, nor did it receive even a cursory analysis. The first known efforts to have it analyzed were Kunitake's, and they all ended in failure. Within a month of the Asahi article of October 10, 1968, however, the poisonous agent was definitively identified by government researchers as polychlorinated biphenyls—PCBs—detected in excessively high concentrations in both Kanemi rice oil and Kanemi dark oil. But for the victims—and the public at large—it was seven months, 20 deaths and thousands of poisonings too late.*

2.

The "accident" that contaminated Kanemi's oils occurred in its Kitakyushu factory in early February 1968. PCBs were used in the deodorizing stage of the oil's manufacturing process, a stage in which the oil is brought to a very high temperature (210 to 230°C). To heat it to this degree, preheated PCBs were circulated through stainless steel pipes running through giant vats. In January, a new vat added to the equipment pushed the heating system above its capacity. Soon afterward, several tiny openings the size of pinholes developed in the steel pipes, allowing PCBs to leak into the oil.

Many disturbing questions regarding the production and sale of the contaminated oils remain unanswered. For example, when feed suspected of contamination was analyzed by the government in November 1968, it revealed a

---

* Kunitake died in May 1972, "oil disease's" eighteenth fatality.

PCB concentration of 1,300 ppm. This would mean a concentration of PCBs in the dark oil of approximately 20,000 to 30,000 ppm, or 2 to 3 percent, before it was mixed with other feed ingredients. The company's production flow chart, however, could not explain how the dark oil became so highly contaminated, since it was supposedly removed before the deodorizing stage. One possible explanation that has been suggested is that scum oil yielded in the deodorizing process was added to the dark oil to increase its volume. Nevertheless, it is odd that the strong chemical smell emitted by a 2 to 3 percent concentration of PCBs did not lead the producers to suspect contamination. It is possible, of course, that Kanemi did discover it but, through either ignorance or irresponsibility, underestimated the toxicity of PCBs and chose to market the product anyway. The one source that could set to rest these nagging doubts is the Kanemi Corporation, which still refuses, six years after the incident occurred, to disclose details of its production or decision-making processes.

Other accusations damaging to the reputation of Kanemi's management and employees have been made. According to *Asahi's* Nishimura, Kanemi failed to make periodic checks of the amount of PCBs flowing through the pipes. No safety equipment capable of detecting an accidental breach in the metal was installed and the pipes were left exposed to the oil without any protective sheathing.

Furthermore, the heating mechanism was not a totally closed system. Water or vapor somehow trickled in and mixed with the PCBs, forming hydrochloric acid which, at high temperatures, caused the pipes to corrode.[4] It is hard to understand how the company's management remained unaware of the sudden increase in consumption of PCBs between January and April 1968; during this period consumption registered a tenfold increase over the normal monthly volume of 20 to 30 kilograms![5]

Some victims claim that Kanemi must have known that the cooking oil was contaminated. The contaminated batch was sold at sharply reduced prices. In addition, perhaps in the hope that it would pass unnoticed, it was marketed in isolated areas such as Tama no Ura. Indeed, even if the company was unaware of the contamination during production, it must have become aware of it after the outbreak of the chicken epidemic. In mid-March, the Fukuoka Fertilizer and Feed Inspection Center sent a team of investigators to Kanemi's Kitakyushu factory in search of the cause of contamination. Kanemi was informed that "dark oil" was under suspicion, and at that point the company had at least two possible and relatively low-cost alternatives for examining the quality of its oils. First, the oils themselves could have been fed to animals to test their alleged toxicity. Second, company officials could have reviewed the consumption rate of poisonous chemicals used in the production process to determine whether any abnormal increases had occurred. Even if production records revealed no peculiarities, a simple toxicity test of the oils would have exposed any dangers. The fact that the Kanemi products were used to make animal feed and a cooking oil should have made the simple toxicity tests imperative.

Yet Kanemi apparently made no attempt to connect the contamination of its dark oil with possible contamination of the cooking oil. While the defective feed and dark oil were tested and retrieved, ending the chicken epidemic by April, people continued to use the rice oil for many months thereafter. In Tama no Ura, victims actually consumed *more* oil as their symptoms worsened, believing that it would help cure them. Moreover, many of the victims did not begin using Kanemi brand oil until May. It is obvious, therefore, that if the company had reacted to the dark oil incident by investigating all its products, halting sales, and retrieving potentially contaminated goods from the market, a great deal of human suffering and death would have been avoided. Instead, the company chose to ignore the implications of the "chicken incident."

Although the Kanemi Corporation may have to bear the brunt of the responsibility for the insidious spread of "oil disease," the inaction of governmental authorities charged with protecting human health and maintaining food and drug standards deserves more than cursory attention. For what were they doing during the months of March through October 1968?

3.

Perhaps the greatest obstacle to earlier recognition of the contamination of Kanemi's products was the lack of communication between the Ministry of Agriculture and Forestry and the Ministry of Health and Welfare. In early March 1968, the Feed Circulation Department of the MAF's Livestock Bureau traced the chicken epidemic to feed manufactured by two companies, Tokyo Ebisu and Rinken. By March 23, the department had pinpointed Kanemi's dark oil, an ingredient common to the two feeds. By the end of the month, it was well aware that dark oil was only a byproduct from the manufacturing of cooking oil intended for human consumption. Nevertheless, except for an off-hand question posed by an MAF inspector in March, the cooking oil was completely ignored during the MAF's investigation of the animal epidemic. Nor did the Ministry of Agriculture and Forestry inform the Ministry of Health and Welfare about possible hazards associated with

Kanemi's oil. An intramural "no-touch" attitude delayed necessary action and contributed to the eventual toll of victims.

One major reason for the lack of communication between the two ministries is the compartmentalized structure of Japan's governmental bureaucracy, a structure said to embody the principles of sectionalism. In practice, sectionalism refers to a set of institutional and psychological barriers that blocks the flow of information between ministries and even between departmental groups within a single ministry. The system leaves individuals and groups within the bureaucracy in a state of perpetual rivalry and mutual isolation. Responsibility for investigating the dark oil incident rested with the Ministry of Agriculture and Forestry because animal feeds were involved. Health problems relating to human foods fell under the authority of the Ministry of Health and Welfare.* Thus, a narrow concept of administrative responsibility compounded by inter-ministry rivalry prevented the MAF from conducting its own investigation of Kanemi's cooking oil or even from communication with the MHW.[6]

Yet even within its own administrative sphere, the MAF's investigation into the dark oil incident seems, in retrospect, to have been seriously inadequate. For it did not include the process of the oil's manufacture, or an exploration of the possible pathways of contamination, a recognition of which would have immediately made the cooking oil suspect. It even failed to isolate the specific causative agent-PCBs. When in April and May 1968 Japan's National Institute for Livestock Hygiene (associated with the Ministry of Agriculture and Forestry) undertook an analysis of the Kanemi dark oil, it focused its attention on possible contamination by heavy metals. Although the oil was manufactured from rice sprayed with agricultural chemicals containing chlorinated hydrocarbons, these chemicals were not investigated.

When asked why Kanemi's manufacturing process was not investigated, a member of the Feed Circulation Department replied that, initially, the dark oil alone was suspected of contamination, and that without express approval from the Ministry of International Trade and Industry, his ministry did not have the authority to review Kanemi's flow-charts. Since dark oil was not registered as an approved feed with the Ministry of Agriculture and Forestry, MAF officials had no legal authority to supervise its use and production. Indeed, when investigators visited the Kanemi factory and requested to be shown its plan of operations, they were reportedly informed by company

---

* In Japan there is no separate agency, such as the U.S. Food and Drug Administration, to monitor and control the safety of products for human consumption; instead, a division of the Ministry of Health and Welfare performs these functions.

management that "there was no need to see it." The officials accepted this narrow interpretation of their responsibility, which no doubt relieved Kanemi's management. The public, however, was to suffer.

Bureaucratic timidity and unwillingness to overstep well-defined administrative boundaries have been attributed to an "insecurity complex" endemic to government officials. As one young bureaucrat explained: "Most high-level officials are afraid of releasing information unless they have a way of protecting themselves from possible consequences. If controversial matters are disclosed, they are almost certain to be attacked in the Diet. In addition, the higher-ups dread causing an emotional panic among the people; they fear that the public will overreact to information. Most of us younger bureaucrats, hoping to rise to the top, follow the example set by our elders."

By no means the psychological tendency of a few individuals, this quest for security is considered by many to be a basic component of the bureaucratic personality (and not only in Japan). In Japan this attitude is often summed up in an aphorism that has become a classic example of bureaucratic wisdom: "Tell them nothing, but make them depend upon you."

Not wanting to "cause unrest among the people before the cause of the disease was identified," the Ministry of Agriculture repressed a possible public reaction which, albeit "hysterical," might have spared many eventual Kanemi oil victims. When asked why the dark oil incident was never made public, a ministry official replied that disclosure was considered unnecessary "because the private parties involved could easily solve the matter among themselves." An impulse to conceal rather than expose helped keep the public in ignorance until October.

The individual's desire to minimize insecurity is magnified in the group or sectional setting. As long as the group acts within its defined role, it retains a strong defensive position against possible criticism. The same reasoning dictates that as long as the individual remains within his own well-defined role in the group, his position is safe and, thanks to the Japanese seniority system, he will, with time, rise in the organization. Unfortunately, the rules of the game often supersede both morality and logic: the scientific proof of dark oil contamination should certainly have generated some investigation of Kanemi's cooking oil.

The inherent psychological tendencies described above are formally institutionalized in a bureaucratic decision-making apparatus: the *ringi* system. The *ringi* method calls for universal consensus before any action can be taken. In practice, consensus is usually reached through long hours of discussion and compromise. A draft proposal is prepared and circulated to each section member, who formally acknowledges his assent by stamping the papers with his personal seal. Although final approval is usually assured by this stage, individuals can delay it by withholding their seal. This procedure, aside from delaying conclusive action, ultimately ends in collective responsibility for the decision. In the process, it dissipates individual anxiety and thereby reduces insecurity. Obviously, this system also discourages individual action without group approval: independent action, in addition to alienating the individual from the group as a whole, would compel one to assume total responsibility for the effects of that action.

In government, the *ringi* system is applied to all official releases of information. During the dark oil incident, this traditional procedure served as an additional barrier to the flow of information from the MAF to both the MHW and the public. An official notification to the press or to other ministries would have required not a majority vote but unanimous consensus that the risks of publicizing the issue were balanced by its importance. The very fact that the dark oil incident was communicated neither to the MHW nor to the press until eight days after the publication of Abe's disclosure of the "oil disease" in the *Asahi* speaks for itself.

The *ringi* system is by no means restricted to the government bureaucracy. The attitudes which underlie it characterize most other organizations in Japan. The medical staff of Kyushu University, the research staffs of the Fukuoka Fertilizer and Feed Inspection Center and National Livestock Hygiene Laboratory, and officials in local health centers all had more than enough information to cast doubt on the safety of Kanemi's cooking oil, but the suspicions were not pursued. In some cases they were deliberately suppressed, leading to later court action and indictments for negligence. As for the moral aspects of seven months of silence, we can only refer to the feudal legacy "to sacrifice moral principles and true courtesy to a punctilious observance of form and etiquette,"[7] a legacy compounded by the need to maintain security amid modern group pressures.

Other important and related groups—the food industry and the LDP and opposition parties—were similarly slow in grasping the meaning of the dark oil incident, and the press, on the whole, lacked a probing attitude. As a result, Kanemi and the government bureaucracy could go on about their business at their own chosen speeds.

It was only after the human victims became conspicuous, as a result of their own cautious efforts, that the full impact of the rice oil poisoning gained recognition by society and its administrative organs. And it was the victims themselves who had to take the initiative in identifying the cause of their disease. They performed the functions that would normally be expected of medical authorities and government agencies. Although this situation mirrors the circumstances surrounding Minamata disease and Yokkaichi asthma, the Kanemi rice oil and similar incidents are not recognized by the government to be "pollution diseases" *(kogai byo)*, but are considered food and drug poisonings. According to the government's definitions, "pollution diseases" are caused *indirectly* by toxic substances that pass through the environment, while food and drug poisonings are caused by "accidents" that *directly* introduce contaminants into food supplies. But this legal and administrative distinction carries little weight with the victims, for the problems encountered in attempting to identify the cause, locate responsibility, and receive adequate compensation and medical treatment have been the same. Thus, the victims of Kanemi rice oil disease insist that they have been afflicted with yet another *kogai byo*.

4.

By identifying the disease as a case of food poisoning, the *Asahi* report established the victims' personal innocence: they had fallen ill through no inherent defect of their own. and in no way did they threaten the welfare of others. But recognition of the disease gave rise to three major problems— medical treatment, official clarification of responsibility, and compensation for damages. At this writing, six years after the outbreak of the disease, these problems remain unsolved.

Up to the present, no effective treatment for PCB poisoning has been discovered, in Japan or elsewhere. Although medicines can relieve minor symptoms, such as headaches and stomach pain, no basic treatment exists to remove or counteract PCBs accumulated in the human body. Like other chlorinated hydrocarbons, PCBs are fat soluble. Some (those containing relatively few chlorine atoms) are gradually discharged, but others remain lodged in fatty tissues in and around the heart and liver. Even in Kanemi victims whose initial PCB concentrations have diminished, however, physical abnormalities persist. These include depression, fever, coughing, pains, irregular menstruation, depressed growth, teeth abnormalities, and skin problems. PCBs leave their mark for life.[8]

Like mercury, PCB compounds cross the placental barrier and have been found to concentrate in the fetus, resulting in the birth of "dark babies" characterized by spots of darkly pigmented skin and poor physical development. Such babies have been born to mothers who themselves are symptomless but who ingested PCBs through Kanemi oil.

One resident of Tama no Ura has given birth to three successive dark babies and her three older children were struck in 1968 after eating fried foods. Although well aware of the nature of her illness and its effects on the fetus, this woman has continued to bear offspring. She is one of a group of "hidden Christians" which has lived in a slightly separated area of the village for centuries and has maintained religious customs introduced into Japan over 400 years ago by Catholic missionaries. Modern methods of birth control are strongly denounced by the local priest and his prohibition is devoutly adhered to. Among many villagers, religious convictions override even the dread realities of PCB poisoning.

In most stricken families, the tragedy is most acute among the young. One parent described the psychological tortures he undergoes: "How do you tell your daughter, who is only ten years old, that she may never marry, because her child would probably be a deformed dark-spotted baby? And what do you say to your son, whose upper teeth have been completely ravaged by the disease, when he explains his failure at school by saying, 'Why should I study? I'm not going to live long anyway.' These are the real agonies of being a Kanemi victim. Even more than the physical pain..."

The Kanemi incident has totally disrupted the lives of every family it has struck, barring the afflicted from acceptance into normal society. The stigma attached to contamination, despite the unwitting manner in which it was acquired, can never be erased. This is particularly true with regard to marriage. One young woman who had been engaged before being victimized by the poisoning had to call off her marriage. "Kanemi rice oil robbed me of my womanhood, my humanity," she said bitterly. "Now, whenever I hear the word 'marriage,' I want to cover my ears and cry."

A high school student, subjected to both physical and psychological abuse because of prejudice, relates that in 1969 "going to school was no pleasure, no fun at all. I didn't have one friend. And I always had to remember, 'Don't let people see your face.' I was always nervous and afraid... Getting ready for an athletic meet was like thinking about death. On the day of the meet, my teacher told the class that people with contagious diseases shouldn't attend school. It wasn't true, but everyone knew he was talking about me. During the games, my partner made an ugly face and made sure that our hands didn't touch. Even now, when I think about that experience, I cringe. I don't know how many times I've thought about dying. But everyone in my family is cursed with this disease, and if I die, what would happen to my parents?"

Excluded both physically and psychologically from Japan's homogeneous society, Kanemi victims are demanding that the company return them to their original condition. But medical research has not yet produced a truly effective means even of reducing the physical pain, much less of treating and reversing the symptoms. Despite official optimism, therefore, victims often say that the disease is beating them.

MHW certification methods have been a major cause of disagreement between the victims on the one hand, and medical experts and government officials on the other. The purpose of the system was to certify victims so that the Kanemi company could negotiate a financial settlement with them. Unlike cases of pollution diseases, in which government accepts some responsibility for medical care, those poisoned by contaminated Kanemi oil have received no government aid, even though their disease was designated incurable by the Ministry of Health and Welfare in 1973. The victims feel that the medical authorities tend to belittle their complaints and deny the relationship between specific symptoms and the intake of PCBs in an effort to keep the number of victims as low as possible. The more victims there are, the more embarrassing it is for the government.

While controversy continues over the problem of medical treatment and the issue of formal certification, Kanemi victims have split into factions over the best way to compel the company (and government) to accept legal responsibility for the disease and provide adequate compensation. Several groups have resorted to litigation, hoping that legal proceedings will clarify the responsibility for causing the disease and force local and central administrations to institute effective measures for medical care and treatment facilities.

But the problems of organizing Kanemi victims into a unified movement are much more complex than in previous pollution disease cases, because the victims are spread over 23 prefectures. Greater intervention by political parties has occurred, and interparty disputes have convinced some patients that they are being exploited for political purposes. Four victims groups have filed civil suits, and the Fukuoka prosecutor's office has brought a criminal suit against Kanemi. Some victims have settled out of court. One family has protested what it considers Kanemi's criminality by carrying out an independent sit-in demonstration in front of the Kitakyushu factory since September 1972.

Animosity between settlement and litigation factions is probably at its worst in Tama no Ura. When, in June 1970, preparations were being made for a second civil suit to be lodged against it, Kanemi initiated negotiations for out-of-court settlements. The company proposed lump sum payments of 400,000 yen ($1,100) for serious cases, 300,000 yen ($860) for moderately serious cases, and 200,000 yen ($560) for mild cases. Victims under 12 years of age would receive 70 percent, and those over 70 would receive 80 percent of the adult payment. The proposal included clauses stipulating that the payments did not imply legal responsibility and that the victims would make no further demands.

It is not surprising that the proposed settlement caused a rift among the victims. One described the meeting at which the split occurred: "My idea was that the children should receive the most money. After all, they have to live under the shadow of this disease for the rest of their lives. I asked the chairman if he had any intention of insisting upon this in further negotiations with Kanemi, and he said he did not. Then I asked if we could negotiate with the company individually concerning the children's compensation, and again he said no. (He was the only negotiator that Kanemi would recognize.) I stood and renounced the proposed settlement, declaring it my intention to fight in the courts." About 100 victims followed his lead and initiated legal proceedings.

Since that fateful evening, relations between the two factions in Tama no Ura have been far from cordial, and their mutual animosities are intensified by religious and subtle regional differences. While the litigation faction is based around the docks in Tama no Ura, the settlement faction is made up largely of the Christians living in the nearby community of Imochi no Ura—among whom hundreds of years of relative isolation have bred a unique dialect and set of traditions. The sudden wealth enjoyed by the settlement group does not help matters. "But still," as one leader of the litigation faction put it, "the basic problem remains. Even those who have received money are suffering. They may have color television sets and automobiles, but money doesn't stop the pain. We still have no cure for the poisons inside us, and our children still have no future."

5.

The industrial accident that produced the Kanemi incident might have occurred anywhere. It is characteristic of the history of such problems in Japan, however, that the incident was ignored or denigrated by administrative agencies until the human victims transformed it into a major social issue, and even then it was treated gingerly. This pattern has been repeated in other cases of food and drug poisonings, perhaps best exemplified by the Morinaga Milk arsenic poisoning case and the infamous thalidomide incident. Both were major tragedies: Morinaga, 12,000 victims with 130 deaths; thalidomide, 1,000 victims with 900 deaths. Although they occurred in 1955 and 1958, respectively, neither case was settled until 1974.

One of the most glaring features shared by these poisonings is the lamentable lack of safety measures taken by the companies involved. The milk poisoning was caused by the Morinaga Company's use of disodium phosphate as a stabilizer to facilitate the dissolving of its powdered milk in water. Even in its purest form, disodium phosphate contains 0.0001 to 0.01 percent of arsenic, and is regarded as dangerous to human health. Morinaga used an inferior grade of the chemical intended for *industrial* use, and the powdered baby's milk that resulted contained 24 to 38 ppm of arsenic! It has since been revealed that the company carried out checks neither on the safety of the additive before introducing it into the powder, nor on the safety of the powder before distributing it for human consumption. Use of the product resulted in symptoms including diarrhea, fever, dark-spotted skin, extreme weakness, and convulsions sometimes ending in death.

Similarly, when Dai Nippon Pharmaceuticals applied to the Ministry of Health and Welfare in August 1957 for a permit to sell thalidomide nationwide, it reportedly failed to provide adequate clinical studies of possible side effects. In addition, the application failed to state the number of animals used in toxicity testing. Although the company did not satisfactorily demonstrate the drug's safety, a lower council of the Ministry of Health and Welfare accepted the application for its production and sale after an hour and a half of discussion. This points to a second factor common to food and drug poisoning cases: the lack of effective government supervision of new products, and the government's apparent unwillingness to enforce self-regulatory mechanisms in industry.

A third feature common to these cases is the government's delayed reaction after being confronted with evidence of contamination. Although Dr. Widuking Lenz of West Germany issued his first warnings about the relationship between thalidomide use and birth defects in November 1961, the only reaction of Japan's MHW was to send an investigator to West Germany. While other countries were banning the sale of drugs containing thalidomide by the end of 1961, the MHW continued to support the drug, and as late as February 1962 allegedly issued a new production permit to another Japanese company. Steps limiting the sale and use of thalidomide were not initiated in Japan until May when, on its own initiative, Dai Nippon Pharmaceuticals halted shipments to retailers. But it was not until the following September that the company began efforts to retrieve the product from the market. At this writing, the Ministry of Health and Welfare has yet to take action against the company, in part because it would raise some embarrassing questions about its own role in the case.

A further weakness in the pattern of government reaction to such public health crises is the lack of adequate medical treatment and follow-up studies provided for the victims. Research carried out by a government team in late 1955 concluded that arsenic poisoning from contaminated milk left no permanent damage, but 14 years later, Professor Hiroshi Maruyama of Osaka University found very serious after-effects, including a high incidence of cerebral palsy and brain damage. The long period of official inaction and silence after the outbreak of the milk poisoning reflects the government's bias in favor of industrial interests. For that matter, the government has yet to undertake a follow-up study of thalidomide; in fact, it continued to deny the cause-effect relationship between the drug and birth defects until December 1973!

The earlier these cases occurred in Japan's postwar history, the lower the rates of compensation offered by industry in its attempt to arrange out-of-court settlements. In 1955, Morinaga paid 250,000 yen ($700) for deaths and 30,000 yen ($80) to living victims, while it refused to grant provisions for future medical complications.

Incredible as it may seem, another case of food oil contamination—this time with international implications—surfaced in April 1973. Salad oil produced by Chiba Nikko Company was contaminated by several derivatives of naphthalene, substances with an acute toxicity about one-third that of polychlorinated biphenyls. Although the company knew from both an abnormal decrease in the level of these substances in the heating apparatus and from subsequent analyses of the products that the oil was contaminated, it did not halt operations, notify the proper authorities, or refrain from marketing affected products. A subcontractor eventually revealed the matter to local health officials. Nikko's president later explained that his company had marketed the salad oil without notifying health authorities because his staff believed most of the poisonous chemicals evaporated during processing. Also, he added, they had judged that consumption of small amounts of the naphthalene derivatives would not be critically dangerous to humans. Luckily, most of the suspect oil was retrieved, including that purchased by 22 Tokyo schools. Subsequent investigations conducted by the Ministry of Health and Welfare in fact showed that the collected oil contained no traces of biphenyl. The ministry's report therefore hypothesized that the missing 45 kilograms of heating medium had, indeed, evaporated during processing.

This MHW announcement in May terminated a brief domestic panic over Nikko's oils. But on September 11, 1973, a disconcerting article appeared in the Japanese edition of the *Asahi* newspaper. Apparently 800 liters of Nikko's waste oil, produced as a byproduct in the manufacturing process and containing high concentrations of vitamin E, were sold to a small company which refined it for export. Its purchasers were several American companies that produced vitamin capsules as a "health food" product. The company's president reportedly said that he "thought the oil safe" and that, furthermore, "there is nothing that can be done about it anyway." An MHW spokesman added that there was no way to retrieve samples of the oil for testing, and that the ministry had "no legal obligation" to inform the American companies. The entire issue has since disappeared from the news and most people consider the incident closed. For the American public, however, the mystery of the exported waste oil, and the question of whether or not it was contaminated, remains unresolved.

6.

Although the Kanemi incident did not spur reforms of food and drug administration practices, it should at least have aroused the Ministry of Health and Welfare to the dangers to human health that environmental PCB contamination might pose. The world's first report of PCB pollution had come in 1966 from Swedish scholar Soren Jensen, and it was followed by similar accounts in *Nature* magazine in 1966 and 1967. Yet no one in Japan, including MHW officials, scientists working on pesticide problems, and doctors involved in the investigation of Kanemi disease, reviewed these papers or informed the public about them. During 1969 and 1970, no government-sponsored PCB research project was undertaken. In fact, annual PCB production in Japan continued to rise, more than doubling between 1968 and 1970.*

In the early months of 1971, an unusual group of individuals concerned about the PCB threat formed a new front. The group was unusual in that it pierced traditional professional barriers and constituted a horizontal communications network. At its core were analytical chemists Ryo Tatsukawa and Kunisato Fujiwara, biologist Naohide Isono, and *Asahi* newspaper reporter Hiroyuki Ishi. These men and the results of their research prodded Japan's slow-moving bureaucracy into action.

The group's first public announcement of PCB contamination in fish, meats, and birds was made in February 1971, soon followed by a report that carbonless copy paper used throughout the nation's post offices, banks, and businesses contained 3-5 percent PCBs. Widespread media coverage of this disclosure set off a mini-panic, and MITI quickly issued an "administrative guidance" recalling all PCB-containing copy paper and directing all industries to cease using the substance. Then came a report that fish, shellfish,

---

* This rise in production was largely influenced by the fact that in 1969 the Monsanto Corporation, principal producer of PCBs in the United States, while aware of environmental problems related to the compounds, formed a joint venture with Mitsubishi to manufacture PCBs in Japan.

water, and mud from Tokyo Bay were also highly PCB-polluted. As the evidence piled up at its doorstep, the government finally allocated funds for a full-scale investigation of PCB contamination, while MITI began limiting the compounds' industrial uses. As their markets disappeared, PCB producers gradually ended their operations, and by June 1972, all PCB production in Japan came to an end.

But between 1954 and 1972, nearly 60,000 tons of the substance had been produced, and the government's measures were far too late to prevent Japan's environment from becoming the world's most heavily polluted with PCBs. The compounds have been found in high concentrations in the soil and in toilet tissue, paper napkins, and newspapers containing recycled carbonless copy paper. Moreover, studies have not only disclosed the presence of PCBs in humans, but among mothers surveyed, *all* samples of breast milk contained PCBs, while in the United States only 38 percent of such samples were contaminated and among England's women contamination was hardly measurable. A March 1972 report of PCB levels of up to 0.7 ppm in Osaka mothers' milk underscored the severity of the problem: For, over a five-month period, Kanemi victims had reportedly ingested a minimum of 0.5 grams of PCBs, amounting for a 50-kilogram adult to a daily intake of 70 micrograms per kilogram of body weight. If a 4-kilogram baby were to drink 1,000 grams of breast milk containing 0.7 ppm of PCBs daily, it would be ingesting 175 micrograms of PCBs per kilogram of body weight—*more than twice the daily intake of Kanemi victims*. No abnormalities have as yet been reported, but a shadow has been cast on the future of many infants.

To quell public anxiety aroused by the discovery of high PCB levels in human breast milk, the Ministry of Health and Welfare set the world's first daily PCB intake tolerance standards at 5 micrograms per kilogram of body weight. Based on Kanemi poisoning statistics, this measure became the basis for additional standards set for foods. When these regulations were presented to the public in August 1972, general concern over PCBs receded. Their lingering threat, however, pressed at the very heart of Japanese society: the health and welfare of its children. Indeed, it had confronted the Japanese with the frightening possibility of a mother unknowingly poisoning her baby with the milk flowing from her own breast.

1. The Million Dollar Night View

Twinkling lights on the Shiohama (Yokkaichi) petrochemical complex led residents to proudly proclaim it the "million dollar night view." Their enthusiasm soon died, however, as the factories' poisonous exhaust fumes caused the onset of "Yokkaichi asthma," a respiratory disease which brought sickness and even death to those living near the industrial complex.

2. Inexpensive solutions

In 1965, in a classic example of early attempts to "solve" pollution problems, Yokkaichi city officials provided all elementary school children with yellow "pollution masks." Two years later, the city's mayor declared the masks completely ineffective.

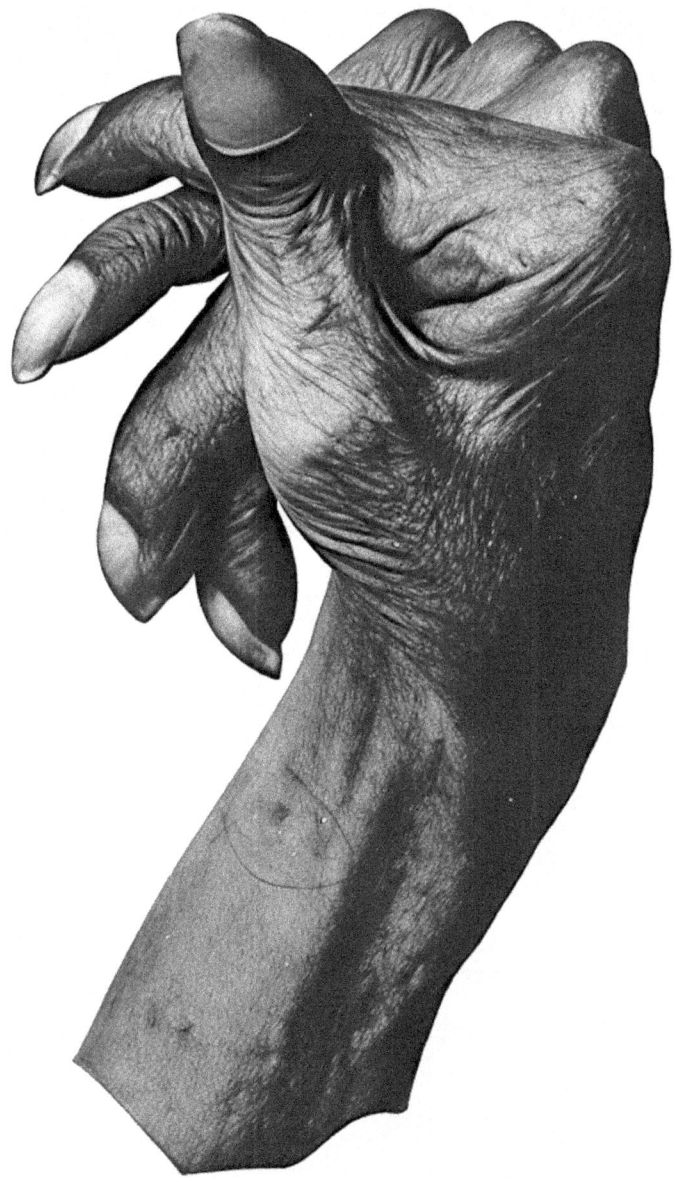

3. Minamata disease

Japan's infamous Minamata disease demonstrated to the world the horrifying consequences of contaminating the environment with organic mercury. The physical and psychological agonies of the victims are excruciatingly painful—and irreversible.

4. The torments of the diseased young

In this case, mercury passed through the placental barrier of the symptomless mother and concentrated in her unborn child. This 18-year-old girl weighs less than 15 kilograms, is unable to speak, walk, or even crawl, and requires constant care.

5. An act of contrition

The president of the Chisso Company bows in deep apology to the victims of the mercury poisoning caused by his Minamata factory. A traditional gesture of humility before one's superiors, the executive's act of contrition was splashed across the front pages of the nation's newspapers.

ISLAND OF DREAMS

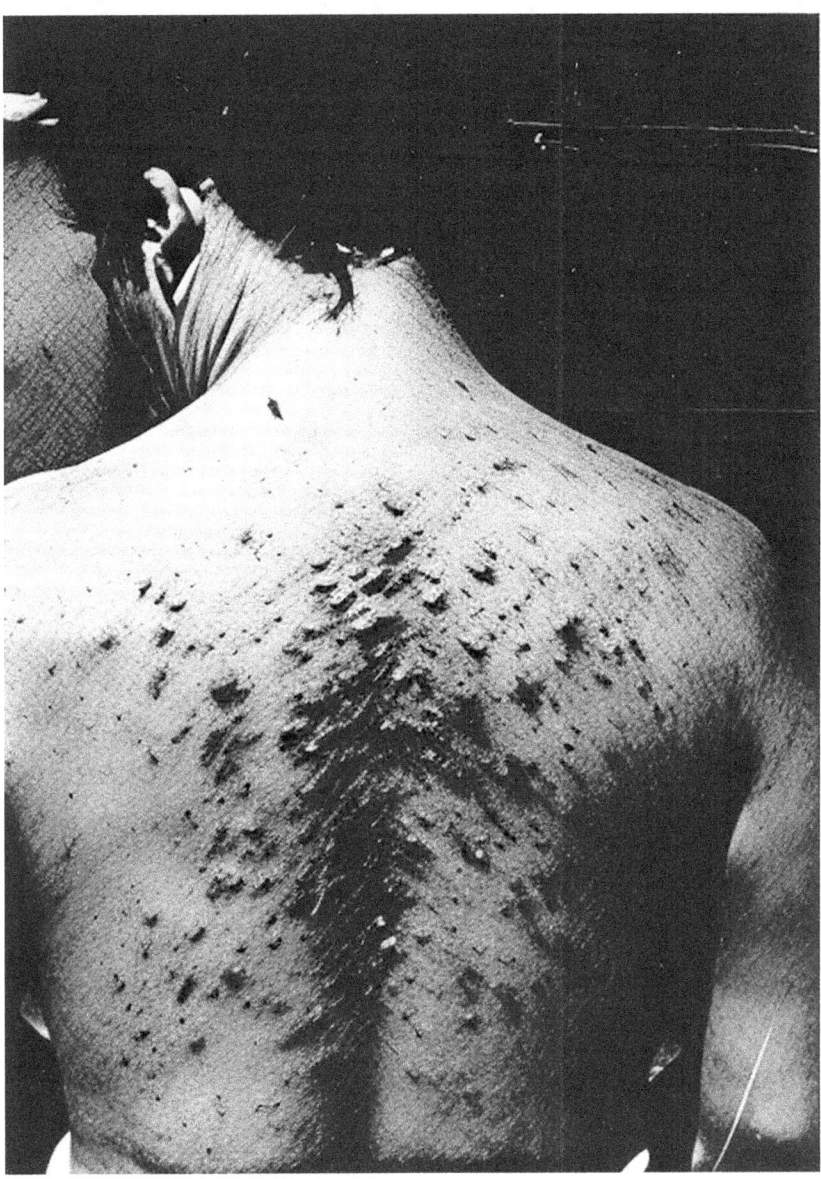

6. Yusho disease

Housewives who fed their families large quantities of Kanemi Rice Oil unwittingly poisoned them with PCBs (polychlorinated biphenyls)—chemically similar to DDT—which contaminated the oil. The primary external manifestation: a very severe form of acne.

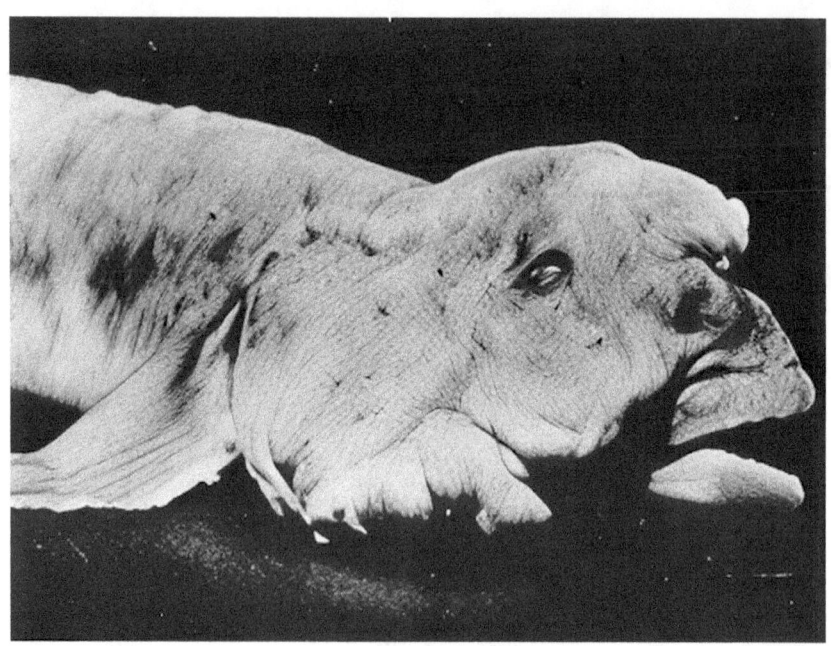

7. Ghost fish

In recent years an increasing number of malformed fish have been caught by native fishermen in Japanese coastal waters. Some scientists cite rising pollution levels as the cause of the mutations and cancer-like growths, and warn that the "ghost fish" may be but the forerunners of human victims.

8. A fishermen's demonstration

Japan's economic policy of growth at all costs has often victimized the nation's fishermen. As a result, fishermen have been a major voice in antipollution protests.

105   ISLAND OF DREAMS

9. Island of Dreams

A vast amount of Tokyo's refuse finds its final resting place in Tokyo Bay, where it is used as landfill. Two islands have already been constructed and a third is nearing completion.

10. Pushers do their work

Tokyo suffers from a state of extreme overcrowding. Here, commuters are helped onto their rush hour train by professional "pushers" employed by the Japan National Railways.

11. Intensive land use

Because Japan's land area is almost 80 percent mountainous, level land is used intensively. In urban areas, houses and factories cluster tightly together, compensating pollution problems.

12. San-chan farming

Japan's postwar development policies drove the farming population into secondary industries. By 1970, nearly two-thirds of the nation's agricultural work force was female and one-third of all male workers were over 60 years of age.

CHAPTER SIX

THE GREAT FISH PANIC

"No gray mullet, no young punctatus, no bass, and no sea eel. It would also be wise to avoid freshwater eel, flounder, and flatfish. No more than two portions of swordfish or raw tuna slices a week; discard all entrails. Infants and pregnant women should give up all fish completely. To be safe, don't eat the same type continuously. I suppose seaweed is alright..."

—CHIEF OF TOKYO METROPOLITAN
GOVERNMENT'S FOOD HYGIENE BUREAU
June 1973

Although they were coming ever closer, pollution diseases had always been "someone else's" problem, and the predominant attitude in Japanese society regarding their "unlucky" victims was one of resigned fatalism. Only the victims knew the agonies of mercury and PCB poisoning, and the fear of untimely death. Only the victims understood the frustration of trying to persuade industry and government to accept responsibility for the diseases a national policy of concentrated economic advancement had left in its wake.

For the great majority of society, pollution diseases were little more than "a fire on the opposite bank." But on May 22, 1973, a report issued by the Kumamoto University Minamata Disease Research Group stunned the apathetic public by announcing the discovery of ten new cases of mercury poisoning. In and of itself, the discovery would not have been earth-shaking, except that these new cases were found not in Minamata or Niigata but in a coastal area bordering the Ariake Sea, a body of water 40 kilometers north of Minamata Bay. Banner newspaper headlines proclaimed "Third Outbreak of

Minamata Disease Uncovered," and the accompanying stories alleged that the Chisso and Showa Denko factories were not the only ones that had been dumping mercury wastes into Japan's coastal waters. There soon appeared reports of suspected victims in other areas (Tokuyama, Oita, Okayama), suggesting fourth, fifth, and sixth outbreaks of the disease. The dam burst, with Japanese everywhere suddenly horrified to realize that they, too, for some 20 years, may have been eating contaminated fish and gradually accumulating heavy metals in their bodies. The nation's anxiety was fed by journalistic predictions of "100 million Minamata victims." Shocked to learn that government and industry had known about the horrors of mercury intoxication since at least 1959 but had done little to curb the spread of contamination, the Japanese reacted in panic.

Government ministries were compelled to act quickly. The Environment Agency and Ministry of Health and Welfare laid the groundwork for a comprehensive investigation of the Ariake Sea situation. MITI initiated a survey of industries that used mercury in their manufacturing processes and began to publicize data for each factory on volumes of mercury consumed and amounts discarded into the environment. For the first time, government officials were openly investigating the extent of mercury pollution in Japan and informing the general public of their findings.

But the Kumamoto University report and the mercury scare that ensued were only the beginning. On June 4, less than two weeks later, the Fisheries Agency made public the results of a nationwide survey of PCB contamination. It was found that more than 80 percent of the fish tested in six major fishing areas exceeded the 3 ppm provisional safety standard set for PCBs by the MHW in August 1972. These six bodies of water were designated as "seriously polluted," and fish caught in them were declared unsafe. Fishermen had no choice but to "voluntarily restrict" their operations.

Panic intensified as newspapers and magazines printed sensational rumors to the effect that since both PCBs and mercury accumulate in the body and pass through the placental barrier, chronic poisoning could cause unknown birth defects and health hazards to future generations. Reports from Tokyo describing the symptoms of cats poisoned by mercury after eating canned and fresh tuna reminded people of the early warning symptoms of Minamata disease. While only a few weeks earlier the public had eaten fish with barely a second thought, it now suspected all seafood of mercury and PCB contamination.

Full and intensive press coverage of the crisis brought a daily flow of disquieting news into every Japanese home. The nation's centralized communications system, enjoying almost 100 percent distribution, exerted its

The Great Fish Panic   **110**

full influence on public opinion,* and the press took a distinctly antigovernment position on the issue.

Thus, with the information media's prodding, the reports of May 23 and June 4 sparked the release of long-suppressed fears. Almost overnight, millions of Japanese removed fish, for millennia a dependable protein staple, from their diet, and turned to foods deemed "safe," such as pork, beef, and frozen foods. Within a few weeks of the scientific announcements, fish sales plummeted by 30 to 50 percent throughout the country. Wholesale markets drastically reduced their purchases from fishermen operating both inside and outside those areas suspected of contamination. The consumer panic thus confronted the national fishing industry with the economic hardship formerly known only in isolated areas like Minamata and Yokkaichi.

One week after the announcement of the Kumamoto University report, the Ministry of Health and Welfare established an ad hoc committee on mercury contamination. The committee met for several weeks and on June 24 startled both the government and the public by announcing recommendations for the world's strictest standards of acceptable mercury levels in foods.† The committee's report called for an adult methyl mercury intake not to exceed 0.17 milligrams per week, an amount equivalent to World Health Organization standards but not as yet adopted by any nation. Specifically, the committee proposed that fish containing an average concentration of total mercury compounds above 0.4 ppm, or of methyl mercury above 0.3 ppm, should be prohibited from sale. These standards, far more stringent than those in Sweden (1.0 ppm) and the United States (0.5 ppm), reflected Japan's heavy consumption of seafoods, the nation's main source of animal protein (55 percent).

In an attempt to make them easier to understand, the MHW converted ppm concentrations into total numbers of fish, by species, that could be safely consumed each week. The published figures were meant as hypothetical examples, but consumers interpreted them as an official decree limiting consumption and confirming the danger of an impending national emergency. Instead of reassuring the public, as was its intent, the MHW announcement backfired, fanning the flames of panic.

---

* Postwar economic wealth, by putting a television set into nearly every household, enables instantaneous dissemination of information to a large audience, while four Tokyo-based newspapers, the *Asahi, Mainichi, Yomiuri,* and *Sankei,* together reach almost the entire adult reading public.

† Strict limits for the daily intake of PCBs had already been set a 72 micrograms the previous August, following the reports of high contamination of mothers' milk.

Two days later, confusing the situation even more, the Ministry of Health and Welfare revised the number of fish that could be "safely" consumed. Pressure from all levels of the fishing industry and political criticisms from the LDP's Executive Council had apparently forced the ministry's bureaucrats to ease their recommendations by sharply increasing the permissible weekly number of fish from, for example, 12 to 46.2 horse mackerel, 1.8 to 6.7 flatfish, 10.3 to 28.3 young bass, or 5.8 to 21.7 mackerel pike.

Ministry officials justified their abrupt reversal by labeling the first guidelines "an unfortunate mistake committed in haste to reassure the public." The earlier standards were said to have been based on the assumption that all fish contained the maximum 0.3 ppm of methyl mercury. The newer set were based on actual surveys of the average level of mercury contamination, which were shown to be about 0.08 ppm, thus permitting considerably higher limits.

While the ministry's revised announcement relieved the fishing industry somewhat, it cast doubt upon the dependability of any ministry recommendation and left most people bewildered. An *Asahi* newspaper commentary of June 29 was entitled "12 or 46?" and compared the ministry's policy reversal to a popular Chinese fable:

> This reminds us of a story told in China. A man liked monkeys very much and kept many monkeys as pets. Since feeding them cost so much money, he decided to cut down on their feed. He told the monkeys, "From now on, I will give each of you three acorns in the morning and four in the evening." But the monkeys became angry. Thereupon he proposed to give them each four in the morning and three in the evening. The monkeys were very happy. Ever since then, "three in the morning and four in the evening" has come to mean hoodwinking. We do not believe the Ministry of Health and Welfare intended to hoodwink the general public, but "12 in the morning and 46 in the evening" may be included in future dictionaries. The description of the phrase will probably be given as "Confusing people with undependable talk; from the Ministry of Health and Welfare saying in the morning it is safe to eat 12 horse mackerel and then changing it to 46 in the evening."[2]

The MHW's ineptitude in handling the proposed consumption limitations only heightened the public's sense of panic. Average monthly fish consumption per family dropped from nearly 5,000 grams in May to 4,000 grams in June, and was still falling in July. Taking up the slack, meat sales jumped 15 to 20 percent and as demand increased, prices soared. During these weeks, the man on the street could be heard bemoaning the fact that the government's new safety standards meant they could no longer enjoy their accustomed weekly allotment of *sushi*, a popular delicacy consisting of thin slices of raw fish served on rice. Some proclaimed that they didn't care what the government said: they would eat their fish and enjoy it, even if it killed them!

2.

The impromptu boycott of marine products by Japanese consumers impoverished fishermen, fish wholesalers, and retailers. And while the consumers' panic struck at the entire fishing industry, it was the little man, the local fisherman and individual retailer, who suffered most. In addition to the economic punch, he was confronted with a dire realization: studies showed that, because fishermen and their families tended to consume five to ten times more fish than the Japanese average, their body tissues contained much higher concentrations of mercury and PCBs than other occupational groups.

The problem confronting Japan's fishermen arose from a combination of industrial irresponsibility and governmental unresponsiveness. Bitterly recalling years of appeals to industry to end the pollution of coastal waters, fisheries' spokesmen complained that their repeated warnings had gone unheeded while polluting enterprises increased the tempo of their activities. They accused local and central governments of having too long sacrificed the environment for the sake of economic growth.

Interviewed by a national television network to publicize his personal plight and that of so many others like him, a fisherman from a small village in Kyushu described the struggle to provide his family with the basic necessities. Out of work for over a month, he told of having already depleted his family's savings and of no longer having enough money to buy the next day's rice. He had finally applied to the local government for welfare benefits, despite an overpowering sense of shame and reluctance to "accept money for nothing." But, he explained, he had no other choice. "I explained it to my children and ordered them to be brave and endure the situation, even if their friends ridiculed them." The effects were repeated in towns and villages throughout the country as the national fish boycott destroyed the financial and psychological security of thousands of fishermen and forced many to give up their trade.

Fish dealers reacted in novel ways to the grave decline in sales. One retailer in Nagoya purchased an expensive device to measure the concentration of mercury in the fish he sold, thus guaranteeing their safety.

The fishing industry and related organizations launched intensive advertising campaigns to persuade the public that most fish were safe to eat and pressured local and central governments into making "safety proclamations." Thus, on July 25, the governor of Wakayama Prefecture, accompanied by an entourage of 20 officials, arrived in Tokyo with four tons of fish, and in a not unsuccessful attempt to lure housewives back to their product, distributed their dubious bounty free. Their slogan: "Our fish are safe." Tuna advertisements appeared in trains and subways proclaiming that "fish caught far out at sea can be eaten with a sense of assurance." Fishermen, for their part, began organized retaliation against those factories believed responsible for the crisis. In angry demonstrations, they dumped tons of unsalable catches at factory gates, demanding to meet with company executives to negotiate compensation. Waving contaminated fish in the faces of industrial spokesmen, they blamed the factories for causing the panic that now threatened their livelihood.

Some unions resorted to even more forceful protest measures. On July 6, 1973, Minamata fishermen escalated their opposition against Chisso by blockading the factory harbor, cutting off supplies of raw materials. By July 17, for the first time in the postwar period, the Chisso factory was forced to cease all operations. The Minamata union's demand of 1.3 billion yen ($4.3 million) for damages incurred since 1961 was met by the company with an offer of 400 million yen ($1.3 million). The latter was accepted and the blockade was lifted.

Throughout the country, fishermen adopted similar tactics against polluting factories. One of the most successful protests occurred in the small town of Saganoseki in Oita Prefecture. Its main objective was to force Nippon Kogyo, whose copper refinery had been dumping wastes into the local harbor for fifty years, to purify the sea. The fishermen blockaded the port and four days later concluded an agreement with the company giving them the right to conduct factory pollution checks and requiring the company to install effective abatement equipment. The company furthermore consented to removing contaminated sludge from the harbor under the fishermen's supervision. As the agreement began to take effect in late summer 1973, antipollution activists throughout the nation praised Saganoseki's fishermen, calling their success "a new page in the struggle that began with Ashio."

Throughout late June and July, fishermen and retailers all over Japan staged demonstrations against local and central governments. On July 6, over 1,500 banner-waving protesters gathered in Tokyo to confront government ministries, the LDP, and the powerful Federation of Economic Organizations

(Keidanren).* Although their protests were primarily oriented toward economic compensation, they marked an important new development in the antipollution movement. They reflected a deepening conviction that politicians, bureaucrats, and business leaders were jointly responsible for neglecting pollution problems and were equally obliged to solve them. It was, furthermore, the first time that fishermen's unions from different geographical regions united in a joint action.

Consumers, in the meantime, were unable to translate their complaints into effective political pressure. Japan's national consumer movements did not protest the industry and government policies that lay at the root of the fish crisis, but merely "appealed to the authorities" to provide guidelines as to which fish were safe to eat. Biologist Naohide Isono later pointed out that consumer demands for "total safety" were not only unrealistic, but contradictory. The shift from fish to meats, he explained, merely replaced the dangers of mercury and PCBs with those of BHC and DDT! Its emotional obsession with "safety" prevented the public from rationally assessing the problems of setting contamination standards for fish and other foods, and from presenting the government with rational demands for environmental controls. Instead, the consumer reaction only aggravated the fishermen's plight and deepened animosities between rural and urban residents.[3]

The government's response was clearly belated. Long before the third outbreak of Minamata disease was reported, government officials must have known that certain bodies of water were seriously contaminated. Since August 1968, industrial effluents, fish, and the hair of local residents had been examined yearly in Minamata and Niigata, and every two or three years in other areas adjacent to factories using mercury.[4] Although the results (which were not made public) revealed abnormally high concentrations of mercury in some areas, the government did not take adequate steps at the time to inform the public or to follow up the studies with appropriate countermeasures.

In addition to being too late, the government's program was also too little. While the MHW announcement set sampling methods to be followed by

---

* The action against Keidanren was especially noteworthy because it was directed against an institution that had hitherto been spared confrontation and public embarrassment. The private equivalent of MITI, Keidanren is composed of the presidents and directors of all major Japanese conglomerates and financial authorities; its elite membership cooperates with government in determining and carrying out national economic policy. Keidanren's previous immunity from the stigma of public demonstrations stemmed from the tradition dating back to the start of Japan's modern era which tended to place a taboo on attacks against big business as a whole. The fishermen's protest against this arm of the Japanese establishment therefore marked the culmination of actions taken against individual firms and industries. It also reflected increasing public suspicion of big business immunity.

prefectural governments, it did not provide mechanisms for indicating where specific catches came from or their levels of contamination. Moreover, the consumption guidelines themselves contained errors and omissions: one species of fish was referred to by the wrong name, while tuna, swordfish, and freshwater fish were excluded, despite their relatively high mercury levels.*

Local governments, too, initiated measures, albeit of dubious effectiveness, aimed at reducing public tension. Hyogo Prefecture directed local fishermen to seal off one PCB-contaminated port with huge nets, in an attempt to prevent further contamination by keeping "PCB fish" from leaving and uncontaminated fish from entering the harbor. In Minamata, the prefectural government sponsored a four-day fish kill. Fishermen retrieved approximately three tons of fish suspected of mercury contamination, then packed them in huge plastic tanks to be buried underground. Although it is difficult to conceive how such projects could ever hope to rid the bay of contamination, the prefecture's announcement that it intended to continue the project once a month met little public criticism.

Indicative of the unbalanced media handling of the whole issue was the fact that, after inflaming the public's response to the fish contamination, the press was quick to drop the story for "fresher" news. The hijacking of a Japanese airliner on July 21 and the tension shared by an emotional public over the fate of its hostage passengers completely displaced the fish panic in both news reports and people's minds, helping, in effect, to "settle" the crisis. The cartoon on page 117 appeared in the July 17 edition of the *Yomiuri* newspaper and speaks for itself.

Indeed, as if the total implications of the crisis were simply too threatening, the Great Fish Panic of 1973 died of its own accord—with the silent acquiescence of government and public alike—only two months after it had begun. By the end of July, newspapers were carrying only occasional references to PCB and mercury contamination, and fish sales were gradually returning to pre-panic levels.

---

* Almost all swordfish and tuna caught in the open seas exceeded the United States limits on mercury concentrations (0.5 ppm), and half exceeded the Swedish level (1.0 ppm). The MHW's only action with regard to tuna was an ambiguous sentence advising those who ate large quantities of the fish to "exercise caution." One ministry official has admitted that the exclusion of tuna and fresh-water fish was "certainly difficult to understand," but explained that their exclusion might have been related to unresolved questions as to whether the source of their contamination was "natural" or "industrial." From the point of view of public health, of course, the source of the mercury was immaterial: both naturally occurring and industrial mercury pose equal dangers. Other factors may have been the ministry's fear of the public's reaction to restrictions on one of Japan's most popular fish and the powerful influence of the Japanese tuna fishing industry.

"What would you like for supper tonight?"
"Tuna fish!"   "Sashimi!"

"All sold out."

"Ha, ha, ha."

"Thanks to the hijack *shokku*—everyone's forgotten about PCBs!"

Still, several important attitudinal changes were occasioned by the panic. Until 1967–68, the government had considered Minamata disease the problem of a single company and of an isolated body of water. The discovery in Niigata of the second outbreak of the disease and official recognition of its cause to be industrial mercury revealed the problem to be more widespread, but still no truly comprehensive surveys were undertaken. The fish panic of 1973 shocked the public and government alike with the fact that mercury pollution had become a national problem. For the first time, a comprehensive nationwide survey of mercury contamination was officially and openly conducted. Nor was the emergence of a public debate concerning the social responsibility of industrial policy-makers of minor importance.

Nevertheless, the basic issue giving rise to the panic—widespread PCB and mercury contamination of the environment precipitated by Japan's commitment to economic growth "at any price"—was lost in the emotional shuffle. Consumers turned the immediate problem back onto fishermen, fishermen focused their demonstrations around economic compensation, while local and central governments responded with ineffective administrative palliatives that were little more than a propaganda campaign to reassure the public. The return to "normalcy" several weeks after the outbreak of the panic reflected the psychological need to repress the panic's implications and restore the nation to its usual self-controlled calm.

3.

PCBs and mercury represent two general classes of toxic agents—chlorinated hydrocarbons and heavy metals—that have infiltrated the Japanese food supply. Minamata disease and the Kanemi rice oil incident exemplify the tragic results of acute poisoning. While sub-threshold amounts of a given substance may not produce distinct health effects, wholesale contamination of the environment by a variety of toxic substances could have long-term detrimental effects both on human health and on ecosystem stability. These long-term dangers, however, remain difficult to predict accurately.

One of the greatest overall dangers, but by no means the only one, is posed by "synergism," the interaction in the body of individual toxins producing a total effect greater than the sum of its parts. It is known, for example, that in less complex animals PCBs combine with DDT or other chlorinated hydrocarbons to generate intensified effects. But because the biochemical mechanisms of synergisms are not well understood, it is difficult to anticipate these complex interactions or their effects on humans. With these questions unanswered, the continued contamination of the Japanese environment has transformed the nation's 100 million inhabitants into the subjects of a vast experiment in chronic toxicology.*

Agricultural chemicals have been a major source of the many chlorinated hydrocarbons that riddle the environment. Following the introduction into Japan of the pesticides BHC (benzene hexachloride) and DDT (dichloro-diphenyl-trichloroethane) in 1945, their use grew exponentially. The production of agricultural chemicals increased twentyfold by 1955, and by 1968 Japan's application of agricultural chemicals per unit of farmland ranked highest in the world. Although intensive use of agricultural chemicals has helped boost agricultural productivity, it has also entailed high external costs: the acute poisoning of farm workers and rural families and the infiltration of ecosystems by highly persistent toxic residues that threaten to "simplify" and thereby destabilize them.

The health of rural farming communities has been most affected by the organophosphates and organic chlorides. Between the years 1959–69, the

---

* One indication that concern may well be justified came in June 1974, when two distinguished doctors announced the results of their joint study. Drs. Takeshi Hirayama and Masabumi Kimura conducted a computer survey of stillborn infants and found that in the last 20 years the rate of occurrence had increased 12 times, while the percentage of deformed stillborns had risen from 0.39 percent in 1952 to 2.02 percent in 1972. Both researchers believe that the probable causes are the combined effects of ingested agricultural chemicals, food additives, and drugs, and both predict that this is only the beginning of a trend that will increase significantly in the future.[6]

number of deaths due to these agricultural chemicals hovered around 800 annually, the great majority of them being suicides. Only 5 percent of all fatalities were due to misuse; similarly, most poisonings not ending in death occurred during normal spraying.[7]

While the Japanese have witnessed the direct effects that pollution may have on man, they are less conscious of the potential consequences of disrupting the stability of ecosystems. For reasons not entirely understood, stability is related to complexity. Ecosystems may be "simplified" by paving them over, planting monocultures, releasing industrial pollutants, or by reducing in size or forcing to extinction some of the component populations. Healthy ecosystems, essential to human survival, supply us with services such as controlling most potential crop pests, recycling wastes, maintaining the quality of the atmosphere, and supplying food from the sea, among others. Without such services (which the Japanese cannot provide for themselves), Japanese society would collapse.

As in other nations, intensive application of agricultural chemicals has disrupted the natural balance between predators and pests. For example, BHC applied to fields and paddies to control the rice stem borer also destroyed spiders. The disappearance of the spiders led to the resurgence of another pest, the leafhopper. Many pest species, thanks to their rapid rate of reproduction and the process of natural selection, have, moreover, been able to develop immunities to agricultural poisons. Since the early 1960s, Japan's endemic rice pests—the rice stem borer, the green leafhopper, and the smaller brown leafhopper—have developed resistance to chlorinated hydrocarbon, organophosphate, and carbamate compounds.[8] These resistant insect populations, documented in all countries that have relied on synthetic pesticides and insecticides, have greatly reduced the effectiveness of agricultural chemicals. Indeed, damage due to blight and insects has not decreased appreciably in Japan during the past 15 years,[9] despite the extremely heavy application of such chemicals.

A striking feature of Japan's use of agricultural chemicals has been its proportionally high emphasis on BHC, a chemical particularly effective in combating rice pests. In the peak year of 1968 alone, Japanese industry manufactured over 50,000 tons of the substance, as compared to only 4,000 tons of DDT. In that year, Japanese farmers sprayed their crops with 41,700 tons of BHC, while about 40,000 tons of DDT were sprayed in all of the United States. As a result, according to one expert, the Japanese absorb from 5 to 16 times more BHC from their food than do Europeans or Americans.[10] Furthermore, while Western food samples contain only a negligible amount of beta-BHC, the most toxic form of the compound, 70 percent of BHC contamination in Japanese foods is of this type.[11] The only other countries with similar contamination patterns are Korea and Taiwan—importers of Japanese BHC production technology.

In July 1969, largely in response to a one-month ban imposed on chlorinated hydrocarbons by the U.S. Department of Agriculture, the Japanese Ministry of Health and Welfare temporarily postponed renewal of BHC and DDT production licenses. In August 1970, the Ministry of Agriculture and Forestry finally banned BHC use on rice. By that time, manufacturers were already switching their production to other synthetics, exporting remaining supplies, or using them for forestry pest control programs. Production for export has continued, and in 1974 the LDP administration was attacked in the Diet for allowing 2,620 tons of BHC and 11 tons of DDT to be sold to Thailand, Malaysia, Singapore, the Philippines, and Australia between January and November of the previous year.[12]

By 1970, BHC residues had spread throughout the Japanese environment: they were detected in Tokyo rainwater, in the fatty tissues of humans as well as fish, in human breast milk and cigarette tobacco. Animal products contained nearly 90 percent of all residues found in human food. A Ministry of Health and Welfare survey carried out in 1972, the year following the total bans on BHC and DDT, revealed beta-BHC and DDT residues in all samples of breast milk at levels 30 to 100 times higher than those detected in the milk of American and European women. Although as of early 1974 BHC concentrations have decreased in fields, crops, food products, and human tissues, DDT levels have not significantly diminished. And because chlorinated hydrocarbons require an estimated four to thirty years in the soil before 95 percent is decomposed, their residues will linger for some time to come.

Organic mercury has been another major source of agricultural contamination. In the early 1950s, it was discovered that organic phenyl mercury was effective against rice blight; alkyl mercurials were also used as bactericides in the soil. Between 1953 and 1971, slightly more than 2,500 tons of mercury were used in the production of agricultural chemicals.[13]

The potential dangers of this practice were first brought to public attention in testimony delivered by Tokyo University's Dr. Hiroji Shiraki to the Upper House Special Committee for the Promotion of Science and Technology in 1966. Shiraki pointed out the similarities between phenyl mercury and methyl mercury—the causative agent of Minamata disease. He then explained that not only was the average level of mercury found in the hair of rural females (mothers) significantly higher than that of urban women (7.31 ppm versus 5.82 ppm, respectively), but mercury concentration in newborn infants was some 30 percent greater than that in their mothers! "The threat is not to us," he concluded, "but to the next generation. We are poisoning our children."[14]

Based on such testimony, a committee resolution called for a scientific review of agricultural chemicals. This was Japan's first move to reconsider its postwar policy of saturating its fields with highly toxic substances. By 1967, restrictions were put on the use of mercury-based insecticides, and three years later, in March 1970, their production and use were banned.

The present extent of Japan's contamination by mercury is indicated in a study conducted by the late Chunoshin Ukita of Tokyo University. Ukita found that mercury levels in the hair of Japanese residing abroad averaged 2.5 ppm, less than half the 6.5 ppm average found among Tokyo residents. Less than 18 months after their return to Japan, the mercury levels of four members of the former group had more than doubled.[15] A similar increase was noted in the case of Shoichi Yokoi, a former Imperial Army corporal, who returned to Japan in February 1972 after 27 years of hiding in the jungles of Guam. The mercury content in Yokoi's hair immediately upon his return registered 2 ppm; within two months it had risen to 4.7 ppm, and in eight months it was 8.2 ppm, more than four times the original concentration.*[16]

Controls on mercurial insecticides, instituted in the late 1960s, have lowered the concentration in rice and have reduced new mercury inputs into the environment. Nevertheless, of the estimated 6,000 tons of mercury discharged into the environment over the past twenty years, only 2,500 originated in agricultural chemicals. Most of the remainder came from industrial wastes dumped directly into Japan's coastal waters.

Cadmium, another heavy metal constituting a potential threat to the health of the Japanese public, now widely pollutes the nation's principal food staple, rice. According to a 1971 Environment Agency survey, nearly 25 percent of 117 agricultural areas surveyed (a total of 11,700 hectares) produced rice which contained cadmium in excess of 1 ppm. Although scientists are still debating the exact health effects of cadmium, studies have linked it to a peculiar and excruciatingly painful bone ailment.

---

* High mercury concentrations in human hair do not necessarily indicate that mercury poisoning symptoms will appear. Seamen on Japanese tuna boats have been found with a maximum hair concentration of 67.0 ppm of methyl mercury, a level approaching the 100 ppm found among Minamata disease victims. So far, these seamen have exhibited none of the early symptoms of acute mercury poisoning. Thus, it cannot be said that the level of mercury in the average citizen (from 4 to 10 ppm), while significantly higher than in his American or European counterpart, foretells a widespread outbreak of the disease.

The disease is said to have first appeared as early as 1910 in a small agricultural village in Toyama Prefecture located on the alluvial plains surrounding the lower reaches of the Jinzu River. In a report presented in 1955, a local medical doctor, Dr. Noboru Hagino, described the disease. Its victims were mainly post-menopausal women who had borne two or more children and who had resided in the Fuchu area for over thirty years. They were completely bedridden, their bones having developed an inexplicable fragility and brittleness. Movement induced painful splinters and fractures. Since pain was vented with anguished cries of *"itai-itai"* ("It hurts! It hurts!"), the ailment came to be known as itai-itai disease.* In the postwar period, over 200 persons in the Fuchu area have been afflicted with it; 130 have died. In addition, an estimated 1,000 local residents have been sufficiently exposed to cadmium contamination to make them potential victims.

In 1961, Hagino and a colleague, Professor Jun Kobayashi of Okayama University, concluded that the cause of the disease was industrial wastes discharged into the Jinzu River by the Mitsui Mining and Smelting Company's facilities located in Kamioka, some 50 kilometers upstream from the affected area. The mine had been producing and refining lead, zinc, and copper for nearly a century. Kobayashi had analyzed samples of victims' bones and tissues and, in addition to large amounts of lead and zinc, found extremely high concentrations of cadmium-amounting in some cases to 10,000 ppm!†

Present-day cadmium contamination in Japan is by no means confined to the area below Mitsui's Kamioka mine. High concentrations are found in most of Japan's zinc deposits, and for the past 100 years, mines and

---

* "Itai-itai" disease has usually been translated as the "ouch-ouch" disease. This English phrase, however, does not express the extreme pain suffered by the victims, as is reflected in the nuances of the Japanese name.

† Mitsui Mining rejected the cadmium hypothesis and was backed up by the local medical association, which contended that the disease was due to nutritional deficiencies. But administration of Vitamin D proved ineffective, and in 1968 the MHW issued an opinion indicting cadmium contamination as one of the disease's intrinsic causes. After meeting corporate denials for seven years, the victims of "itai-itai" disease resorted to legal action, and the case became one of the four major pollution litigations of the period. Unlike the litigations in Niigata, Minamata, and Yokkaichi, itai-itai disease plaintiffs did not have to establish the company's negligence; Article 109 of the Mining Act (enacted in 1939) imposed strict liability upon mining facilities for damages caused by their activities, regardless of the presence of negligence, in a type of "no-fault insurance." The law required only that causation be proved, making the question simply this: did cadmium cause the disease or not? The decision handed down by the Toyama district court on June 30, 1971, was a total victory for the plaintiffs. Moreover, it recognized that, in the presence of no conflicting pathological or clinical evidence, epidemiological proof of causation sufficed as legal proof of causation. This principle was to serve as a helpful precedent in other pollution litigation.

refineries have discarded cadmium released in the refining process into the environment. In the postwar period, with the proliferation of newly developed uses for cadmium, contamination spread from predominantly rural areas near mining operations to urban centers. Garbage incineration plants have contributed to the contamination of cities by releasing cadmium in the combustion of plastic refuse. Despite improvements in pollution control technology, a wave of cadmium pollution has swept over Japan during the past 25 years.

The Japanese government initiated measures to combat cadmium pollution in May 1968 by setting provisional standards for acceptable cadmium concentrations in water and unpolished rice, and by setting human consumption and industrial discharge levels for the substance. Initially, the maximum concentration of cadmium in unpolished rice was set at 0.4 ppm. In July 1970, however, revision of the Foodstuffs Hygiene Law reset the tolerance at 1 ppm for unpolished rice and 0.9 ppm for polished rice, new criteria triggered by the realization that Japan's extensive cadmium contamination would otherwise render unmarketable huge quantities of the rice crop. As mentioned earlier, a full 25 percent of all farmland surveyed in 1972 could not yield grain able to meet even these relaxed standards.

Debate regarding the relationship of cadmium to itai-itai disease has yet to be stilled.* But greater public awareness of the extent of cadmium pollution has resulted in increased pressures on mining companies and refineries, as exemplified by an April 1972 damage suit calling for compensation of 620 million yen ($2.0 million), filed by over one hundred Gumma Prefecture farmers against the Toho Zinc Company. The plaintiffs are demanding compensation for damage to crops and the environment that have resulted from cadmium and other heavy metals discharged by the company's refinery during the last 30 years of its operations. Protest actions carried out by residents in other areas are forcing mines to reduce the levels of their pollution and finance the purification of farmlands.

4.

While the world watches Japan as a multivariable study in chemical pollution, the Japanese watch the Seto Inland Sea. Factory effluents, untreated sewage,

---

* Kobayashi and Hagino claim that they have discovered victims of the disease in other cadmium contaminated regions of Japan, proving the cause-effect relationship, while other scientists and industry researchers deny it. The Japanese government has refused to recognize any victims outside the Fuchu region until the scientific world reaches a consensus.

and agrochemical runoff have transformed this once crystal clear body of water into a chemical soup. Nets that once hauled in fish renowned for their taste and purity now bring up refuse and plastic, while whatever fish catch materializes is suspect of PCB and mercury contamination. Every year, more and more Inland Sea fishermen abandon their trade and resort to employment in nearby factories. Those who once proudly referred to their waters as "Japan's Marine Treasure House" have bitterly renamed it "Japan's Inland Sewer."

Water quality in the Inland Sea began its sharp decline during the 1960s, proportional to the increases in the population and industrial density on its borders. Although massive investments in the fishing industry during this period modernized fishing technology, the region's total annual catch increased only slightly, while its quality declined. Less desirable species, somehow more pollution-resistant than the more valued species, came to comprise the great bulk of the catch.

The most obvious problem besetting the Inland Sea is its "red tides," rapid proliferations of plankton which turn the color of the water a dirty reddish-brown. Starting in 1965, outbreaks of red tides in the Inland Sea increased rapidly in frequency, extent, and duration. Between 1967 and 1972, the number of annual outbreaks increased almost 3.5 times, and in the eastern region near Osaka the tides developed into a year-long phenomenon.[17] In 1971, fishing losses due to red tides were estimated at one billion yen ($2.8 million). In 1972, damages to the yellowtail fish culture industry alone exceeded 7.1 billion yen ($23 million), as more than 14 million fish died in one week from Japan's worst outbreak of the plankton explosions.*

Huge fishing losses have spurred research into the multi-factor causative mechanism of the tides. The Environment Agency reports that the basic requirements for their outbreak are distinct temperature strata in the water accompanied by minimal vertical circulation, abundant sunlight, and nutritive bases of phosphorous and nitrogen. Within this environment, plankton explosions can be triggered by various possible factors,† causing the population to rise from its normal concentration of less than 10 cells per mil-

---

* Since this species is raised in nets, it is particularly susceptible to the tides; a fisherman's entire stock can be destroyed in a single day, leaving him impoverished—and with no source of compensation, since it is difficult to determine legal responsibility for damages. Nevertheless, in October 1973, a group of yellowtail breeders filed suit against the central government, local governments, and major industrial enterprises in the Tokuyama area, where effluents are suspected to be the causative agents. They accused government of having contributed to the sea's decay by failing to take proper protective measures.

† These include: 1) physical stimulation resulting from a decrease in chlorine due to rain or waters

liliter to as much as 100,000 cells per milliliter, giving the water its characteristic reddish tint. Depending upon the type of plankton, scientists speculate that the microorganisms cause the mass fish deaths in one of two ways: either they suffocate the fish by clogging their gills or by releasing toxins; or they may create oxygen-deficient or other toxic conditions simply by their massive presence after decomposition.

Between 1965 and 1970, industrial wastes discharged into the Inland Sea increased from 9.7 to 14.7 billion tons annually and urban sewage reached 2.3 billion tons. In addition, during 1972, 220 tons of nitrogen and 10 tons of phosphorous poured in daily. This enrichment of the sea's nutritive base, known as eutrophication, is one of the necessary conditions for the tides' outbreak. Even if eutrophication could be halted, however, the Environment Agency is pessimistic about restoring the Inland Sea to its former state, for eutrophication resembles the accumulation of PCBs: neither is easily reversible.

Deterioration of the Inland Sea's water quality has brought with it an increasing number of deformed sea creatures. Because of their twisted backbones and ugly cancer-like protrusions, these creatures are referred to as "ghost fish." Fishermen tend to oppose efforts aimed at investigating the phenomenon because of the panic that the results of such an investigation might provoke. Some, after cutting off abnormal growths, have managed to market "ghost fish," for once trimmed and filleted, it is impossible to distinguish them from the normal variety.

These monsters have aroused uneasiness among fishermen, scientists, and the general public alike, and the issue is raised briefly from time to time by the news media. Some authorities fear that the situation in the Inland Sea resembles that noted in Minamata: the appearance in fish, cats, and birds of the first indications of biological aberrations that eventually found their way into humans. Yet, amazingly, research into the causative mechanisms of the cancer-like growths and genetic defects in fish species has barely begun. One MHW official explained that the deformities in question pose a particularly complex problem because of the many different causative factors that may be responsible. Critics of the ministry's attitude fear that if the government follows precedents set in other cases, support of research will come only after it is too late.

---

discharged from rivers, an increase in the plankton's absorption of certain chemical substances, or an increase in the supply of stimulants brought by river waters; 2) the enhancement of spore germination due to lack of oxygen at the bottom of the sea, or the dissolving and mixing of stimulants; 3) the addition of vitamins such as B1 and B12, trace metals such as iron, cobalt and nickel, pulp mill effluents, and the decomposition and production microorganisms and proteins.[19]

The Great Fish Panic of 1973 hastened the implementation of measures aimed at preventing further decay of the Inland Sea's fisheries. Previously, administrative actions had been obstructed by "sectionalism" among central government ministries, and with no consensus inside the central bureaucracy, it was impossible for it to coordinate the bureaucracies of the eleven prefectures that border on the sea. The public outcry against mercury and PCB contamination in fish during May and June 1973 moved Japan's politicians to overcome their differences and challenge the bureaucracy's sluggishness. The LDP and opposition parties cooperated in drafting the Seto Inland Sea Conservation Act, Japan's first environmental preservation law for a specific area. Although valid for only three years, it included regulations prohibiting new land reclamation and industrial expansion projects. These regulations offer hope for at least checking the tempo of the sea's demise.*

The Great Fish Panic was also a much-needed stimulus to increasing research on mercury and PCB contamination of fish, and the results of newly undertaken studies began to emerge in the fall of 1973. The Environment Agency reported that most of the fish from nine areas suspected of mercury contamination fell below the danger level set in June: only fish coming from Minamata Bay (all species), Tokuyama Bay in the Inland Sea (four species), and Yatsushiro Sea to the west of Kumamoto Prefecture (one species) exceeded the limits; local governments of these three areas were "advised" to ban fishing. A study by the National Institute of Public Health further showed that only one out of 895 families surveyed exceeded the daily provisional standard for PCB intake set at 250 micrograms per person. Finally, in March 1974, the Environment Agency's Experts Committee on Mercury Pollution concluded, after careful examination, that cases suspected of being new victims of Minamata disease were not. In sum, scientific evidence, channeled through the government bureaucracy, seemed to justify a return to relative calm—at least for the time being.

---

* The rupture in December 1974 of a huge oil storage tank at the Mizushima industrial complex in the city of Kurashiki has added immeasurably to the area's troubles. Some 50,000 barrels of oil poured into the Inland Sea, tarring 100 miles of scenic coastline and causing losses to the fishing and edible seaweed industries of an estimated $40 million. The Mizushima oil *shokku* has aroused increasing opposition to the government's plans for building more storage tanks to maximize reserves for use if Middle Eastern supplies are again cut.

CHAPTER SEVEN

URBAN EXPLOSION

"On a bright spring day
Boatmen go up and down the Sumida River;
And drops from their oars spread like flowers.
To what can I compare this sight?"

—A MEIJI ERA POEM STILL LEARNED
BY JAPANESE SCHOOL CHILDREN

"The Sumida River is a stinking open sewer."

TOKYO FIGHTS POLLUTION
Tokyo Metropolitan Government
March 1971

Urbanization, industrial concentration, and rising affluence have occasioned environmental disruption in almost every major city of the world. Densely populated and eager for prosperity, postwar Japan has known some of the worst dislocations to date. For in its self-propelled transition to a developed state, Japan has grafted modern urban patterns onto a premodern framework. The result has been an exaggeration of the ills besetting the twentieth-century city.

During the first decade of the postwar period, Japan's urban problems were mostly restricted to its larger industrial cities, areas already suffering from the effects of a century of little controlled industrialization. During the 1960s, however, Japanese leaders encouraged the relocation of rural populations to smaller and newer cities in the Pacific industrial belt and oversaw the construction of huge industrial complexes there. While these development policies helped transform the Japanese economy into one of the world's most productive, the rapid concentration of population and industry was not matched by sufficient investments in social overhead capital or industrial waste treatment facilities. Every major Japanese city quickly fell victim to severe urban blight.

Between 1950 and 1970, the percentage of Japanese living in cities with populations greater than 50,000 rose from 33 to 64 percent, while the proportion of the population living in cities of more than 100,000 increased from 25 to 52 percent. In only two decades, therefore, Japan transformed itself from a rural into a predominantly urban society. By 1970, some 70 percent of the Japanese lived in urban areas and approximately one-third were clustered within a 50-kilometer radius of the three huge metropolises of Tokyo, Osaka, and Nagoya, in a combined land area of about one percent of the entire archipelago. The Greater Tokyo Metropolitan Region* alone comprised about 22 million people—almost 21 percent of the total national population—and registered a population density of nearly 8,000 people per square mile.

According to an Economic Planning Agency report issued in 1973, the Tokyo commuting district, despite deteriorating environmental conditions, was continuing to expand in radius and population. It predicted that if this population migration is left unchecked, about one-third of the Japanese population will be concentrated in the capital region by 1985. The report warned that this could create a nightmare of paralyzed urban systems, chronic water and electricity shortages, severe traffic congestion, and choking photochemical smog.

---

* The nomenclature used for the various administrative regions around Tokyo can be quite confusing (see Fig. 2). We have used "Tokyo" or "metropolitan Tokyo" to refer to the Tokyo Metropolitan Government, which includes the 23 central wards, what we call the "ward area" or "Tokyo proper" and used to be the prewar City of Tokyo, plus the suburban counties to the west. The Greater Tokyo Metropolitan Region includes Metropolitan Tokyo and the three neighboring prefectures of Chiba, Kanagawa, and Saitama. This roughly falls within a 50 kilometer radius from Tokyo's central business district. The third major administrative division is the National Capital Region which includes the Greater Tokyo Metropolitan Region plus the four additional prefectures of Yamanashi, Gunma, Tochigi, and Ibaragi. This administrative planning region is approximately enclosed within a 150 kilometer radius from the central business district.

Fig 2. The Capital Region

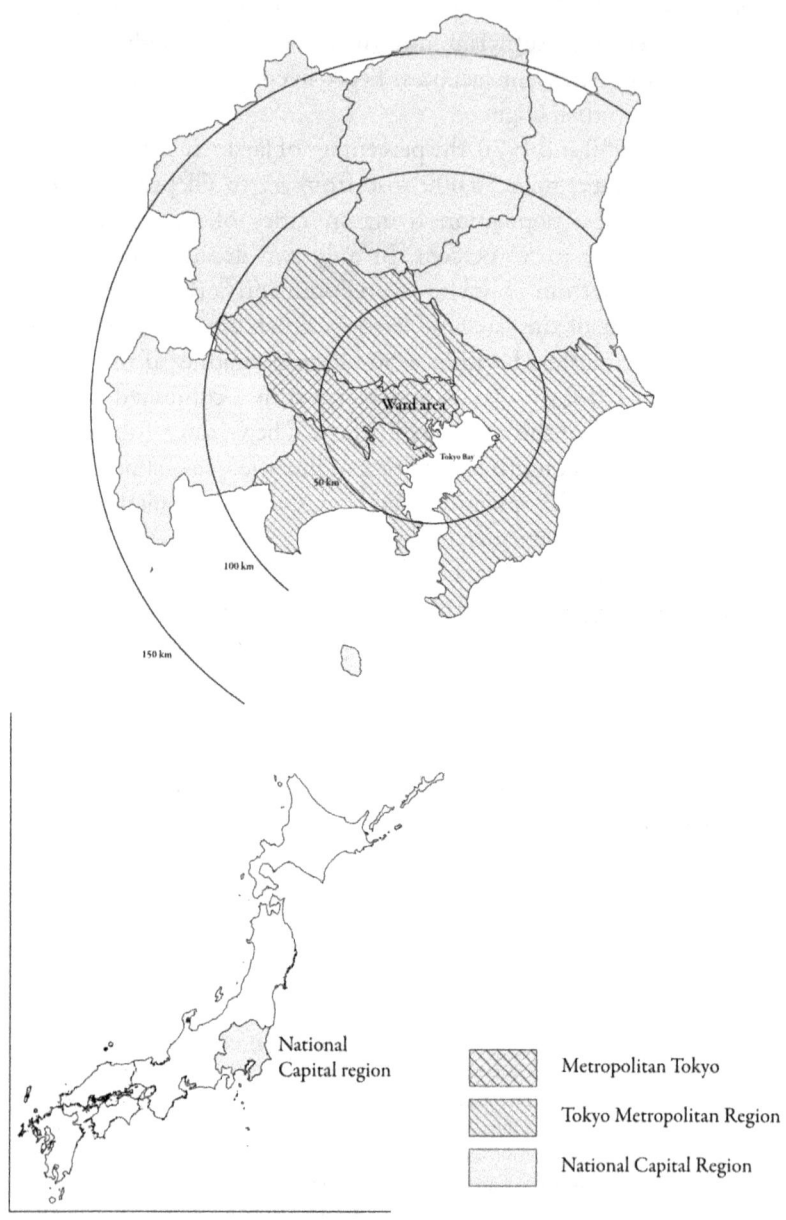

ISLAND OF DREAMS

The severity of Tokyo's problems arises in part from its historical development. A relatively new city, with a history of less than 400 years, Tokyo achieved prominence in 1603, when Ieyasu Tokugawa, Japan's first *shogun*, chose the small fishing village of Edo as his capital. The area grew rapidly, and from the end of the seventeenth to at least the end of the eighteenth century it housed the largest single urban population in the world, surpassing the million mark by around 1800. To provide for military defense, Edo was designed in the style of feudal castle towns, with narrow streets radiating from the central manor in a zigzag pattern. This feudal ground plan has persisted to the present day, to the consternation of most modern city planners.

The insurrectionist samurai who gained control over Japan in the 1867–68 Meiji Restoration retained Edo as their capital, renamed it Tokyo (Eastern Capital) and made it the base of their efforts to centralize and develop the nation. The city grew quickly, encroaching on the surrounding countryside and gradually absorbing outlying districts and towns.

Most of the model industries established by Meiji leaders were located in the nation's capital. Similarly, aware of the importance of maintaining close ties with government leaders, many of Japan's early industrialists located their head offices there. By the turn of the century, private homes and bustling factories clustered together in a disorganized jumble, due to a total disregard of zoning concepts.

Somehow, opportunities to rezone the city in the wake of the Great Kanto Earthquake of 1923 and the firebombings of 1945 were largely missed, and this haphazard commingling of industrial and residential areas has added to the frustrations of modern planners.

The transferral of the Emperor's residence from Kyoto to Edo in 1868 made Tokyo the new spiritual and cultural capital of the nation. Soon, in addition to serving as the managerial nerve center of modern Japan, Tokyo became the home of most of the country's leading universities and research and cultural institutions. Today it is the center of the business, banking, financial, and publishing world, the center of all mass communications media, and the headquarters for all political parties, labor unions, and trade associations. Almost all top Japanese corporations have their headquarters in Tokyo. "It is as if Washington, D.C., New York, Chicago, Philadelphia, Pittsburgh, Boston, and Detroit were rolled into one," writes Chitoshi Yanaga, professor emeritus of political science at Yale University.

> Such a concentration of power is unknown in the United States. To create an analogous situation, it would be necessary to locate

the head offices of America's hundred largest corporations in Washington, D.C., together with their presidents, board chairmen, and directors, many of whom would be related by marriage not only to each other but to influential political leaders and government administrators. Furthermore, these top-level executives would, for the most part, claim the same alma mater, belong to the same country clubs, have ready access to government offices, maintain daily contact with government officials by phone or over the luncheon table, enjoy intimate relations with influential senators and congressmen, and also serve on government advisory bodies and administrative commissions. The impact of this sort of concentration of political, economic and social power can be far-reaching indeed.[1]

Due to this concentration of power and information, almost all important political and economic decisions are made in Tokyo, including those affecting the most remote areas of the country. For people eager to be in the political, economic or social mainstream, living in or near Tokyo is imperative. "Tokyo is like a contagious disease," said one student who came to the capital from the countryside three years ago. "I hated it when I first arrived because it was so dirty and noisy. But now, I can't imagine going back to my native village." A young Tokyo-based salesman tells of a colleague who was transferred from Tokyo to Osaka: "He often telephones me to see what's happening in Tokyo; he says he feels so out of touch with the changes going on in Japan." The total ascendancy of Tokyo is reflected even in the language of the national railway system. Tokyo-bound trains—whether coming from the north or the south—are spoken of as going "up" to Tokyo, while all trains leaving the capital are described as going "down"—to somewhere else.

Tokyo's leadership in all areas of modern Japanese life has resulted in environmental chaos. The problem has been compounded by its continued population and industrial growth. Now that city officials have begun to consider what factors are necessary for a healthy urban environment, many of their belated efforts at redevelopment are frustrated by the shortage of available space and the prevalence of extremely high land prices. Social overhead investments in housing, sewage, and refuse treatment plants, delayed in the past for the sake of economic growth, tend now to be "postponed" because of the difficulties met in acquiring building sites. New houses and apartments are forced to locate within several meters of busy rail lines and highways, refuse treatment plants are being constructed in residential areas, and in some sections of Tokyo and other cities, the world's fastest commercially operating trains whip over the heads of nearby houses once every fifteen minutes, jolting the residents with high levels of noise and vibrations.

One of Tokyo's most pressing problems is its critical housing shortage. According to government statistics for 1968, 810,000 households, nearly one-quarter of all families in metropolitan Tokyo were experiencing "housing difficulties." By 1973, 790,000 Tokyo households were still living under inadequate conditions, with 90 percent of the housing "difficulties" attributed to "overcrowding."

Skyrocketing real estate prices have made it very difficult, if not impossible, for the average citizen to accumulate enough money to buy land or a house of their own. The Japan Real Estate Institute reported in early 1974 that the average detached house within commuting distance of Tokyo cost at least 20 million yen ($72,000). A small two-room apartment with a kitchen and dining area was quoted at more than 10 million yen ($36,000), a sum equal to an average wage earner's lifetime savings. While Japan's GNP increased ninefold between 1955 and 1970, the price of land increased an average sixteen-fold, with the highest advances made in the major urban areas of Tokyo, Osaka, and Nagoya. In the first six months of 1973 alone, Tokyo land prices rose in some cases as much as 30 percent. While some Tokyo residential areas (notably the westernmost suburbs) still contain a considerable number of open lots, these are not always for sale. Many landowners prefer to retain ownership of their property as a hedge against inflation, and when they do sell, it is often to real estate agents representing big business. Speculative trends have made land even less available to the average citizen.

One consequence of the high cost of Tokyo real estate, particularly in the 23 ward area of Tokyo proper, is that all available space is utilized intensively. Instead of being used for "unprofitable" parks or recreational areas, open spaces tend to fill up with high-rise apartment dwellings or office buildings. Tokyo's per capita park area, 1.2 square meters, is less than half the national average for Japanese cities, and is far below the goal of 6 square meters set by the Ministry of Construction.

Tokyo's population distribution also reflects intensive land use patterns. Tokyo proper is composed of relatively low buildings, densely packed and evenly distributed. The result is that crowded conditions are felt everywhere to be a pressing part of daily life.

The Tokyo land situation has forced urban planners to consider two alternative solutions to the housing crisis: building "up" high-rise apartments, or building "out" to the suburbs. Both directions are now being taken, but rather than solving the basic problem of inadequate housing, they are creating new, equally difficult ones. High-rise dwellings, although an apparently logical solution to Tokyo's housing shortage, have encountered two formidable obstacles. Ward governments have vigorously opposed metropolitan government plans to build multistoried housing units in their midst because they believe that a new influx of residents would only add to the existing overload on public facilities. Local ward budgets, they say, cannot afford the land necessary for building additional schools and hospitals. Moreover, past experience has taught the skeptical citizen that housing associations and construction companies often neglect the qualitative aspects of new apartment dwellings and, in some cases, fail to provide adequate sewage facilities.

The massive presence of such high-rise buildings poses a problem in itself. Since even in Tokyo proper the average building is less than two stories high, taller buildings inevitably block the flow of sunlight to preexisting homes. Sunlight is particularly important to the Japanese because of the lack of central heating facilities in most homes, combined with Japan's cold, damp winters. Previously sun-filled rooms are cast into darkness, destroying the traditionally valued interplay between internal and external living environments. This lack of sunlight brings about a sharp depreciation of land values (50–70 percent) and limits the field of prospective buyers. Underscoring the importance to the Japanese of the natural asset of sunlight, newspaper advertisements placed by construction companies and real estate agencies emphasize "good sunlight" as one of their main selling points!

Since the late 1960s, more and more Tokyoites have refused to live in the cold shadow of concrete. Legal proceedings have been initiated both to gain compensation for the loss of sunlight and to prevent the erection of new buildings. In November 1970, residents' groups from 24 regions of the Tokyo area united to form the Construction Kogai Countermeasures League, and within two years the number of participating groups increased to 520. By late 1972, 19 of the 26 cities within the Greater Tokyo Metropolitan Region had passed ordinances limiting the height of new buildings. In July 1972, the metropolitan government established a Sunlight Consultation Office, and in less than two and a half months, Tokyo residents had filed 368 complaints to the new agency, equaling the total number of complaints received during the entire previous year. The movement to protect the right to sunlight climaxed in June 1972, when the Supreme Court ruled that "a home's sunlight and ventilation are essential living requirements for a comfortable and healthy life."[2]

Despite these protests and the laws recently enacted by constituent city governments, most of metropolitan Tokyo's newest buildings continue to grow in height. The percentage of newly constructed buildings higher than six stories increased from 22.2 percent in 1968 to 32 percent in 1970, while the national average was still below 10 percent. In a report entitled "Tokyo and New York in the 1970s," Ryohei Kakumoto, one of Japan's foremost transportation experts, soundly criticized Tokyo's imitation of New York's design:

> Precisely when New York is rethinking its whole urban planning philosophy, Tokyo has now become absorbed in following measures similar to those taken by New York planners of the past. For example, city planners in Tokyo are allowing unlimited construction of high-rise buildings, as long as the ratio of floor space to land is maintained in accordance with municipal regulations. The outcome of this is clear: small empty lots will appear throughout the city with no other function than to satisfy this ratio requirement: dismal urban land spaces and traffic congestion will reduce further the livability of the city. What is most needed is to plan urban growth from a holistic point of view.[3]

The exodus to Tokyo's suburbs has also created a multitude of new problems. Skyrocketing land values in the city have contributed to rapid population growth in outlying cities and the surrounding prefectures of Saitama, Chiba, and Kanagawa. From 1965 through 1970, these three prefectures led the country in population increase, with total increments amounting to a five-year average of 25 percent for each. The 23 wards of Tokyo proper experienced a population increase of only 5 percent. The suburban communities sprouting up in Tokyo's neighboring regions, however, are only "bedroom towns," for the vast majority of their residents remain tied to Tokyo where, in work or school, their first loyalties lie.

Morning and evening, trains connecting these communities to downtown Tokyo are crammed with commuters, many of whom travel up to two hours each way in coaches filled to two or three times their intended capacity. Futurologist Hidetoshi Kato, director of Japan's Communications Design Institute, warns that these abnormal crowding conditions could permanently damage the Japanese psyche by giving rise to a "cocooning" response. Animals and humans exposed to overcrowded environments, Kato writes, tend to wrap themselves in "psychological and spatial cocoons."

> Millions of commuters ride trains as crowded as nineteenth-century slave ships but show no signs of mutiny. Even with some-

one's newspaper shoved in their face and someone's elbow jammed in their side, they remain resigned and indifferent.

That indifference is a danger sign... It shows that Japanese have unconsciously already begun a psychological defense against overcrowding. Withdrawal and passive tolerance of overcrowding are part of the cocooning syndrome that dehumanizes people, and... can lead to greater disruption of social behavior.[4]

One response to the inhuman overcrowding in public transport systems is the rise in popularity of the private motor car for commuting from the suburbs. Although the desire to reduce traveling time and increase personal convenience—as well as the new thrill of mobility provided by one's own car—have contributed to the automobile's popularity, the motor car's role as a "spatial cocoon" may well be an added incentive for driving into Tokyo. The addition of commuter automobiles to the 2.34 million private motor vehicles owned by central Tokyo residents has worsened air pollution and transformed the city into a mass of traffic jams.

2.

By the end of the 1960s, criticism of Japan's "automobiles first" policy was beginning to gain increasing popular support. Urbanites and the news media took to attacking the automobile for the carbon monoxide, nitrogen oxides, hydrocarbons, and lead spewed forth in its exhaust fumes and indicted it for contributing to outbreaks of photochemical smog. In addition, angry voices were raised against the automobile's invasion of Japan's narrow living space, bringing with it dirt, noise, vibration, obstruction of public transport, psychological tension, and traffic deaths. The construction of overhead expressways, roads, parking lots, and garages came under active opposition because of the loss of sunlight, the sacrifice of green areas, and the displacement of children's playgrounds.

Nevertheless, production and sales of automobiles continued to boom. Between 1961 and 1971, the number of four-wheeled vehicles in use increased more than tenfold, while the production of passenger cars for domestic consumption increased twentyfold and that for export an amazing hundredfold. Between 1968 and 1972, the number of persons per passenger vehicle dropped from 19.5 to 8.6, indicating a more than twofold jump in car ownership in four years. By 1973, 22 million motor vehicles clogged the roads, with 400,000 more being added each month. With 480 registered vehicles per square mile, or roughly eight times the concentration of motor vehicles in the United States, Japan ranked first in the world in terms of motor vehicle density. Still, auto industry spokesmen continue to justify expansion of the domestic car market by pointing to the disparity in terms of number of persons per car in Japan versus the United States. It is clear from density considerations, however, that Japan has reached the point of automotive saturation.

Since 1963, the Japanese government has supported a major program of highway construction to keep pace with the rapid increase in the number of motor vehicles rolling off the nation's assembly lines. By 1970, Japan had 2.5 kilometers of road per square kilometer of area, a density ratio second only to that of Belgium. During fiscal 1972, 365 kilometers of expressway were opened, raising the total length of such highways (1,348 km) to the present levels of Great Britain (1,232 km) and France (1,538 km). Nevertheless, the government announced in April 1973 that, as part of its Basic Economic and Social Program for Constructing a Dynamic Welfare Society, it plans to construct an additional 10,000 kilometers of superhighways by 1985. This equals nearly one-quarter the total length of expressways in the United States as of 1969, in a country roughly the size of California!

Postwar government support of the automotive sector has made the industry a major pillar of the nation's economy. Originally export-oriented, the automobile industry has spurred the expansion of the entire economy by its reliance upon a multitude of related activities: the importing and processing of raw materials,* the construction industry, production subcontractors, and the spare-part industry, among others. The recent increase in the number of drivers has engendered a booming service industry of driving schools, automobile accessory shops, and roadside restaurants and motels. Thus, the Japanese economy, like its American model, now depends on "more cars" for continued growth.

It is urban areas which have been most damaged by the marriage of modern Japanese society to the automobile. By 1970, more than 2 million motor vehicles were registered in Tokyo. While this was only slightly more than the ratio of vehicles-to-population boasted by New York City (4.9 and 4.5, respectively), an average of only 12.5 percent of the land area in the 23 wards of Tokyo was used for streets, as compared with 30 percent in New York. Further complicating Tokyo's traffic problems (and those of Japan as a whole) is the fact that narrow roadways were once used almost exclusively for walking and bicycling. Until the reconstruction of Japanese cities after World

---

* Automobile manufacture absorbs 52 percent of all rubber imports, 67 percent of all spring manufacture, 62 percent of all aluminum die-casts, and 69 percent of all metal alloy production.

War II, sidewalks were almost nonexistent. Even in present-day Tokyo, the great majority of city streets do not distinguish between lanes for pedestrians and for motor traffic. As more and more cars and trucks race through the city's narrow streets, traffic accidents rise. Pedestrians are forced to compete with machines for the existing space, and annual statistics on death and injury in the capital indicate only too clearly who loses.

The Tokyo metropolitan government has responded to problems of urban traffic congestion by increasing expenditures to improve the capital's roads and keep the traffic moving. The governments of Tokyo and other cities have undertaken expensive projects of building pedestrian overpasses across busy thoroughfares. But building more roads and pedestrian bridges does not promise to solve the traffic problem. When road space is doubled, the number of automobiles tends to increase fourfold, while overall traffic problems multiply by a factor of eight![5] Thus, in Japan's cities the automobile's original value—that of providing rapid, convenient door-to-door service—is greatly diluted: the suburban commuter who abandoned public transport to save 15 minutes by driving to work now often finds that traffic congestion and parking problems deprive him of his savings—although of course his car may still afford him the benefits of a "psychological and spatial cocoon." Perhaps as an index of the importance of this latter benefit, the number of automobile commuters continues to rise.

While automobiles aimed at foreign markets have been outfitted with exhaust control equipment in order to meet standards set by other nations, cars manufactured in Japan for domestic consumption were unencumbered with such devices until September 1970. Since 1973, mass emission controls have been enforced on carbon monoxide, hydrocarbons, and nitrogen oxides, and emission regulations are slated to be tightened after 1975.* Although Japan had a slow start in regulating automobile exhaust gases, the present standards are about as strict as those currently enforced in the United States. Still, the earlier rapid growth of cars in Tokyo without adequate emission con-

---

* On December 2, 1974, the Environment Agency succumbed to the arguments of the automobile industry and postponed for two years the implementation of controls on auto emissions which would have cut the permissible level of nitrogen oxides to 0. 25 grams per vehicle from fiscal 1976. The agency has, however, stated its intention to give preferential tax treatment to low-pollution cars and increase taxes on old cars. Citizen groups, particularly in areas suffering from attacks of photochemical smog, have been extremely critical of the decision and have expressed the hope that the government will impose stricter levels than those proposed (0.6 grams for cars under 1 ton and 0.85 for larger cars). They have also criticized the auto industry for making insufficient efforts to develop new technology, noting that Toyo Kogyo, one of Japan's largest auto manufacturers, has already announced that cars could be manufactured that would emit only 0.4 grams of nitrogen oxides.[6]

trols contributed to a significant deterioration in the city's air quality and to the generation of its photochemical smog.

In the summer of 1967, a downtown Tokyo monitoring station detected the presence of photochemical oxidants at concentrations high enough to bleach or spot various species of vegetation. But it wasn't until three years later, on July 18, 1970, that Tokyo's photochemical air pollution was generally acknowledged to be a serious problem. In the early predawn hours of that summer day, a thick fog rolled over the city. During the course of twenty-four hours, over 6,000 people in 13 Tokyo wards and 12 suburban cities complained of unusual attacks of sore eyes, sore throats, and difficulty in breathing; eight girls exercising in a high school playground fell unconscious and required several days' hospitalization; several species of trees shed or underwent bleaching of their leaves.

The dreadful smog hung over Tokyo for two more days, panicking the city's residents and disconcerting government officials. The head of the Institute for Environmental Protection Research announced that if the air pollution continued to worsen, Tokyoites "would have to wear gas masks when going out."[7] The metropolitan government responded by dividing Tokyo into four districts and setting up three more oxidant monitoring stations. When the hourly average of oxidants exceeded 0.15 ppm, the government would issue a "warning"; when it reached 0.3 ppm, it would sound an "alarm" calling for factories to lessen sulfur emissions, schools to cease outdoor exercises, and citizens to report to the nearest health center when irritation of the eyes or throat was felt. The public was advised to refrain from driving.

The annual number of Tokyo's photochemical smog victims increased nearly threefold between fiscal 1970 and fiscal 1971, jumping from 10,064 to 28,223 . In neighboring Kanagawa Prefecture, home of the Kawasaki heavy industry belt, the rise was twentyfold, from 638 to 13,138 . Similar outbreaks of photochemical smog began to occur throughout the country, mainly in large urban and industrialized regions. Environment Agency statistics disclosed that automobile exhaust was the main source of the hydrocarbons and nitrogen oxides giving rise to smog in the Tokyo Bay area. During the years 1960–1970, automobile hydrocarbon emissions increased threefold, while the emission of nitrogen oxides rose fivefold. In 1970, 231,800 tons of hydrocarbons and 173 tons of nitrogen oxides were spewed into Tokyo's atmosphere by automobiles alone. Nearby petroleum refineries added to the total of the former, while power stations and industrial installations contributed handsomely to the latter. The Environmental Agency predicts that the total volume of both pollutants will continue to increase in the Tokyo Bay area as the number of motor vehicles grows and industrial plants expand. Given present policies, therefore, photochemical smog conditions can be expected to worsen.

In the early summer of 1972, frequent and lengthy attacks of the smog again incited widespread protest, and Tokyo's governor Ryokichi Minobe was pressured into considering the implementation of measures to reduce the number of automobiles in the city. The government requested suburbanites to refrain from commuting to work by private car and instituted stringent parking regulations, while expanding school zones and encouraging all city officials to use public transport (at least during periods of heavy smog alert). Although a later survey indicated that these requests and the stricter enforcement of parking regulations reduced the volume of traffic somewhat, the decreased flow did not abate smog outbreaks. On the contrary, they increased both in frequency and in terms of the area they affected throughout the remainder of 1972 and the summer of 1973.

In addition to its air pollution problems, private car congestion paralyzes public bus transportation. On an average day (7:30 A.M. to 7:30 P.M.) in 1972, according to police statistics, serious traffic paralysis in different parts of the city lasted for a total of 783 hours, more than three times the average recorded in 1968. Furthermore, between 1968 and 1972, the average length of Tokyo traffic jams was said to have increased greatly. Urban bus traffic has slowed to a crawl along many routes, plunging bus companies deep into debt as increasing numbers of passengers turn to private automobiles.

Traffic congestion has also contributed to the streetcar's gradual disappearance from Tokyo and other cities. Japan's oldest form of mass transit, the streetcar reached a peak of performance in the early 1960s, after which, paralleling the surge in private car ownership, it gradually fell into relative disuse. In 1973, streetcars were still operating in ten cities, but only those in Nagasaki and Hiroshima were running in the black.* The city of Kyoto possesses an extensive network of streetcar lines which the city administration has, nevertheless, been trying to remove for several years, due to large deficits. Such action has been delayed, however, by opposition from residents who claim that streetcars are not subject to traffic jams and harmonize better than cars with the traditional atmosphere of Japan's former capital.

While the city of Kyoto has been reluctant to preserve its streetcars, it has been having second thoughts about automobiles as well. Kyoto's progressive

---

* Their successes were due largely to ordinances banning automobile traffic from the tracks, to active attempts to reduce costs, and to advertising aimed at increasing the number of passengers carried.

mayor, Motoki Funabashi, took a drastic step on November 5, 1973, by declaring that Japanese tourists arriving in private cars would no longer be welcome there. Similar restrictive moves are being considered in Kamakura and Nara, two other historic tourist centers. Several shopping districts in downtown Tokyo and elsewhere have begun to ban all motor vehicles on Sundays (Japan's major shopping day), and the resulting "pedestrian paradises" have met with widespread approval.

There is some evidence, though, that even before such measures were instituted, automobile use per owner was beginning to decline. The Tax Administration Agency has calculated on the basis of fuel consumption figures that the average Japanese car owner used his vehicle 42 percent less in fiscal 1972 than he did ten years earlier.[8] For the private car user, congestion and rising operating costs have apparently begun to outweigh at least some of the advantages. More and more cars have become mere status symbols, waxed, polished, and taken out for "exercise" once or twice a week.

Despite general recognition of the negative impact exerted by automobiles on the urban environment, the public appears unwilling to surrender its automotive prerogatives. This was stunningly demonstrated during the oil crisis of 1973. While European and Americans were enduring strict curbs on Sunday driving, the Japanese were still crowding the highways. An acquaintance employed as a reporter for a national newspaper suggested to her colleagues that they run a campaign against private car use. But her managing editor refused the idea, saying that since the reporter and her husband had no children, she could never understand the importance of the "family Sunday drive." If this opinion-maker's attitude is any gauge, therefore, the public will in all likelihood continue to resist the imposition of strict governmental controls.

3.

In feudal times, the right to own "luxury items" was granted to a privileged few. After the Meiji Restoration, military and industrial priorities preempted investment in improved living standards, leaving the vast majority of Japanese in a state of relative poverty. The Great Depression of the 1930s, the experiences of the Second World War, and more recently the efforts to recover from wartime devastation required personal sacrifice from all. But military defeat cut the spiritual bond tying the individual to the Emperor and, in this sense, secularized the act of labor. Defeat, followed by American Occupation Forces' indoctrination, oriented the Japanese toward renewed material prowess as a nation and the acquisition of personal wealth as individuals.

Paralleling productivity, average per capita income skyrocketed from $123 in 1950 to $1,658 in 1970, sparking an explosion of consumerism. The consumer revolution first began about 1953. Fueled by steadily rising personal income, it snowballed into a tidal wave that has transformed the nation's traditional life style. The Japanese availed themselves of the full buying power of their incomes during the 1960s. Between 1958 and 1972, the percentage of households owning black-and-white television sets rose from 15.9 to 75.1 percent;* refrigerators from 5.5 to 93.5 percent; and washing machines from 29.3 to 96.2 percent. For most, this was the first taste of "modern" material amenities. Prodded by intensive advertising campaigns, the public kept buying and learned to like it.

A domestic mass-consumption society was the logical consequence of a mass-production industrial base. But its emergence required that traditional Japanese frugality give way to the "rationality" of planned obsolescence and the economic patriotism of the "throwaway" culture. And give way it did. It quickly became more economical to buy a new product than to search for and pay a skilled repairman to restore an old one. By 1970, the Japanese scene had come so close to resembling America's that even products in good working order were discarded and replaced with new, "improved" versions. But as manufacturers continued to place new products on the market, and as consumers continued to purchase them, immense quantities of refuse began to accumulate.

Frugality was also abandoned by the owners and managers of Japanese industry. When the nation entered its period of rapid growth, imported resources were available and relatively inexpensive; industrial users had little incentive to recycle materials or reuse their wastes. Industry made few moves to develop treatment facilities for factory effluents, much less to channel precious capital into research and development of recycling techniques. The aluminum industry, for example, extracted usable ore from imported bauxite, then dumped the remainder—about three-fourths of the initial volume—into the ocean, the wastes coming to be known as "red mud." Sludge generated by the plating industry and containing chrome, lead, copper, and zinc was also discarded, with no thought given to retrieving the metals. In their drive to produce goods at the lowest cost, Japanese industrialists, like those elsewhere, assumed air and water to be "free commodities" to be used and contaminated at will; wastes were disposed of with maximum cost-efficiency, given the technology then available.

---

* Ownership peaked in 1965 at 95 percent, then fell as color television ownership rapidly rose from 0.4 percent in 1966 to 65 percent in 1972.[9]

Naturally, Tokyo set the pace for Japan's new "throughput" economy. During the years 1960–1970, the amount of garbage generated in Tokyo increased threefold. By 1968, refuse collected from Tokyo's 23 wards accounted for 16 percent of the nation's daily garbage production of 62,000 tons, although Tokyo's population comprised only 11 percent of the nation's total. Furthermore, thanks to the shortened lives of appliances and rising purchasing power, bulk wastes discarded by Tokyoites between 1961 and 1970 increased from 41,000 to 193,000 tons. By 1972, the capital was producing 13,000 tons of wastes daily, which, if hauled by one-ton trucks traveling 40 kph and spaced 20 meters apart, would stretch the line of garbage trucks for 314 kilometers. According to the metropolitan government, the flow of goods and materials into Tokyo is four times greater than the outflow, and it predicts this gap will widen. Sooner or later, most of these goods end up as refuse, creating an unwieldy problem for the municipal government.

Most of Tokyo's refuse is used in land reclamation or landfill, or it is disposed of by incineration. Although landfill and reclamation were the main means of disposal during the early years of economic development, by 1970 the volume of garbage incinerated had increased eightfold over the 1961 level and comprised over half of the total volume of garbage disposed. The landfill system offers the advantages of a relatively simple technology which can dispose of large amounts of garbage at relatively low cost. On the other hand, it can pollute surrounding areas, and therefore requires that sites be selected with extreme care. Again, some varieties of refuse limit the uses to which reclaimed land can be put. While most organic matter decomposes, for example, plastics retain their original form and can weaken land foundations.

The shores of Tokyo Bay constitute the only space available for reclamation in the capital. Between 1966 and 1971, some 10 million tons of garbage were dumped into a section of the bay known as Site No. 15, or more popularly, as Island of Dreams; an additional 273,000 square meters along the coast, an area called New Island of Dreams, was completely filled in by the end of 1973; and New New Island of Dreams, a third plot—and the last available—is expected to be filled by 1976.

In early 1974, the *Japan Times* reported, several firms from Taiwan and Korea approached the Tokyo metropolitan government with the unusual offer to buy up some of the dreams discarded in Tokyo Bay. The businessmen hoped to use the waste plastic, iron, and steel for producing handicraft items in their home countries. The metropolitan government is said to be considering the deal, which would signal the emergence of a new Japanese export item.

Coastal landfill requires the transport of garbage from relatively distant parts of the city. Each day in Tokyo, over 5,000 garbage trucks on their way to the reclamation site pass through socioeconomically depressed Koto Ward, plaguing its residents with traffic jams, stench, noise, hordes of flies, and torrents of scattered litter. Trucks coming from such areas as Suginami Ward in the west must travel nearly 25 kilometers to reach the site, a journey that can take an hour and a half in congested traffic. To prepare for eventual restrictions on land reclamation and reduce the financial and social costs of transporting refuse across the city, the metropolitan government has proposed that by 1975 each ward become self-sufficient in disposing of its own garbage—mainly through incineration. In 1967, the Tokyo government began searching for a suitable incinerator site in Suginami Ward. But persistent opposition by Suginami's middle- and upper-class residents caused repeated delays. Even with delicate negotiations underway, however, some 620 tons of their garbage continued to pass *daily* through Koto Ward. Finally, the residents of Koto decided that they would no longer tolerate the exploitation of their living environment by the wealthier residents of the city. Antagonism between the two wards flared into emotional confrontations, turning the Tokyo metropolitan government's widely publicized "war on garbage" into a resident's "garbage war." Twice in 1973, the Koto Ward Assembly declared boycotts against garbage trucks coming from Suginami and lifted them only after the intervention of metropolitan governor Minobe. But despite metropolitan government assurances that Suginami's incineration facilities would be modern and nonpolluting and that heat generated by the incinerator would be used to warm a municipal swimming pool and other community facilities, Suginami's residents have remained adamant in their opposition.

There are good reasons for Suginami's opposition to the project. Although garbage disposal by incineration increased eightfold in Tokyo between 1961 and 1970, the practice suffers from a number of chronic problems. First, there are the problems posed by plastics, which comprise 8 to 10 percent of Tokyo's refuse by volume. The intense heat required for their combustion tends to wear down facilities, while the minute amounts of cadmium they contain are released into the local environment. In addition, PCBs contained in incinerated paper and plastic wastes are discharged into the air virtually intact. Finally, the presence of municipal garbage and waste facilities depresses land values while nearby landowners go uncompensated.

For these reasons, residents of many wards are reluctant to see an incinerator go up in their neighborhood. Even if the plant itself were improved, they insist, the objectionable noise and smell that accompany the constant flow of garbage trucks to and from the site would be unavoidable. To deal with these problems the metropolitan government is investigating the possibility of deodorizing garbage trucks with aromatic sprays.* Suginami Ward residents, meanwhile, remain opposed to construction of the incinerator, despite the fact that the general public has sided with the people of Koto Ward and the news media have repeatedly criticized them for their "selfish" attitude. The Suginami matter has thus become a test case for the metropolitan government's goal of every ward's burning its own trash.†

Even if incinerators were constructed throughout the city, however, the fundamental problem in Tokyo and Japan as a whole would remain unsolved. Efforts have so far been directed primarily at trying to solve the problem of *disposal*; the continued—and growing—generation of waste is assumed. Instead of placing top priority on reducing waste and developing comprehensive recycling systems, the metropolitan government has tended to concentrate on finding new coastal areas that can be reclaimed, and on convincing citizens of the necessity of installing huge incinerators in their midst. Perhaps the epitome of this trend is the government's plan to locate an enormous incinerator in the heart of Shinjuku Ward, the area earmarked to be the new center of Japan's capital. These are stop-gap measures, at best.

Were the volume of wastes generated by a society a reliable indicator of the level of its affluence, all doubts would vanish regarding Japan's entry into the club of elite consumer nations. According to the Environment Agency, the total volume of wastes produced in Japan since 1965 has increased at a rate of approximately 11 percent a year, paralleling the rise in the nation's GNP. The Environment Agency further predicts that by 1975, Japan will be creating garbage at a daily rate of 1.2 kg per person, for a yearly national total of well over 45 million tons.

A truly effective solution to the garbage problem may require of the Japanese, as of the inhabitants of other industrial nations, a surrender of some newly acquired tastes and values in favor of a more traditional frugality and degree of self-sacrifice.

---

* One municipality in Aichi Prefecture has already adopted such a system: its garbage now smells like peppermint, and trucks that haul it blare happy music. The tactic has met a mixed reaction.[10]

† The eight-year-long "garbage war" came to an end on November 25, 1974, in an out-of-court agreement reached between the Tokyo Metropolitan Government and the residents of Suginami. The agreement—the first of its kind—provides for local participation in the plant's administration. Tight restrictions on dust, gases, and waste water were set, based on total amounts discharged as well as ppm density. If pollutants exceed levels set, local residents can call for suspension of plant operation or operation at a reduced rate. The plant will be completed by 1977.[11]

4.

Tokyo's befouled air has given rise to an endless series of anecdotes, many of which are true. There is the one about the woman who lived in the countryside several hours north of the city. Traveling to the capital for the first time in a half-dozen years, she was shocked to see the sky suddenly darken, a signal she took as a portent of rain. Since atmospheric conditions over the metropolis usually moved quickly to the north during the warmer months, she telephoned her daughter to remove the day's laundry from the line. The punchline, of course, is that there was no rain, for while Tokyo's skies are often foreboding, it is not necessarily rain that is in the offing. It is said that young schoolchildren, born and reared in Tokyo, now paint the sky gray in their pictures and are pleasantly disoriented when, visiting the countryside, they can see the heavens full of stars at night. United States Senator Edmund Muskie, interviewed by reporters in July of 1973, commented dryly on the city's air: "It certainly lives up to its reputation."[12]

Until 1955, the principal sources of Tokyo's air pollution were boilers and winter heating facilities. Conditions worsened as the number of local factories and their production output increased and as the economy shifted from coal to heavy oil for its fuel requirements. The major contaminants thrown off during the combustion of coal were particulate matter and sulfur dioxide. During the early 1960s, the consumption of heavy oil surpassed that of coal and the amount of soot in the air decreased, but sulfur dioxide concentrations increased rapidly. By 1964, when the number of motor vehicles in the city exceeded the one million mark, automobile exhaust fumes were complicating the problem. Confirmation in 1967 of the presence of photochemical oxidants revealed a further hazard, which has increased in severity every year since.

The concentration of sulfur dioxide in Tokyo's air, found to be directly related to the incidence of respiratory diseases, increased during the years 1964–1967, but has since then gradually declined. Factory smokestacks are its main source, and its highest concentrations are found along the borders of Tokyo Bay, in the industrial zones along the Sumida and Arakawa rivers, and over the central commercial and business districts of the city. A major portion of Tokyo's sulfur oxides are blown into the city proper from the high smokestacks of factories located in Kawasaki and Yokohama. The relief of intense "spot-source" pollution by means of higher stacks in these nearby industrial areas has thus extended the overall area affected. Tokyo metropolitan and Kanagawa prefectural government cooperation on remedial action is hard to achieve because of bureaucratic obstacles and conflicting interests.

In August 1973, a group of researchers reported to the Environment Agency that concentrations of metallic dust, in some cases several hundred times greater than those deemed acceptable, were detected in the air over Tokyo, Osaka, and other major cities. The dusts included nickel, cadmium, chrome, iron, copper, manganese, zinc, lead, titanium, and aluminum residues, all of which have been found to be carcinogenic in humans if inhaled in excessive amounts. Alarmingly high concentrations of more than 10 metals were detected near Tokyo's Haneda Airport and in the air over other portions of Tokyo's Ota Ward, and residents in these areas, the report noted, were known to suffer an exceptionally high rate of respiratory ailments. The high concentrations of metallic substances have been attributed to daily household and industrial processes, principally fossil fuel combustion, metal refining, and chemical plant and incinerator wastes.[13]

Dr. Takeo Suzuki of the National Institute of Public Health points out that although the causal relationship between these suspended particles and human illness has yet to be conclusively affirmed, the likelihood of a correlation is very strong. Indications are that a correlation also exists between traffic congestion and the incidence of cancer due to human inhalation of carcinogenic 3-4 benzyprene emitted in automobile exhaust fumes. A joint survey conducted by six ward health offices in Tokyo has disclosed that a high incidence of lung cancer was found in three areas characterized by excessively heavy traffic. As a result, Japanese environmental experts are urging that more detailed studies of possible correlations between exhaust fumes and the incidence of cancer be carried out.

The 1973 National Environmental White Paper reported a total of 8,737 "certified" air pollution victims throughout the nation who were suffering from obstructive respiratory ailments such as chronic bronchitis, asthma, asthmatic bronchitis, and pulmonary edema. Since enactment in December 1969 of the Law Concerning Special Measures for the Relief of Pollution Related Patients, the number of certified victims (who are eligible for government compensation) has rapidly risen, and each year the Environment Agency recognizes several new "heavily polluted districts" (there were ten in 1973). Although Tokyo has yet to be classified by the national government as a heavily polluted district, the metropolitan government established its own victim certification system and by March 1974 had designated almost 14,000 official victims.* This is in addition to the nearly 50,000 Tokyo residents who reported in as temporarily disabled by photochemical smog during the period 1970–72.

---

* Only minors (under 18 years of age) are eligible for this classification.

Humans and animals are not the only forms of life being slowly smothered by Tokyo's air. A disturbing report issued in 1972 by the Resources Council of the Science and Technology Agency warns Tokyoites that, if air quality continues to deteriorate at the present rate, most of the city's plant life may disappear within fifty years. Tokyo's rapid urbanization has already destroyed forests that once existed within metropolitan district limits. Green areas decreased from 80 percent of total land in 1932 to a mere 30 percent in 1965, and the trend continues. This sacrifice of plant life, which serves to purify the air, in favor of dwellings, roads, and office buildings has contributed inestimably to the "graying" of the city. The Environment Agency has further pointed out that, once man has destroyed natural green areas, it is extremely difficult to restore them to their original condition.

Tokyo has also been in the forefront in the deterioration of inland and coastal waters. Pollution of Tokyo's Edo River by the Honshu Paper Company gave rise as early as 1958 to violent protests by local fishermen, and these protests served to hasten the enactment of Japan's first laws aimed at water pollution control.* Unfortunately, these ordinances were never strictly enforced (in Tokyo or elsewhere) and the quality of Japan's rivers rapidly worsened. Between the years 1962 and 1969, industrial consumption of Japan's total water supply increased from 35 to 50 percent, causing a sharp intensification of the effluent burden. And the unrelieved concentration of industrial enterprises in Japan's cities has naturally speeded the degradation of urban waterways. In 1971, metropolitan Tokyo boasted the presence of 83,000 factories, including such heavy polluters as food-processing facilities (4,201), paper pulp and paper producers (3,414), chemical plants (1,078), and metal products manufacturers (14,150).

By the early 1970s, one of Tokyo's most contaminated waterways was the Sumida River.† Over the last twenty years, industrial and household wastes have transformed this once picturesque waterway from a source of poetry into a source of depressing pollution reports:

> As a result of the pollution, the famous events which once took place on the river—swimming meets, regattas, and fireworks displays—have vanished. The gases rising from the river corrode metals, blacken copper- and silver-ware, and shorten the life of sewing machines and TV sets. Sometimes they endanger human

---

* See pp. 200–201

† See p. 127

life. Besides offensive odors, the high incidence of respiratory diseases among residents along the river is attributed to its pollution.[14]

Another of Tokyo's major rivers, the Tama, is the site of a huge dam with a water storage capacity of 190 million tons. The dam and river serve as Tokyo's main source of drinking water. The quality of the Tama's water has so deteriorated since 1961, however, that by 1968, the cost of purifying it in its lower reaches was ten to twenty times that of purification in the upper reaches. Consumption has had to be suspended on several occasions due to cyanide contamination traced to metal plating factories located along the Tama's banks. Frequent fish poisonings are on record, and the metropolitan government estimates that, because the Tama is also used for irrigation, its ammonia and nitrate content has contaminated some 2,471 acres of agricultural land in the greater metropolitan area.

The increasing quantity and changing quality of household wastes have also contributed to the degradation of Tokyo's water resources. Although the city's population rose only 5 percent between 1965 and 1970, the volume of household wastes increased a full 30 percent. Other rapidly urbanizing prefectures showed similar tendencies: over the same period, Saitama's population grew 28 percent, but the volume of its household effluents nearly doubled. The popularity of synthetic detergents adds to the burden on water systems by introducing non-biodegradable contaminants into them; huge accumulations of soap bubbles in Tokyo's waterways have become a common sight, not only limiting recreational activities but, in many cases, rendering unusable important sources of drinking water.

Water problems are further exacerbated by the glaring inadequacy of urban sewage treatment systems. Since large-scale sewage facilities, when they exist, have generally been installed only after the construction of new housing, household wastes have often been dumped untreated into nearby rivers and streams. As of 1970, only 21 percent of the nation's homes were linked to a common public sewage system, and the nation's goal was to provide services to additional 17 percent by 1975. Even assuming the target is met, it would still be far below that enjoyed in England (90 percent), Holland (90 percent), the United States (68 percent) and other developed countries. Tokyo is somewhat better serviced than the rest of the country—43 percent of all homes in the city are connected to the sewage system—but is still far below foreign urban standards which often approximate total coverage. The policy reasons for such a low level of social overhead stock in the world's third strongest economic power have been outlined in previous chapters, but an additional factor is public aversion to the construction of sewage treatment plants. Although nearly three-quarters of all Tokyo households have installed flush toilets, many remain unconnected to treatment facilities. No popular movements have called for improved treatment facilities; on the contrary, it has not been uncommon for residents to oppose their construction because of their "unclean" image and the depreciation of land values they trigger. One public health official criticized this attitude, complaining that "everyone in the city wants a flush toilet but no one wants a sewage treatment plant." This aversion may be reinforced in Japan by a long-standing tradition for the individual to "keep one's own garden clean" but to be unconcerned about public spaces.

The quality of many of Tokyo's waterways improved slightly as a result of the metropolitan government's purification efforts begun in the later half of the 1960s. Still, in 1969, more than three-quarters of the capital's rivers continued to be burdened with an average BOD (biological oxygen demand) in excess of 5 ppm, making it impossible for fish to survive in them. Nevertheless, Tokyo's inland waters were in better condition than Tokyo Bay. Bordered by Chiba Prefecture to the north, metropolitan Tokyo to the west, and Kanagawa Prefecture to the southwest, Tokyo Bay has an area of 1,100 square kilometers (about 400 square miles) and measures 40–50 meters at its deepest point. The narrow channel connecting it to the Pacific Ocean is only some 8 kilometers wide, making the bay an excellent natural harbor; unfortunately, it also makes it a receptacle for the vast quantities of wastes that pour into it daily. The bay has accumulated such a variety of pollutants that it is reportedly possible to develop photographic negatives in its waters without the use of additional chemicals! When entering the bay, ships' captains are said to navigate their crafts with special care lest propeller blades get entangled in plastic refuse.

When asked if Tokyo Bay can ever be restored to a healthy condition, most government authorities throw up their hands. By the 1960s, red tides had become a chronic problem, effectively destroying the bay's once-rich fisheries. After initiating land reclamation projects during the mid1950s, Tokyo's metropolitan government purchased the fishing rights of some 4,000 fishermen for the sum of 33 billion yen ($92 million). A few fishermen, however, refused to sell and still protest the continued contamination and reclamation of their waters. One such Kawasaki-based protest group composed the following song:

> Black and filthy Tokyo Bay,
> Tokyo Bay, where fish cannot live,

> What can we do?
> We must all take care of you.
> Black sea, deceptive sea,
> Mercury and sludge-filled sea that died,
> You were everyone's treasure...
> Oh, how clean your waters used to be.
> Everyone bathed in your waters,
> Shellfish, seaweed and fish lived in them.
> You were a rich sea, belonging to the people,
> Now... you have been stolen away.
> Black sea, who did this to you?
> Industrial priorities are cruel...
> Give us back our clean sea.

Despite sporadic public protests and general awareness of the bay's acutely deteriorated state, Tokyo Bay continues to ingest a seemingly endless flow of refuse and effluents. Many Japanese, including government authorities, are fearful that the bay could someday disgorge its contents. As a result of industrial pumping of underground water, much of the earthquake-prone capital's downtown area—the political and commercial heartland of the nation—has sunk below sea level. A major quake could bring a tidal wave that would sweep large parts of the city—and leave devastating epidemics in its wake. Experts believe earthquakes of such magnitude are likely to occur in the region once every fifty to one hundred years. The last major quake occurred in 1923; the next one is being nervously awaited.

5.

In May 1969, the government of Eisaku Sato announced a New Comprehensive Development Plan aimed at solving some of the problems caused by previous policies of population and industrial concentration in Tokyo and the other major urban centers of the Pacific Belt. Taking 1965 as its base year and setting 1985 as its target, the plan was designed to serve as the "basic direction" for national development. Recognizing the inevitable catastrophe that would ensue if industrial concentration and rural migration to the cities continued unchecked, the Sato plan aimed at reforming the pattern of land utilization and population distribution. Through these reforms, it hoped to realize a more "balanced" development of the entire country. The drafters of the plan pointed to the "shrinking" of the nation as a result of improved transport and communications technology, and called for Japan to enter boldly into the Information Age.

The superrational structure of the plan—labeled "dehumanizing" by its many critics—was based on the concept of the post-industrial society:

> Japan will continue to develop and there will be rapid progress in the so-called "Second Industrial Revolution" based on the information revolution, internationalization, and technological innovation. As a result, a new society, which may be termed the "information society," will come into existence.
>
> Manpower was replaced by machinery in the first industrial revolution. In the second industrial revolution, a portion of man's intelligence will be replaced by machinery by means of a rapid advancement of automation. This will free men for higher intellectual activities. In the process of transformation to the new society, drastic changes will take place in social and economic aspects.
>
> Men will be required to adapt themselves to this new society...[15]

To enter fully into the information age, the plan called for establishing a nationwide transport and communication network that would enable the high-speed transmission of labor, goods, and energy. The implementation of these networks would enable the country to function as a single unit. Management operations were to be located in urban areas which, the plan envisioned, would become "knowledge banks." Although Tokyo would continue to be the central focus of the nation, greatly reduced time distances between Tokyo and other major cities (thanks to an expansion of highways, super-express trains, and air travel systems) would enable a dispersal of many management functions to other cities.

Urban areas were to be surrounded by "broad activity zones," the basic units for regional development, and planners recognized that each zone needed a separate development plan that would reflect local needs and characteristics. Regional programs would include development of the agricultural, fishing, manufacturing, tourism, and recreational industries. The main objective of the plan, however, was the dispersal of industry to less-developed areas of the nation in an effort to ease the environmental problems confronting the heavily industrialized Pacific Belt and to boost ailing economies in the countryside. Industrial production was to increase fivefold in the process.

To meet increasing international competition, the Sato development plan called for the construction of huge kombinats on a scale previously undreamed of. It predicted that by 1985 steel production would increase by 400 percent, petroleum refining by 500 percent, and petrochemicals by a staggering 1,300 percent. These increases in output presupposed a four- to fivefold rise in energy requirements. Although most of the latter would be supplied by petroleum, it was envisioned that by 1985, 10 percent would be generated by nuclear power plants. Mammoth atomic (30–40 million kw) and thermal power stations were to be located in remote areas, their output channeled to the rest of the nation through an extra-high voltage power transmission network.

Thus, in the late 1960s, the response at the highest levels of government to the problems of urban environmental deterioration was to propose large new development projects based on the kombinat formula. Yet by 1969, the complexes already in operation were being severely criticized—particularly for their pollution of local environments. Nevertheless, the scale of the kombinats envisioned in Sato's plan exceeded anything that had ever before been proposed: Although government announcements proclaimed that these huge projects would bring modern employment and material prosperity, many rural residents, aware of the environmental experiences of their city cousins, felt deep concern. They agreed that development was necessary, but they wondered if this was the kind of development they wanted.

CHAPTER EIGHT

RURAL DEMISE

"It's a dilemma: it seems that the only way we can improve our environment is to allow government and industry to destroy it."

–KISO KIMURA
Rokkasho farmer
May 1973

The adage "you can't keep 'em down on the farm" is as applicable to Japan as it is to the United States and other areas of the world. While in Japan a sentimental identification with one's rural birthplace still persists, traditional filial obligations which once gave practical form to that sentiment have been greatly undermined. Sociologist John Bennett notes that even in the early 1960s the number of eldest sons migrating to urban areas was approximating that of younger progeny.[1] This trend indicated a loosening of family ties occasioned by the legal abandonment of primogeniture after the war and the rapidly decreasing popularity of farming as an occupation. By the end of the decade, the values of a money economy had so infiltrated Japanese society that many farm families had resorted to paying the eldest son cash wages to keep him home.[2] Such a thing would have been unthinkable in prewar households ruled by a father who received dedicated service, particularly from the eldest son who would inherit the homestead.

As an economic venture, however, Japanese agriculture is confronted by many problems. For one, increases in farm labor productivity have been dwarfed by those in other industries. The agricultural production index (1965=100) for the decade 1960–70 rose only 23 points (from 89 to 112), while that for secondary industries rose 156 points (from 58 to 214). During the same period, the farming population decreased from 34.3 to 26.3 million persons, while the number of farm households dropped from 6.1 to 5.3 million. But even in 1970, 68 percent of the remaining farm households still worked plots less than one hectare in size. Operating on such a small scale, Japanese agriculture is unable to compete with large-scale American, Canadian, and Australian agribusiness farming. Consequently, the government has imposed protective tariffs on many agricultural imports and has provided domestic agriculture with hefty price supports. But recent American trade deficits increased American demands for a liberalization of Japanese import tariffs, and under intense international pressure, the Japanese government reduced the number of restricted food items from 68 in October 1969 to 24 in April 1973. Upward revaluations of the yen in August 1971 (16.88 percent) and February 1973 (16.05 percent) further diminished the competitive edge of Japanese farm products relative to their foreign counterparts. Despite continued government price supports, therefore, Japanese farmers have been hard hit by the liberalization of imports.

The majority of Japanese farming families have been unable to keep pace with the rising living standard enjoyed by the population as a whole. In 1970, the minimum annual agricultural income required by a farm family to be self-supporting was estimated at 1.5 million yen ($4,200), and only 7 percent of all farming households could meet that criterion. In almost all parts of the nation, farmers and members of their families were compelled to seek supplementary sources of income in the form of factory or office work. Many men between their late teens and mid-forties and women in their late teens and early twenties have moved from their ancestral homes to the cities, leaving the farm work to wives, parents, and grandparents.

Between 1960 and 1970, the number of farmers engaged in supplementary occupations rose from 66 to 84 percent, demonstrating an increasing dependence on nonagricultural incomes. Agriculture in Japan has consequently become known as *san-chan nogyo*, or "three-*chan* farming"; the three *chans* are *okaachan* (mommy), *obaachan* (grandma) and *ojiichan* (grandpa). By 1970, nearly two-thirds of the nation's agricultural labor force was female, and one-third of all male workers were over 60 years of age. Gradual suburbanization and the growing number of nonagricultural workers taking up residence in once-rural regions have further changed traditional community work patterns. These changes have made it increasingly difficult to engage in the collective production methods that characterized Japanese agricultural villages in the past. The government's 1972 White Paper on Agriculture observes:

> With more and more members of farming families commuting daily to their nonagricultural work and an increasing number of nonagricultural workers and their families flowing into rural areas, suburban farming communities are turning into a mixed community of famers, half-farmers and non-farmers. There, coordination of will and activity regarding agricultural production has become increasingly difficult to attain.[3]

The daily commute to nonagricultural work is possible only in areas located close to urban centers. In places like Hokkaido and northern Honshu, more remote regions with shorter growing seasons, a large number of farmers have been forced to find employment as migrant workers. These men work on their farms from spring planting time until the harvest, and then seek seasonal employment in relatively distant industrial centers. In 1973, an estimated 300,000 farmers participated in the annual migration. Farmers from mountainous areas characterized by low agricultural yield and no supplementary employment opportunities have migrated semipermanently to the cities, returning only during the busiest times of planting or harvesting, or briefly for the New Year holiday and midsummer *Bon* festival held in honor of the souls of departed ancestors.

During the 1960s, rural depopulation became a particularly acute problem, and in 1970, the government enacted a law providing emergency measures to assist affected areas. Nevertheless, by February 1973, 1,047 cities, towns, and villages had been officially designated as "depopulated areas"—comprising 32.4 percent of all municipal bodies in Japan, 8.6 percent of the nation's total population, and 41.7 percent of the total land area. In sharp contrast to extreme congestion in urban areas, these rural areas, with their abandoned farmhouses and fields, are now lifeless.

Of course, it is primarily the young who leave for the cities, attracted by education, employment, and recreational opportunities unavailable in the countryside. Because the expansion of Japanese industry has depended heavily upon an abundant supply of young, cheap labor, corporate planners and personnel managers have actively recruited the rural young, usually for unskilled positions. At the same time, the wider postwar educational base has provided many rural offspring with skills for which employment can only be found in urban areas. The Japanese educational system and mass communication media have encouraged this emigration from the farms by transmitting the image of the white-collar salaried worker as the desirable norm.

Many young adults find rural life restrictive, almost claustrophobic: "I sneeze, and the next day the person at the far end of the village asks me if I'm catching a cold." The generation gap and rural resistance to new cultural values and "modern" psychology also contribute to youthful dissatisfaction with village life. Young men are often heard to complain that casual dating is impossible in the traditional village context, since merely being seen alone with a girl almost necessitates eventual marriage. For many, therefore, urban anonymity and individual freedom are welcome changes. Cities attract the young with their excitement, stimulation, and variety, all of which contrast sharply with the perceived monotony of the countryside. But continuous migration to the cities only abets the vicious circle of depopulation: the departure of the young further devitalizes the area, encouraging still others to leave.

Depopulation is accompanied by a decline in the quality and variety of public services. Steady rises in personnel and operating costs, coupled with a decline in the number of passengers carried, have forced Japan's National Railway system to reduce the number of trains running to and from depopulated areas. In extreme cases, local lines have been completely abolished. Bus companies in depopulated areas have encountered similar difficulties and have drastically cut back or suspended services.

Medical and educational services in depopulated areas are sorely deficient. Although Japan boasts a national average of 117 doctors to serve each thousand people (1971), the majority of practitioners are clustered in urban areas, driving down the ratio in rural regions to 65 doctors per thousand. In many depopulated areas, there are no medical services at all and local residents must travel substantial distances to secure them. Similarly, these regions are confronted by a severe shortage of qualified teaching personnel. This shortage, combined with the small size of many depopulated communities and commuting difficulties between individual settlements, forces many schools to combine different grades under the guidance of one teacher. Because practically none of these areas is endowed with a high school, most local children end their formal schooling after middle school. Those who elect to attend high school in the nearest large town usually find it difficult to readjust to country life.

Japan's pattern of population movement is not, however, unidirectional. Since about 1962, the nation has been experiencing a "U-turn" phenomenon in which former migrants to Tokyo, Osaka, and Nagoya are returning to their native prefectures. Many of the "U-turners," still relatively few although growing in number, are men in their forties who, after profiting from the higher wages and wider opportunities of the cities, are returning to manage their ancestral holdings. Many young migrants, fresh from the clean rural environment, have grown increasingly discontented with Japan's overgrown, dirty metropolitan centers and have begun a move toward the previously bypassed middle-size cities, particularly the prefectural capitals. Industries relocated in these smaller urban centers now provide them with more convenient employment opportunities. Thus, while growth of Japan's largest cities is beginning to level off, the middle-size cities are still expanding and, in the process, are falling victim to similar types of environmental disruption.

Environmental pollution itself has contributed to the shift in employment patterns from primary to secondary or tertiary industries. Fishing communities located near heavily industrialized areas have been particularly hard hit. Declining yields due to severe water contamination have forced many fishermen to give up their trade, often, ironically, to take jobs in the very factories that destroyed their fishing grounds. In areas near large industrial complexes, pollution of coastal waters has actually encouraged the expansion of production facilities, in a pattern describable as a "domino effect." After a kombinat begins operation, its effluents soon begin to downgrade neighboring fishing areas. Since fishing rights for these areas were not purchased by industrialists when they reclaimed land and set up the complex, their fishermen go "uncompensated" for fishing rights. The more unprofitable fishing is made, however, the more willing these fishermen become to sell their rights when the original complex is expanded. *Their* neighbors, however, working one step further removed from the kombinat and still able to support themselves from the sea, oppose the sale bitterly. Once the new additions to the complex are built, however, *their* fishing grounds are now adversely affected, which leads to the issue of their own "compensation." Thus, once a single fishermen's union is toppled, it becomes very likely that surrounding fishing grounds—and the will of their fishermen—will also deteriorate.

The degree to which environmental disruption has hastened the phenomenon of rural depopulation is not precisely known, but it is a factor that cannot be neglected. The 1971 Agricultural White Paper notes that damage from polluted irrigation water is the most extensive, affecting approximately 3 percent of Japan's total cultivated land area. Cadmium pollution of the soil has rendered rice crops unfit for human consumption.* In areas such as Ashio and Tokyo's Tama River basin, pollutants in river water used to irrigate farmlands have stunted or killed a variety of farm crops. On farms located near industrial zones, soot, smoke, and poisonous gases have rendered many yields unusable. In 1970, crops worth an estimated 22 billion yen ($61 million) were damaged by contaminated water alone, a nearly five-fold increase in ten years.

The economic dislocations wrought by acute pollution problems speak for themselves, but it remains to be seen what long-range, chronic effects

---

* See pp. 121–123

Japan's ecologically unsound farming practices will have on her intensively cultivated land.

The desire to increase output has motivated most agricultural producers to take labor-saving shortcuts, simplifying and "rationalizing" agricultural operations. In 1960, for example, 63 percent of Japan's total farming households specialized in a single farm product; by 1971, the percentage had risen to 88 percent. But monoculture, although it raises labor productivity and cash-crop yield over the short run, simplifies the ecosystem and results in a long-term decline in soil fertility. And there are already signs that the overuse of chemical fertilizers, pesticides, herbicides, and fungicides have also taken a toll in more ways than just the pollution of fresh-water systems by run-off: In 1972, Tochigi village (Hokkaido) potato farmers added six times as much inorganic nitrogen to the soil as they did in 1955, but their potato yield was only slightly higher. Fed too much synthetic fertilizer, the soil becomes desiccated and deoxygenated, and is denuded of the microbes needed for soil decomposition and plant nourishment. As in Tochigi, farmers throughout the nation have switched to chemical fertilizers at the price of considerable damage to soil structure and long-term fertility. The shift away from traditional organic manures and compost has been most abrupt during the past decade. Until 1965, farmers used on the average some 5.5 kilograms of manure per hectare of land, but this ratio has decreased by over 10 percent every year since. Rice straw, too, is no longer used for composting in many areas. The abandonment of diversified farming methods and the wholesale acceptance of "modern" chemical treatment of plants and soil presents a particularly severe problem in Japan because of the sheer volume of chemicals in use. In 1967, Japan's total consumption of toxic agrochemicals almost equaled that of the entire United States! Indeed, unless the decline in the structure and fertility of Japan's soil is reversed, the nation's agricultural base could be headed for a catastrophe of massive proportions.

2.

When first announced in May 1969, the New National Comprehensive Development Plan of Prime Minister Eisaku Sato was generally well received. Concern over environmental and development problems was overshadowed in the public mind by the issues of inflation, the renewal of the U.S.-Japan Security Treaty, and the reversion of Okinawa. By mid-1971, however, public anxiety over rapidly worsening environmental conditions had grown more insistent, and Kakuei Tanaka, then Minister of International Trade and Industry, responded to the changing domestic climate by proposing a new plan ostensibly of his own devising. First presented in a 24-page pamphlet entitled

"The Basic and Major Policies: My Proposal for the People," the plan was later expanded into a book, *Remodeling the Japanese Archipelago*, which quickly became a red-hot best seller. Tanaka's three principal goals were 1) to encourage the development of a new, prosperous agricultural base and the rise of small and medium-size industries; 2) to build a viable regional society; and 3) to prevent further pollution and generally rescue the environment. Although the Tanaka plan was never officially adopted by the Japanese Diet and has been bitterly attacked by opposition intellectuals and politicians, its contents and initially wide popularity suggest that in 1971–72, many government and business leaders still supported the basic concepts at the root of earlier economic plans. For the Tanaka plan, like all others, assumed that continued rapid economic growth was the only answer to Japan's burgeoning problems.

Tanaka cited uneven distribution of population and industry, a state of "underdevelopment-overdevelopment," as the cause of many of Japan's domestic ills. As did earlier development plans, his proposals to remedy this imbalance rested on the premise that people will tag along after economic opportunity; hence, industrial relocation would lead to population redistribution. Tanaka advocated the establishment of new towns at key provincial locations. Each would be formed around an industrial nucleus and boast a population of approximately 250,000, comprised mainly of factory, office, and service workers and their families who would move away from existing metropolises once the new industrial facilities were set up. Residential and recreational areas in the new towns would be separated from the central industrial zone by a green belt. Native residents of nearby rural communities could also find employment in the new towns, facilitating a reorganization of farming on a larger scale.

Many agreed that, on paper, these new towns seemed very attractive, but a closer look at the proposals disclosed hidden problems. Not the least of these was how to persuade existing individual enterprises or whole industries to relocate, since moving to new locations would involve heavy outlays and astronomical bank loans. But this prerequisite was made somewhat more palatable by several advantages which the plan offered industry. For example, the less industrialized conditions of a rural area would legally allow a given factory to pollute more there than in a highly developed region. Also, the introduction of the most modern, labor-saving equipment in rebuilt facilities would mean long-term savings from reduced manpower requirements. Not surprisingly, it was just these "attractions" that were quickly attacked by residents of the proposed new town sites. The Tanaka remodeling scheme, they charged, would simply serve to spread pollution throughout the country, and since new machinery required less manpower, unions would snap up the best jobs and leave only the less desirable positions for the local labor pool. A significant increase in the size of individual farming units was also highly unlikely, critics said, because most people leaving the land would wish to retain ownership of their property, both for sentimental reasons and as a hedge against inflation. Many came to perceive the new town concept as a threat to intimate human relations built up over centuries. As one man put it: "If these new towns are built, they will destroy the sense of community we have developed in our villages; we'll just end up 'little Tokyos,' where people are all strangers."

As a means of generating the funds the government would need to finance a national transformation of this scale, Tanaka proposed a steep surcharge on corporate taxes. This would further encourage relocation by making it increasingly uneconomical to remain in the cities. Many critics deemed it highly questionable, however, whether Japan's powerful corporate elite would allow such a tax to be imposed. Given industry's strong influence over political decisions, its tacit consent would first have to be secured. But even with industry's consent, it was noted, revenues deriving from the "Tanaka tax" would in themselves be insufficient to finance both the internal relocation costs and the additional social overhead investment that would be required. Tanaka himself estimated that roughly 450 trillion yen ($1.5 trillion) would be necessary to carry out his plan. This astronomical sum, he believed, could be garnered from a combination of private institutional loans and a national bond issue, in addition to the new corporate tax. It was convincingly argued, however, that any action taken on these proposals would only aggravate the rampant inflation already besetting the nation: between 1965 and 1969, the Consumer Price Index had risen 15.2 percent; after Sato announced his New National Comprehensive Development Plan, inflation accelerated even further, and the Consumer Price Index climbed another 13.5 percent by 1971. As it turned out, the mere publication of Tanaka's proposals was enough to fuel corporate speculation, contributing to an inflationary spiral of consumer prices which by 1973 were racing ahead at a rate of 28.6 percent.

The underlying objective of the Tanaka plan was to prolong the spectacular economic growth that Japan had enjoyed for the preceding decade and a half. Tetsuro Nishizaki, an economic critic, wrote in early 1974:

> Tanaka considers himself a favorite disciple of the late Prime Minister Hayato Ikeda, an economic expansionist who proposed the "income doubling" policy of the early 1960s. Like his mentor, Tanaka believes the Japanese economy will keep growing at an

average rate of 10 percent until attaining a US$ one trillion GNP level by 1985.[4]

A gross national product of these dimensions, requiring a fourfold increase in 15 years, would equal that achieved in the United States in 1972. The opposition parties have denounced this continued emphasis on GNP and high growth, claiming that in addition to worsening environmental and economic problems at home, it completely lacks an international perspective. Instead of recognizing that the ready availability of raw materials in the buyers' market of the 1950s has been replaced in the early 1970s by a growing trend for developing countries to insist on utilizing their domestic resources to promote their own development, the Tanaka plan proposes vast increases by 1985 in the annual consumption of energy and raw materials. It calls for four times the oil, six times the ethylene, and over twice the steel consumed in 1970.

Criticisms have been leveled at nearly every aspect of this scheme, and the course of events in the world economy since its first publication have lent heavy weight to the arguments of its detractors. Economist Shuichi Miyoshi warned in 1971 that growing nationalism in developing countries would result in a diminished flow of resources to the developed nations—a squeeze that would be felt most severely by resource-poor Japan. The nation's already massive consumption of raw materials (third in the world after United States and the Soviet Union) and nearly total dependence on imported resources, he said, made the realization of the scheme's economic goals unlikely.[5]

Japan's most obvious Achilles' heel is its near total dependence on oil imports. Well before the partial Middle Eastern oil embargo of 1973, the petroleum and ethylene requirements set by Tanaka's plan were raising a number of informed eyebrows. In 1971, Japan imported 99.7 percent of its crude oil requirements, refined 210 million kiloliters of petroleum, and produced 4.8 million tons of ethylene. The Tanaka plan called for an increase in oil imports to 750 million kiloliters by 1985—amounting to one-fourth of the world's predicted total consumption. Even if Japan were able to meet the Tanaka target, critics insisted, transport problems would be enormous. Tankers of the 200,000 DWT class would have to be strung out continuously at less than 40 kilometer intervals in a line stretching from the Persian Gulf to Tokyo Bay. Once it reached Japan, the crude oil would then have to be transferred to huge storage depots which the plan envisioned would be built along Japan's seacoasts. The scheme then called for a central transport system, comprising some 7,500 kilometers of pipelines, to connect oil depots with the super-kombinats where the oil would be refined and processed.

Besides the huge quantities of oil, Tanaka estimated that by 1985 the volume of goods transported throughout the country would total 1,320,000 million tonne-kilometers, half of which would be transported by sea and half overland. The prime minister proposed that some 500,000 tonne-kilometers be carried by rail, which would mean that lines presently carrying passengers would be utilized primarily for freight. Passengers, the plan postulates, would be carried by a new network of bullet trains.

The distance covered by paved roads would have to increase from 1,900 kilometers in 1972 to 10,000 by 1985, and Tanaka notes that "By the beginning of the 21st century, we will have to pave about one-fifth of our level land just to cope with the vast road traffic demand."[6] This massive transport program would be complemented by equally extensive development of data transmission systems, which would help solve the problem of inferior medical care and educational facilities in the countryside. As he envisioned it, a health office employee or a patient would eventually need only to press a few buttons and receive from a computer both a diagnosis and a recommendation for treatment.

Opponents argue that computers should not be viewed as a replacement for doctors and teachers, that an additional 8,000 kilometers of highways would eliminate vast amounts of Japan's remaining arable land, and that increased numbers of motor vehicles would substantially raise Japan's overall pollution level—unless new technology and restrictions make it possible to tighten exhaust standards and clean up automobile production processes. A wider network of Japan's famous bullet trains would, it is argued, benefit only a limited number of people while increasing noise pollution in the areas through which the trains passed. It, too, would eat up some of Japan's best (most level) arable land. Finally, many have pointed out that, while concentrating on economic growth, the plan totally ignored the cultural identity crisis and decline of traditional values that has accompanied the rise of materialism. It also completely failed to deal with fundamental problems in the content and approach of Japan's educational and healthcare systems.

Perhaps the most significant resistance to Tanaka's plan, however, has come from the residents of sites selected for the placement of the super-kombinats. Government and private land transactions at two of these sites—Rokkasho village in northeastern Honshu and the Shibushi Bay area in southwestern Kyushu—began in earnest in 1971. They have met with such strong local opposition in Kyushu that the government has apparently shelved the whole project there. The situation in Rokkasho, however, is more complex, and its outcome is still in doubt. It is perhaps more representative.

3.

Rokkasho village is composed of six small settlements with a total population about 13,000 strung along the Pacific coast of the Shimokita Peninsula on the northeastern tip of Honshu. It has always been one of the poorest areas of Aomori Prefecture. Its short growing season, rough terrain, low agricultural productivity, and fierce winters have traditionally driven many of its inhabitants to urban areas for employment as seasonal laborers. In the early days of Japan's economic takeoff, its young people headed south to the booming cities of the Pacific Belt; many adjusted to city life and never returned. Since the mid-1960s, new industrial complexes in Aomori City, the prefectural capital, and Hachinohe, a once quiet coastal town some 40 kilometers to the south, have siphoned off much of the area's remaining labor supply. Between 1965 and 1970, Rokkasho's population decreased by 1,100 persons—about 10 percent of the total.

Rokkasho's scattered population is served by totally inadequate transportation, educational, and medical facilities. Most of the region's roads are unpaved, bus service is infrequent, and no train lines venture north of Misawa, about 30 kilometers to the south, or Hachinohe. Although Rokkasho has three elementary schools and one middle school, older children are forced to go to Misawa or Hachinohe to attend high school; about two-thirds of the children simply drop out after completing middle school. In 1973, Rokkasho still had no hospital and only four doctors served the entire population. There is no dentist, and many of the region's inhabitants suffer from severe tooth decay.

Rokkasho can be divided into three zones: north, central, and south. The northern zone is the most mountainous and harsh; the land dips briefly as it nears the ocean. This zone supports a few coastal settlements that subsist on a meager income derived from fishing and the cultivation of tiny rice paddies and potato fields.

The mountains retreat in the central zone, permitting somewhat larger-scale agricultural production. The major source of income in this area is rice, corn, and legume cultivation. Tractors first replaced horse-drawn plows and hoes in the late 1960s. Although villagers engage in some fishing to supplement their diet, ocean currents are not very favorable. Two saltwater bays extend nearly halfway through the peninsula and in places form broad marshlands that in the autumn fill with migratory birds which attract hunting parties. The majority of Rokkasho's population lives in this central area in a series of communities separated from one another by little more than a few kilometers. A number of small shops, restaurants, and inns have sprung up to cater to local residents and seasonal hunters and fishermen. Most villagers here have strong ties with the land, which has been handed down from father to eldest son for generations.

South of the bays, Rokkasho stretches out into a broad expanse of rolling hills, much of which was once owned by the central government. After World War II, the government sold its holdings to Japanese returning from Manchuria. Although some of the settlers in this zone continue traditional farming and fishing practices, most have come to use their relatively larger but less fertile properties for cattle raising or soybean cultivation.

The potential productivity of the land in this southern zone, however, has been offset by a series of inconsistent and shortsighted agricultural programs and administrative directives issued by the prefectural and central governments. In 1954, for example, government officials supported a program aimed at importing Jersey milk cows from the United States and Canada, and within five years, the southern zone of Rokkasho boasted the second largest number of milk cows in all of Japan. As it turned out, however, the Jersey strain was unable to withstand the severe cold of Rokkasho's winters: the cows yielded only half the amount of milk that Holsteins normally produce and the quality of their meat was inferior. As a result, anticipated markets never materialized, and by March 1971, the bovine population had fallen to a mere 30 percent of its peak.

In 1962, the prefectural government directed farmers to concentrate on beet production and persuaded a sugar factory to relocate just outside Rokkasho's southern border. For five years, the farmers grew beets by the cartload and the program seemed a success, but the first liberalization of agricultural imports in 1967 forced a drastic reduction in the market share enjoyed by domestic beets. The farmers, unable to compete against cheaper beets imported from abroad, lost again. The Minister of Agriculture, canceling the beet order, agreed to purchase that year's crop; the factory soon fired its workers and folded. Soybeans and corn, which had also been encouraged, suffered as well when import barriers were lowered.

In 1963, the government urged Rokkasho's farmers to grow more rice. In 1969, due to massive national overproduction, the government reversed its stand and subsidized farmers who let their fields lie fallow. Not surprisingly, the seesaw nature of this "guidance" has planted a widespread sense of mistrust of government in Rokkasho residents.

Then in May 1969, Prime Minister Sato's new National Comprehensive Development Plan proposed the construction of a petrochemical complex in the Rokkasho area. According to journalist Sadahiko Koizumi, it was Aomori's governor, Shunkichi Takeuchi, who persuaded Keidanren and MITI officials to choose this region not only because of its wide coastal plains but because he believed the residents' poverty would facilitate purchase of their land and enable their relatively painless relocation. In August 1969, only three weeks after the announcement of the Sato plan, the Planning Division of Aomori's Development Office published a small pamphlet bearing the inconspicuous title, "Mutsu Bay and Ogawara Lake: Regional Development." Despite its subdued packaging, the plan was anything but modest. It called for construction of a kombinat four times the size of Japan's Kashima complex, the largest then in operation. Located on 17,500 square hectares of land, it was to include an oil refinery with a production capacity of 1.5 million barrels per day, a petrochemical plant capable of manufacturing 2.6 million tons of ethylene equivalent yearly, and a thermal electric power plant of the 10.5 million kilowatt class. Larger than any industrial complex the world had ever seen, the plans for the Mutsu Ogawara (Rokkasho) kombinat were heralded as an important economic and technological step. Having failed to provide the Rokkasho area with a viable economy based on agriculture and fishing, the government proclaimed it would do so by means of the most modern industrial development.

Much to the surprise of central government and prefectural officials, however, the plan provoked fierce opposition from a substantial number of Rokkasho's residents. Furthermore, Rokkasho's village mayor, Rikisaburo Terashita, gained national prominence by his stubborn refusal to cooperate. He explained: "We are not against development, but we want the kind of development that will really help the people living here—doctors, schools, dentists, paved roads and good work—not just menial jobs in heavily polluting factories." Terashita bitterly criticized the government's disregard of Rokkasho's desires. "The planners didn't bother to ask us what kind of development we wanted; they merely handed us their proposal and demanded 17,500 hectares of land."

Prefectural officials reacted by revising the plan which appeared in a final version in June 1972. In the interim, however, Rokkasho's local residents still had not been consulted. To the consternation of prefectural officials, Terashita flatly refused to discuss the project. "What they're proposing isn't development; it's destruction. As an elected official, it is my job to represent the interests of Rokkasho's citizens, and as long as my constituents oppose that plan, I will represent them." An envelope tacked to the wall of Terashita's office contains his written oath, entered into with another leader of the opposition movement, vowing ritual suicide should either of them convert to the group favoring the petrochemical complex.

Local residents fear that pollution from the superkombinat would irreparably damage both their living environment and their health. Many residents have visited nearby industrial complexes in Hachinohe and Sendai, and over 400 traveled to Kashima to see firsthand the toll its kombinat had taken and confer with members of the local antipollution movement.

Realizing that modern technology has been incapable of maintaining a healthy environment in existing kombinats, Rokkasho residents are wary of Aomori official assurances that the far larger Mutsu Ogawara kombinat will be "pollution free." When it was pointed out to prefectural officials that before its construction the Kashima kombinat had been proclaimed the "victory of humanity" but that now everyone conceded that it had caused severe pollution problems, they reiterated, "Yes, but Mutsu Ogawara's kombinat will *really* be pollution free." When asked if they could *guarantee* that to Rokkasho's residents, they admitted that "this was the plan's main problem."

Interpretations of what constitutes a "pollution-free" facility differ markedly among the various groups involved. Prefectural officials, backed up by industry and government planners, consider that contamination of the environment up to the national standards set by Environment Agency is "pollution-free." Environment Agency bureaucrats, on the other hand, fearing this loophole in the law could pave the way for eventual well-distributed contamination of the entire country, are considering methods to prevent degradation of clean areas, but are confronted by the strong countervailing forces of big business in need of new industrial sites. At present, therefore, Environment Agency officials, too, view the question as one of whether or not pollution resulting from new installations will exceed present ambient standards. For local residents who oppose the plan, however, the concept of "pollution" goes far beyond the question of sulfur oxides in the air or oil slicks in the bay. They feel that both the loss of natural landscape to the unsightly presence of modern factories and supertankers and the spiritual and physical changes in life style which would come from sudden massive industrialization would degrade the quality of life in Rokkasho. These factors tend to be totally ignored by developers; government and industry leaders operate on the assumption that modernization, despite its unavoidable "external" costs, should be the aspiration of all "poor farmers." Thus, the core of the debate over the permissible level of environmental contamination is a fundamental conflict of values.

Since 1971, in its attempts to design a model "non-polluting" kombinat, Aomori Prefecture has commissioned several scientific surveys of local geological features and meteorological conditions, and of water currents and marine resources in Mutsu Bay and Pacific coastal waters. The results of at least one survey have challenged the wisdom of the prefecture's plan for turning Mutsu Bay into an industrial port capable of docking 500,000-ton supertankers.

A study conducted in 1973 by Professor Masakichi Nishimura of Hokkaido University concluded that because of Mutsu Bay's narrow mouth and internal currents, just one oil spill of major proportions would spread throughout the bay and destroy valuable marine life and seriously damage beaches.

Partially in response to protests and criticisms such as these, prefectural officials have twice altered the kombinat's master plan. The changes that have been made, however, sometimes suggest greater rather than diminished environmental disruption. By referring to the accompanying tables, one can see that although Chart 1 indicates that the total land area of the development region and the factory zone were reduced by some 50 percent in the plan's second draft, Chart 2 suggests that the amount of land earmarked for factory use actually increased by some 50 percent, as oil refinery facilities were enlarged and installations were packed together more densely. The predicted scale of production also increased from 1.5 to 2.0 million barrels a day at the oil refinery, and from 2.6 to 4.0 million tons of ethylene equivalent per year at the petrochemical plant. The June 1972 report shows manpower requirements quadruple the figure in the original draft plan. While capital-intensive land was reduced by 50 percent, the green belt slated to protect nearby residents was slashed by some 67 percent. In sum, the plan's modifications decreased the total land area required by over 50 percent; while *increasing* industrial land usage by an equivalent amount. Some productivity goals were raised more than 30 percent and manpower requirements jumped 400 percent.

A further inconsistency of the plan relates to the water supply and estimated needs. The plan indicates that industry will use 1.8 million tons of fresh water daily, of which 1.2 million tons will be fresh and 0.6 million tons recycled. Current prefectural government estimates, however, set the region's present water limit at 1.2 million tons per day, although there are plans afoot to build additional dams in the region to bring total available supplies to 1.5 million tons. Assuming that the estimates of available supplies are correct* and that industries would, in fact, recycle their 0.6 million tons, only 0.3 million tons per day would be left for irrigation, drinking, and household uses. But increased manpower figures suggest an enormous spurt in total population and growth of kombinat-related secondary industries, all of which would further strain fresh-water supplies. By all indications, the prefecture is planning to use every available drop of fresh water in the area and is no doubt praying for more rain.

---

* A number of scholars reject these estimates as too high, pointing out that the Shimokita Peninsula has a shallow water table. Pumping up large amounts of groundwater might induce saltwater seepage into fresh-water supplies. This has, in fact, happened in the Kashima region, damaging agricultural land.

Fig 3. The Mutsu Ogawara Kombinat

CHART I.	Draft Plan #1 (1969)	Draft Plan #2 (1971)	Basic Plan #1 (1972)
1. Land Area			
Total Area of Development Region (in hectares)	17,500	7,900	7,900
a) Factory zone	9,500	5,000	5,000
b) Port	1,200	820	820
c) Green belt	6,800	2,080	2,080
d) Government-owned land	4,580	3,990	3,990
e) Public land	0	450	450
f) Privately owned land (total)	12,920	3,460	3,460
1) Residential	320	60	60
2) Rice paddies	1,812	470	470
3) Other agricultural fields	2,728	1,020	1,020
4) Mountains and open fields	8,060	1,910	1,910
2. Factory Production Scale			
Oil refining facilities (in barrels/day)	1.5 million	2 million	2 million
Petrochemical facilities (in tons ethylene/year)	2.6 million	4 million	4 million
Thermal electric power plant (in kilowatts)	10.5 million	10 million	10 million
3. Required Manpower	8,155	12,040	35,000

CHART II.	Draft Plan #1	Draft Plan #2	Basic Plan #1
Breakdown by Industry of Factory Land (in hectares)			
Oil refining facilities	1,950	2,600	2,600
Petrochemical facilities	1,180	1,900	1,900
Electric generating plant	500	500	500
Total	3,530	5,000	5,000

CHART III.	Basic Plan #1
Fresh Water Requirements (in tons/day)	
Total requirements	1.8 million
Used once	1.2 million
Recycled	0.6 million
Presently Available Fresh Water	1.2 million
Estimate of Future Available Fresh Water	1.5 million

The most immediate and emotion-packed problem facing Rokkasho's residents is the issue of land. Because of spiraling land prices throughout the country, a farmer's selling of his land implies relocation to an inferior plot.

After the announcement of the first draft plan in 1969, Rokkasho's farmers loudly objected to the proposed transfer of 6,500 of their number to less fertile areas. Aomori officials responded by cutting the land requirement and reducing the number of farmers to be relocated to around 400. Those most eager to sell are Rokkasho's "newcomers," those who live on the poorer-quality but larger-sized tracts in the southern zone. Long-time residents feel that these postwar immigrants lack a real attachment to their land and can therefore part with it more easily. But Kokichi Kawamura, a journalist who has covered the Rokkasho area for many years, points to more concrete incentives: "These people have suffered so many hardships that they see this chance to make money as their first real break. They don't want to think about the long-term disadvantages."

For those owning large plots, temptations to sell have often outweighed misgivings about the development project. Hordes of real estate speculators have driven land prices from $1 per square meter in 1969 to over $100 per square meter in late 1972. Pro-development village assemblymen, acting as "mediators" in arranging the sales, have reportedly earned sizable commissions during the past few years. Terashita says, "People here are poor and aren't very clever at dealing with businessmen who flash large amounts of money in front of them." He laments that even those who don't want to sell nevertheless find it difficult to resist the handsome sums offered by the "men in suits." Those who have sold out have built new homes and drive expensive cars; their children are well dressed and have lots of pocket money. Those who refuse to sell remain poor. "This division has pressured people into selling, and has split the community," Terashita complains.

A variety of pressures have been exerted on Rokkasho's landowners. The prefecture reportedly encouraged the local farmers cooperative to sell new household furnishings to those farmers who had received fallow rice-field subsidies, sparking a minor construction boom. It also encouraged banks to ease restrictions on loans to local residents and to accept land as collateral. The prefecture then offered to pay the interest on loans to farmers who agreed to sell out. Their debts have made many farmers increasingly dependent on implementation of the development plans, for cancellation would send the price of their land tumbling.[7]

There are also certain non-monetary aspects of Rokkasho's development plans that tempt residents. For example, the prefecture is offering a "package deal" with numerous fringe benefits in the form of improvements in the agricultural and fishing industries, social welfare, educational institutions, and so on. Government and industry planners have learned that bigger and better incentives are now required to quell protests against new industrial complexes, and they are promising to deliver the goods. Kiso Kimura, an active member of the Rokkasho group opposing the development plans, considers these tactics a form of bribery. "In essence, they're saying, 'If you accept these development plans, we'll build you schools, roads, medical facilities and many other good things.' The implication is that if we *reject* the plans, they won't give us anything. But it is our *right* as citizens of Japan to have good schools, roads, and a decent medical system. Some people forget this and are afraid that if we refuse this form of development we won't get another chance. It's a dilemma: It seems that the only way we can improve our environment is to allow government and industry to destroy it."

By mid-1973, once-peaceful Rokkasho had become divided into two bitterly hostile camps. The conflict reached a climax in June 1973, with attempts to recall Rokkasho's two top political leaders: Katsushiro Hashimoto, chairman of the village assembly and head of the pro-development faction, and village mayor Terashita, head of the anti-development faction. Both votes fell short of the required number, leaving the situation in a stalemate, but those opposing the kombinat were gradually losing momentum. In September 1972, the Tanaka Cabinet approved the Mutsu Ogawara development plans and by the end of 1973, the prefectural Mutsu Ogawara Development Corporation had acquired 57 percent of the land required and felt another 13 percent was within reach.

In December 1973, the anti-development faction suffered a major setback: Terashita was voted out of office by a narrow margin of 79 votes. The new village mayor, Isematsu Furukawa, represented the "development-with-conditions" faction, claiming to support "non-polluting" progress. His position is clearly pro-kombinat. He hopes to have the oil refinery and petrochemical plant in operation by 1980, and he wants to see construction begin as soon as possible. The anti-development faction, led by Terashita, continues to oppose the plan, but at this writing their future seems bleak.

One thing, however, is certain: animosity between the two factions in Rokkasho is still strong and will not be quickly assuaged. Similar conflicts are being repeated wherever the kombinat approach is applied to achieve rapid rural "modernization."

The Rokkasho conflagration demonstrates that many of Tanaka's proposals for remodeling Japan are being implemented even though the full scheme was never formally approved by the National Diet. Expansion throughout Japan of the super express "bullet train" network is underway, and vast new industrial complexes are springing up in Akita, Niigata, Toyama, and Fukui on Honshu, for example, and in Tomakomai on the southern coast of Hokkaido. Although the plan failed to deal effectively with urban problems and other crucial issues, and while it threatened to spread environmental pollution throughout the country, its basic assumptions were tacitly accepted by ruling party politicians, government bureaucrats, and business leaders. Its momentum, however, was not of its own making. As an official of the Economic Planning Agency explained, "all Tanaka did was to take the old development plans, which are difficult to read and understand, and rewrite them in a popularized form." Thus, while nominally only Tanaka's "personal vision," the remodeling plan in fact perpetuated the basic policies that have brought the nation to its present impasse. "Economic growth" remained the catchword, and Japan's ruling elite continued to view rapid industrial expansion as the nation's only means of survival in the modern world. And while recognizing that international circumstances may pose obstacles to the scheme's realization, it continues to view domestic resistance as regrettable but in no way insurmountable. It is still convinced that it knows best.

In fact, however, domestic resistance may be stronger than the ruling elite would like to admit. Although opposition appears to be crumbling in Rokkasho, it has held up more effectively elsewhere. While opposition political parties have been unable to block Tanaka's "bulldozer tactics" in the Diet, public opinion has caused other proposed heavy industrial complexes near Sukumo Bay (Kochi Prefecture, Shikoku) and Shibushi Bay (Kagoshima Prefecture, Kyushu) to be postponed, if not aborted. The construction of an artificial port slated to be the world's largest has been at least delayed in Tomakomai. In each case, the juggernaut was slowed, if not defeated, by the concerted action of local citizens' groups, and it is to them that we turn next.

CHAPTER NINE

THE DRIVE FOR CITIZENSHIP

Attention, residents of Shimuzu! We will not stand by silently and allow a dangerous petrochemical factory to be built near our homes. We, too, are farmers and understand the difficulties faced by agriculture these days. But is that any reason to sell your valuable land to the first factory that comes along? In Nakazato we thought about our children's health and the troubles a refinery would cause to all Mishima citizens, and we decided to oppose Fuji Petroleum and not sell our land. We ask you to do the same. Don't let yourselves be fooled by government or industry. And, most important, don't sell your land to Sumitomo or any of its related companies. This has been a broadcast from the residents of Nakazato. Thank you for listening.

–AN APPEAL, 1964

It was 1964, the heyday of Japan's economic expansionism, and most communities were sparing no efforts in trying to lure modern industries within their borders. But in one area earmarked for development, Japan's economic planners received a shocking rebuff: the residents of Mishima, Numazu, and Shimuzu, three small cities located about 60 miles southwest of Tokyo, organized a broad-based movement against a vast petrochemical complex slated for the area and, after a year of unrelenting community action, forced the government to abandon the project. Battling the nation's bureaucracy and big business leaders, an aroused citizenry channeled its energies into a movement that was to become known as the first major domestic challenge to the nation's postwar economic policies. The fervor underlying it signaled a turning point in the people's awareness of the dangers posed by pollution, and the movement's tactics provided a ground plan that would later be adopted by other groups. It was a new pattern of popular action facilitated by the structural and conceptual framework of Japan's postwar American-style "democracy," and its success was truly historic.

By the early 1960s, developers were eyeing the coastal region of Shizuoka Prefecture, located in the burgeoning industrial belt, as a prime site for a new kombinat. The first decisive moves followed announcement of the National Comprehensive Development Plan, and in July 1963, the East Suruga Bay Region was designated a "special industrial area." Not anticipating much opposition, the prefectural government informed the public in December that a Fuji Petroleum oil refinery would be built in Mishima, that a Sumitomo petrochemical plant would be based in Shimizu, and that a Tokyo Electric Company thermal power plant would be constructed in Numazu. The new complex was to be one of Japan's largest, with production on a scale far exceeding that of Yokkaichi.

The first sparks of local protest directed against the East Suruga Bay kombinat originated not from concern over environmental pollution, for such concern was still minimal at the time, but from dissatisfaction with plans to administratively consolidate the three cities involved. Consolidation of this type was a common prelude to industrialization: it increased the efficiency of planning and implementing large-scale development, while it multiplied the political and economic powers of the newly formed municipal government. Shizuoka Prefecture began promoting the merger of the three municipalities in May 1963, but only Mishima residents resisted. They suspected only vaguely that the moves to consolidate might be tied in some way to industrialization plans—until the prefectural government announced that the merger's purpose was indeed to facilitate construction of a kombinat. This announcement exposed as false the prefectural government's previous assertion that they were two separate matters.*

In response, various cultural groups, labor union federations, and political parties organized the Mishima Citizens Kombinat Countermeasures Roundtable to investigate the effects of industrialization on their city. Studying the government's plans, they found themselves confronted by a number of disconcerting ambiguities: What would happen to local finances? In what ways would the welfare of local residents be enhanced by support of the project? What effect would the new industries have on the National Genetic Research Institute, located in Mishima? Would the kombinat pollute

---

* Another consequence of such mergers has been to increase the distance between local city halls and the populace, eroding even further the already weak influence exerted by citizens on the decision-making process and weakening the impact of residents' movements. In 1963, however, these considerations were not significant in Mishima's opposition to the consolidation plans.

the region's air? What would happen to the city's famous Kakita River, fed for centuries by the snows of Mount Fuji? In February 1964, members of the roundtable put their questions to Shizuoka's governor, but his vague reassurances did little to assuage their concern. The residents decided that in order to protect the environment it was necessary for them to conduct their own research into the plans, and publicize their findings.

As a first step in self-education, the citizens visited operating petrochemical complexes to observe firsthand what a kombinat was and how it influenced the lives of local populations. Between February and April 1964, some fifteen Mishima study groups explored the complexes in Yokkaichi, Chiba, Mizushima, and Kawasaki. Indeed, it seemed as if nearly everyone in town—from LDP politicians to representatives of the local innkeepers union—was on the road, recording the environmental impact of Japanese-style heavy industrialization. As a result of these excursions, farmers living in the Nakazato district of Mishima slated for development by Fuji Petroleum became convinced that a local oil refinery would not improve their livelihood. In March they circulated a petition calling for the boycott of all land sales to the company, and by mid-April almost all landowners at the proposed site had signed it.

Mishima's mayor, Taiso Hasegawa, a member of a progressive faction of the conservative Liberal Democratic party, adopted an unusually independent stance. When, for the first time in Japan's postwar history, MITI and MHW commissioned a group of scientists to investigate methods for reducing pollutants in the new industrial complex, Hasegawa countered by establishing his own committee to review the kombinat's environmental implications. The government group, headed by Masataka Kurokawa, included some of Japan's foremost meteorologists and public health experts. The municipal group, headed by geneticist Kiyoji Matsumura, recruited local scientists and included specialists in agriculture, industrial chemistry, and water utilization, in addition to meteorology and public health. On May 5, several months before the Kurokawa team issued its report, the Matsumura group published its findings—Japan's first environmental impact statement—concluding that air and water pollution would very likely result from the proposed installation. When an opinion poll conducted shortly thereafter by the municipal government revealed that 90 percent of the city's residents disapproved of the oil refinery, Mayor Hasegawa announced the city's official opposition to it. Fuji Petroleum, he declared, would not be coming to Mishima.

Hasegawa's rejection of the refinery shocked politicians at both the prefectural and national levels. Although the mayor's decision to challenge government and big business sprang partly from his progressive leanings and lack of close connections with the prefectural governor, it is doubtful that he would have made the May announcement without strong urging from the well-organized Mishima citizens' movement. At the core of the citizens' group were the housewives' association and land-owning farmers of Nakazato. These activists, in turn, were emboldened by the area's location and economic base. Unlike Yokkaichi and other regions where large companies had earlier come to employ a majority of the local labor force and control civic activities, the Mishima-Nakazato area was predominantly rural and free of such conflicts. At the same time, Shizuoka Prefecture's position at the heart of Honshu and its mild climate, far different from Rokkasho's northerly isolation, gave its farmers good reason to hope for alternative forms of development. Financially stable, they could resist the temptations of short-term gains from selling their land.

Although the Nakazato agricultural community provided the foundation for opposing the oil refinery, support from the citizenry of Mishima as a whole was crucial to the movement's ultimate success. In addition to progressive political parties, various clubs and cultural societies joined in the protests against the kombinat and conducted fund-raising campaigns to assist Nakazato residents' activities. The unusual dynamism and independence of Mishima citizens can be partly explained by historical circumstances. During World War II, many intellectuals eager to escape political repression and American fire-bombings emigrated to Mishima from Tokyo and transformed it into a sort of refuge for progressives. In the early years of the Occupation, they formed a "citizens' university," bringing together factory workers, farmers, housewives, businessmen, and office workers to discuss the meaning of Japan's new "democracy." Although it was disbanded in 1950, the university's brief life planted seeds of self-government that were to bear fruit more than a decade later.

Cancellation of the refinery plans brought intensified opposition to the kombinat in Numazu and Shimizu.

Dissatisfied with the cancellation of the Fuji Petroleum project alone, the farmers of Nakazato launched an energetic public relations campaign aimed at convincing their neighbors not to sell their land to Sumitomo Chemical. Each morning for several months, loudspeakers bellowed anti-kombinat announcements across Shimizu's rice paddies.* The opposition of Nakazato's farmers, maintained even after they had defeated development plans slated for their own area, thus acted as a catalyst for continued protest.

---

* See p. 173.

Numazu's anti-kombinat movement, however, lacked the pre-existing progressive tendencies which helped support Mishima's organization. In order to mobilize grassroots resistance, several of Numazu's high school teachers and medical practitioners began, in February 1965, to hold study meetings in a number of private homes. According to Akio Nishioka, an instructor who was to become a key leader of the antipollution movement, "We had to explain the problems in a way that could be understood by both young and old. To do this, we presented slides and recordings of farmers, fishermen, and others already suffering from air and water pollution, and arranged contacts with people living near kombinats." These study groups quickly became the foundation of the Numazu residents' movement, and in one year nearly one thousand such sessions were held.

An important function of the movement was to collect and process useful information for the study groups. Twenty thousand copies of a report on the effects of air pollution in Yokkaichi, for example, were distributed throughout Numazu. Various "outside" social and natural scientists were also invited to speak with residents about pollution and the problems of industrialization and regional development. Specialists in regional development and pollution-control technology visited the area, establishing a vital precedent of direct contact between academic activists and local residents.

This helped balance the usually biased information disseminated by government and industry, thereby providing concerned citizens with a broader perspective on regional development.

The residents' movement also conducted its own scientific research. High school teachers and their students observed the colorful paper carp streamers, commonly flown in May, to determine wind direction simultaneously throughout a wide region and found that exhaust gases from the industries, if they were constructed, would blow into residential areas. This and other research activities heightened the residents' awareness of the issues and of their options. Despite the fact that many of the movement's participants had never before opposed prefectural, much less central, authority, opposition to the kombinat snowballed.

Unlike Mishima's mayor Hasegawa, however, the Numazu mayor and his officials were staunch mainstream supporters of the Liberal Democratic party. After Mishima's mayor canceled construction of the oil refinery, Numazu's residents petitioned their city council representatives, demanding that they clarify their position as being either "for" or "against" the kombinat. The residents "inquired" from a position of strength: several hundred confronted each council member at his home and, hinting broadly at the possibility of political recall, demanded that he sign the petition. These tactics convinced twenty-four of thirty-six councilmen to pledge their opposition to the proposed thermal electric generating plant. On June 10, 1965, the petition was presented to Numazu's mayor and, on the following day, he announced the plans would be canceled. Tokyo Electric Company complied.

But on July 27, when the national government's Kurokawa team made public its findings, the cancelled plans were reactivated by central government and industry officials. Moreover, the proposed Fuji Petroleum refinery, previously sited for Mishima, was to be relocated on Thousand Pine Beach, a public bathing area located on the western border of Numazu. Several days later, the Kurokawa and Matsumura teams met in Tokyo to compare their studies. A comparison of their reports showed that only the local team had examined the kombinat comprehensively—including related problems of city planning, noise pollution, and inadequate water supplies. The Matsumura report also emphasized that the residents themselves should be given the final decision as to whether or not to construct the complex. The national team, on the other hand, had concentrated almost exclusively on problems of air pollution, suggesting methods for minimizing the discharge from the various potential sources. Although Kurokawa repeatedly claimed that his report was "purely scientific," and that it neither recommended nor opposed construction of the factories, the study in effect took construction for granted, offering neither criticisms of nor alternatives to the government's proposals. Had it not been for the local Matsumura report commissioned by Mishima city, the Kurokawa study would undoubtedly have passed unchallenged and would have proved a powerful ally to the advocates of construction.

Despite the resident's opposition and the Matsumura report, the central and prefectural governments remained blindly resolved to carry out their plans. Their intentions were finally jolted on September 13, when twenty-six thousand Numazu residents—nearly one-fifth of the city's total population—demonstrated against the plan in front of city hall. Widespread press coverage of the incident forced Numazu's mayor to yield to his constituents' demands. Several days later he traveled "up" to Tokyo to confer with officials of Fuji Petroleum and MITI. He then met with Shizuoka's governor. On September 18, the mayor announced final and irreversible cancellation of the petrochemical installation; one month later, Shimizu's town council issued a similar statement. The kombinat had been resoundingly defeated.

2.

The Mishima-Numazu anti-kombinat protest of 1964–65 marked the beginning of a period of public agitation against environmental pollution. Residents' groups adopting similar tactics have sprung up in every corner of the nation and have become the primary voice calling for the amelioration and prevention of environmental disruption. At the same time, they have initiated significant changes in traditional ways of thinking. By stressing self-preservation and basic human rights, these grassroots movements are contributing to lowering the traditional endurance threshold of the Japanese people, at least with regard to environmental problems, and are increasing pressure on government and industry at all levels. These phenomena, in turn, are restructuring the relationship between the governing and the governed by establishing a type of political and social interaction not observed previously in Japanese history. It is a process heralded by some as the first phase in the emergence of a new civic spirit of participatory democracy. Dr. Michio Hashimoto, counselor to the Environment Agency, goes so far as to declare the antipollution residents' movements "Japan's cultural revolution."[1]

Protest itself, even that directed against environmental contamination, is not new in Japan. One such protest occurred as far back as the 17th century, when farmers living in present-day Hitachi (Ibaragi Prefecture) forced the closure of the local Akazawa copper mine. Sociologist Nobuko Iijima notes that similar protests during the early Tokugawa period were uniformly occasioned by agricultural and fishing damages caused by mining operations and were apparently not centered on demands for compensation. Resorting to direct and often violent action, the victims were largely successful in putting an end to the operation of individual mines.[2] But slowly, the balance of power began to shift. During the latter years of the premodern period, as Japan's feudal leaders began to give greater priority to the mining industry, protests enjoyed less success.

With the rapid growth of Japanese industry after the Meiji Restoration, the protesters came to include urbanites as well as farmers and fishermen. Not insignificantly, these protest movements were influenced by contemporary "democratic" ideas and liberal activists. For example, Japan's first movement espousing democratic principles, the Freedom and People's Rights Movement, was active in the late 1870s and early 1880s and was instrumental in setting up elected prefectural assemblies in 1879 and in laying the foundations for the convening of the first elected National Diet in 1890. It was Shozo Tanaka, a one-time activist in the Freedom and People's Rights Movement, who was the sole Diet member who persistently attacked the government for its treatment of the Ashio Copper Mine problems.* Many of the Christians, socialists, and students who supported the victims of Ashio were likewise influenced by the political thinking and ideals of the proponents of democracy. This ideological interpretation of industrial pollution set a new pattern linking political and social issues to the human suffering occasioned by environmental disruption.

After interludes of militarism coinciding with the Sino-Japanese, Russo-Japanese, and First World Wars, Japan entered a period of dalliance with liberalism referred to as "Taisho democracy" that saw Diet passage of the Jury Law of 1923 and the Universal (Male) Suffrage Law of 1925. During the Taisho era (1912–26), some significant advances were made by victims of air pollution. In Hitachi and Besshi, mining and industrial magnates were compelled to resolve pollution conflicts by paying monetary compensation and implementing more effective technological controls over effluents. In 1918, the court decision in the Osaka Alkali case stipulated that industries were obliged to use the most advanced technology to prevent environmental contamination. The rise of labor organizations in the 1920s increased protest against deplorable working conditions, and Ashio mine workers joined with local farmers to fight the mine's contamination of both its own and neighboring environments. Although antipollution actions during the Taisho era did not generally receive direct aid from democratic movements, they undoubtedly benefited from the liberal mood of the times. But after the late 1920s, when the dominant mood waxed conservative, anticommunist, and militarist, all activities perceived to even remotely challenge the "national interest" were sharply and forcibly curtailed. It once again became the duty of the populace to endure pollution silently.

Then, in the late 1940s, radical constitutional and legal reforms instituted by the Occupation provided Japan with the framework for an American-style democratic system of government. Its potential, however, was not immediately realized because of the psychological carryover of wartime authoritarianism, demands of economic recovery, and a deep-rooted feeling that the postwar Constitution had been "imposed" by a foreign power and was not really a Japanese document. For more than a decade protests against pollution remained minimal as the nation strained to recover its economic base.† Massive demonstrations occasioned in 1960 by the ratification of the U.S.-Japan Mutual Security Pact, however, coming on top of renewed

---

* See pp. 4–7.

† The only noteworthy antipollution movement came in 1954, in reaction to American hydrogen bomb tests at Bikini Atoll which injured crew members of a Japanese fishing vessel and resulted in one death from radiation poisoning.

economic stability, may be viewed as a turning point in postwar social history. Although most Japanese subsequently returned to the business of developing the nation's economy, the conflict gave rise to renewed debate regarding the problems of Japanese democracy. It was in the wake of these debates that "resident power" in Mishima and Numazu blocked the local kombinat and gave birth to a new sense of community-based public interest.

Since the Mishima-Numazu incident, citizens' action groups have gradually broadened the scope of their activities from movements against local pollution problems to attempts to alter Japan's traditional "vertical" society and free communities from the tradition of unquestioning obedience to directives handed down by national and prefectural governments. Residents' movements have overtly defied central governmental authority, have demanded control of local political affairs, and have organized "horizontal" information flows on local and national levels. Using the press and the courts, they have insisted on the individual citizen's right to governmental and corporate information, to participation in decision-making processes, and to a clean and healthy living environment.

Popular movements against pollution take two basic forms. "Victims' groups," typified by the movements in Ashio, Yokkaichi, and Minamata, sprang primarily from a single segment of society directly harmed by industrial pollution. Motivated by an emotional sense of having been victimized, such groups overcame strong cultural pressures calling for endurance for the sake of social harmony, and pressed instead for public clarification of responsibility and monetary compensation. Once the damages incurred were politicized through the press, these groups usually developed numerous horizontal ties with a wide variety of sympathizers, but the victims themselves remained the core of the movement. Although victims' movements have developed into the primary force compelling government and industry to respond to industrial pollution, they have tended to remain *ad hoc* organizations with limited goals. "Citizens' groups," on the other hand, usually include a cross-section rather than a single homogeneous segment of local society, and therefore enjoy broad-based support and greater political leverage. Of course, these groups, too, are motivated by the desire to protect their health and livelihoods but, in contrast to victims' movements, they are typically prevention-oriented. In addition, many of these groups entertain long-range goals of modifying local and national decision-making processes that presently ignore the opinions of affected citizens. Holding to the principle that "residents must do it themselves," they try to avoid domination by outside organizations and institutions while utilizing the services of scientists, lawyers, and opposition political parties to advance their cause.

Although in practice the distinction between victims' and citizens' groups is rarely hard and fast, the two may be conceptualized as two ends of a single historical continuum. Until the Meiji Restoration, Japan countenanced neither the concept of "citizenship" nor "citizen's rights"; indeed, the words themselves did not exist at that time. Up to 1945, the rights of citizenship were guaranteed on paper but rarely achieved tangible expression. The Japanese were loyal subjects burdened with obligations, not citizens endowed with rights. Protests against pollution in the prewar and early postwar periods, therefore, were not typically based on the abstract values generally associated with Western political thought but arose only after concrete damages to the living environment had become overwhelming. An emotional sense of victimization was prerequisite to protest because, as subjects, the Japanese felt they had no "rights" to demand, while as "victims" they could act with justification.

Similarly, early protests against pollution did not originate in a popular sense of outrage against the spoilage of nature, despite the common Western image of traditional Japanese culture. Rather, they began as a reaction to personal sickness, death, and loss of livelihood. Indeed, it may well be that in Japan a special sense of "harmony" with one's natural surroundings actually contributed to the worsening of environmental blight. For in premodern times, harmony with nature meant an acceptance of the cycles of nature—their malevolent as well as beneficent manifestations. The Japanese conceived of human and nature as interacting within a single unified sphere in which people lived in awe of natural powers. This sense of harmony thus entailed a degree of resignation and endurance: One had to wait for natural disasters to eventually subside and beneficent conditions to return. Human examination and domination of nature via modern science were conceptual imports that were introduced along with Western technology. In the process of modernization, nature was secularized, but the sense of harmony in the form of resignation to the caprices of nature still persists. History of science professor Masao Watanabe writes that, "still immersed in nature itself, the Japanese people do not quite realize what is happening to nature and to themselves, and are thus exposed more directly to, and are more helpless in, the current environmental crisis."[3]

In its use of scientific data to organize a mass movement and counter government reports, the Mishima-Numazu movement marked an important shift away from this pattern. But like most citizens' movements of the 1960s, its activities centered on concrete issues such as "protecting our water and air" and "saving our children's health" rather than on abstract rights. In 1970, the latter were consolidated into a single concept when Michigan University professor Joseph Sax introduced into Japan the legal notion of "environmental rights."[4] The concept soon became the slogan of many residents' groups and, not long afterward, the basis of several legal actions. The speed with which Japanese antipollution activists adopted the idea is indicative not only of a maturing popular consciousness with regard to pollution problems, but also of the growing emphasis on recognition and enforcement of constitutionally guaranteed citizens' rights of all kinds. Nevertheless, as University of Hawaii Law School professor Julian Gresser notes, "Environmental rights ... are conceived of as man's rights to the purity of his environment. Somewhat curiously, no thought has been given in Japan, with its Buddhist-Shinto tradition, to the proposition that the environment itself has 'rights' to its own integrity, a concept becoming accepted in the West."[5]

Acceptance of the "human environmental rights" concept has been accompanied by increased recourse to legal action. The Japanese have come a long way since 1969, when the desperate fishermen of Yokkaichi's Isozu turned to the public law as a last resort. Courtroom debate is now generally recognized as an effective means of resolving conflicts and informing the public; moreover, court action is now taken much more quickly. These changes in the public's legal consciousness are due in large part to the favorable decisions handed down in the Minamata, Yokkaichi, Niigata, and itai-itai disease cases, known collectively as the four major pollution litigations. These favorable rulings marked the climax of the major postwar victims' movements, dramatically demonstrating the growing strength of antipollution residents' power.

These cases were effectively brought to national attention by concentrated news media coverage. Beginning in the late 1960s, the press waged a campaign to educate the public about pollution and its causes, the plight of its victims, and the failure of government and industry to accept responsibility for its occurrence. The press raised national awareness of the problem to the point where the announcement of nationwide contamination in the 1970s could set off genuine and widespread panic. Coverage of the major litigations provided rallying points for growing antipollution sentiment, and inspired the rise of new movements. In the 1960s, newspaper and television coverage of pollution problems increased approximately tenfold, and by 1973, hardly a day passed without a pollution-related story hitting the news. To a large extent, the media have succeeded in fostering public acceptance of protesters. The latter are today no longer considered unpatriotic or treasonous but, on the contrary, are perceived to be concerned citizens striving to protect their well-being and their livelihoods. In the years 1970–72, the official count of residents' movements throughout the nation increased fourfold. Citizen action groups have appeared in opposition to every imaginable form of environmental disruption, from noise and air pollution to highway construction, and range in size from single individuals to groups of over 40,000 members. This sudden increase in citizen activism has been encouraged by the realization that Japan's environmental problems are no longer merely local issues but are a serious nationwide threat.

In many respects, these new citizens' groups represent a popular forum for social debate as well as an intensive educational exercise in "democracy in action." Their participants are learning how to express grievances and make demands upon government rather than to submit passively to authority. They are meeting their elected officials face to face, using scientific data and legal and constitutional arguments to challenge authorities on specific issues. In the process, new personal friendships and professional relationships have grown up between previously isolated groups: Schoolteachers, farmers, housewives and fishermen, businessmen, and office workers have joined together to solve community pollution problems, making for a union of forces and social strata rarely encountered in Japanese society. Antipollution activities also comprise a training ground for potential leaders of the future: many young men and women are gaining invaluable political experience and knowledge related to the functioning of their local communities and the political and economic realities of contemporary Japan.

In contrast to the United States, however, Japan's antipollution movements are dominated by their older members. Many of the movements' elder participants and leaders, not a few of whom have come out of retirement, are forced to face, perhaps for the first time in their lives, questions of how government in fact operates, how it should function, and what industrialization and "development" have come to mean. Local leaders assert that this process of individual awakening is important in itself and contributes to the ultimate success or failure of each movement. Both within homogeneous communities such as apartment buildings and in heterogeneous communities such as those found near industrial areas, citizens' movements are creating a new sense of community spirit, grounded in a willingness to work together to protect the common living environment.

In addition to contacts between formerly isolated social groups within a single region, exchanges between groups in different areas of the country have also increased. One example of this trend is the federation of residents movements formed in Oita Prefecture in November 1972, as a forum for the exchange of information and as a medium for cooperation on common problems. A poignant example of the effects of contacts between groups related by shared problems rather than common geographical location is the 1964 meeting of the Minamata and Niigata mercury poisoning victims. The two groups not only recognized their common plight; their contact renewed the anti-Chisso movement in Minamata.*

These new contacts have established a two-way flow of people in areas designated for industrialization. Local residents travel throughout Japan inspecting factories and talking with officials and citizens in already industrialized areas, while politicians and independent scholars visit still undeveloped areas to inform residents of the pros and cons of proposed development. Personal contacts of this type have become indispensable to the success of local antipollution movements.

Contact between groups has been amplified by several loosely organized information networks that characteristically revolve around a single personality. These operations are deliberately non-centralized and do not attempt to exert control over local antipollution groups. This is at least partly a reaction to the wartime experience of excessive governmental repression, but also to a strong distinction, long an important element of Japanese social psychology, made between the residents of a given community and outsiders. Locals tend to resent the intrusion of outsiders into their affairs, particularly those coming from cosmopolitan Tokyo. And although they do little political "lobbying," at least as it is conceived in the United States, the groups that do exist maintain influential contacts in local movements, the press, and opposition political parties. Through these connections, they function as service groups and as clearinghouses for information.

Three important networks are the Independent Study Group, the Pollution Problems Research Association, and the *Chiiki Toso* (Regional Struggle) magazine. The Independent Study Group, guided by the personality of Jun Ui, a teacher of urban engineering at Tokyo University, is one of few that have developed viable international connections. Ui's organization was responsible for sending a group of Japanese pollution victims to the United Nations Stockholm Conference of 1972 and for publishing an English account of Japanese environmental problems, *Polluted Japan,* which goaded the government into hurriedly publishing three "supplementary" booklets on pollution diseases for the conference. The Pollution Problems Research Association is composed of activists formerly associated with Japan's Socialist party, and its political connections are useful for securing government materials and access to bureaucrats and politicians. *Chiiki Toso* is based in Kyoto, and is published by a group which shares its formal name, Rocinante, with Don Quixote's mule, its purpose being to bear some of the weight of the residents' burden. The magazine is an attempt to provide information linkages between different regions

---

* See p. 74.

and different groups, or, as one of its editors put it, "to create order within disorder." National conclaves of local residents' groups confronting similar problems are also uniting Japan's citizenry in new ways. Such conclaves have been held on issues relating to thermal and nuclear electric power plant construction, environmental rights trials, highways and urban transportation problems, and noise and vibration pollution from the super express bullet trains. These meetings have been called primarily for the purpose of exchanging information and strengthening personal relationships, and have been important in contributing to mutual support and creativity through a sort of "cross pollination" of ideas and experiences. They have not, however, resulted in an effective nationwide lobbying organization, although such a potential exists. In this sense, Japan's residents' movements remain local in nature, although they are willing to provide support to other groups "on request."

While the scattered and decentralized "organization" that characterizes Japan's antipollution movement may on the surface seem ineffective, concentration of effort at the local level has nevertheless been one key to success. "We haven't the desire or the surplus time or money to participate in national organizations," explained Hitoshi Koyama, leader of an anti-highway movement in Osaka; "We've got our hands full as it is." Each group values its integrity and the freedom of making its own decisions and therefore is reluctant to be placed under the direction of an "outsider." Strong group consciousness permits almost obsessive concentration on a single purpose, although it leaves individual groups nearly powerless on a national level. Nonetheless, despite traditional obstacles to horizontal contacts in Japanese society, geographical and problem-oriented "solidarity" groups have also been organized, and their political leverage is gradually increasing. Moreover, residents' groups are bringing together formerly separated groups within local communities and are gaining greater influence on the decision-making process in local government. They are both a sign and an instrument of changing social consciousness in contemporary Japan.

3.

Residents' movements have been aided, and sometimes hindered, by other groups not principally concerned with environmental problems: political parties, the press, labor unions, student groups, and a wide variety of scientists and professionals. Several general patterns of cooperation and conflict have emerged which have both helped and obstructed initiatives to protect the environment.

Inasmuch as they seek to resolve specific disputes by influencing the policies of local and central governments, residents' movements are by nature political pressure groups. Moreover, since traditional conflict-resolution mechanisms—appeals to authority followed by negotiation and compromise—have often failed to satisfy residents' demands, these citizens' groups have characteristically acquired anti-bureaucratic, anti-LDP, and anti-big business leanings. They have come to associate local pollution problems with laxity and irresponsibility on the part of business enterprises and government officials. Although many members of such groups were at one time either apolitical or LDP supporters, the failure of the conservative government has driven them to take a more progressive stance. As one Tokyo resident put it: "Frankly, my neighbors and I didn't really like the Japan Communist party, but when we complained about a high-rise building that was planned for our area, the JCP representative was out here every day collecting information and talking to the people. We've had to revise our opinions of the communists because, unlike the LDP, they've taken the time to come and listen to us."

A common pattern of organizational support emerged in areas such as Yokkaichi and Niigata in the mid-1960s. Key assistance came from local opposition parties and branches of large labor federations, mainly Sohyo (the General Council of Trade Unions), which is in turn closely tied to the Socialist party. Organizational aid comes primarily in three forms. First, support groups are able to mobilize manpower for mass demonstrations. Second, opposition party and labor union professionals, far more experienced than the average citizen in the methods of political confrontation and organizational management, provide invaluable tactical advice and assist at meetings with government spokesmen.

Third, important support is provided by opposition political parties in Tokyo. Their interrogation of ruling administration officials in the National Diet compels cabinet ministers to take a formal stand on specific issues. In many cases, residents' movements provide the political spokesmen with the data, questions, and policy statements used in these sessions. Although such confrontations have contributed to the growing popularity of the opposition parties and have served to publicize specific environmental problems, they have not, for the most part, resulted in fundamental changes of government policy. Nevertheless, in individual cases, the parliamentary process has proved helpful. In introducing residents' spokesmen to high- and middle-level bureaucrats, opposition politicians also play an important role as middlemen. A journey to Tokyo to make the rounds of the bureaucracy remains an important symbolic demonstration of protest, and traditional etiquette requires a formal introduction to a new acquaintance, especially a government official. The participation of political leaders at such meetings lends crucially important psychological status to the residents and their cause. In addition to their symbolic importance, such meetings also serve to improve the notoriously poor flow of information regarding local problems to government ministries.

Pollution in Japan is, therefore, a highly politicized and partisan issue, due in part to the structure of the political system and the vast gap in ideology and power that separates the ruling LDP and the nation's four opposition parties (Japan Communist, Socialist, Democratic Socialist, and Clean Government parties). Moreover, relations between Japan's opposition parties tend to be highly competitive, and are even further complicated by a deep-rooted factionalism within the individual parties themselves. The parties' main point of agreement is their strong opposition to the Liberal Democrats, and this limited consensus is often unable to smooth over emotional and ideological rifts between the parties on concrete issues. Under such circumstances, the pollution issue, for as long as it remains an important focus of popular discontent, is a tool that can be used by the opposition parties to gain leverage against the government. Thus, adoption of an outspoken antipollution stance by the progressives is considered by many observers to be largely a political expedient. While grateful for political services, therefore, residents tend to be wary of political motives. The ability to maintain a position of autonomy and avoid becoming entrapped in factional disputes varies from group to group. One which has been notably skillful in enlisting the aid of all the parties, including even the LDP, is the Osaka-based Nakatsu anti-highway movement. As one of the movement's leaders put it, "We welcome any politician willing to help our cause. When the communists come, we round up a welcoming committee composed of our more progressive residents—the university professors, for example; when the LDP comes, we call out our housewives, company presidents, and business executives. We try to keep everybody happy."

In some areas, political and ideological splits among political support groups have seriously interfered with antipollution efforts. The principal conflict in Minamata and elsewhere is between the communist party and unaffiliated groups and individuals. Among the latter are numbered former JCP members and sympathizers who left the party ranks and have since been branded "Trotskyites"* for their more independent and critical attitudes. In Date (Hokkaido), for example, a communist lawyer approached by the local

---

* This term was first widely used in reference to the leadership faction of the National Student Federation (Zengakuren), which renounced international communism and criticized Khrushchev and Mao Tse-tung around the time of the Security Treaty demonstrations of 1960. Those pollution activists labeled as "Trotskyites" dismiss the term as a part of the factionalism in the Japanese political left and as an attempt by the JCP to blackball citizen activists as anarchists.

residents' movement refused to handle an environmental rights case because one of the group's leaders bore the Trotskyite label. The "Trotskyites," in turn, accuse the JCP of exploiting the pollution issue for political purposes.

Company unions have been even slower than political parties and associated national union federations in recognizing their potential role in helping to ameliorate and prevent pollution problems. Since most of Japan's unions are organized on a company rather than an industry-wide basis, they have very weak horizontal ties and are inordinately susceptible to management control. It is not unusual for a given company to pay its union leaders' salaries, and the pervasive corporate atmosphere of paternalism encourages the speedy resolution of "family" spats through compromise and negotiation. When, on rare occasions, a union dares to challenge company opinion overtly, management commonly responds by forming a "second" union, as happened in Minamata, to woo the misled sheep back into the fold. At the root of company union inactivity, however, is a conflict between labor's personal economic interests (especially in times of inflation), which argue for the continued growth of industry, and increasing social pressure calling for labor to assume greater responsibility for the company's pollution of the environment. Furthermore, as one frustrated worker explained: "Our first priority, before dealing with *external* pollution, is to get a healthy environment *inside* our factory."

Individual employees who have linked hands with antipollution groups have been subjected to extra psychological pressures in addition to those inherent in the Japanese corporate structure. They have not been fired but "relieved" of their work duties; in Japanese terminology, they have been "hung out to dry." One employee of the Kojin Paper Company in Saeki (Oita Prefecture), who passed information regarding company violations of effluent regulations to a local residents' movement, continued to appear at work, but spent his days sitting in a chair doing nothing. The company, reluctant to fire him because of its traditional lifetime employment system, resorted to ostracizing him from the company group. Reprisals and threats of delayed advancement in the company hierarchy, combined with residual feelings of obligation and loyalty to the company employer, have effectively prevented most individuals from acting on impulses of conscience. Perhaps the most tragic example of such a failure to act on higher principles was provided by Chisso's Dr. Hosokawa. Nevertheless, with increasing labor mobility accompanied by a gradual relaxing of the traditional sense of devotion to the company, the number of "indicters from within" will probably be on the rise.

One possible solution to labor's often paralyzing conflict of interests was adopted by factory employees in the small city of Ishinomaki (Miyagi Prefecture) which boasts a variety of local industries and is beset by an equal variety of pollution problems. Unable to object to the policies of their own company, employees of factory A vigorously protested against the pollution caused by factory B, while workers engaged by factory B protested the effluents discharged by factory A. For the most part, however, company unions, comprising the great majority of labor organizations in Japan, remain apathetic and inactive, effectively controlled by corporate management.

Students, too, were slow to realize the full implications of pollution problems. It was not until after the campus riots of 1968 and the period of "self-reflection" that followed—all of which roughly coincided with the initiation of legal proceedings in Minamata and Yokkaichi—that college students and faculty became widely concerned with the plight of industrial pollution victims. Frustrated by their inability to bring about significant changes in the nation's educational system, many student activists turned to social problems outside the academic community. Direct student participation was most pronounced in the Narita Airport struggle, where local farmers supported by student activists fought against the government's arbitrary imposition of a new international airport in their midst. Resembling that of Ashio in many ways, the struggle ended in a violent confrontation with Japan's riot police. Students at Kyushu University have formed a group to research and publicize pollution problems in northern Kyushu and several groups have moved into Minamata to help mercury victims fish and farm, as well as to participate in demonstrations. Still, the numbers of students actively involved with pollution problems is small, although concern among them is on the rise. Many local movements, however, reflecting the psychological distinction made between "residents" and "outsiders," are not oriented to using student volunteers, and not a few would prefer their absence.

Another group of "outsiders" important to the antipollution movement is composed of interested specialists, particularly medical and physical scientists and legal attorneys. Here again, a few began investigating and publicizing pollution problems in the 1960s, but the great majority remained indifferent until the student riots of 1968 and the worsening pollution conditions of the early 1970s. The Seto Inland Sea Investigation Team, made up of students and faculty from 18 universities in the Kyoto-Osaka-Kobe area, is representative of the recent trend. In 1971, and again in 1973, this group spent several months analyzing the problem, and the report they issued, still the most complete survey of Inland Sea contamination, preceded a government study by two years. Similar research groups have sprung up at other universities and have been accompanied by an increase in direct exchanges between local residents and academics. But here, too, political and ideological differences have interfered with the scientific and legal exploration of environmental issues.

Those leaders of residents' movements labeled "Trotskyites" have been cut off from the JCP-dominated Japan Scientists Association and from JCP-affiliated lawyers. Moreover, it seems unlikely that the fragmented political atmosphere surrounding pollution issues will significantly improve in the near future.

The staunchest and most reliable supporters of antipollution efforts to date have been members of the press. In addition to serving as a check on the activities of the power elites, they have educated the public on the issues and, at times, have provided the spark that incited effective protest.

In general, the Japanese public tends to view its press as predominantly antigovernment. According to the *Asahi* correspondent in New York, Yukio Matsuyama, the press's antigovernment stance is a reaction to the autocratic power of the executive branch and to the fact that mass media feel responsible for having cooperated with the military during the war. He also sees in it a catering to the public's predilection for news that provokes tension. Finally, he cites the "erratic" policies of the United States, which in "close company with those of the Liberal Democratic Government ... invite, even require, public criticism."[6] Richard Halloran, Tokyo correspondent for *The New York Times*, holds a somewhat different view of the Japanese press, seeing it as a "participant, a communicator among the other elements of Japanese leadership, and the mouthpiece of the Establishment." Press criticisms of the government, Halloran maintains, are "only part of the the consensus-making—an aspect of a family fight that goes on in the open."[7] Whether "in" or "out" of the Establishment, the press is undeniably a powerful opinion-molding force which Halloran ranks as equal in clout with Japan's bureaucrats, LDP politicians, and big business leaders. Its high-powered, albeit at times sensational, coverage of environmental problems has been a major force in the rise of antipollution movements.

In sum, it can be fairly said that local residents' movements could well represent a transitional step in Japan's modernization. They embody the traditional elements of group orientation while emphasizing the value of human rights, participatory democracy, and legal and scientific debate. In this sense, environmental disruption in Japan has posed a challenge to the very social, political, and economic systems that have brought that disruption to its exaggerated state.

4.

Although the struggle against unresponsiveness in government and irresponsibility in industry has made appreciable headway, antipollution groups may have to change their present tactics if lasting gains are to be made.

Industry spokesmen often criticize antipollution movements for being overly emotional and for lacking a firm, scientific basis. Chie Nakane, professor of anthropology at Tokyo University, summarizes the general attitude held by elite circles toward all "opposition groups":

> "Any criticism of authority tends to be seen as heroism ... And ... such deeds are today labelled as democratic action. Often it is merely opposition for opposition's sake; it is nearer in essence to emotional contradiction, than to rational resistance from which further reasonable development might be expected..."[8]
>
> "[T]rade or students unions and other popular movements, in spite of the strong appeal of radicalism and violence, have little social significance, in that they are unable to stir the majority, even of those in the same category."[9]

How applicable are Nakane's observations to Japan's antipollution movements? Can the movements' accomplishments to date be said to have "little social significance?"

In addition to the weaknesses it may represent, it is worthwhile to note the cultural determinants of emotionalism in the antipollution movement, and the short-term purposes it serves. Anthropologist Masao Kunihiro has pointed out that Japan has no cultural tradition of rational dissent. Conflicts, he explains, have traditionally been resolved by unspoken mutual understanding, the "art of gut communication," rather than through verbal and intellectual debate. Historically, when understanding of the former type could not be achieved, a given issue was not "argued" on the basis of facts: protesters either surrendered in conformity with the tradition of resignation to authority or exploded in direct action.

In Numazu, for example, it was not scientific debate between the Kurokawa and Matsumura investigatory teams that forced the government to cancel Suruga Bay's planned petrochemical complex but rather the angry demonstration of 26,000 Numazu residents. While a David-and-Goliath atmosphere may at times pervade antipollution activities, therefore, it must be remembered that whatever emotionalism and irrationality these groups may display are nothing more than a reaction to the attitudes and behavior of Japan's ruling authorities. It is, after all, a two-way street.

Once Japan's ruling politicians, government bureaucrats, and big business executives decide upon a given course of action, they tend not to alter that decision in response to "rational resistance" alone. The general impotence of rationality is reinforced by the ruling triumvirate's tendency to treat environmental pollution as a political or social rather than a scientific problem, although lip service has been regularly paid to the value of science. Thus, in Minamata, fishermen's verbal protests against Chisso, based on the observation of dead fish near the factory's drainpipe, were rejected by corporate executives and governmental officials as "unscientific," implying that they did not merit rational scrutiny. It was not until the fishermen rioted in 1959 that the company began to consider the scientific treatment demanded by common sense. Even then, Chisso paid disease victims and fishermen monetary compensation to quell their protests and politically neutralize the issue. The pollution problem was considered "solved." In Yokkaichi, scientific data on the effects of environmental degradation upon human health were disregarded as government and industry planners continued to expand production facilities. Only direct, forceful, and repeated emotional outbursts succeeded in compelling the authorities to recognize the seriousness of the situation. Thus, considering the history of government and industry response to pollution problems, one must wonder if the resort to scientific rationality alone would have been sufficient to bring about change.

Dr. Takeo Suzuki, assistant director of the National Public Health Research Institute, comments that the Japanese "have not really taken Western science to heart, and that without an incident to incite the public and produce emotional panic, scientific surveys are simply not undertaken."[10] This certainly seems to be the case. Although researchers detected photochemical oxidants in Tokyo's air in 1967 and requested funds to study the problem, they received no major support until the summer of 1970, when the hospitalization of a number of high school students due to photochemical smog had already caused a veritable panic. Similarly, one Environment Agency bureaucrat welcomed the 1973 fish panic because, he explained, it made it easier for the agency to obtain funding from the Finance Ministry!

Where environmental protection is concerned, Japan's central authorities are still primarily "reactive" rather than "proactive." Once committed to a program of action, agreed upon by consensus and allowed to filter down to the populace, major modifications of that program are rarely initiated from within the power elite; they come, rather, from outside pressures. And when such external pressures appear, they often give rise to extreme reactions. At the time PCBs were identified as the toxic agents responsible for the Kanemi rice oil poisoning in 1968, for example, the government initiated no studies of possible environmental contamination by the chemicals but, on the contrary, authorized additional factories to produce them and oversaw the doubling of their production by 1970. It was not until 1971, largely in reaction to widespread emotional panic at home and foreign precedents, that the government moved, first to restrict and then to place a total ban on PCB use. In so doing, however, it failed to recognize those situations where the substances' noncombustible properties are necessary for safety and where the substance could be prevented from contaminating foods or the environment. This pendulum-like behavior, the sudden and emotional swing from one extreme to its opposite, is to be found in the responses of the power elite to international as well as domestic issues, as will be shown in Chapter 10.

Seen in the light of Japanese social and political behavior, therefore, the emotionalism underlying antipollution tactics has its place and plays a vital role in influencing governmental actions. Press-induced panic may well be indispensable to achieve environmental improvement. Such emotionalism also fuels the determination and dedication that characterize environmental groups. Undoubtedly, however, efforts grounded in emotionalism alone are bound to be short lived; like the farmers' riots of the Tokugawa period and the Great Fish Panic of 1973, they cannot be sustained or channeled toward long-range goals. In this sense, Nakane's point is well taken. Nevertheless, there is evidence that antipollution residents' movements have broadened their goals in the process of dealing with immediate issues and have wrought significant changes among their participants, at least in terms of individual attitudes toward the role of citizens in political decision-making processes.

But are environmental pollution problems enough of a shock to the body politic to evoke truly significant cultural change? Perhaps. In 1973, Numazu's local antipollution movement, backed by the four progressive parties, toppled the LDP's candidate in the mayoral election and placed a member of its own organization in the city's highest office. This political change has been accompanied by surveys of the local environment, tree-planting projects, and greater overall citizen participation in local government. Nor are these changes limited to this one region. By 1973, non-LDP "progressive" administrations had been voted into office in Japan's seven largest cities—Tokyo, Osaka, Nagoya, Yokohama, Kawasaki, Kyoto, and Kobe—and more than 150 local governments had switched their prime allegiance from the LDP to one or another of the opposition parties. Such shifts have been accompanied by changes in the relationship between local government and residents' movements. Mutual defiance has given way to cooperation. Some city governments are said to subsidize antipollution groups, while residents' participation on local committees, inquiry commissions, and policy boards is on the rise.

Progressive administrations, however, have not been able to unravel the complex web of urban problems endemic to Japan's large cities. Moreover, residents opposed to super expressway construction in Osaka and the laying of new railway tracks in Yokohama criticize their local progressive administrations for supporting these projects. "The party label has changed," charges one activist, "but the bureaucracy has not. All we have now is a progressive bureaucracy!" On the other hand, residents' movements, as witness the role of Suginami Ward residents in Tokyo's garbage war, have sometimes opposed "public welfare" projects, bringing down on themselves such charges as that of "egoism."

Such unwillingness to submit to government projects for the "public welfare" seems to be on the rise in all developed nations,* but it poses a particularly difficult problem in Japan, where social "harmony" has been a cherished value for centuries. Worsening environmental disruptions and increasing popular demand for better living conditions have caused the number of complaints to soar, and the apparently "unbearable" discontent represented by such dissatisfaction threatens to unravel some of the nation's taut social fabric. In 1970, the number of reported complaints of all types lodged with official agencies throughout the country reached 63,000, an increase of 55 percent over that of the previous year, and by 1973 it totaled 87,800. Thus, it seems that the traditional Japanese reluctance to protest is being eroded by the negative effects of modernization.

But can a solid majority of Japan's population be meaningfully activated by the problem of environmental pollution? A public opinion survey conducted by the Prime Minister's Office in 1972 revealed that 77 percent of the respondents expressed an interest in environmental problems, while 49 percent believed that pollution should not be tolerated for the sake of economic development. The latter statistic represented an increase of 22 percent over a similar survey conducted in 1966. A 1971 survey indicated that 51 percent of the public agreed that pollution should be eliminated even if it

---

* University of California Professor Melvin Webber, an expert on city planning, proposed at a seminar held in 1973 at the Japan Regional Development Center that the concept of "public interest" has become a mirage for the United States and other highly industrialized nations. While solutions to "easy" problems of the past (improving housing conditions, treating disease, paving roads) tended to win rapid consensus, the issues of advanced societies are more controversial. Webber maintained that today's problems are more "difficult" since they require deciding how to build what and where to do it. "In a situation where some gain and others lose, such as constructing a superhighway through a dense urban residential area, there simply are no technical, scientific or economic answers as to what is right. The answer is in the decision-making process and in introducing citizens into decision-making: It is to professionalize the amateurs." Webber's statements evoked interesting responses from the Japanese attending the meeting. One city planner employed by the progressive Yokohama government noted that in Japan "the way the central government usually accomplishes its aim is by sending in the riot police to drag off protesters." This view was countered by a young bureaucrat from the central Economic Planning Agency, an arm of the Prime Minister's Office. "The problem in Japan today is that the system of planning is too democratic and too inefficient ... I worry that decentralization will burden the local citizenry with the problem of self-reliance."

involved minor sacrifices in economic growth. These findings add up to a change in public consciousness and personal values occurring on a relatively wide scale; they indicate that Japan's overriding national consensus may indeed be fading under the onslaught of environmental degradation and rising expectations regarding the quality of life. Meanwhile, more and more citizens' groups demand control over the fate of their communities. Thus, residents' movements may be riding the crest of a gathering wave.

Nevertheless, antipollution groups are encumbered by serious limitations. Most are exclusively local phenomena that have arisen from specific problems and are confined to particular geographic regions. While their grassroots origins and narrowly defined goals have assisted them in achieving short-term goals, their deep-seated parochialism may jeopardize their long-term effectiveness. Moreover, as presently constituted, most residents' movements are antipollution rather than environmental: they tend to be motivated by the appearance of an objectionable phenomenon in their midst rather than by the broader concepts of ecology. The emotionalism of these movements must come to encompass scientific and theoretical understanding of the full domestic and international implications of Japan's pollution problems if the nation's concerned citizens are to exert a positive impact on the ecocrisis confronting Japan and the rest of the world.

The lack of a holistic ecological philosophy is to be seen in the example of movements' neglect of intrinsically related environmental problems. While pre-packed vegetables no longer bear the proud English label "chemically grown," for example, most Japanese seem to have accepted contaminated and industrially denaturalized foods as unavoidable adjuncts of modern life.* Similarly, there is depressingly little interest being paid to developing nonchemical pesticide techniques, reviving traditional methods of agriculture, or exploring ways to rejuvenate deteriorated soils.† This fragmented perception

---

* Consumer groups have, however, begun to put increasing pressure on the government to tighten its controls over chemical food additives, such as AF-2, a synthetic germicide which has been shown to cause mutations in human cells and bacteria. In response to growing consumer anxieties, the Health and Welfare Ministry announced that during fiscal 1974 it will recheck the safety of some 37 controversial chemical substances included in the total of 337 food additives that are legal in Japan. Nevertheless, as consumer activist Katsuko Nomura noted, "It took us one full year of hard work to force the government to place a ban on AF-2, a single additive. Checking 337 other additives may take years."

† This attitude seems to be slowly changing. A few groups and individuals have begun to rent plots of land to cultivate by natural means, and some farmers have responded by producing "organic" (and higher priced) rice and vegetables. Also, in late November 1974, a representative from the

of the environmental problem is reinforced by the distinct gap between consumers' groups and antipollution organizations.

Antipollution groups have undeniably succeeded in gaining a measure of influence in local political affairs. Their political victories make it all the more urgent that the emotionalism which sparked their initial thrust become more informed with the technical and legal ability required for city management and environmental planning. It is also vitally important that residents' movements avoid entanglement in narrow political issues and develop a perspective in which political processes are seen as a means to realizing ecological goals rather than as ends in themselves.

And perhaps of greatest importance, there is the role to be played by the Japanese on "spaceship earth" in relation to the vital international problems of population, resources, the oceans, and the export of pollution. Despite Japan's heavy dependence upon the oceans and her disproportionate complicity in despoiling them, there is in the nation today little action dedicated to treating the problem of declining world fisheries or general ocean contamination. This challenge of internationalism may be the hardest of all to meet, for it means overcoming the vestiges of a long history of isolation while necessitating the resolution of genuine and complex conflicts of interest. It is in dealing with problems of international import that Japan's antipollution groups, like many such groups elsewhere, are at present most unprepared and inexperienced.

Independent Study Group attended a natural farming conference in France. An Okinawa-based group is producing natural salt, and a Tokyo group imports eggs from a countryside farm that have been laid by non-mechanized chickens that are allowed to roam and peck "as they used to."

CHAPTER TEN

THE BIG SQUEEZE

> "In the last eight years I have come very close to a belief that the Japanese have, in effect, discovered or developed an ability to grow, economically, with a rapidity that is unlikely to be surpassed in the period at issue— that might well result, late in the twentieth century or early in the twenty-first in Japan's possessing the largest gross national product in the world."
>
> —HERMAN KAHN
> *The Emerging Japanese Superstate,* 1970

> "Japan is an octopus that is eating its own legs."
>
> —A JAPANESE FISHERMAN, 1972

Although the Japanese government has made efforts to alleviate the nation's environmental problems in the postwar period, measures have too often been instituted only reluctantly in the face of critical environmental disruption and in reaction to loud and sometimes violent popular protest. Moreover, even after the enactment of pollution control legislation, pressures from industrial and financial circles have often blocked efforts at effective enforcement. Pressure from citizens' groups, the press, and the opposition parties over the past five years has finally compelled the government to initiate belated efforts in the worst stricken areas—and these have not been without some success. Nevertheless, the root causes of Japan's environmental problems—an industrial structure based on the heavy and chemical industries, a throughput mass-consumption economy, inadequate social overhead capital and a commitment to rapid economic growth—have been, until only recently, largely disregarded.

The first postwar attempts to grapple with pollution were made not by Japan's central government planners but by Tokyo metropolitan government officials. In 1949, the city adopted an industrial pollution control ordinance, followed by laws restricting noise (1954), and smoke and soot (1955). Unfortunately, these municipal measures had little effect. By the mid-1950s, thousands of small factories had sprung up throughout the city, making the separation of industrial and residential areas all but impossible. Moreover, politically powerful big business interests within the capital area could disregard local ordinances with relative impunity.*

The Ministry of Health and Welfare was the first to investigate pollution on a national level. In 1953, after recording the number of incidents and victims of pollution outbreaks, it drafted the Act to Control Environmental Contamination. Vigorous opposition from governmental and financial circles and lackadaisical popular and press support, however, prevented enactment of the bill. As a result, Japan entered its period of intense economic growth unhampered by environmental restraints.

It required a riot to finally spark enactment of the government's first pollution control laws. In June 1958, after the effluents discharged into the Edo River by the Honshu Paper Company caused a massive fish die-off and appeals to the Tokyo metropolitan government failed to bring any response, some 1,000 fishermen stormed the paper factory. In response, the government oversaw speedy Diet ratification of the Water Quality Conservation and Factory Effluents Control Laws in December 1958. It was at this time that the residents of Yokkaichi and other cities hosting industrial complexes were first beginning to complain of air pollution and the diseases and general discomforts associated with it. Four years later, in belated response, the government enacted the Smoke and Soot Regulation Law of June 1962.

These earliest national legislative measures, like Tokyo's, left many loopholes. The Smoke and Soot Law, which declared it necessary to maintain "harmony between preservation of the living environment and the healthy development of industry," applied only to seriously contaminated areas, and even there was completely ineffective in controlling "invisible" pollution caused by sulfur oxides and automobile exhaust. In fact, early legislation was largely designed to appease angry elements of the populace while, in effect, according higher priority to the "healthy development of industry" than to

---

* Despite Tokyo's limited success in establishing effective ordinances, due recognition must be accorded to the government's attempt—especially considering that during the 1950s, cities elsewhere were actively competing to attract industries and considered pollution control a disincentive to be avoided. As recently as 1965, only 8 of the 46 prefectural governments had established pollution control divisions. By 1970, however, nearly every prefecture had one.

human and environmental well-being. Although an Environmental Pollution Division was set up in the Ministry of Health and Welfare in 1964, its powers were severely limited by the government's overall bias.

In 1963, the Ministry of Health and Welfare initiated "discussions" regarding the need for broader environmental legislation that culminated four years later in the Basic Law for Environmental Pollution Control. This new ordinance was a significant advance in that it defined the types of pollution to be brought under control and outlined the regulatory roles to be played by industry and local and national governments. But even in 1967, the concept of environmental protection as embodied in the Basic Law was watered down by the inclusion of a clause specifying that such protection was to occur in "harmony with the healthy development of the economy." This "harmony clause" provided industrial circles with legal justification for pressuring government to weaken environmental standards and for delaying the costly indemnification of pollution disease victims. Realizing its implications, the press and opposition parties accused the government of favoring big business at the public's expense. In December 1970, the Diet revised the law by removing this reference to the economy. During this same session, the government introduced, and the Diet quickly approved, fourteen bills related to environmental protection. Known as the Pollution Diet, this legislative session gave Japan the world's most complete legal framework relating to environmental protection. In July 1971, following the precedent set by the United States several months earlier, the government established an Environment Agency to implement the new laws.

Since its inception, the Environment Agency has made significant progress in several areas. By taking over the functions of environment-related "sections" previously dispersed throughout half a dozen other ministries, it has coordinated and strengthened the antipollution voice in government deliberations. By urging tighter effluent standards and drafting pollution-control laws, the agency has introduced greater environmental concern into the decision-making process. It has steadily expanded the scope and number of its scientific surveys, and since March 1974, has been operating its own research and analysis laboratories. The agency has channeled public concern into the governmental process of "rolling consensus," and at times has taken action to the direct benefit of residents' movements. Although its overall character and influence has varied with successive directors-general, the Environment Agency has achieved modifications in a number of industry-supported projects.

The agency's effectiveness, however, has been severely limited by its organizational characteristics. First, many of its members are recruited from other ministries and retain close ties to their "home offices." Only temporarily assigned to the Environment Agency, they are scheduled to return to their former ministries after two or three years of "exile." This mixing has diluted efforts to protect the environment. Although the Air Quality Bureau—staffed with a contingent from the former MHW Environmental Division—has drafted several relatively progressive air pollution control bills, the Water Conservation Bureau—its staff drawn largely from MITI and the Economic Planning Agency—has taken a weaker stance on water pollution, refusing, for example, to sponsor legislation to protect the Seto Inland Sea.

A second internal weakness is the result of Japan's endemic sectionalism, which obstructs cooperation between the various bureaus of the agency. Sectionalism is particularly self-defeating when applied to environmental concerns, since the biosphere is, after all, indivisible. Artificially partitioning it into atmosphere, hydrosphere, and lithosphere (air, water, and earth) defies its ecological oneness. Thus, tightening air but not water pollution standards could tempt an irresponsible polluter to discharge a greater percentage of wastes into water systems.

External barriers between the Environment Agency and other ministries are even more difficult to overcome. Although the EA assumed many previously scattered administrative functions, several others, such as food and drug administration, and sewage and water treatment plant construction, have remained in their original ministries. Potential dangers inherent in this separation of powers, vividly revealed in the Kanemi rice oil case, remain.

Because of its newness, the Environment Agency has been relegated to a relatively low rank in the hierarchy of ministries. In addition, although budget expenditures for the environment increased nearly sixfold between 1967 and 1973 (a proportional rise twice that of the total national budget), the agency lacks the industrial and LDP support to stand up to the Ministry of Finance or MITI. Because government bills presented to the Diet must receive the approval of all related ministries and cabinet officials, the agency has been forced to compromise on its pollution control legislation in "adjustment negotiations" with the staunch patrons of industrial interests.* The major

---

* The gradual strengthening of controls over sulfur dioxide is a typical case in point. Although the government knew as early as 1961 that sulfur dioxide gases were causing health problems in Yokkaichi, it did not institute national controls over the pollutant until February 1969. At that time, the government set ambient air quality "goals" calling for annual average hourly concentrations of less than 0.05 ppm, and 88 percent of hourly levels to be held to less than 0.1 ppm. By 1972, an Environment Agency survey of 236 cities showed that 95 percent met the standards (including Yokkaichi), and only 12 cities still exceeded them. But the Yokkaichi court decision served as an impetus to review the standards, and in March 1973, a committee of specialists, concluding that the existing standards were far too lenient, recommended new

impetus for criticizing environmentally hazardous policies has therefore come largely from the opposition parties, the press, and popular movements.

In general, the EA has shied away from encouraging or developing ties with grassroots antipollution movements. Although the agency tends to be more receptive than other government bodies to requests from residents' groups, the flow of information between it and people in local areas is still far from what it could be. Unlike its American counterpart, the EA has not officially assumed a policy of encouraging citizens' group activities, perhaps partly because of traditional Japanese concepts of ruler and ruled, but also because of the political implications such a policy would entail. The Environment Agency remains part of a conservative, big-business-oriented government that associates antipollution activities with the opposition. Nonetheless, the general spirit of the agency, particularly among its younger members, is dedicated to reducing pollution and is sympathetic to the overall goals of the residents' movements.

While the Pollution Diet has helped moderate the most severe instances of air and water pollution, environmental disruptions have continued to increase in extent, frequency, and duration throughout the country. Although use of low sulfur oil, higher stacks, desulfurizers, and electrostatic dust-collectors have helped reduce the national average atmospheric concentrations of sulfur dioxide and particulates, concentrations of nitrogen oxides and hydrocarbons have continued to increase due to steady rises in the production and number of motor vehicles on the nation's roads. (The latter two pollutants have interacted to exacerbate the secondary pollution problem of photochemical oxidants.) By 1974, official pollution victims of obstructive respiratory ailments in twelve designated areas totaled nearly ten thousand.

The state of Japan's waterways is no less discouraging. The annual nationwide water pollution survey published in October 1972 reported that although concentrations of heavy metals had diminished from the previous year, the general quality of Japan's rivers, lakes, marshes, and coastal waters had further deteriorated. Despite four- to fivefold increases in water pollution control capital stock in the major industries of foodstuffs, pulp and paper, textiles, and chemicals between 1968 and 1971, they treated only 20 percent of their total BOD output. Moreover, because production expanded rapidly,

---

standards three times as strict. Promulgated in May 1973, these were met by only 35 cities, while pollutants in 213 urban areas exceeded the level now deemed necessary for the maintenance of good health. It is worthwhile to note that the original advisory committee studying sulfur oxides had, as early as 1968, proposed regulations similar to the standards adopted in 1973, but, due to opposition from industrial circles, MITI, and the Ministry of Health and Welfare, had been forced to weaken them.

the total volume of untreated BOD actually increased. Spreading suburbs added to the burden.

Pollution abatement investment has increased rapidly over the past few years. Between 1970 and 1974, MITI reports, the ratio of pollution prevention equipment to total equipment investments rose from 5.3 to an estimated 12.6 percent, or from a total of 163.7 billion ($454 million) to 618.9 billion yen ($2,000 million).[1] But, again, the effectiveness of these substantial investments has tended to be offset by rapid increases in production. Between the years 1960 to 1970, the total annual social costs of environmental pollution rose from 936 billion yen ($2.7 billion) to 6,101 billion yen ($16.9 billion).[2] Moreover, investments have tended to concentrate in air pollution control, leaving other crucial abatement mechanisms sorely neglected. In 1969, for example, only 27 percent of the 58 million tons of discharged industrial wastes was recycled, while 53 percent went into land reclamation and 11 percent was burned or simply dumped into rivers, trash heaps, and the ocean.

Some Japanese scientists and technologists are optimistic. A report compiled by the Science and Technology Agency predicts that air and water pollution will be solvable by 1985, and that sensory pollution problems (noise, vibration, and offensive odor) could be eliminated shortly thereafter.[3] The report foretells that by 1990, advanced technology will make it possible to construct no-waste, noiseless, vibrationless, and odorless factories in residential areas, and new techniques of natural resource management and land-use planning will make it possible to end all environmental disruption. Full implementation of this technology could begin around 1985, after the nation has achieved a $1 trillion economy and can then afford to "clean its nest." The survey reflects one vision of the "new" New Japan: worry-free people swimming in waters bordering on petrochemical plants; a modern garbage incinerator in the center of Shinjuku, the new center of Tokyo; huge factories interspersed among residential areas. The apparent goal is to technologically "de-pollute" industrial processes so that man and his creations may continue to grow in mutual "harmony." It is, of course, rooted in a faith in the ability of technology to solve the problems its misuse has created, and fails to consider that there may be cases of irreversible environmental deterioration before which even the most advanced technology may be ineffective.

The achievement of these technological solutions has received an increasingly high priority in both private and governmental circles. Although Japanese industry has traditionally relied upon imported technology, the increase in domestic demand has sped many firms into basic research and development. In some areas, such as sulfur dioxide abatement and automobile engine technology, noteworthy advances have been made. Between 1970 and 1972, private and government investments in pollution abatement research nearly quadrupled, reaching 4.76 billion yen. As a result, pollution prevention and control has now become an important Japanese industry.

Even after industries install abatement equipment, though, there remains the administrative problem of seeing that it is properly used. Many concerned citizens have expressed suspicions that because operating the equipment is expensive, industries often turn it on only during daylight hours or official inspection tours. There are cases of individual factories being forewarned of such inspections, allowing them to clean up beforehand. After several such incidents in the Kashima industrial complex, local residents concluded, "We should invite government officials to come every day—then, maybe, we'd have clean air." One way of checking whether equipment is being used properly is through monitoring systems, and while computerized systems (such as the telemeter system) for monitoring ambient air quality and factory effluents have become fairly widespread, many local residents remain skeptical about the uses to which the data is put.*

Two basic Japanese environmental policies have been the compensation of pollution victims and the mediation of pollution disputes. Although based on the "polluter pays principle," compensation measures were not designed as an industrial pollution deterrent, but more as a harmony-restoring mechanism. Based on the Law Concerning Special Measures for the Relief of Pollution-Related Patients, enacted in 1969, the system provides relief to pollution victims whether or not civil liability has been established. Victims living in designated areas and certified by screening committees may receive hospitalization, out-patient treatment, and nursing expenses. The company or companies responsible provide one-half the expenses, with municipal, prefectural, and national governments sharing the remainder. For victims who

---

* Public fears were substantiated in early 1974 when a major scandal broke involving the Japan Institute of Analytical Chemistry. The Institute had been commissioned by the Science and Technology Agency to survey radioactivity in harbors during port calls by American nuclear-powered submarines. The Institute's management had disregarded scientific data collection procedures and forged 30 percent of the graphs included in reports submitted to the government in 1972. The falsification of data was reportedly an "open secret" among the Institute's staff, but was not publicized until it was discovered by a Communist Party Diet member. The same Institute had been commissioned by the Environment Agency and local governments to examine water, soil, plant, and animal samples for contamination; needless to say, the radioactivity testing scandal immediately made all its analyses suspect and the Institute was disbanded.

A second case occurred in March 1974. The factory director of Toyo Zinc instructed his subordinates to alter MHW cadmium contamination survey material. Publicity of this incident further contributed to the public's skepticism about the validity of official pollution reports.

wish to clarify cause-effect relationships and questions of responsibility, yet avoid litigation, the government has established four semi-judicial arbitration procedures.

To reduce future environmental deterioration, Japan is presently considering the adoption of environmental and technological "assessment" procedures. The legal mechanisms for these systems have not yet been finalized, but in late 1973, the EA published a manual proposing guidelines for "pre-assessing" development plans and "re-assessing" ongoing projects. Derived from concepts embodied in the United States National Environmental Policy Act of 1969, these guidelines are basically a checklist for measuring environmental impact, then correcting for possible disruption by means of technical revisions. Noticeably absent from these provisional guidelines are key points of the American act: public access to government information and assessment results, and public participation in the preparation of alternative plans and in the assessment procedure.* This reflects the predominant view within the Japanese government that pollution can be solved by technology alone, without changes in decision-making procedures. It is, in effect, a move to bypass the nascent attempts toward self government being made by the residents' movements.

But will technological advancements alone be sufficient to prevent continued environmental decline due to vigorous economic expansion? This question is dealt with in a sobering report entitled "Long-Term Prospectus for the Preservation of the Environment" issued in December 1972 by the Planning Committee of the Central Council for Environmental Pollution Control, an advisory body to the Environment Agency. The report noted that the government's main activities have so far been to establish environmental standards, support pollution control measures, and encourage the installation of abatement equipment. But these measures alone, it claimed, would not produce a desirable living environment or minimize the depletion of Japan's resources. Using a multivariable computer simulation model to predict future environmental conditions, the authors of the report recommended that the

---

* These deletions are in line with a general move toward tighter measures to enforce government and corporate secrecy. The Legislative Council, an advisory body to the Justice Minister, is undertaking revisions in Japan's Penal Code and has recommended criminal punishment for civil servants who disclose official secrets, and imprisonment and fines for company executives who leak secrets to third parties "without justifiable reasons." It is generally feared that these revisions, based on a draft prepared in 1941, could provide a legal basis for limiting the freedoms of speech and press. Antipollution and consumer groups see the revisions as a direct attack on their primary sources of incriminatory information.

nation's leaders adopt a more basic approach which would include "proper management of human activities, particularly production and consumption."

The study is, in effect, Japan's own "limits to growth" report.

The prospectus presents a disturbing picture of the archipelago's future. Assuming the rate of industrial and economic growth remains unchanged, the report predicts that between 1970 and 1985 the total annual amount of sulfur produced would increase from 2.0 to 7.2 million tons, of BOD from 6.4 to 21.1 million tons, and of solid wastes from 34.7 to 78.9 million tons. While advances in technology will continue to reduce the percentages of these pollutants released into the environment, their *total volume* will in all likelihood increase. Most of the pollution burden, however, will shift from densely populated to rural districts, as a result of an implicit national "pollution-sharing" policy, causing a general worsening of environmental conditions throughout the islands. To make matters worse, an Economic Planning Agency survey in August 1971 revealed that 16 percent of the coastal areas scheduled for industrial development by 1980 are adjacent to or included in national parks, while development in another 42 percent could cause damage to nearby centers of relatively high population or of tourism. Apparently, Japan's central planners still deem greater destruction of the natural environment to be unavoidable and acceptable.

The prospectus concludes that a continuation of present administrative policies can check environmental deterioration to a certain degree, but will not return Japan's environment to a healthy state. Rather, industrial structure and consumption patterns must change and environmental preservation must become a top priority in all "economic" planning. Otherwise, the report warns, the Japanese environment is in for still more deterioration.

2.

Gradual environmental strangulation is not the only threat lending urgency to the reform of Japan's economic structure and consumption patterns. The global resource crunch poses an even greater obstacle to the continuation of present trends. Because of its "economic middleman" function and reliance on foreign supplies of food and raw materials, Japan has been likened to a "fragile blossom," a nation whose surface wealth rests upon shaky foundations that are heavily dependent upon international trade for survival. At the same time, Japan's long centuries of isolation, racial homogeneity, and distinct language and culture have bred a close-knit nation that feels itself separate from both East and West. This combined sense of isolation and uniqueness has given the Japanese a heightened sensitivity to what they have sometimes perceived as international victimization on racial grounds. In the 1930s and 1940s, these feelings were skillfully manipulated by chauvinistic militarists to fuel a war fought largely for resources and markets. Although postwar Japan has renounced war "as a sovereign right of the nation," the economy's growing demands for natural resources put it in an increasingly precarious diplomatic position.[4]

One of Japan's most important imports is petroleum. In 1973, 99.7 percent of its oil supplies came from abroad. In terms of sheer volume, annual crude imports rose almost fiftyfold between 1953 and 1973, to 270 million kiloliters. This rise reflected an increase in petroleum from 17.1 to about 70 percent of the nation's total energy needs.* In terms of volume, Japan imported far more petroleum than any other country in the world in 1970, and by 1971, was importing 16.5 percent of the world's total oil exports. While so exploiting this resource to power its rapid economic growth, Japan became popularly referred to as a "petroleum culture."

Another important characteristic of Japan's dependence upon foreign petroleum supplies is the predominance of Middle East oil in the total (77.3 percent in 1973), which not only makes Japan susceptible to political and military disturbances in the area, but also contributes to domestic pollution problems because of the oil's high sulfur content (2.0 percent or more). An additional source of concern is that nearly 70 percent of all oil flowing into Japan is controlled by non-Japanese international oil companies, whose first allegiance is to their home countries.

Japan's oil consumption pattern further increases the economy's vulnerability: petroleum accounts for nearly three-quarters of the total primary energy supply, of which 35 percent is used in the general industrial sector—the highest rate among all industrially advanced nations. Furthermore, high energy-consuming industries, such as paper and pulp, steel, aluminum, and chemical, use 77 percent of all petroleum allocated to manufacturing industries. Thus, both Japan's high demand for petroleum and its vulnerability are fundamentally due to the economy's bias in favor of heavy and chemical industries.

In addition to underplaying the environmental consequences of its energy policies, the Japanese government failed to foresee the end of the era of low-cost energy supplies. The oil crisis of 1973 shook the economy to its roots, creating at its outset nothing short of a panic that resembled the fish

---

* Thus, in 1970, imports filled about 75 percent of Japan's total energy needs, compared with the United States ratio of 10 percent in 1970 and a predicted 30 percent in 1985; this rate of dependence nearly doubles those of England and West Germany in 1970.

crisis six months earlier. When, in late October, Arab countries announced a 25 percent production cut accompanied by price hikes, Japanese officials predicted that the world's major oil companies would reduce their supplies to Japan by as much as 35 percent; the nation perceived itself to be in its "greatest postwar crisis." In response, Japan announced an abrupt diplomatic shift in favor of the Arab states, labeled even by native pundits "a diplomacy of unprincipled expediency."[5] Over two decades of diplomatic "neutrality" quickly gave way to the requirements of maintaining the nation's oil lifeline.

That the government and oil industry initially exaggerated the effects of the oil crisis became clear by early 1974, when doomsday predictions of zero or negative growth gave way to estimates ranging from 3 to 8 percent. Even in the face of this crisis, the government displayed no intention of altering its basic economic plans. The emphasis was put on securing oil at any cost: higher prices would be offset by passing them on to consumers, streamlining production, and stepping up export sales.

Environmentally, oil price increases brought mixed blessings. On the one hand, industries began demanding a relaxation of pollution control standards, which increase operating costs. On the other hand, higher gasoline prices at the pump—$1.30 or more a gallon—may well reduce both the domestic use and sales of automobiles. Oil price increases will also push up electricity costs, since the electric power industry depends on petroleum for 80 percent of its raw materials. The new power costs may give energy-intensive industries added reasons to relocate outside Japan. Such moves could contribute to reducing the domestic pollution load.

Oil price increases also provided a new incentive for research into alternative sources of energy. In early 1974, MITI's Agency of Industrial Science and Technology launched "Project Sunshine"—Japan's answer to "Project Independence"—to investigate technologies using pollution-free solar, geothermal, substitute natural gas, and hydrogen gas energies. At the same time, the program for nuclear power was given new impetus. In 1972, nuclear power provided 3 percent of Japan's electric output, but by 1985, nuclear output is expected to increase approximately thirtyfold to 60 million kilowatts, and even more rapidly thereafter. The environmental dangers of this plan for Japan are manifold, due to the country's high susceptibility to earthquakes. problems in importing uranium and exporting used fuel to be reprocessed, and unresolved questions regarding the safety of the light water-cooled type of reactor chosen for use in Japan. Yet the nation is designing some of the world's largest nuclear power plants; one of them, planned for

Shimokita Peninsula in the north, will have a 20 million kilowatt capacity. This load will dangerously magnify inherent safety problems.*

Japan's vulnerability to coordinated action taken by resource-producing nations applies to other vital raw materials besides oil. In 1973, Japan depended on imports for 98.3 percent of its total iron ore supply, 85.4 percent of its copper concentrate, 81.4 percent of its bituminous coal for coking, and 100 percent of its bauxite, uranium, nickel, and tin. Here again, Japan's near total dependence on imports and foreign corporations for these crucial supplies makes the nation particularly susceptible to external pressures.†

To secure a stable flow of resources, Japanese industries have been increasing their investments abroad. The Export-Import Bank of Japan notes that although Japanese foreign investments are still low compared with other developed countries, they are increasing rapidly. Most of these investments have been concentrated in the development of iron and copper ores, coal, oil, rubber, and timber, but are expanding to include natural gas, uranium, and fluorite ore production. Rather than trusting completely in the goodwill of

---

* The Japanese government apparently assumes that effective control of potential nuclear pollutants will take care of itself. Estimating that 80,000 cubic meters of radioactive wastes would be generated in 1985, a government advisory report issued in 1975 noted that these could be disposed of either by using them as landfill—a solution which, in earthquake-prone Japan, would be dangerous to say the least—or by dumping them into the sea. The problem with this latter course is the danger that radioisotopes will accumulate in fish and other marine products and pass up through the food chain to humans. These isotopes can cause leukemia, bone cancer, and genetic damage. Despite the nation's high dependance on marine food products and its experience with Minamata disease, the level of public and government awareness of this latter danger seems shockingly low.

Another serious problem facing nuclear power plant advocates is that of how to dispose of the vast amounts of warmed sea water used as a secondary coolant. Little is known yet of the effects thermal pollution will have on the environment, particularly as nuclear plants begin to proliferate on a wide scale over the entire earth. In addition, the government will be forced to deal with nuclear reactors after they go into disuse: the light water-cooled reactor (LWR) now used in Japan has a lifespan of only 20 to 30 years, after which it can neither be used nor dismantled because of intense radioactivity. Finally, questions regarding the reliability of inspections have also been raised. In Japan, responsibility for the two functions (of promoting nuclear power generation and of conducting technical, safety, and maintenance inspection of plants) is located in the same two agencies—the Science and Technology Agency and MITI. The problems surrounding nuclear power generation have given rise to citizen movements in every area where plants are in operation or under construction.[6]

† The copper-producing countries of Chile, Peru, Zaire, and Zambia have already formed a combine to discuss possible joint actions, and in early 1974, the bauxite-producing nations of Australia, Guyana, Guinea, Yugoslavia, Sierra Leone, and Jamaica organized the International Bauxite Association. Because of their political differences, it is expected that the member nations of these organizations will be unable to intimidate industrialized nations as effectively as did the Arab oil states, but price increases and nationalization of foreign concerns are not unlikely.

international corporations, the government has been encouraging more direct agreements with resource-producing nations. While such efforts may successfully procure foreign resources over the short term, dependence upon raw material imports can only become more impelling as production continues to expand. This dependence will almost inevitably contribute to greater international tension and competition.

Japan is heavily dependent not only on imported mineral resources, but also on foreign food and feed supplies to provide for the needs of its growing and increasingly affluent population. Since the early postwar years, the nation has worked hard to raise farm productivity by applying modern agricultural technology and synthetic fertilizers and chemicals to the land. Although agricultural production per acre has kept pace with that of America and Europe, Japan's limited and decreasing farmland and emphasis on rice production have forced her to depend increasingly on foreign food supplies. Between 1960 and 1972, Japan's self-sufficiency rate in farm produce dropped from 90 to 73 percent, and despite domestic production of all her rice needs, in 1972 she relied on imports for 57 percent of all grains.

Although Japan comprised only 3 percent of the world's total population in 1970, the nation imported 10 percent (in dollar value) of all agricultural products sold on the world market that year, including 27 percent of all soybeans, and 21 percent of all corn. With only 5 percent of the total Asian population, Japan monopolized food imports into that region: 55 percent of all cereals, 70 percent of the soybeans, almost 60 percent of the meat, over 60 percent of the meat meal, more than 25 percent of the milk, and over 60 percent of the fish meal. Without these imports (much of them destined for animal feeds), the Japanese population would be reduced to near starvation; their calorie and protein intake would drop by about one-third and fat consumption would drop by about 60 percent of its 1971 level. The *Asahi Evening News* concluded, "The rich dietary life of the Japanese people is a house of cards."[7]

The necessity for imports is due, in part, to a growing shift from the traditional diet of rice, vegetables, and fish to a more varied diet of meats, dairy products, and breadstuffs. Although about 50 percent of consumed protein still consists of seafood, Japan has undergone a sharp rise in meat consumption. Stimulated by the new dietary trends, domestic meat production between 1964 and 1972 rose 71 percent, to 1.824 million tons. Domestic production, however, has been unable to keep pace with rising demand, forcing the nation to almost quadruple its meat imports during this period, primarily from Australia, the United States, and Argentina. Combined meat imports reached 429,000 tons in 1972.

Rising domestic meat production has caused a sharp increase in feed grain imports. Hogs and poultry were fed about 90 percent of the corn, sorghum, and other feed grains in 1972. Rather than liberalize meat imports, which would threaten domestic producers with extinction, Japan has chosen to import the feed grains necessary to raise as many animals as possible at home. This has not only increased the nation's grain imports but, because the same grains serve as food in developing countries, it has increased international competition and antagonism.

In a series of articles on the global population and food problems, the *Asahi Evening News* questioned the morality of Japan's increasing use of cereals as animal feed in the face of mounting global food shortages. The *Asahi* pointed out that because of the low efficiency rates of animal as compared to vegetable proteins, the amount of sorghum needed for each Japanese to have just 100 grams more of pork each *month* would feed 4 million Indians for a year. Thus, although worldwide grain shortages in the early 1970s are partially due to abnormal weather, the *Asahi* explains that a further underlying cause is the steady rise in world demand for feed grain, which "seems to punch a hole in the widely accepted view that a future food crisis will come from the population explosion in developing countries."[8]

Demand for meat and feed grains, however, is continuing to rise rapidly. But already, according to the *Asahi*, Japan's heavy grain buying has begun to antagonize food-short nations. Although all industrialized nations rely upon imports to some extent, in 1973 Japan imported 97 percent of her wheat, 78 percent of her sugar, and almost all supplies of soybeans, maize, and kaoliang, putting her in a particularly precarious position as competition for existing meat, cereals, and other foods intensifies.*

In addition to agricultural products, the Japanese rely heavily upon distant supplies of fish protein. Its fleets encircle the globe—from the waters

---

* America's soybean crop failure and subsequent brief embargo on exports in 1973 provided an ominous warning of what might happen to Japan in the future were global crop failures to ensue, international trade to break down, or nations to bargain with food exports to gain political objectives. The unexpected embargo shocked the government and news media into thinking seriously about Japan's heavy dependence on imported foodstuffs. The oil crisis and the 1974 World Food Conference in Rome are also credited with having revealed a "big defect" in Japan's economic fabric, but one of which few Japanese are aware. In December 1974, the Agricultural Problems Council, established by leaders of Japanese business and agricultural organizations, urged Prime Minister Miki to bring about a change in the nation's agricultural policy from one which submerged the agricultural sector in favor of industrial growth and food imports to one of self-sufficiency.[9] A spokesman for the policy board of the Bank of Japan has pointed out, however, that "the self-sufficiency rate will keep falling, no matter how much energy is put into agricultural uplift," until the Japanese face the vital issue of how to change their modern food habits and return to more traditional dietary patterns.[10]

off Baja California, to the Caribbean, the South Atlantic, the Mediterranean, and the Indian Ocean. In 1972, nearly three-fourths of Japan's fish supplies came from the open seas (about 7.5 million metric tons) and the nation's total haul accounted for 16 percent of the global catch. Nevertheless, Japan found herself short of fish and imported an additional 190,000 million yen ($611 million) worth—60 times more than in 1962—pushing per capita consumption levels to four times the world average. But Japan may find it increasingly difficult to maintain this rate of fish consumption in the coming years. As rising world population pressures stimulate greater demand for ocean food resources, Japanese domination of the international fishing scene may face severe challenges.

Evidence of this trend was very visible at the Sixth Conference on the Law of the Sea in the summer of 1974, as the developing nations of the world expressed vigorous demands for a more equitable share of ocean resources and called for broad extensions of territorial waters. Japan, whose diminutive land area simply could not produce anywhere near the amount of animal protein presently derived from the oceans, is more affected by these demands than any other nation. Moreover, spoliation of much of her coastal waters is one more reason why the nation's fishing vessels have been forced to concentrate their operations in other parts of the world. Although Japan's seafood haul increased by approximately 3 million metric tons between 1962 and 1972, the increase came almost entirely from ocean catches.

A great unknown is the maximum sustainable yield of the world's oceans. In 1969, the United Nation's Food and Agriculture Organization estimated that developable marine resources might equal about 120 million metric tons. Other more optimistic marine biologists set the limit at 200 million tons. Biologist Paul Ehrlich points out, however, that such estimates depend on "doing everything right" which, he says, we are not; indeed, since 1969, the global catch has not increased substantially and at least one year registered an absolute decrease. Ehrlich writes:

> Roughly half the stocks of marine fishes now exploited are being overfished. A vast variety of toxic substances is being added daily to the oceans by mankind, mostly to the water close to shore, waters where more than 95 percent of the ocean's fisheries productivity is concentrated. Ironically, some of these toxic substances are pesticides, added to the seas in the course of attempting to grow more food on land. Furthermore, human activities such as dredging and filling are destroying estuaries around the world. At one stage or another of their life cycles, more than one-half of

commercially harvested marine fishes may be dependent on estuaries. Deterioration of the environment caused by human activities as well as a lack of control of harvesting threaten to prevent mankind from even approaching theoretically obtainable yields.[11]

The Japanese whaling industry, which takes in some 40 percent of the global whale catch, has come under heavy fire for its exploitation of this marine resource. In June 1972, the United Nations Conference on the Human Environment adopted a resolution calling for a 10-year blanket moratorium on commercial whaling, aimed particularly at the Japanese and Soviet fleets. The Japanese Whaling Association reacted to growing international complaints by criticizing the emotionalism of "ban whaling" advocates and arguing that a moratorium would strike a hard blow at the Japanese who, unlike other peoples, use whale meat as an important source of protein, noting that it accounted for 9 percent of total Japanese meat consumption in 1970.* Supporters of the moratorium argue that the 10-year period would enable some over-harvested whale stocks to replenish themselves and allow time for comprehensive studies of whale populations and for the creation of an effective international whaling agency. The present International Whaling Commission, they charge, failing to act in this capacity, has set limits that have been completely ignored.

Despite real threats to the world's oceanic fisheries, no broad popular movement has arisen in Japan to challenge continued over-harvesting of the seas. Partially related to a generally low level of ecological awareness, this apparent indifference also reflects Japan's inordinate dependence on the ocean's "free" resources. In addition, some Japanese feel that the movement to protect whales may spring from other than pure conservationist motivation. A Japanese journalist attending the 1972 Stockholm conference commented critically on the scene of Americans "parading to protect the world's whales while ignoring the deaths of Vietnamese people and the ecological destruction of that nation caused by American bombs." Valid or not, this criticism is a possible indication of what the future response of Japanese may be in the face of approaching environmental crises. As greater competition for food and resources restricts Japan's ability to expand imports, some Japanese may

---

* Although the Japanese do indeed use whales less wastefully than other peoples, the comparison of whale meat consumption with that of other meat is misleading since animal meats, excluding fish, account for less than 20 percent of the total Japanese protein intake. Most grades of whale meat are considered "inferior" and annual per capita consumption has declined steadily from 2 kilograms in 1960 to only 1.2 kilograms in 1971.

interpret the cutting off of supplies as thinly veiled "racial discrimination." At the same time, increasing competition for global resources will doubtless contribute to greater international (and interracial) tensions among the developed and developing nations; these could easily be focused against Japan because of her high share in world markets. If nothing else, these rising tensions, which will provide more ready excuses for conflict, present one of the central challenges to peaceful international diplomacy in the coming decades.

3.

Although domestic food supplies and natural resources are already insufficient for Japan's 100 million inhabitants, the nation's population continues to increase at a rate of approximately 1.2 million people per year. Experts predict that even if all families keep to an average of only 1.8 children, Japan's population will reach 126 million by 1985 and level off only after it reaches 130 to 140 million near the year 2000. At the beginning of the Meiji era, Japan's population density was already four times the present density of the United States; today, at approximately 293 people per square kilometer, it is about thirteen times that of the United States and fourth highest in the world. Despite this grim picture of overpopulation, however, the Japanese have set an example for the world by reducing the birth rate in an unprecedentedly short time. Japanese population experts note with justifiable pride that while it required 75 to 150 years to complete the transition from high fertility and mortality to low fertility and mortality in the West, the same transition required only 30 to 35 years in Japan.

Population control in Japan has a long and variegated history. Infanticide and abortion were routinely practiced throughout the feudal period, particularly at times of severe crop failure and economic hardship. These practices were outlawed after Japan opened itself to the West, and the dynamic setting of the Meiji period further stimulated the birthrate, which continued to rise unabated until the 1920s. The economic slowdown which came in the wake of World War I and growing doubts about the future livelihood of industrial workers occasioned the first attempts to disseminate birth control information on a wide scale. These efforts were initiated by labor leaders and contemporary socialists, and not by the government, which opposed the idea at that time. Indeed, when Margaret Sanger, leader of the American birth control movement, visited Japan at the invitation of a publishing company in 1922, the Japanese government tried to prevent her from landing and finally permitted her to enter only on the condition that she give no public lectures and confer only with medical doctors. Widely publicized, this incident helped to spread word about birth control throughout the country, and, with the encouragement of the socialists and labor leaders, population growth slowed during the 1920s. After the Manchurian Incident of 1931, however, the government's pronatalist policies came increasingly to the fore, and in 1935, the birth control movement was forced to disband. For the duration of the militarist period, large families were the norm and prizes were awarded to women who bore ten or more children.

The economic misery of the immediate postwar years was compounded by the repatriation of over 6.5 million Japanese, bringing the nation's total population to nearly 70 million. The return of men from the front resulted in a flurry of marriages and the resumption of normal family life, nurturing a baby boom between 1947 and 1949, marked by an average of 33.6 births per thousand population. Growth in numbers was further magnified by a rapidly falling crude death rate. The death rate had begun to decline in the early Meiji period and had received further impetus in the 1920s by improvements in hygienic and sanitation facilities. Following the postwar introduction of DDT, antibiotics, and other medicines, the death rate plummeted sharply.

Confronted by a domestic population explosion in the midst of severe economic dislocation, the Japanese became acutely aware of the need to limit family size. The seeds of the birth control movement, sown in the 1920s, came to new life. In 1948, the government replaced the 1940 National Eugenics Law—which allowed abortion to "protect the quality of the race"—with a new Eugenic Protection Law that legalized abortions deemed necessary to "protect the life and health of the mother." The law was amended during the following year to include abortions for "a mother whose health may be affected seriously by continuation of pregnancy or by delivery from the physical or *economic* viewpoint" (emphasis added). In 1952, the bureaucratic procedures for obtaining an abortion were greatly simplified, and since then, approximately one million legal abortions have been performed annually in Japan.* The abortion trend peaked in 1955, and then tapered off due to wider use of contraceptives. The net reproductive rate also began to drop noticeably, averaging 17.58 per thousand in the decade between 1956 and 1965. The year 1966, Japanese zodiacal year of the Fire and Horse, was believed to be a bad year to give birth to baby girls, as females born under that sign are believed doomed to lead unhappy lives and destroy their husbands if they marry. In that year the birthrate dropped to 13.7 per thousand population, indicating that the Japanese were able to exert a high degree of control over their fertility.

---

* Dr. Minoru Muramatsu of the National Public Health Institute, a leading population expert, estimates that the actual number may be twice that.

Postwar demand for labor increased with rapid economic recovery, and by the mid-1960s, full employment had been achieved. Japanese industrial planners suddenly found themselves short of young workers whose low wages in the Japanese seniority system made them a key element in the economy's continued expansion. A call soon arose to increase the birthrate by restricting abortions, and the idea was supported on moral grounds by religious groups. In August 1969, the Ministry of Health and Welfare's Council on Population Problems, headed by the late Minoru Tachi, presented a report on the contemporary state and future direction of Japan's population to the MHW. Acknowledging the nation's extremely high population density, the report noted that if Japan's birthrate—"one of the lowest in the world"—remained as low as it was, the population level would start to decline within some thirty years.* Therefore, the council concluded, a higher birthrate was desirable. The report, produced under pressure from industrial interests, sparked indignant opposition in scientific circles. Among many Asian nations, too, it aroused unpleasant memories of Japan's pronatalist policies during her period of militarism. Nevertheless, the government of Eisaku Sato called in 1969 for an increased birthrate and proposed a revision of the Eugenic Protection Law to eliminate the clause permitting abortions for "economic reasons." Only determined opposition from scientists and women's groups forced the government to temporarily shelve the proposal.

In 1971, Dr. Tachi wrote that Japan's industrial enterprises must adjust themselves to an inevitable labor shortage beginning in the 1970s. Tachi suggested four countermeasures: moving from a labor-intensive to a capital-intensive economic structure; improving labor mobility by increasing the availability and quality of vocational training (and possibly revising the lifetime employment system and the seniority wage structure); making more effective use of middle-aged and old-aged labor (including a hike in the retirement age from 55 to 65); and upgrading the activities of women in the labor force.

Although most demographers supported Tachi's suggestions, government and industrial circles continued to persist in their efforts to stimulate the birthrate. The government introduced measures in both the 1972 and 1973 Diet sessions proposing revisions of the Eugenic Protection Act. Their passage was blocked by the heated opposition of demographers, geneticists and other scientists, and women's groups.

---

* The report neglected to mention that, before starting to decline, the population would increase to 130 or 140 million.

Drs. Ei Matsunaga and Motoo Kimura, members of the National Genetics Institute, argued that the Eugenic Protection Law had been instrumental in halving Japan's postwar birthrate and in making rapid economic recovery possible. The scientists warned against "simplistic thinking," pointing out that a net reproductive rate as low as 1.8 offspring per family meant a population as large as 140 million by the year 2005, an increase which would have to be accompanied by enormous expenditures in housing, schools, hospitals, sewage and refuse treatment facilities, and other public services. Japan's limited size and natural resources, they argued, made a static population imperative in order to maintain a "healthy and peaceful society." The Family Planning Federation of Japan warned that the government move would lead to an increase in "back street" abortions, concluding that if the government really wanted to reduce the abortion rate, it should disseminate contraceptive information more effectively and liberalize use of the birth control pill.

Although Japanese family planning organizations favor the pill, the government has continued to oppose its liberalization for birth control purposes on the grounds that its safety has yet to be scientifically validated. Dr. Takashi Wagatsuma, a leading expert on oral contraception at Tokyo University's School of Medicine, has noted that there are many other medicines commonly sold in Japan that are much less tested and less safe. The main obstacle blocking the pill's liberalization, says Wagatsuma, is the "lack of support given the move by the Japan Society of Obstetricians and Gynecologists. This powerful branch of the Japan Medical Association quite naturally wants to protect a primary source of its members' incomes, i.e., abortions." In addition, Wagatsuma points out, the Japanese have begun to be wary of all orally administered drugs, particularly since the thalidomide tragedy. Although the pill is available and can be prescribed by physicians for contraceptive purposes, the government stance and the pill's relatively high cost* have delayed its acceptance by the general public.

Acceptance of the IUD as a birth control device has also been delayed, but the issue is now under review by the Ministry of Health and Welfare, and the IUD is expected to receive official approval sometime during 1974.† Although the government's reluctance to give official approval to the pill and the IUD doubtless reflects in part its concern over their possible ill effects, a

---

* The pill costs approximately 1,500 yen ($5) per month; the prescription must be renewed monthly.

† Approval was granted to the IUD in August 1974.

far more compelling reason may well be industry's concern over the impending young-labor shortage.

The government's advocacy of increased numbers seems to reflect its view of the population problem as primarily one of distribution. By relocating industries to rural areas, planners hope to reverse the influx to the cities and ease over-concentration. Although such a policy may somewhat relieve overcrowding in large cities, it can by no means "solve" Japan's population problem. Because the consumption rate of resources and the impact of environmental disruption increase directly with population, every increment in Japan—as in other industrialized countries—exacerbates domestic and global environmental problems. Population redistribution policies ignore not only the per capita impact of each new baby but disregard the ecological costs of creating new industrial cities. In addition to the inevitable contamination of the environment from industrial effluents and increased levels of human activity, valuable arable land is lost to housing, roads, parking lots, and other urban facilities.

Japan is at present just beginning to become aware of the grave problems of global population growth and of the particularly severe situation in Asia. Although the Japan Organization for International Cooperation in Family Planning (JOICFP), a private agency established in 1968, has worked hard to increase the government's contributions to the United Nations Fund for Population Activities and the International Planned Parenthood Federation, Japanese grants to these institutions amounted to only $2 million in 1972, and $2.5 million in 1973. Bilateral assistance, too, has been minimal, partly because the Japanese government has been reluctant to involve itself in so delicate a political issue, preferring to wait until asked to do so by a developing country. The reports of the Club of Rome (1972), the United Nations Conference on the Human Environment (1972), and the United Nations ECAFE* Asian Population Conference (1972) have, however, helped make some of Japan's influential political and industrial leaders more aware of the seriousness and magnitude of the world's exploding population. In October 1973, a twenty-nine-member population problems study team, headed by former Prime Minister Kishi and including Dietmen, government officials, and family planning experts, spent two weeks touring India, Thailand, Indonesia, and the Philippines. The members of this mission, the first of its kind, were greatly impressed by both the gravity of the problem and the high expectations Asian nations placed on Japan to help them solve it. Upon their return, the members of the mission called on the government to raise the ratio

---

* In 1974, the organization's name was changed to ESCAP—Economic and Social Commission for Asia and the Pacific region.

of population assistance by up to 10 percent of present grants, augment bilateral assistance, and double Japan's contributions to UNFPA, bringing it up to $5 million in 1974.

The international problem cannot be separated from the question of Japan's own future growth, and there are some indications that government attitudes are changing. On April 15, 1974, the Population Problems Council submitted its first Population White Paper in fifteen years. In it, the council urged the nation to exert greater efforts to curb its population growth, increase awareness of the problem among politicians and administrators, and work to set up a system for collecting information on the global question. A move by the Diet in June 1974 to force through the lower house a revision of the New Eugenics Protection Law that would outlaw abortions for economic reasons, however, countered this extremely positive document. Because the move was made on the last day of the Diet session, no action was taken on it in the upper house and the bill died—for the time being. But the incident revealed the tension surrounding present population policy in Japan.

4.

Japan's political and economic leaders have come to recognize the necessity of change. An April 1973 report by the Industrial Planning Roundtable examined Japan's role in the converging global crises of pollution and resources, concluding that it was necessary to revamp the nation's petroleum, petrochemical, iron and steel, power, and transportation industries. Keidanren echoed this opinion and announced that Japan had "depended too much and, perhaps, too long on the heavy and chemical industries."[12] The government's Economic White Paper of 1973 came to similar conclusions and, in December, Prime Minister Kakuei Tanaka admitted before the National Diet that "a structural reformation of economic activity to conserve energy and natural resources" had to be undertaken.[13] A consensus was being reached that the time had come for the goals of "growthmanship" to yield to the requirements of establishing a "welfare state."*

---

* The concept of the welfare state was given tangible political expression with the rise of Takeo Miki to the post of prime minister in December 1974. A former director-general of the Environment Agency, Miki is relatively sensitive to environmental problems and is an advocate of "stable" rather than "high" growth. His administration's policy shift, however, cannot be attributed solely to environmental concerns. The regime has come into power when the resources problem, inflation, and other "economic" troubles were already forcing a move away from the policy of rapid economic expansion. Furthermore, because Miki's power base is tenuous, many political observers doubt he will remain in office long.

Proponents of this transformation advocate the replacement of high resource- and energy-consuming activities with new, knowledge-intensive, minimally polluting industries (computers and information processing, aircraft, communications and fashion, among others). Existing industrial installations would be redistributed and thinned out after a Tanaka-like remodeling scheme, while an emphasis would be placed on developing advanced transportation and communication networks and expanding parks, playgrounds, sewage systems, waste-treatment facilities, and medical and other social services. By no means, however, would economic growth come to a standstill: rising personal consumption and increasing expenditures on public facilities, research and development, pollution abatement equipment and the like would prolong a relatively high rate of economic growth. "Simple" pollution, such as contamination of air and water, would be held in check by means of technology, while Japan's citizens would become steadily more affluent. The Japanese would have more money, more leisure time, fewer polluting factories, and the latest technological devices for recreation, communication, and transport. The "New New Japan" would be the epitome of an ultramodern post-industrial society.

To achieve this goal, economic planners propose transferring dirtier industrial production to developing nations eager to emulate Japan's domestic miracle. Thus, the imperative need for restructuring Japan's domestic economy is seen to dovetail with the rising economic aspirations of developing nations. The key concept underlying this transformation is the "international division of labor." Over-industrialized, inflation-plagued and resource-poor Japan would transfer its production facilities—or simply sell its technology—to foreign nations which enjoy rich deposits of natural resources, offer plentiful, cheap labor, and, as Keidanren puts it, "have more elbow room from an environmental viewpoint."[14] Japan's technologically sophisticated populace would serve as a central information locus in Asia, guiding, directing, and financing development in the region; the nation would expand imports of semi-processed raw materials to support its new "clean" industries. Southeast Asian agricultural production, boosted by Japanese technology, would ensure a steady source of agricultural products. For Japan, therefore, the international division of labor concept holds the potential of preempting domestic antipollution movements, while improving prospects for continued growth, rising affluence, and heightened international prestige. Demonstrating what Peter Drucker praises as the Japanese ability to "steer by the international economy,"[15] the planned transformation would, in many respects, bring into being a sort of East Asia

Co-Prosperity Sphere and perhaps make the twenty-first century the "Japanese century."

The industrial exodus from Japan has already begun. Japanese enterprises are producing steel in Malaysia, drilling for oil off Indonesia, assembling cars in the Philippines and televisions in Taiwan. Investments in the Southeast Asian agricultural sector, in Australian resource-development projects, and in overseas heavy, chemical, mining, and refining industries have risen dramatically since the late 1960s. In the United States, Japanese paper mills are now in operation in Washington and Alaska, there is an aluminum plant in Oregon, and the governments of Mississippi and Puerto Rico are actively striving to recruit Japanese investments. Nearby South Korea and Taiwan have patterned their domestic economies after the Japanese model, while government and economic leaders in Singapore, Thailand, and elsewhere welcome inputs of Japanese technology and capital.

Native reaction to increased Japanese penetration of Southeast Asian economies has not been unmixed. Well received by those who profit most directly from it, expanding Japanese influence has sparked indignant and sometimes violent resentment from others. During his visit to five Southeast Asian nations in January 1974, former Prime Minister Tanaka was greeted by angry mobs of students condemning Japan's alleged economic exploitation of their nations' resources and markets. Throughout Southeast Asia, the Japanese investor is being accused of indifference to local cultures, reviving the legacy of ill will left by Japanese wartime occupation of the region. Throughout most of the area, the "ugly American" is said to be giving way to the "ugly Japanese" as a focus of domestic criticism.

The Japanese businessman's alleged cultural insensitivity and excessive concern for profits have made his motives for participating in the economies of his host nations highly suspect. The installation of sophisticated, capital-intensive technology, which forces native firms to adopt similar types of equipment in order to remain competitive, and the importation of managerial personnel from Japan have undermined the illusion that foreign investment provides opportunities for widespread employment and leads to technological independence. Japanese manufactured goods, meanwhile, have flooded Asian markets, adding to hefty deficits in balances of payments. And while Japanese capital is acquiring substantial political as well as economic influence in these nations, mammoth industrial complexes similar to Japan's own kombinats may be planting the seeds for future environmentally related social conflict.

Although this new distribution of industrial activities yields short-term advantages, it could be a future source of international conflict. Aware of this possibility, government and industrial officials have initiated efforts at devising a code of behavior for enterprises operating abroad. At this writing, however, the difficult problem of how to deal with possible environmental disruption caused by foreign-based factories remains unsolved. According to one MITI official, the present consensus of opinion views the imposition of standards on overseas installations as an "infringement" on the laws of the host country—as well as being an economically disadvantageous tactic. The official felt, however, that this consensus of opinion may prove to be "extremely short-sighted," since pollution "could provide a concrete issue around which anti-Japanese sentiment could be rallied."*

From a long-term, global perspective, Japan's move toward a welfare state, characterized by the transfer of some of its pollution load to developing countries while maintaining its mass-consumption, high-growth economy, is little more than a stop-gap measure. Although the Japanese—perhaps more than any other people of the industrialized world—have become aware of the dire effects of pollution on human health, they remain little cognizant of a much more serious aspect of environmental deterioration: man's assault on the integrity of the life-support systems of the Earth as a whole. Japanese political and economic leaders remain committed to the economic values and techniques imported and modified during the past one hundred years. What they have yet to grasp, however, is that "the main problems of the environment

---

* A widely publicized incident in September 1973, was read as a possible portent of the future. The Thai Asahi Caustic Soda Company, a subsidiary of Japan's Asahi Glass, was attacked in the Thai press for having polluted the Chao Phraya River with hydrochloric acid and mercury effluents. Residents living near the factory complained of foul odors, withering rice seedlings and dying fish. A local newspaper, the *Siam Rath*, reporting that some persons were suffering skin diseases allegedly caused by contaminated water, launched a campaign under the headline: "Don't repeat the tragedy of Minamata disease in Thailand." Wide media coverage of the incident in Japan sparked antipollution demonstrations in downtown Tokyo, while fishermen picketed the company's Chiba factory. An Asahi Glass official dispatched by the home office to investigate the situation reported that the faulty equipment that had leaked the pollutants into the river had been repaired and that, except for the *Siam Rath*, there was as yet no active "opposition to pollution" in Thailand. Soon thereafter, however, three Thai universities sponsored an environmental exhibit— the country's first, but doubtless not its last—introducing the Japanese archipelago's pollution tragedies in detail.

Reports of the Asahi Glass incident in the Japanese press criticized the nation's industries for "exporting pollution" and for its "division of labor" policy. In an attempt to prevent the repetition of similar occurrences, antipollution groups have begun channeling information related to Japan's experience to interested parties in other countries. Most Japanese officials, however, tend to underplay the diplomatic or commercial problems that may result from future incidents of environmental disruption abroad. For the most part, government leaders in developing nations— and the bulk of local populations as well—continue to welcome Japanese-style development in spite of the risks it may entail.

do not arise from temporary and accidental malfunctions of existing economic and social systems ... (but) are the warning signs of a profound incompatibility between deeply rooted beliefs in continuous growth and the dawning recognition of the Earth as a spaceship, limited in its resources and vulnerable to mishandling."[16]

The ecological demands placed upon the global environment are intensifying under the weight of rapidly increasing economic activity. A growing body of scientific evidence indicates that the indiscriminate use of the atmosphere as an "industrial sewer" may be upsetting the balance of natural forces controlling global climatic conditions. Of perhaps even more immediate concern is the possibility that uneven distribution of energy use on the Earth's surface may be influencing local climatic patterns. Although human beings have a relatively wide tolerance range for temperature variations, many plants vital to sustaining human life are acutely sensitive to even small fluctuations.* Millions of tons of sewage, heavy metals, oil, inorganic materials, fertilizers, and pesticides dumped directly or carried by rivers or rain into the oceans every year and the drastic overfishing of many species may be setting the stage for a major collapse of the world's fisheries.

These assaults on the global environment come at a time when only one-third of the world's nations have entered the industrial age. Wanting to repeat Japan's economic "miracle" and coming increasingly under Japan's tutelage, many developing nations seem all too willing to imitate Japan's economically successful, but ecologically catastrophic, use of the biosphere. Such nations interpret recent efforts by the advanced nations to promote strict effluent standards as but another attempt to maintain the present inequitable allocation of the Earth's resources. If Japan is to serve as the model for modernizing nations, we are likely to see the conflict between economy and ecology become increasingly prevalent.

In fact, the air and the oceans are mankind's common heritage, and toxic substances dumped into them know no sovereign boundaries. At present we know little about how nature absorbs or purifies these poisons (if it can), nor do we know the limits of nature's ability to handle them. We do know, however, that as the world's population grows and per capita consumption, production, and demand increase, we are running the danger of passing those ecological limits.

In most respects, Japan, like other highly industrialized nations, is reluctant to acknowledge the enormity of the impending crisis. Its political and

---

* Laboratory-produced plants such as those used in the much-publicized Green Revolution are particularly susceptible to temperature changes,

economic leaders prefer to avoid the basic issue of reducing industrial growth and its impact on global ecosystems, and instead design stop-gap measures to preserve the status quo. Until very recently, Japanese opinion makers tended to be obsessed by the goal of leading the world economy in growth and size. Although the 1973 oil crisis shocked them into reassessing this long-term objective, the primary reaction of Japan's leaders was to maintain the flow of supplies at any price. Reduction in energy demand was minimal and temporary. While political progressives may accuse the ruling triumvirate for bringing on Japan's present difficulties, they too have failed to espouse a policy of limiting demand, much less one of "no growth." And they are unlikely to do so unless a vast change in the public's thinking occurs, including an awakening to the inherent ecological contradictions of increasing affluence and reducing pollution.

In many respects, it is tempting for the Japanese to lay the blame for the world's present impasse upon the West. It is equally tempting for the West to criticize Japan's "overweening ambitions," its thirst for an economic glory and power that far exceeds the nation's size and resources. The Japanese, in turn, reply: "Nature has been unfair with us, but we have managed, by dint of hard work and self-sacrifice, to transform our necessities into virtues and build our nation. Why should we be forced to limit ourselves in the world economy solely because of the poverty of our islands?"

Indeed, given the criteria of economic "success" that presently prevail in the world, it would be manifestly unfair to criticize the Japanese for playing the production game as efficiently as they do. Nor is it reasonable to expect that organizational changes in Japan alone could significantly alleviate the crisis we all confront. The Earth's problems are obviously far too complex, rooted as they are in the values motivating *homo industrialis* and our present system of unbridled exploitation of our planet—what University of California Biology Professor Garrett Hardin calls "the tragedy of the commons."* In a global commons possessing ecological limits, says Hardin,

---

* The tragedy develops in this way: in a pasture open to all, the "rational herdsman" seeks to maximize his gain by keeping as many cattle as possible on the commons. Sooner or later, the number of cattle increase to the carrying limit of the commons. At this point the "tragedy" remorselessly unfolds. Each herdsman asks himself, "What is the utility *to me* of adding one more animal to my herd?" "This utility," says Hardin, "has one negative and one positive component." Since the herdsman receives all profit from the sale of each animal, his "positive utility" is close to +1. The "negative component" (i.e., the overgrazing damage caused by each additional animal) is shared by all the herdsmen, making it only a fraction of -1 for any particular herdsman. "Adding together the component partial utilities, the rational herdsman concludes that the only sensible course . . . is to add another animal to his herd. And another and another . . . But this is the

complete and unprincipled freedom—freedom to breed, to pollute, to exploit resources—will "ultimately bring ruin to us all."[17]

But at the same time, as long as such "freedom" governs our behavior, anyone refraining from all-out exploitation for reasons of "conscience" senses that he will be secretly condemned "as a simpleton who can be shamed into standing aside while the rest of us exploit the commons."[18] For the Japanese, the satisfactions gained by following the dictates of "conscience" might well provide little compensation for the potential loss of face brought about by a posture of self-restraint before the nations of the West. Nor would they balance the economic privations that would ensue upon expulsion from the elite club of industrial nations. Indeed, it is this unwillingness to appear as a simpleton, coupled with a deep-rooted spirit of competitiveness, that reinforces Japanese defensiveness on mercantile issues and tends to make the Japanese suspect that United States advocacy of international pollution controls is little more than a disguised attempt to check the Japanese export drive.

According to Hardin, freedom must be limited by responsibility grounded in definite social arrangements. He advocates a system of "mutual coercion," capable of ensuring the universal observance of rules "mutually agreed upon by the majority of people affected" because they recognize the "horrifying alternatives" that stem from a narrowly conceived freedom of action. Surely, seen in long-term perspective, Japan's great dependence on the world's shared resources should serve as a strong incentive for that nation to support restrictions on ecologically harmful patterns of freedom in the commons. Yet, while participating in United Nations sponsored projects to investigate global environmental problems, Japan has refrained from taking a noticeably dynamic role. In 1974, Japan criticized the demands voiced by developing nations to extend the limits of territorial waters, labeling such proposals an infringement upon the principle of "freedom of the seas." In the long run, however, it is Japan that is most vulnerable to major ecological breakdown, dislocations brought ever-nearer by the exploitative behavior in which she herself is engaged. Moreover, it would seem only reasonable that Japan's unparalleled experience with pollution would orient her toward taking a leading role in preventing further global as well as domestic environmental destruction.

Japan could play a very important role in effecting the necessary transition from an economy of waste and ecological assault to one of

---

conclusion reached by each and every rational herdsman sharing a commons. Therein is the tragedy. Each man is locked into a system that compels him to increase his herd without limit—in a world that is limited."

conservation and ecological harmony. Few other nations have proved themselves so capable of implementing sweeping and rapid social change—precisely what is called for today—or have so successfully engineered themselves to adapt to domestic and international circumstances. The peoples of few other nations have been as capable of so uniformly orienting themselves to their leaders' chosen goals, and, in a remarkably short span of time, reforming their systems of education to inculcate the values and information necessary to achieve those goals. And perhaps no other nation can tap so deep a psychological reservoir of self-discipline and self-restraint.

When confined by the Tokugawas to the limited area and resources of "spaceship Japan," the Japanese evolved and refined a cultural tradition embodying precepts whose rejuvenation may well be called for to meet the requirements of "spaceship Earth": a respect for nature, an appreciation of simplicity, a high value placed on thrift, durability, and craftsmanship, an esthetic sense, a deep awareness of community, and a high estimation of spiritual intangibles. The potential offered by these still-accessible traits are acknowledged by the Japanese themselves. When faced with the oil crisis of late 1973, Saburo Okita, perhaps the single most prominent figure responsible for masterminding Japan's economic miracle, announced that the Japanese "have begun to doubt [their] constant pursuit of wasteful, luxurious consumption," and, in the face of the resource crunch, "are ready to return to *hibachi* and *kotatsu* simplicity. Instead of heating the room we can heat our bodies. If the burdens are shared equally, the people will cooperate."[19]

The Japanese are endowed with a contradictory nature. They can be brave and self-sacrificial, or timid and self-indulgent. They are a rigid people, and yet a highly adaptable one. They are inveterately conservative, and yet hospitable to new ways. They are motivated by a deeply ingrained sense of historical purposefulness and national destiny and have proved themselves capable of a global perspective, yet they can recoil into periodic isolation and xenophobia. They are deeply achievement-oriented, but are receptive, judging their own performance against criteria established by others. They are capable of ingenious procedural and technological innovations, but may work best from an imported blueprint. Their unusual ability to function effectively in groups and dedicate themselves to a particular goal could enable them to make important contributions to international cooperative efforts aimed at solving the global population-resources-environment crisis.

But if Japan should feel isolated or betrayed by other nations who fail to recognize her needs and accord her due status, the national consensus could shift to embrace a new militarism. All in all, it is highly unlikely that the Japanese will move to an ecologically low-impact society unless guided by a strictly monitored *international consensus* to which all adhered. The Japanese cannot, will not, and should not be expected to go it alone. There is every reason to believe, however, that their contributions to a global effort at ecological survival could be every bit as historic as the successes they have scored using older and increasingly outdated criteria. In all likelihood, it will remain for the nations of the West to take the initiative. But if the burdens are shared, the Japanese will cooperate.

AFTERWORD
BY RALPH NADER

The silent, cumulative violence called pollution that pours throughout Japan from the jaws of her industrial baronies is just beginning to be traced and chronicled. The preceding pages have described the horrors undergone by those victimized by a relentless devastation of the air, soil, and water in a nation's suicidal drive for economic growth. Like those in other societies, the Japanese have cruelly soiled their own nest, but because of Japan's small land area and comparatively high population and industrial density, its environmental backlash is more grotesquely graphic than that seen elsewhere.

The calculus of contamination is simple—and thereby doubly tragic. To save a little capital in the short run, Japanese industry is imposing huge costs in terms of both economic and qualitative welfare on millions of innocent people living today and on unborn generations of the future. Although able to apply corrective technology to prevent or diminish the outflow of the poisons of industry, these corporations heave those poisons on other shoulders and other public and private properties. The result is death, injury, waste, ugliness, and eventually waves of self-destruction. The peril of old pollutants is made even greater by the proliferation of new dangers, such as that posed by the numerous nuclear power plants slated to cover Japan and their associated risk of radioactive catastrophe. It could be otherwise. There is no inevitability about the present course of brutalizing technology. But to pursue the course of humane technology requires a much deeper sense of impact, of what has been and is going on.

Impacts on the individual are inseparable from impacts on oceans, stratospheres, and genetic material. National boundaries are fictions as far as the spread of global contamination is concerned. In a very real sense, this book is about pollution in the United States, since Americans are exposed to the fish, air currents, and other aspects of the environment shared in common with the Japanese. But language barriers have posed real obstacles to a spreading perception of the unity of the planet's victimization. The authors have provided Americans with a view of another industrialized society's pollution problems and power plays that should sensitize us to our own industrial pillages.

The Japanese experience teaches us of the potential abuses inherent in a close, centralized corporate-governmental interlock and of the need for decentralized points of access by citizens to shape their own legislative, executive, and judicial power. It also teaches us that to wait for the hideous symptoms to reveal themselves, and then wait longer until more proof erupts, as in the dreaded Minamata and itai-itai epidemics, is to doom the victims by contrived inaction and to free the perpetrators by the mere passage of time. Above all, it teaches the need to recognize the unities that must underlie the philosophies and strategies required to bring about genuine change.

There is, for example, the unity of all the earth's people in the recognition that one nation's pollutants is another's torment. There is the unity between workers and consumers, whose diseases stem from common sources. There is the unity of parents and progeny inherent in the ecological trust that must be administered by one generation for the next. And, finally, there is the unity of man and nature which, when ignored, is replaced by an attitude of severance that views the despoliation of nature as somehow separate from and uneventful for man.

The delicate life relationships that fuse man and nature took millions of years to develop and only a few to disrupt. To reverse this macabre tide requires much closer international citizen cooperation and more effective methods of organization within each society to support full-time activists and advocates. If this volume helps bring more Japanese and Americans together toward such citizen objectives, one of its greatest values will be in multiplying our options for successful action.

Who can deny that our respective countries possess the ready or readily available economic and technical means to make lives livable and minds humane? Never in human history has a generation had to give up so little in order to achieve so much. By the same token, should our generation refuse to make the necessary commitment, we may well be the last generation permitted the choice.

Ralph Nader
Washington, D.C.
1974

NOTES

PREFACE TO THE FIFTIETH ANNIVERSARY EDITION

1. George Santayana, *The Life of Reason*, 1905. ["Aquellos que no pueden recordar el pasado están condenados a repetirlo."]
2. "Many Minamata Disease victims still waiting for overdue relief." Editorial. *Asahi Shimbun*. 29 April 2021. Accessed 6 October 2024 at: https://www.asahi.com/ajw/articles/14340051
3. Minamata Disease Municipal Museum. Website. Accessed 6 October 2024, at https://minamata195651.jp/guide_en.html
4. Yamaguchi Keiko. "Ill health plaguing children, grandchildren of 1968 oil poisoning victims in Japan: survey." *The Mainichi*, 8 May 2022. Accessed 6 October 2024, at: https://mainichi.jp/english/articles/20220506/p2a/00m/0li/035000c
5. Michael R. Reich and Aya Goto. "Towards long-term responses in Fukushima." *Lancet*. 2015; 386: 498–500.
6. Nina Agrawal. "What experts want you to know about microplastics." *New York Times*. May 20, 2025. Accessed May 20, 2025 at https://www.nytimes.com/2025/05/20/well/microplastics-health-risks.html
7. "Great Pacific Garbage Patch." National Geographic Society. Updated September 18, 2024. Accessed 6 October 2024 at: https://education.nationalgeographicsociety/resource/great-pacific-garbage-patch

CHAPTER ONE

1. Johannes Hirschmeier, "Shibusawa Eiichi: Industrial Pioneer," in William W. Lockwood (ed.), The State and Economic Enterprise in Japan (Princeton, New Jersey: Princeton University Press, 1969), p. 236.
2. George DeVos, Socialization for Achievement (Berkeley: University of California Press, 1973), p. 195.
3. Kanson Arahata, Yanaka Mura no Metsuboshi (The Ruin of Yanaka Village) (Tokyo: Shinsensha, 1970), p. 39.
4. Yoshiro Nomura, Zoku: Kogai to Ho no Chishiki (Sequel to a Manual of Pollution and the Law) (Tokyo: Teikoku Chiho Gyosei Gakkai, 1971), p. 20.
5. Shobei Shioda, "Ashio Dozan Kodoku Jiken" (The Ashio Copper Mine Poisoning Incident) in Juristo (Jurist), August 10, 1970, p. 15.
6. Arahata, op. cit., p. 67.
7. Edwin O. Reischauer and John K. Fairbank, East Asia: The Great Tradition (Tokyo: Charles E. Tuttle Co., 1958), p. 619.

8. M. Y. Yoshino, Japan's Managerial System (Cambridge, Massachusetts: The MIT Press, 1968), p. 75.
9. Ibid., p. 78.
10. The Japan Times, January 3, 1974.
11. Shuichi Kato, personal communication.
12. W. G. Beasley, The Modern History of Japan (New York: Praeger, 1963), p. 276.

CHAPTER TWO

1. Eiji Ono, Genten: Yokkaichi Kogai Junen no Kiroku (The Origin: Ten Years of Yokkaichi Pollution) (Tokyo: Keiso Shobo, 1971), pp. 57–8.
2. Ibid., p. 59.

CHAPTER THREE

1. Masao Kunihiro, personal communication.
2. R. E. Ward, "The Legacy of the Occupation," in Herbert Passin (ed.), The United States and Japan (Englewood, New Jersey: Prentice-Hall, 1966), p. 35.
3. Ibid., pp. 34–5.
4. Saburo Okita, "Causes and Problems of Rapid Growth in Postwar Japan and Their Implications for Developing Economies" (Tokyo: Japanese Economic Research Center, March 1967), p. 11.
5. Report on the Activities of Trading Companies, Fair Trade Commission, January 1974.
6. Asahi Shimbun, February 12, 1974.
7. Robert Scalapino and Junnosuke Masumi, Parties and Politics in Contemporary Japan (Berkeley: University of California Press, 1962), p. 79.
8. Ken'ichi Miyamoto, Chiiki Kaihatsu wa Kore de Yoi ka (Is This Regional Development Good?) (Tokyo: Iwanami Shoten, 1973), p. 28.
9. William W. Lockwood, "Japan's 'New Capitalism,'" in William W. Lockwood (ed.), The State and Economic Enterprise in Japan (Princeton, New Jersey: Princeton University Press, 1965), p. 468.
10. Michitaka Kaino, Director of the Tokyo Metropolitan Environmental Research Institute, personal communication.
11. Kiyohiko Yoshitake, Public Enterprise in Japan (Tokyo: Nippon Hyoronsha, 1973), p. 316.
12. Sankei Shimbun, January 4, 1973.
13. Scalapino and Masumi, op. cit., p. 122.
14. Ekonomisto (Economist), November 13, 1973.

CHAPTER FOUR

1. Masazumi Harada, Minamata Byo (Minamata Disease) (Tokyo: Iwanami Shoten, 1972), p. 10.

2. Minamata Byo Kenkyu Kai (Minamata Disease Research Association), Minamata Byo ni Tai Suru Kigyo no Sekinin (The Corporate Responsibility for Minamata Disease) (Kumamoto: Minamata Byo o Kokuhatsu Suru Kai, 1970), pp. 189–91.
3. Jun Ui, Kogai no Seijigaku (The Politics of Pollution) (Tokyo: Sanseido, 1968), p. 42.
4. Ibid., p. 32.
5. Harada, op. cit., p. 180.

CHAPTER FIVE

1. Barry Commoner, "Workplace Burden," Environment, Vol. 15, No. 6, p. 17.
2. Kevin Shea, "PCB: The Worldwide Pollutant That Nobody Noticed," Environment, Vol. 15, No. 9, pp. 26–7.
3. Mikio Nishimura, "Hachi Kagetsu no Kuhaku o Tsuikyu Suru" (Examining Eight Months of Silence), in Hiroyuki Ishi (ed.), PCB (Tokyo: Asahi Shimbunsha, 1972), p. 71.
4. Ibid., pp. 76–8.
5. Naohide Isono, PCB no Kako to Gendai (The Past and Present of PCB) (Tokyo: Jishu Koza, 1974), p. 37.
6. Makoto Kohanawa, "Niwatori (PCB Konnyu) Daku Oiru Chudoku Jiken o Kaerimite" (Looking Back on the Chicken (PCB-Containing) Dark Oil Poisoning Incident), Kagaku (Science), Vol. 44, No. 2, p. 118.
7. Edwin O. Reischauer and John K. Fairbank, East Asia: The Great Tradition (Tokyo: Charles E. Tuttle Co., 1958), p. 619.
8. Gensyu Umeda, "PCB Poisoning in Japan," Ambio, Vol. 1, No. 4, pp. 132–4.

CHAPTER SIX

1. The Japan Times, June 28, 1973.
2. Asahi Evening News, June 29, 1973.
3. Naohide Isono, "Retto ni Afureru Suigin" (The Archipelago Overflowing with Mercury), Asahi Jyanaru (Asahi Journal), August 8, 1973, p. 25.
4. "Suigin ni Yoru Kankyo Osen no Zantei Taisaku Yoryo" (An Outline of Provisional Measures for Mercury Contamination of the Environment), administrative guidance by Chief of Environmental Bureau, Ministry of Health and Welfare, August 1968.
5. Nihon Koshu Eisei Kyokai (Japan Public Health Association), "Suigin Kankyo Osen Chosa Kekka" (Results of the Examination of Mercury Environmental Contamination), August 1970.
6. Mainichi Shimbun, June 28, 1974.
7. Ministry of Health and Welfare statistics.
8. Takafumi Sasaba and Keizi Kiritani, "Pest Control in Paddy Fields: Past, Present and Future," Technocrat, Vol. 5, No. 1, p. 51.

9. Naohide Isono and others, "PCB no Kiroku" (The PCB Record), (Tokyo: Shiryo Tsushin, 1972), pp. 138–40.
10. Ibid., p. 121.
11. Toshikazu Wakatsuki, "Noyaku ni Yoru Kankyo Osen" (Environmental Contamination Due to Agricultural Chemicals), Dai 12 Kai 'Noson Igaku' Kaki Daigaku Koza (12th Rural Medicine Summer University Lectures), July 1972, p. 55.
12. The Japan Times, February 24, 1974.
13. Isono, op. cit., p. 23.
14. Hiroji Shiraki, "Minamata Byo to Suigin ni Yoru Kankyo Osen" (Minamata Disease and Environmental Contamination from Mercury Agricultural Chemicals), Dai 12 Kai 'Noson Igaku' Kaki Daigaku Koza (12th Rural Medicine Summer University Lectures), July 1972, pp. 34–5, 46.
15. Chunoshin Ukita, "Suigin Kagobutsu ni Yoru Chudoku to Kogai" (Poisoning and Pollution from Mercury Compounds), Kagaku (Science), Vol. 36, No. 5, 1966.
16. Mainichi Shimbun, May 24, 1973.
17. Seto Nai Kai no Akashio Genjo to Taisaku (Red Tides of the Seto Inland Sea: Present Conditions and Countermeasures), Seto Nai Kai Suisan Kaihatsu Kyogi Kai (Council for Development of Seto Inland Sea Marine Products), 1971, p. 61.
18. Seto Nai Kai no Akashio Showa 47 (Red Tides of the Seto Inland Sea 1972), Suisancho Seto Nai Kai Gyogyo Chosei Kimukyoku (Fisheries Agency Seto Inland Sea Fisheries Regulation Bureau). Tokyo, 1973, p. 10.
19. Quality of the Environment in Japan (Tokyo: Environment Agency, 1972), p. 100.

CHAPTER SEVEN

1. Chitoshi Yanaga, Big Business in Japanese Politics (New Haven: Yale University Press, 1968), p. 26.
2. Ryoichi Mitakura v. Hisashi Suzuki, Hanrei jiho Vol. 669 (Supreme Court, June 27, 1971).
3. Ryohei Kakumoto, Tokyo and New York in the 1970s (Tokyo: Japan Transport Economics Research Center, 1973), p. 12.
4. Hidetoshi Kato, "A View of Densely Populated Societies," The Wheel Extended, Spring 1972, p. 15.
5. Tokyo Municipal News, Vol. 22, No. 6, August 1972.
6. Asahi Evening News, December 3 and 28, 1974.
7. Administrative Perspective of Tokyo (Tokyo: Tokyo Metropolitan Government Report, 1972), p. 38.
8. Japan Times, September 9, 1973.
9. Government White Paper on the Citizens' Livelihood, 1973, pp. 440–41.
10. The Japan Times, December 14, 1973.

11. The Japan Times, November 26, 1974.
12. Press interview with Senator Edmund Muskie, Tokyo, June 1973.
13. Asahi Evening News, October 17, 1973.
14. Tokyo Fights Pollution (Tokyo: Tokyo Metropolitan Government Report, 1971), p. 94.
15. New Comprehensive National Development Plan (Tokyo: Economic Planning Agency, May 1969, revised October 1972), pp. 3–4.

CHAPTER EIGHT

1. John Bennett, "Japanese Economic Growth: Background for Social Change," in R. P. Dore (ed.), Aspects of Social Change in Modern Japan (Princeton, New Jersey: Princeton University Press, 1967), p. 438.
2. George DeVos, personal communication.
3. 1971 White Paper on Agriculture, p. 7.
4. Business Community, Fall 1973.
5. Shuichi Miyoshi, "Japan's Resources at a Turning Point," Japan Quarterly, July–September 1971.
6. Kakuei Tanaka, Building a New Japan, A Plan for Remodeling the Japanese Archipelago (Tokyo: The Simul Press, 1972), p. 126.
7. Sadahiko Koizumi, "Mutsu Ogawara," Jurisuto (Jurist), May 25, 1973, p. 119.

CHAPTER NINE

1. Interview with Dr. Michio Hashimoto.
2. Nobuko Iijima, "Nihon Kogaishi Kenkyu Noto" (Research Notes on Japanese Pollution History), Kogai Kenkyu (Pollution Research), January 1974, Vol. 3, No. 3, pp. 58-60.
3. Masao Watanabe, "The Conception of Nature in Japanese Culture," Science, Vol. 183, January 25, 1974, p. 282.
4. This occurred at the International Symposium on Environmental Disruption in the Modern World, held in Tokyo during the summer of 1970.
5. Julian Gresser, "Japan Environmental Center," Ecology Law Quarterly, Vol. 3, No. 4, p. 766.
6. Yukio Matsuyama, The New York Times, January 3, 1973.
7. Richard Halloran, Asahi Evening News, December 6, 1973.
8. Chie Nakane, Japanese Society (Berkeley and Los Angeles: University of California Press, 1970), p. 103.
9. Ibid., p. 150.
10. Interview with Dr. Takeo Suzuki.

CHAPTER TEN

1. "Private Equipment Investment Trend in Industrial Pollution Prevention," Ministry of International Trade and Industry, Background Information No. 73-54, December 10, 1973.
2. Keizai Shingi Kai NNW Kaihatsu Iinkai (Economic Advisory Council Subcommittee on the Development of Net National Welfare), Atarashii Fukushi Shihyo (New Welfare Indicator) (Tokyo: Ministry of Finance, 1973), p. 140.
3. Gijitsu Yosoku Hokoku Sho (Report on the Future of Technology) (Tokyo: Science and Technology Agency), June 1971.
4. For more information on the question of the rebirth of militarism, see Albert Axelbank, Black Star Over Japan: Rising Forces of Militarism (New York: Hill and Wang, 1972).
5. Minoru Shimizu, "Japan's Arab Diplomacy" The Japan Times, February 7, 1974.
6. The Japan Times, January 6, 7, and 8, 1975.
7. Asahi Evening News, July 14, 1973.
8. Ibid., July 28, 1973.
9. The Japan Times, January 3, 1975.
10. Asahi Evening News, Interview with Shiro Tahata, January 11, 1975.
11. Paul Ehrlich, The Population-Resource-Environment Crisis: With Special Reference to Japan, copyright 1973 by Paul Ehrlich, p. 2.
12. Keidanren, May 1973 Bulletin.
13. Asahi Shimbun (evening edition), December 1, 1973.
14. Keidanren, op. cit.
15. Peter Drucker, The Age of Discontinuity (London: Pan Books, 1971), p. 90.
16. The Ecologist, A Blueprint for Survival (London: Penguin Books, 1972), p. 26.
17. Garret Hardin, "Tragedy of the Commons," Science, Vol. 162, December 13, 1968, p. 1244.
18. Ibid.
19. Newsweek, December 17, 1973.

BIBLIOGRAPHY, 1975

GENERAL WORKS ON JAPANESE ENVIRONMENTAL PROBLEMS

Air Pollution Control in Japan, Environment Agency, 1972.

Gresser, Julian, "Japan Environmental Center," Ecology Law Quarterly, Vol. 3, No. 4.

Hashimoto, Michio, Kogai o Kangaeru (Thinking About Pollution), Tokyo: Nihon Keizai Shimbun, 1970.

NHK Shakaibu, Nihon Kogai Chizu (Japan Pollution Map), 2nd edition, Tokyo: Nihon Hoso Shuppan Kyokai, 1973.

Nomura, Yoshiro, Kogai to Ho no Chishiki (A Manual of Pollution and the Law), Tokyo: Teikoku Chiho Gyosei Gakkai, 1970.

Nomura, Yoshiro, Zoku: Kogai to Ho no Chishiki (Sequel to a Manual of Pollution and the Law), Tokyo: Teikoku Chiho Gyosei Gakkai, 1971.

Pollution Related Diseases and Relief Measures in Japan, Environment Agency, 1972.

Quality of the Environment in Japan, Environment Agency, 1972.

Quality of the Environment in Japan, Environment Agency, 1973.

Shoji, Hikaru, and Miyamoto, Ken'ichi, Osorubeki Kogai (Terrible Pollution), Tokyo: Iwanami Shoten, 1964.

Ui, Jun ed., Polluted Japan, Tokyo: Jishu Koza, 1972.

Ui, Jun, Sonoda, Kyoichi, and Iijima, Nobuko, Environmental Pollution Control and Public Opinion, Tokyo: unpublished manuscript, 1970.

White Paper on National Life 1973, Economic Planning Agency, 1973. Zu de Miru Kankyo Hakusho (Environment White Paper with Charts) Environment Agency, 1972.

CHAPTER ONE

Beasley, W. G., The Modern History of Japan, New York: Praeger, 1963.

DeVos, George, Socialization for Achievement, Berkeley and Los Angeles: University of California Press, 1973.

Feis, Herbert, The Road to Pearl Harbor, Princeton: Princeton University Press, 1950.

Nakane, Chie, Japanese Society, Berkeley and Los Angeles: University of California Press, 1970.

Reischauer, Edwin O., Japan: Past and Present, 3rd edition, Rutland, Vermont: Charles E. Tuttle Co., 1964.

Shioda, Shobei, "Ashio Dozan Kodoku Jiken" (The Ashio Copper Mine Poisoning Incident), Jurisuto (Jurist), August 10, 1970.

Storry, Richard, A History of Modern Japan, Baltimore: Penguin Books, 1960.

Yoshino, M. Y. Japan's Managerial System, Cambridge, Massachusetts: The MIT Press, 1968.

CHAPTER TWO

Kuto, Kazuo, "Yokkaichi Taiki Osen" (Yokkaichi Air Pollution), Jurisuto (Jurist), August 10, 1970.

Ono, Eiji, Genten: Yokkaichi Kogai Junen no Kiroku (The Origin: Ten Years of Yokkaichi Pollution), Tokyo: Keiso Shobo, 1971.

Sawai, Yoshiro, "Yokkaichi," Jurisuto (Jurist), May 25, 1973. Yokkaichi-shi no Kogai no Genjo to Taisaku (Pollution Conditions and Countermeasures in Yokkaichi City), Yokkaichi City Environment Bureau, Pollution Countermeasures Division, 1973.

CHAPTER THREE

Bennet, John W., "Japanese Economic Growth: Background for Social Change," in R. P. Dore, ed., Aspects of Social Change in Modern Japan, Princeton: Princeton University Press, 1967.

Brzezinski, Zbigniew, The Fragile Blossom, Crisis and Change in Japan, New York: Harper and Row, 1972.

Drucker, Peter, The Age of Discontinuity, London: Pan Books, 1971.

Emmerson, John K., Arms, Yen and Power: The Japanese Dilemma, Tokyo: Charles E. Tuttle Co., 1972.

Honjo, Masahiko, "Study of Regional and Urban Development in Japan and the Japan Center for Area Development Research," The U.S.-Japan Conference on Regional Development, Tokyo: Japan Center for Area Development Research, 1971.

Kaplan, Eugene, Japan: The Government-Business Relationship, Washinton, D.C.: U.S. Department of Commerce, 1972.

Lockwood, William W., "Japan's 'New Capitalism,'" in William W. Lockwood, ed., The State and Economic Enterprise in Japan, Princeton: Princeton University Press, 1965.

Miyamoto, Ken'ichi, Chiiki Kaihatsu wa Kore de Yoi ka (Is The Regional Development Acceptable?), Tokyo: Iwanami Shoten, 1973.

Okita, Saburo, "Causes and Problems of Rapid Growth in Postwar Japan and their Implications for Developing Economies," Tokyo: Japanese Economic Research Center, March 1967.

Patrick, Hugh, "Cyclical Instability and Fiscal Monetary Policy in Postwar Japan," in William W. Lockwood, ed., The State and Economic Enterprise in Japan, Princeton: Princeton University Press, 1965.

Scalapino, Robert, and Masumi, Junnosuke, Parties and Politics in Contemporary Japan, Berkeley and Los Angeles: University of California Press, 1962.

Vogel, Ezra F., Japan's New Middle Class, Berkeley: University of California Press, 1967.

Yanaga, Chitoshi, Big Business in Japanese Politics, New Haven: Yale University Press, 1968.

Yoshitake, Kiyohiko, Public Enterprise in Japan, Tokyo: Nippon Hyoronsha, 1973.

CHAPTER FOUR

Harada, Masazumi, Minamata Byo (Minamata Disease), Tokyo: Iwanami Shoten, 1972.

Ishimure, Michiko, "Pure Land Poisoned Sea," Japan Quarterly, Vol. 18, No. 3, July-September 1971.

Kurland, Leonard, and others, "Minamata Disease," World Neurology, May 1960.

McAlpine, Douglas, and Araki, Shukuro, "Minamata Disease, an Unusual Neurological Disorder Caused by Contaminated Fish," The Lancet, September 20, 1958.

Minamata Byo Kenkyu Kai (Minamata Disease Research Society), Minamata Byo ni Tai Suru Kigyo no Sekinin (The Corporate Responsibility for Minamata Disease), Kumamoto: Minamata Byo o Kokuhatsu Suru Kai, 1970.

Putnam, John, "Quicksilver and Slow Death," National Geographic, Vol. 142, No. 4, October 1972.

Tomita, Hachiro (pen name for Jun Ui), Minamata Byo (Minamata Disease), Kumamoto: Minamata Byo o Kokuhatsu Suru Kai, 1968.

Ui, Jun, Kogai no Seijigaku (The Politics of Pollution), Tokyo: Sanseido, 1968.

Ui, Jun, "Minamata Byo" (Minamata Disease), Juristo (Jurist), August 10, 1970.

Ui, Jun, and Kitamura, Shoji, "Mercury Pollution of Sea and Fresh Water, Its Accumulation into Water Biomass," submitted to the 4th Colloquium for Medical Oceanography, Naples, October 2-5, 1969.

CHAPTER FIVE

Commoner, Barry, "Workplace Burden," Environment, Vol. 15, No. 6, July/August 1973.

Doguchi, Masao, "Chlorinated Hydrocarbons in the Environment in the Kanto Plain and Tokyo Bay, as Reflected in Fishes, Birds and Man," in F. Coulston and others, eds., Methods in Environmental Chemistry and Toxicology, Tokyo: International Academic Printing Company, 1973.

Fujiwara, Kunisato, PCB no Kyoi (The Threat of PCB), Tokyo: Dalsan Bunmeisha, 1973.

Ishi, Hiroyuki, "Kenkyusha, Yakunin, Shimbunsha" (Researchers, Bureaucrats and Reporters), in Hiroyuki Ishi, ed., PCB, Tokyo: Asahi Shimbunsha, 1972.

Ishi, Hiroyuki, "Nihon ni Okeru PCB Osen" (PCB Contamination in Japan), Kankyo Hoken Repoto (Environmental Health Report), Nihon Koshu Eisei Kyokai (Japan Public Health Association), No. 14.

Isono, Naohide, PCB no Kako to Genzai (The Past and Present of PCB), Tokyo: Jishu Koza, 1974.

Jensen, Sören, "The PCB Story," Ambio, Vol. 1, No. 4, August 1972.

Kamino, Ryuzo, "Bubetsu to no Tatakai" (Struggles with Human Contempt), in Hiroyuki Ishi, ed., PCB, Tokyo: Asahi Shimbunsha, 1972.

Kohanawa, Makoto, "Niwatori (PCB Konnyu) Daku Oiru Chudoku Jiken o Kaerimite" (Looking Back on the Chicken PCB-Containing) Dark Oil Incident), Kagaku (Science), Vol. 44, No. 2, February 1974.

Namisaba, Yoshiyuki, ed., Kore ga Yusho da (This Is the Oil Disease), Kitakyushu City: Kanemi Raisu Oiru Higaisha o Mamoru Kai, 1969.

Nishimura, Mikio, "Hachikagetsu no Kuhaku o Tsuikyu Suru" (Examining Eight Months of Silence), in Hiroyuki Ishi, ed., PCB, Tokyo: Asahi Shimbunsha, 1972.

Shea, Kevin, "PCB: The Worldwide Pollutant that Nobody Noticed," Environment, Vol. 15, No. 9, November 1973.

Umeda, Gensyu, "PCB Poisoning in Japan," Ambio, Vol. 1, No. 4, August 1972.

CHAPTER SIX

Hoshino, Yoshiro, Seto Nai Kai Osen (Seto Inland Sea Contamination), Tokyo: Iwanami Shoten, 1972.

Isono, Naohide, "Retto ni Afureru Suigin" (The Archipelago Overflowing with Mercury), Asahi Jyanaru (Asahi Journal), August 8, 1973.

Kobayashi, Jun, "Itai-i ai Byo" (Itai-itai Disease), Jurisuto (Jurist), August 10, 1970.

Sasaba, Takafumi, and Kiritani, Keizi, "Pest Control in Paddy Fields: Past, Present and Future," Technocrat, Vol. 5, No. 1.

Seto Nai Kai no Akashio Genjo to Taisaku (Red Tides of the Seto Inland Sea: Present Conditions and Countermeasures), Seto Nai Kai Suisan Kaihatsu Kyogi Kai (Council for Development of Seto Inland Sea Marine Products), 1971.

Seto Nai Kai no Akashio, Showa 47 (Red Tides of the Seto Inland Sea 1972), Suisancho Seto Nai Kai Gyogyo Chosei Jimukyoku (Fisheries Agency, Seto Inland Sea Fishing Regulation Office), 1973.

Shiraki, Hiroji, "Minamata Byo to Suigin Noyaku ni Yoru Kankyo Osen" (Minamata Disease and Environmental Contamination from Mercury Agricultural Chemicals), Dai 12 Kai 'Noson Igaku' Kaki Daigaku Koza (12th Rural Medicine Summer University Lectures), July 1972.

Wakatsuki, Toshikazu, "Noyaku Kogai" (Agricultural Chemical Pollution), Jurisuto (Jurist), August 10, 1970.

Wakatsuki, Toshikazu, "Noyaku ni Yoru Kankyo Osen" (Environmental Contamination from Agricultural Chemicals), Dai 12 Kai 'Noson Igaku' Kaki Daigaku Koza (12th Rural Medicine Summer University Lectures), July 1972.

CHAPTER SEVEN

Administrative Perspective of Tokyo, Tokyo Metropolitan Government, 1972.

"Garbage Disposal in Tokyo," Tokyo Municipal News, Vol. 22, No. 2, March/April 1972.

Kakumoto, Ryohei, Tokyo and New York in the 1970s, Tokyo: Japan Transport Economics Research Center, 1973.

Kato, Hidetoshi, "A View of Densely Populated Societies," The Wheel Extended, Spring 1972.

References on Photochemical Air Pollution in Japan, Environment Agency, Air Quality Bureau, 1973.

Tokyo Fights Pollution, Tokyo Metropolitan Government, 1971.

Utilization of Resources and Protection of the Environment in High Density Area, Resources Council, Science and Technology Agency, 1971.

CHAPTER EIGHT

Ebato, Akira, Postwar Japanese Agriculture, Tokyo: The International Society for Educational Information Press, 1973.

Hoshino, Yoshiro, "Remodeling the Archipelago," Japan Quarterly, Vol. 20, No. 1, January-March, 1973.

Koizumi, Sadahiko, "Mutsu Ogawara", Jurisuto (Jurist), May 25, 1973.

Tanaka, Kakuei, Building a New Japan, A Plan for Remodeling the Japanese Archipelago, Tokyo: The Simul Press, 1972.

U.S.-Japan Conference on Regional Development (Honolulu, Hawaii January 4-6, 1971), Japan Center for Area Development, 1971.

CHAPTER NINE

Chiiki Toso (Regional Struggle), Rocinante (publ.), 1972-1974.

Iijima, Nobuko, "Chiiki Shakai to Kogai" (The Community and Pollution), Tokyo University Master's Thesis, unpublished, 1968.

Glickman, Norman, "Conflict Over Public Facility Location in Japan," Area Development in Japan, Japan Center for Area Developmeht Research, No. 6, 1972.

Huddle, Norie, and Reich, Michael, "Pollution and Social Response," Area Development in Japan, Japan Center for Area Development Research, No. 7, 1973.

Nishioka, Akio, "Mishima-Numazu-Shimizu, Hitoshi Futacho, Sekiyu Kombinato Hantai Undo" (Mishima-Numazu-Shimizu: The Petroleum Kombinat Protest Movement of One City and Two Towns), Jurisuto (Jurist), August 10, 1970.

Simcock, Bradford, "Environmental Pollution and Citizens' Movements: The Social Sources and Significance of Anti-Pollution Protest in Japan," Area Development in Japan, Japan Center for Area Development Research, No. 5, 1972.

CHAPTER TEN

Long-term Prospectus for Preservation of the Environment-An Interim Report, Planning Committee of the Council for Environmental Pollution Control, 1973.

Miyoshi, Shuichi, "Japan's Resources at a Turning Point," Japan Quarterly, Vol. 18, No. 3, July-September 1971.

Oil: The Present Situation and Future Prospects, Paris: Organization for Economic Cooperation and Development, 1973.

Reference Materials for Seminars in Population/Family Planning, Japanese Organization for International Cooperation in Family Planning, Inc., 1970.

Sangyo Keikaku Konrankai (Industrial Planning Round Table), Sangyo Kozo no Kaikaku (Reformation of the Industrial Structure), Tokyo: Daisei Shuppansha, 1973.

Ward, Barbara, and Dubos, René, Only One Earth, New York: W. W. Norton, 1972.

INDEX

abortion, 216

accidents

    industrial, 57, 87–88. See Also Kanemi Cooking Oil

Asahi Evening News, 211–212, 271

Ashio Copper Mine incident, 2, 180

birth control, 94, 215–216, 218

Buddhism, 8

Bushido, 10, 14

cadmium, xiii, 121–123, 143, 146, 157, 205

Capitalism, in Japan, 11

Chiba Nikko Company, 98

Chisso Corporation, x, 60, 66–67

company unions, 189–190

Confucian ethic, 9

copper poisoning, 1, 4–5, 7. See Also Ashio Copper Mine incident

Dai Nippon Pharmaceuticals, 97

daimyo (feudal barons), 9–10, 12

Dutch learning, 9

Edo (Tokyo), 9, 22, 130

Ehrlich, Paul, 213

Eisenhower, Dwight D., 51

Ekonomisuto, 57

family structure, feudal, 15

food and drug poisonings, 93, 96. See Also Kanemi Cooking Oil, disease

Furukawa, Ichibei, 3, 5, 7, 37, 170

Great Fish Panic of 1973, 116, 126, 194

Greater East Asia Co-Prosperity Sphere, 18

Gross National Product, xv, 161

Halloran, Richard, 191

Harada, Masazumi, 61
Hasegawa, Taiso, 175, 177
Hashimoto, Hikoshichi, 68, 73
hydroelectric power development program, 47
Ikeda, Hayato, 51, 160
Imamura, Yoshiichiro, 34–35
immigration, 17
Inaba, Emon, 22
Income Doubling Plan, 51
INDEX, 243
Irukayama, Katsuro, 72
Ise Bay, 21, 31
Ishihara Industries, 23
Isozu, 25, 28–33, 36–37, 40
Itai-Itai disease, 122
Japan Communist Party, 76, 187
Kaino, Michitaka, 232
Kakumoto, Ryohei, 134
Kanemi Cooking Oil
    disease, 84
Kato, Hidetoshi, 134
Kato, Shuichi, 18
Kishi, Nobusuke, 51
Korean War, 24, 44
Kunihiro, Masao, 42, 192
Kunitake, Tadashi, 85–87
Liberal Democratic party, 30, 46, 175, 177, 257, 261
MacArthur, Douglas, 42
Masumi, Junnosuke, 46, 232
Matsuyama, Yukio, 191
Meiji Restoration, 1, 3, 12, 16, 130, 140, 179, 182
mercury poisoning, x, xiii, xviii, 59–60, 65, 73, 76, 78, 80, 103, 109, 121, 184
Ministry of Agriculture and Commerce, 4
Ministry of Agriculture and Forestry, 67, 87, 89–90, 120

Ministry of International Trade and Industry (MITI), 49, 53, 67, 73–74, 90, 236, 257

Mitsubishi Petrochemical plant, 25

Miyoshi, Shuichi, 161

Morinaga Milk case, 96

National Comprehensive Development Plan, 51, 158, 160, 164, 174

National Institute of Public Health, 65, 126, 146, 263

Nishimura, Masakichi, 167

Nishizaki, Tetsuro, 160

nuclear power plants, x, 152, 209, 229, 263

Okita, Saburo, 43, 227

Otani, Kazohiro, 38–39

petrochemical industry, 24–25, 49–50

Pollution Diet, 201, 203

recycling systems, 144

San-chan Nogyo, 154

Sanger, Margaret, 215

Sato, Eisaku, xiv, 150, 158, 160
    New Comprehensive Development Plan, 150

Scalapino, Robert, 46

Shibusawa, Eiichi, 2

Showa Denko, 73–75, 77, 110

Showa oil refinery, 25

Sino-Japanese War, 16

Statistics Research Council, 37

Storry, Richard, 8

Suzuki, Takeo, 146, 193

Taisho Democracy, 17, 180

Tanaka, Shozo, 4

taxation system, 52, 56

Terashita, Rikisaburo, 165, 169–170

Thalidomide case, 96

Tokugawa society, 10–11

Tokugawa, Ieyasu, 130

Tonemoto, Kiyoshi, 56

Ui, Jun, 68, 71, 73, 78, 185

Umesao, Tadao, 15

victims
- and air pollution, 60
- Ashio Mining, 5
- attitudes of, 77
- factionalism among, 76, 80, 95
- Minamata, 61–62, 64, 67–68, 74, 243

Ward, R.E., 42

water pollution
- and legislation, 147
- contamination of supplies, 148
- cultural factors in, 149
- effects on fishing industry, 157
- household waste and, 148
- in Tokyo Bay, 149

whaling industry, 214

Yanaga, Chitoshi, 130

Yokkaichi, 21
- as a case history of industrial growth, 21–26, 28–31, 33, 35–40
- development of, 21–23
- legislation in pollution case, 56
- pollution in, 54

Yokkaichi asthma, xviii, 31, 36, 40, 56, 93

Yoshida, Katsumi, 32, 36

Yoshida, Katsuro, 24

Zaibatsu, 23–24

APPENDIX

INTRODUCTION TO THE 1987 EDITION BY NORIE HUDDLE

Over ten years have passed since *Island of Dreams* was first published, yet the message contained in these pages has grown more timely and more urgent.

The first and most obvious theme of this book is the Japanese version of "David and Goliath," the story of how desperate pollution victims banded together with concerned citizens to force political and industrial leaders to halt the most extreme forms of environmental assault.

The second theme, which emerged to startle us toward the end of our long quest to understand Japan's pollution problems, is how that country's environmental crisis rang the warning bell to alert the rest of the world to our deepening *global* environmental crisis. This second theme, which we were piecing together while the Club of Rome was developing its well-publicized report, *Limits to Growth*, can be sketched out in a few bold strokes:

> Imagine a country that is one-twenty-fifth the size of the United States (about the size of California) and make it 80 percent mountains. Cram into this small land mass 130 million people, approximately *half* of the population of the United States, concentrating them in the non-mountainous regions. Then, into those same areas of flat land, put in farmland, living space, and one-quarter of the total industrial production of the United States!
>
> Place this small country off the coast of a country (Korea) which Japanese traditionally refer to as "the dagger pointed at the heart of Japan," and near two enormous communist nations, the Soviet Union and the People's Republic of China. Then place the largest body of water in the world between Japan and her closest ally, the United States.
>
> In conclusion, give this nation practically no natural resources, making it highly dependent on the goodwill and partnership of the rest of the world.

Being a small country with a large population and very few mineral resources, the Japanese have been quick to understand how dependent they are for their survival on the rest of the world. Today, we all need to learn this lesson of mutual global interdependence.

Given their unique "pressure-cooker" conditions, the Japanese now have an opportunity to play a unique and historic role on the global stage. Can they, and the rest of us, break free of the predominant "dance step" being rigidly ground out to the persistent and monotonous tune of "the-one-with-the-most-power-and-money-wins?" Or, can we reexamine our basic human values and goals in a systematic way and chart a new course as a global community?

As a growing number of countries seek to develop their economies to get a measure of the material good life, our Earth's natural systems are being increasingly strained. Japan's environmental crisis is, therefore, merely the tip of an enormous iceberg, and indeed is only one of the more visible examples of the emerging global environmental crisis.

In the Eastern tradition, however, the word *crisis* has a dual meaning. The Chinese character for *crisis*, *weichi*, is comprised of two independent ideographs: *wei* means *danger*, and *chi* means *opportunity*. The implication is that we tend to continue in our normal habits or patterns until they become so clearly dysfunctional that we realize we must change or be destroyed.

The crisis is severe. Briefly sketched, we are witnessing a skyrocketing planetary population, a growing stockpile of nuclear warheads, increased pollution and forest decimation, the expansion of desert into once arable land, the inability of our antiquated socio-political structure to resolve these issues, and an economic and financial system which most agree needs major overhaul.

Fortunately, over the last decade there has also been a growing body of citizens in the United States, Japan, Europe, and elsewhere who have begun cleaning up and transforming their environment, their values and goals, and the world around them.

In some cases, we draw from our past, from enduring values and customs which we can see have withstood the test of time: truth, love, beauty, collaboration, and synthesis of the best that is available in every discipline. In other cases, we draw upon fresh creative wellsprings and dreams of new possibilities.

Some of the questions which we—Japanese, Americans, and all people—must now address are these:

- What values, goals, laws, institutions, and individual and group behaviors are required for our collective human survival and fulfillment?

- What will motivate us to make the needed changes?
- Can we redesign our laws and institutions to encourage constructive participation, rather than merely punishing obvious negative behavior when we are able to discover it?
- Rather than viewing Japan as a "sometimes devious trade competitor" interested only in her own benefit, can we restructure our relationship with this uniquely talented country in a way which will benefit Japan, the United States, and all nations?
- Can we, together with Japan and other nations, prioritize the problems, outline the opportunities, lay out a realistic strategy, and mobilize our people and our resources... and do this in time to avoid the major disasters which have been predicted by so many well-informed observers?

On a more personal level, we each have the opportunity—and hopefully the desire—to ask ourselves the key question on which will hinge our collective fate:

- What can *I* do, individually and together with others, that will contribute maximally to this enormous transformation in a way which will continually nurture and inspire us?

It is my deep hope that these and other vital questions will be raised in classrooms and organizations all over the United States and around the world, for I am convinced that no less than our survival is at stake. We have a narrow window of opportunity in which to more effectively catalyze and coordinate the efforts of a critical mass of people to carry out the needed changes in time to halt major catastrophe.

We are coming to see that we are one planet and one human family. We have seen ourselves from the startling and inspiring perspective of outer space: a lovely blue and green pearl of priceless life suspended in the vastness of the universe. Our Earth's fate rests in *our* hands.

Today, a vast array of new technologies have not only enabled us to step off the Earth, but we have begun to unravel the mysteries of the atom and of DNA, to discover that all life we now know is constructed with the same extraordinary basic building blocks.

At the same time, our ingenious telecommunications technologies, which encircle the Earth and act like a vast global nervous system, report back to us that we human beings everywhere are fundamentally quite similar. We care deeply about the same things: love, security, family, friends, education, good health, wholesome food and water, confidence and dignity in our daily living, a sense of purpose and meaning in our lives and in the work we do, and a genuine sense of hope for a better tomorrow for ourselves and our children.

As this edition of *Island of Dreams* goes to press, a new form of organization called a "working net"—clusters of friends who meet regularly to talk about these and other questions of deep personal and mutual interest—have been springing up around the world to develop joint projects out of a shared base of values and concerns.

In conclusion, I wish to add that we all owe the victims of pollution in Japan and elsewhere a deep—and aching—debt of appreciation: they have warned us of the impending crisis with their suffering and deaths. It remains for us, the living, to learn these lessons in time and to make the fundamental transformation required to ensure our collective human survival, well-being, and fulfillment.

Norie Huddle
Alexandria, VA
June 1986

ISLAND OF DREAMS REVISITED IN 1987 BY MICHAEL REICH[1]

The suggestion to revise a ten-year-old book presents an author with a dilemma. While a source of pride and good feeling that some readers are still interested in the volume, the query also provides "a problem of conscience," as another author reported:

> It is only too clear that in such a long time not only has scholarship as such gone forward, but also the opinions of the author himself, even if fundamentally unchanged, have been altered in many details.
>
> To take this development into account would be possible only if the author could bring himself to write a completely new book probably three or four times as big; but for this he lacks the time, the strength, and—to speak frankly-the inclination.[2]

As the product of a particular historical moment, *Island of Dreams* reflects the vision of Japan's environmental crisis in the early 1970s, when the antipollution movement of that country reached a peak of activism. The vision looked back on the past and forward to the future, and helped create the fabric of a worldview, woven throughout the book, which could not be easily amended for updating. In addition, the book resulted from a unique collaboration among coauthors, a cooperative effort that would seem to defy resurrection. These factors make updating and revising the book seem a daunting if not impossible task, at least to this author.

Yet, a reader who approaches this book ten years after its initial publication deserves some indication of what has changed. What has happened to Japan's environmental crisis and the deteriorating air and waters? How have the institutions of government and business adapted? Where are the protest movements and the activists who marched and rallied against the destruction of Japan's natural resources and who organized to help the human victims of pollution? Rather than update these details, this introduction briefly reviews the changes in three areas related to the environment—the problems, the institutions, and the movement.

The ten years from 1965 to 1975 could aptly be called Japan's environmental decade. Many new policies were introduced and implemented by central and local governments and by private corporations, while citizens movements created a new political force pushing for reforms. These changes in social policy and politics have been described and analyzed in a vast literature in Japanese, which this introduction does not even attempt to summarize.[3] A substantial literature also exists in English. A small growth industry appeared among American academics, who produced a flow of Ph.D. dissertations,[4] scholarly articles of social and political analysis,[5] and law journal articles,[6] as well as full-length books on the subject.[7] *Island of Dreams* was among the first English publications on Japan's environmental crisis.

The Problems

In the past ten years, the quality of environmental problems in Japan has changed in important ways. While significant improvements have been made for some kinds of pollution, the overall record is more complex and mixed. In general, the government has worked to address the worst offenses, often with advances in control, while more complex forms of pollution remain problematic or continue to worsen. Noise from automobiles, aircraft, and Shinkansen bullet trains, for example, persists as a major environmental complaint.[8] Below, I briefly review the progress and problems of air and water quality, and hazardous wastes, and then note recent concern with "amenities."

Air and water quality: One important improvement in environmental quality is the ambient level of sulfur dioxide. As mentioned in Chapter Three, air pollution from sulfur oxides results mainly from the combustion of petroleum fuels, which increased rapidly in the 1950s and 1960s. The average annual concentration of sulfur dioxide reached a peak of 0.059 ppm (parts per million) in 1967 and has declined each year since then, at least according to fifteen general air pollution monitoring stations, falling to an average of 0.013 ppm in 1982. These average values, however, could mask changes in certain industrial areas of Japan. In 1978, for example, the Environment Agency stated that "the monitoring stations which failed to meet the criteria have increased in large cities and their nearby areas in Chiba, Tokyo, and Osaka."[9] In 1984, however, the agency noted that the number of monitoring stations that satisfy quality standards is increasing year by year, although problems have persisted in some areas.[10]

Lowering the ambient level of sulfur oxides resulted from a three-pronged approach in government policy: (1) lowering the sulfur content of imported fuel; (2) desulfurizing heavy oil; and (3) desulfurizing stack gases.[11] The ability to achieve this improvement depended partly on the relatively simple nature of the problem—sulfur oxides produced from burning petroleum that contained sulfur—which allowed for relatively simple technical solutions. Japan's slowdown in economic growth from the mid-1970s and the shift in industrial structure towards the service sector contributed to lower levels of sulfur oxides. The improvement also depended, however, on government support and subsidies to encourage importing low-sulfur fuel, developing petroleum desulfurization devices, and developing stack gas desulfurization equipment. As a result, Japan made faster progress than the United States in the development and use of sulfur oxide control technology.[12] But Japan's efforts to control these pollutants also resulted from the pressure of the Yokkaichi decision[13] in favor of the victims and the threat of additional legal suits against industry in other cities (see Chapter Four).

Other areas of Japan's environment have not improved so dramatically. The national ambient level of nitrogen oxides, for example, increased during the 1970s. This air pollutant is produced through combustion by both stationary and moving sources, that is, by both factories and automobiles, and the combustion process is not as amenable to technical controls as sulfur oxides. The increasing number of automobiles, especially in major urban centers, makes it difficult to reduce the ambient level of nitrogen oxides. In 1982, air pollution stations in Tokyo, Osaka, and Kanagawa Prefecture recorded values exceeding the quality standard for nitrogen dioxide.[14] In 1984, the Environment Agency recorded an increase in monitoring stations that exceeded the standard for nitrogen dioxide, and attributed it to the rising use of cars in major cities and to weather conditions during the year.[15] Public concern about nitrogen oxide pollution surged recently, when the Tokyo municipal government reported a study showing an association between air pollution levels and higher mortality rates, including respiratory diseases and lung cancer in women.[16]

Water pollution control in Japan also has a mixed record. Marked improvements have been made since the 1960s in controlling the flow of toxic substances in factory effluent, thereby increasing the compliance rate for heavy metals and toxic chemicals in rivers and streams. Levels of organic substances in water (measured as biological or chemical oxygen demand) have decreased in the worst rivers and streams, but not as rapidly in other rivers and water bodies, if at all. For the Tama River, which runs through Tokyo, a 1980 report showed improved water quality in the lower river, due to stricter effluent control and expanded sewerage systems. But water quality of the river as a whole remained the same or worsened between 1973 and 1978, with the middle segment far exceeding the water quality standard of 5 ppm biological oxygen demand.[17]

Water pollution remains a serious problem for Japan's closed water bodies, such as lakes and marshes, and for many rivers. In fiscal 1981, water quality continued to decline in closed water bodies, due to pollution by nitrogen and phosphates and to problems of eutrophication.[18] In fiscal 1984, a survey of public waters showed a decline in the percentage meeting quality standards, especially in rivers near urban areas.[19] For example, Osaka Prefecture's main water source, the Yodo River, has exceeded environmental standards for nine years through 1984, and, in the same year, only 28 of the prefecture's 64 rivers passed the standards.[20] Significantly, controls over artificial detergents (with phosphates) were first instituted in Shiga Prefecture as a result of persistent activities by consumer organizations.

The causes of continued water pollution problems are complex, and include socio-economic and geophysical factors. In many areas, population growth continues to exceed sewer construction, making household waste water a major problem. Water runoff from non-point sources, such as farmland and land reclamation sites, poses difficult problems of control. And limited water exchange in closed water areas provides ripe conditions for deterioration. In these ways, Japan's economic success continues to exacerbate water pollution problems.

Technological progress also contributes to water pollution problems in Japan, for example, through toxic organic chemicals (such as trichloroethylene) used in producing integrated circuits. These chemicals have leaked into water bodies—similar to pollution problems in California's Silicon Valley—contaminating groundwater sources and causing great concern. The Environment Agency warned in its 1985 report that "high-tech pollution" could become a major problem in Japan, especially since chemical contamination cannot easily be reversed.[21]

Hazardous wastes: In the United States, the problem of toxic wastes and hazardous dumps became a major issue of national policy in the late 1970s and 1980s. The tragedies of Love Canal and Times Beach symbolized how wastes discarded long ago could harm the health and disrupt the lives of unsuspecting citizens. In Japan, the issue of hazardous wastes emerged with the case of hexavalent chromium buried near a factory in Tokyo. In 1978, the Environment Agency observed that "illegal dumping of wastes still accounts for more than half the pollution offenses each year—one indication that securing proper disposal is still a problem."[22] Problems associated with the disposal of mercury batteries have become an environmental and social issue raised by citizen groups. Almost 80 percent of Japan's municipal governments have responded by collecting mercury batteries separately from other household garbage and storing them, pushing the central government to convene an expert committee to examine the problem. In 1985, the group reported that existing procedures should be adequate to prevent mercury contamination of the environment, but it still recommended that battery producers make every effort to recall used mercury batteries and reduce the mercury content and that the government establish area-wide disposal centers.[23]

In the early 1980s, toxic wastes became a major environmental issue in Japan. In November 1983, the highly toxic chemical dioxin, a contaminant in herbicides and in Agent Orange in Vietnam, was detected in ashes and dust in the incinerators of seven major Japanese cities, provoking alarm among health and environmental officials. Similar discoveries had been made in Europe and the United States in the late 1970s. In 1984, Professor Ryo Tatsukawa, of Ehime University, detected minute levels of dioxin in fat tissues obtained from thirteen people. He criticized the lack of research on dioxin pollution in Japan, and urged the Japanese government to take fast action against dioxin pollution.[24]

Amenities: Japan's official concern with the concept of amenities as an element of environmental policy began in the mid-1970s. In many ways, it emerged from the report on Japanese environmental policy by the Organization for Economic Cooperation and Development, which concluded that "Japan has won many pollution abatement battles, but has not yet won the war for environmental quality."[25] The report went on to say that Japan's policies concentrated on pollution abatement because popular discontent focused on pollution and not on environmental quality. This interpretation, however, ignores the many protests of the 1960s and 1970s which voiced popular concern with both environmental quality and amenities, the latter defined in the report as "quietness, beauty, privacy, social relations and other non-measured elements of the 'quality of life.'" [26]

In the late 1970s and early 1980s, Japan's Environment Agency adopted the concept of amenity as an objective for policy, and introduced the word directly into the Japanese language. The Environment Agency's director-general and high-ranking government officials now use the English word in Japanese without hesitation, and the 1984 agency budget included 200 million yen for the promotion of environmental amenities. As one agency official put it, "To define a new issue for policy, it is sometimes useful to have a word that no one understands." But the acceptance of this concept also reflects Japan's increasing official concern with protecting scenic, historical, and green areas, as part of the new national image of a maturing, rich society.

The Institutions

Government agencies: The creation of Japan's Environment Agency in 1971 marked a major accomplishment in the administrative realm for pollution control. The decision by top Liberal Democratic party political leaders to consolidate environmental administration into a single entity, with specific jurisdiction, represented a key change in the ruling party's policy from the previous approach of coordinating environmental policy through an interministerial committee. That decision, as noted in Chapter Ten, represented a governmental response to increasing social and political conflict around pollution issues—especially from opposition parties and citizen groups. The ruling party thus sought to contain conflict and challenge through institutional change and symbolic reassurance.

Creation of the Environment Agency provided an official administrative voice for environmental concerns. The quality of that voice has varied under different directors of the agency, with the terms of Buichi Oishi and Takeo Miki standing out as the most supportive of environmental protection. (In the United States as well, the quality of the EPA's voice has varied under different directors, with an all-time low reached by Anne Burford Gorsuch in the Reagan administration, who managed to achieve an almost anti-environmental record.) In 1981, Oishi, the agency's first director-general, criticized his successors at a public rally, saying it was regrettable that some of them had "sold out their souls to industry."[27] The establishment of the agency nonetheless transformed ad hoc and decentralized environmental concerns in the government into formalized and more centralized procedures and institutions. Countries without a central agency, such as Spain and Italy in the early 1980s, experience enormous difficulty in instituting an effective environmental policy.

But Japan's Environment Agency continues to suffer various organizational weaknesses. Internal conflicts persist between bureaucrats hired directly by the agency or assigned from the Ministry of Health and Welfare and those assigned to the agency for several years from the Ministry of International Trade and Industry and elsewhere. Growing numbers of bureaucrats with a primary allegiance to the Environment Agency have provided a voice of commitment to environmental management within the central government's policies. But the agency still remains relatively weak in comparison to other ministries, such as transportation and construction. That position in the power structure of the central government has contributed to the agency's difficulties in pushing new elements of environmental policy, such as the environmental impact statement.

The agency nevertheless has carried out important administrative tasks, including preparation of an annual report, with an English translation. This report provides a record of agency activities and a presentation of compiled data. As is typical of bureaucratic reports, however, the annual white paper seeks to justify the agency's existence through two standard tactics: by documenting continued environmental problems that require official action, and by presenting successful agency efforts to control some environmental hazards. Overall, however, the annual reports reflect the transformation of environmental problems and government administration during the past ten years.

The Environment Agency in the 1970s also expanded programs to build up the capabilities of local environmental administrations in prefectural and city governments. Local administrations in Japan are responsible for implementing and enforcing much of the environmental policy. The agency began a training institute for pollution control in 1973 and by March 1980 had trained 4,506 administrative and 1,415 technical personnel.[28] But in the 1980s, Japanese local governments have witnessed a decrease in the number of independent environment sections, which have been combined with other sections. Budgets for local pollution control have been cut, and environmental issues have declined in importance for political campaigns.

In the international environmental arena, Japan's administration has a similarly mixed record. One U.S. legal scholar observed: "Despite her enthusiastic pledge of environmental good citizenship at the 1973 Stockholm Conference on the Human Environment, Japan has consistently taken anti-environmental positions in international negotiations."[29] That evaluation is supported by another analysis, illustrated with three case studies on the proposed Japanese supertanker port in Palau, Japan's role in the Law of the Sea Conference, and Japan's activities in international negotiations to restrict whaling.[30] The Japanese government has also neglected implementation of the Convention on International Trade in Endangered Species of Wild Fauna and Flora, and resisted efforts to curb such imports to Japan. A regional meeting in Malaysia in October 1984 on implementing the convention issued a resolution that sternly criticized Japan by name for consistently failing to meet its main obligation.[31]

On the other hand, in the 1980s, Japan has adopted a more international perspective on certain environmental issues. For example, the Environment Agency has sent assistance teams to Southeast Asian countries, as well as to Brazil, to help those countries introduce environmental policies into development strategies. But as one former agency official stressed, developing countries need to learn from Japan's failures as well as its successes;[32] and whether government bureaucrats can adequately teach both is doubtful. Moreover, while Japan ten years ago looked to the United States for innovations in environmental policy, today many Japanese think that the United States has much to learn from Japan in this field. This change in attitude, of course, applies far beyond the Environment Agency, reflecting Japan's extraordinary economic strength and expanding political responsibilities in the international arena.

In sum, Japan's national environmental administration has become institutionalized, with both benefits and problems. The Environment Agency has become an accepted (if relatively powerless) piece of the national bureaucracy and has established environmental concerns as a national value. But in the process, environmental problems in the government have become more routine, as another part of the administrative machinery. In some sense, the government needed to make the problems routine for the issues to become accepted.

Environmental assessment: Some of these administrative and political problems appeared in the debate over environmental impact assessments. While the United States has nearly fifteen years of experience with a national system of environmental impact statements (EISs), Japan's experience has been one of fragmentation among governmental agencies, and resistance to the idea by central government and business. This experience illustrates some of the difficulties in establishing a new environmental program, especially in the Japan of the late 1970s and early 1980s.

In the United States, the environmental impact process came under attack in the mid-1970s for causing excessive delays and paperwork and for being of little use to decision-makers. As a result, the Council of Environmental Quality put together a new set of regulations to simplify the EIS process, regulations that took effect on July 30, 1979. The Environmental Protection Agency also performed an analysis of the costs and benefits of doing an environmental impact assessment. According to the Council of Environmental Quality's annual report in 1980:

> The EPA analysis concludes that the EIS substantively changed decision-making. They were not simply a pro forma paperwork exercise. Significant long-term protection and enhancement of environmental resources were attributable to the EIS. Thus the EIS process protects the environment at the same time that it helps improve the cost-effectiveness of projects.[33]

Yet Japan has failed to adopt a system for environmental impact assessment.[34] The need for a systematic assessment of public and private development projects has been debated in Japan since the early 1970s. Various governmental development plans included a requirement for some assessment procedures. But opposition from industry and conflict among ministries prevented passage of a general law on environmental assessment. Among the controversial issues were types of projects to be assessed, methods of assessment, relationship of the Environment Agency to other government bodies, the legal nature of the environmental impact assessment, and procedures for public participation of affected residents. In the early 1980s, despite numerous attempts to get a bill through parliament, the Environment Agency could not muster sufficient political power. The stalled situation at the central level encouraged a number of prefectures and cities to prepare and pass their own local environmental assessment ordinances. The effectiveness of these local efforts, however, has been seriously questioned.[35]

The need for "proper" assessment of environmental impact "is generally recognized" in Japan, at least according to the Environment Agency.[36] In 1972, the cabinet approved a resolution "On Environmental Conservation Measures Relating to Public Works," which encouraged some form of environmental assessment in Japan.[37] Subsequently, in the 1970s, various laws were amended to require prior assessment of public projects for environmental disruptions.

But that resolution and its consequences have many problems. The assessment procedure remains informal, ambiguous, and discretionary for the agency involved. Moreover, the procedure is carried out within the agency and without meaningful public review. As Frank K. Upham put it:

> There is no legally enforceable duty which would give Japanese environmentalists an opportunity to challenge an assessment's adequacy in the courts, similar to the NEPA requirement in the United States. Furthermore, in the current [1979] period of economic recession in Japan, there are frequent signs that the assessments are halfhearted at best and *pro forma* in many cases. The value of these informal assessments is further lessened by the agencies' extreme reluctance to open up the assessment process to substantial participation by environmental groups.[38]

An important indication of these weaknesses is that the Environment Agency's annual report in 1980 described the various assessments that had been performed, but provided no information about ways in which projects had changed as a result of the assessments.[39]

Yet, in the Japan of the 1980s, performing an environmental assessment for public projects has become standard procedure, according to one former agency official. Private companies exist to perform assessments and issue reports, as in the United States. Even without a general law, assessments are commonly performed for roads, for sewage plants, and for projects of private companies. Ten years ago, no budgets and no plans existed for environmental assessments, while today both are included in most public and private projects. These changes reflect basic shifts in public and private consciousness. Whether the changes are sufficient remains a debatable point.

In 1984, after four years of parliamentary efforts, the Environment Agency gave up its attempt to push a general law through the Diet and settled for a cabinet decision on the implementation of Environmental Impact Assessment. The failure to enact a general law resulted from many obstacles.[40] Opposition from Japan's business community remained strong, especially from the electric power companies and from Keidanren, the Federation of Economic Organizations. Within the government, the most important constraint was the rigid institutional resistance to opening up the process of making decisions. Important public decisions are still made in remarkably private ways, without meaningful public hearings and with little public access to official documents. In addition, the fragmentation of interests among ministries in the central government blocked a general law. Individual ministries wanted to control the assessment procedure for their own projects, to protect their own constituencies, to protect their own interests, and to decide what they believed was the best course. They opposed the idea of the Environment Agency having legal authority to review assessments and dictate changes. Finally, resistance to the law within the Liberal Democratic party delayed and weakened the proposal at each step of the parliamentary path.

The difficulties in enacting the assessment law also reflected a deeper and more general problem: the environmental movement's declining influence in political institutions. Indeed, in both Japan and the United States, the declining political influence of the environmental movement has paralleled the declining power of the government's environment agency.

The Movement

Environmental organizations: Japan's environmental movement in the 1980s is certainly different from the movement of the 1970s. Two U.S. academics, in analyzing the movement, predicted that it would either die out or become bureaucratic, following the view of organizational theory on the fate of social movements.[41] A hasty review might suggest both have happened. For example, the activist organization based at Tokyo University, Jishu Koza (The Independent Study Group), described in Chapter Nine, disbanded in 1985, and its leader, Jun Ui, moved to Okinawa University. Other groups, such as the Consumers Union of Japan, have become relatively stable institutions, with weekly newsletters, annual meetings, and regular activities, and some observers might identify bureaucratic elements. The movement generally seems less powerful and less political, reflecting the downfall of progressive local governments throughout Japan. But this view, and the academic prediction, disregard the new ideas and new forms that environmental activism has taken in Japan and the extent to which the movement has become part of daily life. A closer analysis indicates that the movement continues to pursue new issues and to influence policy, although usually in a calmer manner.

A recent protest movement in Zushi, a bedroom city 30 miles southwest of Tokyo, illustrates some of these trends. Two groups, the Citizens' Association for the Protection of Nature and Children and the Ikego Green Operation Center, have opposed plans to build U.S. military housing in the Ikego Ammunition Storage Area, which now serves as a nature conservation area. The local groups, typical of many in Japan, are based on housewives who organized to protect their home environment. The groups mobilized local, national, and international support, but fundamentally relied on democratic methods at the local level: the recall of a mayor who supported the plan in September 1984, the formation of an independent political body to elect their own mayor in November 1984, the collection of comments on a draft environmental impact report (required by Kanagawa Prefecture), the recall of the city council in March 1986 for supporting the plan, and the successful resistance of efforts to recall the mayor in the same month.

The mayor of Zushi has called the protest "a symbol for grassroots movements for the preservation of nature in Japan." The movement's success to date has depended on its combination of diverse elements: nature protection, worries about soldiers, peace activism, and concerns about maintaining a good suburban environment for children. While perhaps including some anti-American tones, the dominant orientation of the movement has been environmental protection.

The Zushi movement represents the continuity of environmental activism at the local level in Japan. Protests against airport noise and airport construction persist in many parts of Japan, with mixed success. The movement against noise at the airbase in Atsugi, used by United States and Japanese military, recently suffered a setback when the Tokyo Superior Court refused to grant an injunction and reversed an earlier decision to pay damages for night flights, citing the larger public interest of national security.[42] Nature conservation groups and local citizens oppose the construction of a new airstrip for U.S. military training on Miyake Island, which belongs to a national park and national bird migratory protection area.[43] And plans to construct a commercial airport on Ishigaki Island in Okinawa have raised local, national, and international opposition, because proposed landfill plans would damage a coral reef and fish resources.[44]

Japan's environmental movement has also focused on nuclear power issues. Japanese activists collaborated with South Pacific groups to block government plans for ocean disposal of Japanese nuclear wastes in that region. Now, Japanese groups oppose the construction and operation of nuclear power plants throughout the nation (producing 23 percent of electricity), and also plans for nuclear fuel reprocessing in Aomori and high-level waste storage in Hokkaido. Litigation against nuclear power plants has proved difficult for citizens groups to win, but the courtroom has provided citizens with a public forum to voice their fears and complaints and thereby influence government agencies to improve some safety review procedures.[45]

Some environmental groups, particularly in Tokyo, have turned increasing attention to international issues, especially problems involving Japanese corporations in poor countries. Japanese groups have cooperated with the International Organization of Consumers Unions in hosting conferences in Japan and in seeking to mobilize Japanese resources for environmental and consumer problems in poor countries. After the chemical disaster in Bhopal, India, a coalition of nineteen consumer, citizen, environmental, and women's groups in Japan formed the Bhopal Disaster Monitoring Group to investigate the tragedy in India and publicize the findings in Japan. Japanese environmental activists have become frequent participants in international movement meetings, although language problems and cultural gaps still occasionally hamper cross-national collaboration. But no doubt exists that one portion of Japan's environmental movement is increasingly integrated into the growing global network of consumer activism.

One outgrowth of Japan's environmental activism is an anti-tobacco movement. That movement emerged in the late 1970s with the new concept of "the right to hate smoking" (*ken'en ken*), and has gained strength every year. Several key anti-tobacco activists previously participated in Japan's antipollution movement and draw on that experience and their nationwide contacts. This movement has received expert support from scientists at Japan's National Cancer Center and National Institute of Public Health. In 1984, a national organization, the All Japan Anti-Smoking Liaison Council, formed and included about twenty groups from around the country. Several activists have sued the Japanese National Railways to expand the number of no-smoking cars. And groups organized Japan's first Anti-Smoking Week in April 1984, and have formed the Association to Promote AntiSmoking Education for school children.[46]

The no-smoking movement has also developed international activities. Several Japanese groups collaborated with the International Organization of Consumers Unions to protest Japanese plans to increase cigarette sales in developing countries, especially in Southeast Asia. The movement also sent protest letters to President Reagan in the fall of 1985, to protest U.S. government efforts to increase U.S. cigarette sales in Japan. And in 1987, Japan will host the International Conference on Smoking.

This movement has achieved significant progress on various fronts, but especially in changing Japanese attitudes towards the rights of non-smokers. Japan's anti-smoking activists are addressing what many people consider the major public health problem of rich countries—tobacco-related illnesses—with enormous economic and political implications. In April 1985, when the Japanese government turned its state tobacco company into a private firm, the no-smoking movement issued a poster with the slogan: "The State Quits (tobacco monopoly), and I Quit (smoking), Too." But much remains to be done, since about 65 percent of adult males are still smokers.[48]

Japan's consumer movement has also developed new ideas and forms for activism. Japan has a well-established cooperative movement, going back to the late 1940s (and perhaps even earlier). A recent development, however, is the Daily Life Cooperatives movement, which seeks to connect consumers with producers, without supermarkets, through a network of small groups that buy food directly from farmers and fishermen. This movement's leaders include former student activists, who are now seeking to introduce ideas of social change into the day-to-day lives of people. The network has grown to 128,000 members, with increasing continuity and stability, and a desire to expand to a national basis. The movement also has a political side, with eight city councilors elected in Tokyo and a monthly newsletter called "Livelihood and Self-Government" (*Seikatsu to Jichi*).

One environmental movement that has persisted is the opposition to the airport at Narita, also known as the New Tokyo International Airport. This movement has existed for nearly twenty years, with changes in form, strategy, and ideology. The alliance between local farmers and radical supporters remains a key feature of the anti-airport struggle. While more violent than most environmental movements in Japan, the protest at Narita nonetheless represents many aspects of environmental conflicts in Japan, including a more general shift in concern from pollution by private industry to problems of government projects, including highways, airports, garbage incinerators, and super-express trains.[49] The anti-airport struggle is now entering another phase, five years after the airport's opening in 1978, as the government tries to clear the land for the second stage of construction. Three of twelve remaining farm families on the site agreed to sell their land in 1985, but the others refuse even to speak with company representatives.[50] And in October 1985, one group of the Anti-Airport Federation organized a demonstration of thousands (14,000 according to sponsors, 4,000 according to police) with helmets, bamboo sticks, stones, and molotov cocktails—who were met by 9,500 policemen with water cannons and tear gas.[51] The struggle at Narita seems unlikely to end soon.

Victims of pollution: Japan's system for the administrative compensation of pollution-related health damage, one of the world's few systems designed specifically and solely to compensate victims of toxic substance pollution, has attracted international attention. The 1973 law has been examined and assessed by Western and Japanese scholars.[52] A bill to create such an administrative compensation system was introduced into the U.S. Congress in the late 1970s, and several hearings were held on the proposal. That bill did not pass, however, and provisions for health damage compensation in the Superfund Law (Comprehensive Environmental Response, Compensation, and Liability Act of 1980) were removed as part of a compromise to get the bill through Congress.

The history of the compensation system illustrates the importance of political pressures. Research on the law's drafting and enactment has shown that industry generally supported the approach of an administrative compensation system. Industry supported the 1969 law to diffuse social issues more than to avoid legal liability. But after the decision in the Yokkaichi case, which found a group of industries jointly liable for damaging people's health due to air pollution, an industry organization drafted a version of what became the 1973 law, in hopes of preventing similar damage suits.[54] It should therefore come as no surprise that Japan's compensation law does not work as an economic incentive to reduce pollution (at least as economists talk about achieving a certain efficient level of emissions based on marginal costs and benefits). The law was designed mainly to serve the political purposes of containing conflict, not to advance economic theories to prevent pollution.[55] Japan's compensation law thus lends support to social theory that views policy as an institutional effort to contain protest and conflict.[56] The experience also suggests that a general compensation law for pollution victims will not be enacted in the United States without a strong victims' movement in politics and in the courts, as happened with black lung.

Japan's compensation system also illustrates a fundamental problem in designing such a system: deciding who should be compensated. Japan's system combines two types of criteria: geographic boundaries and individual symptoms. For general air pollution-related health damage (class 1 areas), the system uses strict geographic boundaries and loose individual symptoms, while for toxic substance-related health damages (class 2 areas), the system uses loose geographic boundaries and strict individual symptoms. As in other environmental controversies, the way of drawing the lines determines the form of controversy.[57] For Japan's compensation system in the 1970s, criticism of the air pollution criteria focused more on the drawing of geographic boundaries for designated pollution areas, while criticism of the toxic pollution criteria focused more on the diagnosis of individual symptoms for certified pollution victims.[58] Controversy in a compensation system is probably inevitable; but the form of controversy can be chosen by the design of the system.

In the 1980s, controversy over the compensation system persisted and expanded. Keidanren, the Federation of Economic Organizations, has launched a major campaign to revise the compensation system and reduce the burden on business. Industry has argued that the compensation system is not based on scientific evidence or rational principles. For example, while the ambient levels of sulfur oxides have declined markedly, the number of patients has continued to increase, although the rate of increase slowed down, especially in the late 1970s and early 1980s.[59] Industry has also complained about the continued designation of air pollution areas, even after sulfur oxide levels were reduced. On the other hand, Japan's victims of pollution diseases have protested persistent delays in providing relief through the compensation system. In 1985, the National Federation of Pollution Victims' Associations appealed to several government agencies to improve the system.[60] To examine these and other problems, in 1983 the Environment Agency requested the Central Council for Environmental Pollution Control to prepare a report on the compensation system for air pollution, and discussions and controversies still continued in mid-1986. In October 1986, the Council recommended a drastic revision in the law, to abolish all air pollution areas and to stop the certification of new patents.

Remarkably and tragically, victims of Minamata disease and Kanemi Rice Oil disease continue to protest and litigate, even in 1986. In Minamata, persons who have applied for certification as official patients have confronted long waits in administrative decisions on their cases, and have initiated several legal suits against the prefectural and central governments. In the latest case, in November 1985, the Fukuoka High Court upheld a lower court decision and ruled that the delays in decisions were illegal after two years from filing, and required Kumamoto Prefecture and the central government to pay compensation to 24 patients.[61] These patients originally filed their suit in 1978, and by 1985, some persons had waited more than ten years for a decision on their application. In October 1985, according to the Environment Agency, 6,052 persons were waiting for local government decisions on their Minamata disease applications, including 5,195 persons in Kumamoto Prefecture.[62] In December 1985, when denied a meeting with the Environment Agency's director-general, patients and supporters began a sit-in at the building, but were ejected by police, as groups were previously in 1978 and 1983.[63]

Minamata victims thus have continued to demand public accountability for government officials, and now demand governmental restitution for damages when those officials do not carry out their public duties. Their struggle, even now, nearly thirty years after the discovery of Minamata disease, is not over. In early December 1985, the Environment Agency announced it would appeal the Fukuoka decision to Japan's Supreme Court. A lawyer for the plaintiffs condemned the action for further delaying compensation to Minamata victims, saying it called into question the Environment Agency's justification for existence.[64] The agency's appeal demonstrated again that victory in court does not easily translate into justice for victims.

In the Kanemi case as well, conflict and litigation have continued long after we completed *Island of Dreams*. About ten years after Yusho broke out, three long-awaited court decisions finally arrived. Two civil decisions (one handed down in Fukuoka City in October 1977, the other in Kitakyushu City in early March 1978) found both Kanemi and Kanegafuchi Companies guilty of negligence and ordered them to pay damages to the plaintiffs: for 44 Fukuoka plaintiffs, 680 million yen ($2.9 million); and for 729 Kitakyushu plaintiffs, 6.08 billion yen ($26.2 million). The criminal decision, reached in late March 1978, found Kanemi's factory director guilty of injury due to professional negligence and found the company president innocent. The Kitakyushu trial in particular raised the issue of the government's liability for not preventing the Kanemi Rice Oil disaster, a point we stressed in Chapter Five.[65]

But these decisions did not end the litigation, as appeals and new trials of various sorts followed.[66] Even in 1985, a new group of 74 Kanemi Rice Oil disease victims filed a damage suit against the two companies, Kanemi's president, and the national government—the fifth group to go to court. Another group of 560 certified victims announced their intention to begin litigation in the near future.[67] And in May 1986, the Fukuoka High Court reduced damages awarded to 342 Yusho victims by a lower court decision in 1982 and rejected the plaintiffs' demand for damages from the central government, the Kitakyushu City government, or the Kanegafuchi Company. This decision reversed trends in five previous Yusho trials and marked a stunning setback for Kanemi victims.[68]

Japan's wheels of justice thus continue to turn slowly—and more frequently against the victims of pollution. Pollution trials in the 1980s have tended to favor defendants over plaintiffs, in contrast to the court decisions of the 1970s. The judicial system no longer provides pressure on the government's environmental policy. And victims whose proceedings have dragged on for years feel increasingly discouraged and isolated.

Metaphors and realities

In 1975, we gave this book the title *Island of Dreams*, to suggest several metaphors about Japan's environmental crisis. We noted in the Introduction that the Japanese people in the first half of this century pursued "a dream of imperial status and military conquest, a dream that ended in nightmare." Then, in the postwar period, they worked to achieve the dream of "national economic power and material wellbeing," which brought with it tremendous environmental and human costs that are too often forgotten today. The third metaphor was the garbage produced by Japan's mass-consumption throw-away culture, and its disposal in Tokyo Bay in landfill sites first called Island of Dreams, then New Island of Dreams, and finally New New Island of Dreams.

What does *Island of Dreams* look like in Tokyo Bay today? In Chapter Seven, we observed that the last plot was expected to be filled by 1976, but Tokyo still continues to truck its garbage and other refuse to the bay to create new land. As a U.S. reporter recently noted, "For future generations, the islands will be turned into parks. That is the only feasible use, as garbage-based land cannot bear anything much heavier than people."[69] More solid refuse materials, including earth, gravel, sludge and ash, are being used to create land for port buildings, a power plant, an apartment complex, and other facilities. The surface of *Island of Dreams* thus has been transformed into attractive parks, exercise areas, public baths, and green trees. But underneath remain Tokyo's wastes. As one long-time public health expert warned, "Who knows what will happen to those wastes in 20 years?"

People captivated by Japan's economic successes today should not forget the wastes beneath the pretty surface—or the costs paid by the victims of uncontrolled economic growth. This book remains a tribute to the victims and a reminder to us all. The dedication to this volume remains the same:

To the victims:
May their suffering not be in vain.

Michael Reich
Cambridge, Massachusetts
June, 1986

NOTES for Island of Dreams revisited, 1987

1. Sections of this introduction are based on M.R. Reich, "Environmental Policy and Japanese Society, Part I. Successes and Failures," and "Part II. Lessons about Japan and about Policy." International Journal of Environmental Studies 20 (1983):191-198 and 20(1983):199-207.
2. E. Panofsky, Idea: A Concept in Art Theory (Harper & Row, New York, 1924, 1960, 1968), cited in A. O. Hirschman, National Power and the Structure of Foreign Trade (University of California Press, Berkeley, 1945, 1980).
3. For a bibliographic review of important sources in Japanese, see: M.A. McKean, Environmental Protest and Citizen Politics in Japan (University of California Press, Berkeley, 1981), 276-278.
4. For example: A.B. Campbell, The Implementation of Water Quality Legislation: A Comparative Study of the United States and Japan, unpublished Ph.D. dissertation, Rutgers University, 1975; M.A. McKean, The Potentials for GrassRoots Democracy in Post-War Japan: the Anti-Pollution Movement as a Case Study in Political Activism, unpublished Ph.D. dissertation, University of California at Berkeley, 1974; B.L. Simcock, Environmental Politics in Japan, unpublished Ph.D. dissertation, Harvard University, 1974; J.G. Lewis, Hokaku Rengo: The Politics of Conservative-Progressive Cooperation in a Japanese City, unpublished Ph.D. dissertation, Stanford University, 1974.
5. E.S. Krauss and B.L. Simcock, "Citizens' Movements: The Growth and Impact of Environmental Protest in Japan," in K. Steiner, et al., eds., Political Opposition and Local Politics in Japan (Princeton University Press, Princeton, 1980), 187-227; M.A. McKean, "Pollution and Policymaking," in T.J. Pempel, ed., Policymaking in Contemporary Japan (Cornell University Press, Ithaca, 1977), 201-238; and F.G. Notehelfer, "Japan's First Pollution Incident," Journal of Japanese Studies 1 (1975):351-384.
6. J. Gresser, "The 1973 Japanese Law for the Compensation of Pollution-Related Health Damage: An Introductory Assessment," Law in Japan 8(1975):91-135; F.K. Upham, "Litigation and Moral Consciousness in Japan: An Interpretative Analysis of Four Japanese Pollution Suits," Law and Society Review 10 (1976):579-619; and F.K. Upham, "After Minamata: Current Prospects and Problems in Japanese Environmental Litigation," Ecology Law Quarterly 8 (1979):213-268.
7. J. Gresser, et al., Environmental Law in Japan (MIT Press, Cambridge, 1981); McKean, op. cit., 1981; N. Iijima, Pollution Japan: Historical Chronology (Pergamon Press, New York, 1980); and W.E. Smith and A. Smith, Minamata: Words and Photographs (Holt, Rinehart and Winston, New York, 1975).
8. Japan Environment Agency, Quality of the Environment in Japan (Environment Agency, Tokyo, 1984), 11.
9. Japan Environment Agency, Quality of the Environment in Japan (Environment Agency, Tokyo, 1980), 173.
10. Japan Environment Agency, op. cit., 1984, 3.

11. Japan Environment Agency, Qutility of the Enyirnment in Japan (Environment Agency, Tokyo, 1978), 190–191.
12. TVA/EPRI/EPA, Sulfur Oxides Control in Japan (U.S. Environmental Protection Agency Interagency Energy/Environment Research and Development Program, Washington, D.C., 1979).
13. Hanrei Jihn, 672:30 (Tsu District Court, Yokkaichi Branch, July 24, 1972).
14. Japan Environment Agency, op. cit., 1984, 5.
15. "Agency Bears Air Pollution Study," Japan Times, December 22, 1985.
16. "Josei no Haigan to Kanren," Yomiuri Shinbun, May 11, 1986.
17. "Report on Environmental Measures for the Tama River Basin," Japan Environment Summary, 3–4 (November 10, 1980).
18. "Pollution Problems Declining But Sources Become Complex," Japan Times, May 19, 1982.
19. "Public Water Quality Worse," Japan Times, December 14, 1985.
20. "White Paper Says Pollution Becoming Worse in Osaka," Japan Times, September 29, 1985.
21. "Haiteku Osen ni Keisho," Asahi Shinhun, May 20, 1986.
22. Japan Environment Agency, op. cit., 1978, 18.
23. "Battery Disposal Safe, Panel Claims," Japan Times, July 26, 1985; and "Body to Set Up Battery Disposal Center," Japan Times, October 28, 1985.
24. "Toxic Substance Dioxin Detected in Japanese," Japan Times, December 26, 1985.
25. Enyirnmental Policy in Japan (Organization for Economic Cooperation and Development, Paris, 1977), 83.
26. Ibid., 87.
27. "Tokyo Rally Protests Environmental Policy," Japan Times, June 28, 1981.
28. Japan Environment Agency, op. cit., 1980, 340.
29. F.K. Upham, "Review of Environmental Law in Japan," Ecology Law Quarterly 10 (1982):181–192.
30. Gresser, et al., op. cit., 1981.
31. Nosei Seibutsu 108(1984):16–17 and 109(1985):16–17.
32. M. Hashimoto, "Kankyo Gyosei no Atana Taido," PPM 12(1984):2–9.
33. Council on Environmental Quality, Environmental Quality-1980: The Eleventh Annual Report of the Council on Environmental Quality (U.S. Government Printing Office, Washington, D.C., 1980), 373.
34. H. Shoji, "Asesumento no Seidoka no Ayumi," Kogai Kenkyu, 12 (Spring 1983):1.
35. Ibid.
36. Japan Environment Agency, op. cit., 1980, 93.
37. Ibid., 94.
38. Upham, op. cit., 1979.
39. Japan Environment Agency, op. cit., 1980, 93–96.
40. For a discussion of the history of efforts to pass an assessment law see: "Zadankai: Kankyo Asesumento Ho Seidoka no Kaidai," Kogai Kenkyu, 13(1983):62–72.

41. Simcock and Krauss, op. cit., 224.
42. Asahi Shinbun, evening edition, April 9, 1986.
43. Shizen Hogo, 287 (April 1986), 4–5; and "Environmentalists Join in the Fight Against Airstrip," Asahi Evening News, May 19, 1986.
44. Shizen Hogo, 286 (March 1986), 8–11.
45. "Genpatsu Saiban no Genkai to Igi," Asahi Shinbun, June 28, 1985.
46. Y. Uchiyama, "Schools Cry Out Against Lighting Up," Asahi Evening News, March 29, 1985.
47. K. Terao, "Japanese No-Smoking Groups Growing Slowly and Quietly," Asahi Evening News, April 11, 1985.
48. See, for example, editorials in the following papers: Asahi Shinbun, April 6, 1984; Tokyo Shinbun, April 5, 1984; Japan Times, April 15, 1984. All supported the movement's objectives and methods.
49. M. R. Reich, "Lowering the Boom at Narita," Environmental Action (July 1, 1978):14–15.
50. "3 Out of 12 Farm Families to Sell Land to Airport," Asahi Evening News, August 28, 1985.
51. "241 Protesters Arrested in Anti-Narita Airport Clash," Asahi Evening News, October 21, 1985.
52. Gresser, et al., op. cit., 1981, 285–319. For a good critical review of the Gresser, et al., book and the Compensation Law, see: B. Aronson, "Review Essay: Environmental Law in Japan," The Harvard Environmental Law Review 7 (1983):135–171. See also a special issue on this subject in: Jurisuto 821 (1984):6–57.
53. S.M. Soble, "A Proposal for the Administrative Compensation of Victims to Toxic Substance Pollution: A Model Act," Harvard Journal on Legislation 14 (1977):683–824.
54. B. Aronson, "Administrative Compensation of Pollution Victims in Japan: A Reappraisal After Seven Years Experience," presented at the Harvard Law School East Asian Legal Studies Program, October 22, 1981.
55. Aronson, op. cit., 156–159.
56. F.F. Piven and R.A. Cloward, Poor People's Movements, Why They Succeed, How They Fail (Random House, New York, 1977).
57. M.R. Reich, Toxic Politics: A Comparative Study of Public and Private Responses to Chemical Disasters in the United States, Italy, and Japan, unpublished Ph.D. dissertation, Yale University, 1981.
58. Aronson, op. cit., 166.
59. Japan Environment Agency, op. cit., 1984, 263.
60. "Pollution Victims Urge Relief Action," Japan Times, June 6, 1985.
61. "Court Upholds Decision in Minamata Disease Suit," Japan Times, December 1, 1985.
62. "Minamata Byo no Nintei Seido," Asahi Shinbun, November 30, 1985.
63. Asahi Shinbun, December 1, 1985.
64. Goto, "Minamata Byo no Nintei o Isoge," Asahi Shinbun, December 16, 1985.

65. See, for example, T. Muroi, "Kanemi Sosho Kososhin Hanketsu ni Tsuite," Jurisuto 816(1984):13–17.
66. For more information, see: M.R. Reich, op. cit., 1981, 140–201.
67. "Kanemi Poison Victims File Damage Suit," Japan Times, December 1, 1985.
68. "342 Food Poisoning Victims Awarded 1.8 Billion Yen in Damages," Japan Times, May 15, 1986.
69. J. Burgess, "Trash Builds New Islands in Tokyo Bay," The Washington Post, January 2, 1986.

ACKNOWLEDGMENTS, 1975

Many people in many capacities have helped us in the preparation of this book. Unfortunately, the limitations of space prohibit our giving full credit to all. Below are a few of the individuals and institutions to whom we wish to express special thanks.

We would like to express our appreciation to the Princeton University Center for Environmental Studies for a grant to aid in the preparation of the manuscript. Other institutions that provided official and personal support were the International Education Center, the International Medical Information Center, the Economic Research Institute of Hitotsubashi University, the Heart Institute of Japan, Jishu (Independent Study Group), the Japan Center for Development Research, the Environment Agency, and the Kogai Mondai Kenkyu Kai (Pollution Problems Research Society).

Friends and colleagues who provided invaluable assistance in collecting research materials included: Tony Carter, Erihisa Ujii, Tadashi Fujino, Julian Gresser, Aiko Iijima, Masahi Iijima, Hiroyuki Ishi, Kokichi Kawamura, Takakore Oda, Chojiro Kunii, Koichi Maruyama, Yayori Matsui, Hiroshi Matsumoto, Akio Matsumura, Nobuo Matsuoka, Uko Matsuzaki, Minoru Muramatsu, Tomio Nakai, Akio Niioka, Kunikazu Ohashi, Yoshiro Sawai, Takuro Uchiyama, Takashi Wagatsuma, and Paul Zimmer. Also, to many friends and students who helped us read reports, transcribe tapes, and type sections of the manuscript, we owe a deep debt of gratitude.

We can never repay the kindness and assistance of the people in the antipollution movements who, during our two and a half month study tour of the Japanese archipelago in the fall of 1972, opened their homes and hearts to us. The intense dedication of these people was a special source of inspiration for this book, and, in a very real way, changed our lives.

Special thanks for personal favors and support during our stay in Tokyo go to Masahisa Ando, Martin Cohen, Peter Hazelhurst, Kenji Hoshino, Eiichi Isomura, Namiji Itabashi, Shuichi Kato, Masao Kunihiro, Katsuko Nomura, Hiroko Sato, Atsuyoshi Takao, Yoshiyuki Tanaka, the Hideichi Yoshida family, and Toshiyuki Yoshida.

The final version of the manuscript reflects our indebtedness to editors William Carter and Jeannine Ciliotta. Others who read the manuscript and provided helpful comments include George DeVos, Richard Diamond, Thomas Lifson, Hugh Patrick, and Douglas Sparks. Particularly vital feedback was provided by Martin Cohen, Anne and Paul Ehrlich, Shironori Hamanaka, and Naohide Isono through their in-depth reviews of several chapters. While we acknowledge the contributions of these various persons, it is we, the authors, who must take final responsibility for the substance of the following pages.

Perhaps the greatest debt we owe is to our publisher and friend, Nahum Stiskin, whose faith in the project and in our ability to see it through was a constant source of energy. And warm thanks to his wife, Beverly, for her unfailing cheerfulness and patience, and Friday-night dinners.

Finally, special thanks to each other for struggling together through the long process of researching, writing, and rewriting.

ACKNOWLEDGMENTS, 1987

We express a brief note of thanks to the persons who helped us in reprinting this volume. We especially appreciate the vision of Alfred Schenkman and the perseverance of his nephew, Joe, who agreed to publish *Island of Dreams*, despite difficult circumstances. Karen Hull expertly guided the editorial process. We also thank a group of good friends who assisted us by commenting on the new introduction, providing materials on recent trends in Japan, and prodding us to get this book back in print: Saburo Kato, Ellis Krauss, Rob Leflar, Kiyofumi Matsumoto, Nobuo Matsuoka, Katsuko Nomura, Cathy Perlmutter, Donna Hodgson Reich, Takeo Suzuki, Eiko Terada, Frank Upham, and Bungaku Watanabe.

ACKNOWLEDGMENTS, 2025

The authors appreciate the many contributions of Johnattan Garcia Ruiz of Decilion for transforming the scanned PDF of the 1987 edition of *Island of Dreams*—along with our many requests for changes—into this Fiftieth Anniversary Edition. Brian Shillue of Digital Scanning provided us with the excellent scan of the 1987 book and then gave Michael valuable guidance on how to navigate the print-on-demand world.

A special thank you to Richard Bell, Editor of the Eastern Shore Cooperator in Novia Scotia and a friend of Michael's from the 1970s, who reread *Island of Dreams* in 2023 and encouraged Michael to republish it, stressing the book's continued relevance today.

Finally, the authors thank each other for our collaboration, 50 years later, reviewing our work from long ago and writing a new preface. In doing this, we were reminded how much the Japanese experience presented in *Island of Dreams* still matters today, as we seek to heal our planet for future generations.

ABOUT THE AUTHORS

NORIE HUDDLE, born in Virginia in 1944, graduated from Brown University in Russian language (1966) and spent two years in Colombia, S.A. with the Peace Corps. Back in America, she studied Chinese and environmental sciences and, in 1971, was given a scholarship to attend a conference in Japan after which she hoped to visit China. But shocked by Japan's deteriorated environment, she stayed to study the problem and write *Island of Dreams* with Michael Reich. A Visiting Scholar with Hitotsubashi University's President Shigeto Tsuru's research center (1973-5), Norie returned to America (1975) to organize "Project America 1976," celebrating America's Bicentennial by bicycling 9 months across America. Her book about this became a bestseller in Japan.

In 1979, Norie founded the Center for New National Security to study national and global security issues, broadly defined. During the 1980s, while participating in numerous US-USSR citizen diplomacy initiatives, she wrote *Surviving: The Best Game on Earth*, a NYTimes bestseller redefining national security. In the 1990s, Norie wrote three more bestsellers and built her house (hands-on) in West Virginia. In 2007, she and her husband, Richard Wheeler, began transforming a semi-abandoned 350-acre farm in Ecuador into the Garden of Paradise. In 2011, they won the first successful Rights of Nature lawsuit in Ecuador and in the world. Today the Garden of Paradise has visitors from all over the world. Norie continues to write, consult, coach and do public speaking. (For more information, see https://noriehuddle.earth).

MICHAEL REICH, born in Ohio in 1950, entered Yale University in September 1968 and, after three years of courses, travelled to Japan in 1971 under the Yale Five-Year B.A. Program. In Japan, Michael first worked as a medical technician at the Heart Institute of Japan (Tokyo Women's Medical University) and then moved to Keio University's International Medical Information Center as visiting researcher. In October 1973, he was appointed as research assistant at the Princeton University Center for Environmental Studies. While in Japan for three years, he wrote *Island of Dreams* with Norie Huddle. He then returned to the U.S.A. in the summer of 1974. Michael graduated with a B.A. in molecular biophysics and biochemistry in 1974, then received his M.A. in East Asian Studies in 1975 and PhD. in political science in 1981, all from Yale.

Michael joined the faculty at the Harvard School of Public Health in 1983 and helped establish the Takemi Program in International Health, serving as director from 1988 to 2023. Among his many publications, he is coauthor of *Six Lives/Six Deaths: Portraits from Modern Japan* (Yale, 1979), author of *Toxic Politics: Responding to Chemical Disasters* (Cornell, 1991), and coauthor of *Getting Health Reform Right: A Guide to Improving Performance and Equity* (Oxford, 2004). He is founding Editor-in-Chief of the journal Health Systems & Reform since 2015, and is currently the Taro Takemi Professor of International Health Policy, Emeritus at Harvard. (For more information, see https://michaelrreich.com)

www.ingramcontent.com/pod-product-compliance
Lightning Source LLC
Chambersburg PA
CBHW060453030426
42337CB00015B/1567